2001 SUPPLEMENT to

CASES AND MATERIALS

ON

TRADE REGULATION

By

MILTON HANDLER
Late Professor Emeritus of Law,
Columbia University School of Law

ROBERT PITOFSKY
Professor of Law,
Georgetown University Law Center

HARVEY J. GOLDSCHMID
Dwight Professor of Law,
Columbia University School of Law

DIANE P. WOOD
Circuit Judge, U.S. Court of Appeals,
Seventh Circuit;
Senior Lecturer in Law,
University of Chicago Law School

FOURTH EDITION

New York, New York
FOUNDATION PRESS
2001

ISBN 1–58778–116–6

TEXT IS PRINTED ON 10% POST CONSUMER RECYCLED PAPER

1st Reprint — 2002

TABLE OF CONTENTS

CHAPTER 1: THE OBJECTIVES AND ORIGINS OF ANTITRUST LAW

Section 1. The Goals of Antitrust Policy

B. Sherman Act and Comparative Legislation

Insert before Treaty of Rome, page 24:

Note: Over time, the jurisdiction of the Court of First Instance of the European Communities has expanded. That court currently has jurisdiction to rule in the first instance on (1) all actions for annulment, for failure to act, and for damages brought by natural or legal persons against the Community, (2) actions brought against the Commission under the ECSC Treaty by business firms or associations, and (3) disputes between the Community and its officials and employees. The Treaty of Amsterdam, which entered into force on May 1, 1999, contemplates that the Court of First Instance may eventually have jurisdiction over all categories of cases now within the jurisdiction of the Court of Justice except for preliminary references from the national courts made pursuant to Article 234 of the Treaty.

In addition to making this change in the power of the Court of First Instance, the Treaty of Amsterdam extensively revised and consolidated the earlier treaties governing the European Union. It renumbered the provisions of the original Treaty of Rome. For competition lawyers, it is important to bear in mind that former Articles 85-90 of the Treaty of Rome are now Articles 81 to 86, respectively. The Competition Directorate of the European Commission (formerly known as DG-IV) now routinely refers to the amended numbers in its official documents. Thus, the treaty provision concerned with cartels and other collective behavior is now Article 81, and the treaty provision concerned with abuses of a dominant position is now Article 82.

More changes are also on the horizon for the administration of competition law within Europe. On April 28, 1999, the Commission published a "White paper on modernisation of the rules implementing articles 85 and 86 [now 81 and 82] of the EC Treaty," Commission programme No. 99/027. See <http://www.europa.eu.int/comm/competition/antitrust/others/modernisation/comm_2000_582/en.pdf>. After a period of consultation and comment, it followed up with proposed regulations issued September 27, 2000, that would amend the system of implementing those two articles. Under the proposed regulations (which are limited to Articles 81 and 82 and thus do not address either merger control or state aids), Regulation 17 would be replaced with a new system of decentralized enforcement authority. Under the new system, notification of business arrangements falling within the scope of Article 81(1) will no longer be required. In addition, the Commission will give up its monopoly on granting exemptions under Article 81(3), and will permit the Member State competition authorities and the Member State courts to decide whether an exemption is appropriate in a given case. As the Commission puts it in the proposed regulation, the national authorities will be able to apply Article 81 in its entirety, rather than being limited as they have been to applying only Article 81(1) and (2). The proposal also expressly contemplates more private enforcement of the competition laws. See Proposal for a Council Regulation on the implementation of the rules on competition laid down in Articles 81 and 82 of the Treaty and amending Regulations (EEC) No 1017/68, (EEC) No 2988/74, (EEC) No 4056/86 and (EEC) No 3975/87, Brussels, September 17, 2000, COM(2000) 582 final, available on the website of the Competition Directorate. (That website is now found at <http://www.europa.eu.int/comm/competition/>.) The proposed changes are far-reaching and will, if passed, have a profound effect on the way European competition law is enforced.

CHAPTER 2: INSTITUTIONAL FRAMEWORK OF ANTITRUST POLICY

Section 1. The Three-Level Antitrust Enforcement Pattern

Delete first full paragraph page 113 and insert:

The Hart-Scott-Rodino Act also required pre-merger notification. Parties, including foreign interests, involved in a merger must file a pre-merger notification form with the FTC and Antitrust Division. Although transition rules are in effect until February 1, 2002 for certain transactions, filings made after February 1, 2001 (under a 2000 amendment to the Hart-Scott-Rodino Act and FTC implementing regulations) must involve a "size-of-transaction" threshold of $50 million (up from $15 million) for the Act to be applicable. The amendment did away with prior "size-of-person" tests for transactions valued in excess of $200 million, and put into effect a graduated scale for filing fees based on the size of a transaction. An automatic waiting period, prior to the consummation of a merger, is mandated, and the waiting period runs for 15 to at least 50 days depending on circumstances and the type of merger.

Insert after second full paragraph, page 118:

During the late 1990's, monetary remedies, both civil and criminal, became much more important in government enforcement efforts. On the criminal side, the Antitrust Division was extremely successful against cartels, particularly international cartels, and unprecedented fines, at times amounting to hundreds of millions of dollars, were imposed under the Criminal Fine Improvements Act of 1987. On the civil side, in FTC v. Mylan, the company allegedly made over $100 million in illegal profits by improperly cornering the market for an essential ingredient. The FTC persuaded a district court, relying on equitable powers, that the proper antitrust remedy in these circumstances would be disgorgement, and an elaborate system was introduced requiring repayment to exploited consumers of over $100 million.

CHAPTER 4: COMPETITOR COLLABORATION ON PRICE FIXING AND DIVISION OF MARKETS

Section 2. Development of the "Per Se" Rule on Price Fixing

Insert after *Appalachian Coals* and *Socony-Vacuum*, page 255:

JTC PETROLEUM CO. v. PIASA MOTOR FUELS, INC.
United States Court of Appeals, Seventh Circuit, 1999.
179 F. 3d 1073.

Before: POSNER, Chief Judge, and EASTERBROOK and ROVNER, Circuit Judges.

Posner, J. The plaintiff seeks damages for violations of sections 1 and 2 of the Sherman Act arising out of the road-repair business in southern Illinois. There are two groups of defendants: the road contractors themselves, called "applicators," and producers of the emulsified asphalt that the applicators apply to the surface of the roads. After the plaintiff, itself an applicator, settled with all three of the producers and three of the six applicator defendants, the district court granted summary judgment for the remaining applicator defendants, who are the appellees in this court. . . .

The plaintiff presented evidence both that the applicator defendants had agreed not to compete with one another in bidding on local government contracts and that the producers had agreed not to compete among each other either, both agreements being (if proved) per se violations of section 1 of the Sherman Act. There is a long history of bid-rigging and related practices of collusion in the road construction and road maintenance business. See, e.g., Gulf Oil Corp. v. Copp Paving Co., 419 U.S. 186 (1974); United States v. Azzarelli Construction Co., 612 F.2d 292 (7th Cir. 1979); In re Western Liquid Asphalt Cases, 487 F.2d 191 (9th Cir. 1973). (In recent years most criminal antitrust prosecutions have been of road contractors.) These are local markets, with a limited number of competitors, selling a rather standardized service to local governments constrained to give their business to the lowest bidder, a constraint that makes it easy for colluding bidders to determine whether one of their number is cheating on the agreement to divide markets. The conditions are thus ripe for effective collusion, making it unsurprising that there is evidence that the applicator defendants in fact colluded with one another to allocate the applicator business in their region. (In discussing the evidence, we emphasize that we are construing it in the light most favorable to the plaintiff, as we are required to do in reviewing the grant of summary judgment to the defendants.)

As for the producers of the asphalt used by these applicators, the record contains evidence that the product is both heavy relative to value and prone to deteriorate when transported long distances, and that as a result the practical radius within which a plant can supply applicators is only about 70 miles. This has limited to three the number of producers that can supply applicators in the region served by the plaintiff and by the applicator defendants. The plants are specialized to the production of emulsified asphalt, meaning that they can't readily be switched to producing other products . This gives the producers an incentive to produce emulsified asphalt up to the capacity of their plants (because there is no profitable use of the plants other than producing this product), and, since it is a fungible product, about the only way of increasing output is by cutting price. But since the demand for emulsified asphalt is inelastic--that is, lower prices do not yield commensurate increases in volume--the effect of price competition would be to diminish profits. So the producers, like the applicators, have much to gain by eliminating competition among themselves. And since the product is standard and the number of competing producers few, an agreement not to compete should not be too difficult to enforce; that is, at the producer level as at the applicator level, cheating should be readily observable and hence quickly checked by a retaliatory price cut. Therefore a cartel agreement would not be quickly eroded by cheating, and so again the conditions for collusion are ripe and again the record contains evidence of such collusion.

But the only defendants remaining in the case are applicators, which is to say the plaintiff's competitors. The producers have settled out. Suppose that all that the plaintiff were complaining about, therefore, was a conspiracy of the applicators to raise prices or (what amounts to the same thing) to allocate customers or markets. The complaint would fail at the threshold. A conspiracy of a firm's competitors to do these things could only help the firm, by providing an umbrella under which it could sell a large quantity at a supracompetitive price generating supracompetitive profits just by setting price in between the conspirators' price and the lower, competitive price that would prevail in the absence of the conspiracy. You want your competitors to charge high prices. The fact that it was in JTC's interest that the other applicators agree not to compete with each other would be irrelevant if the Department of Justice were suing the applicators, but it is not; this is a private suit by a competitor that, since it cannot show harm to itself from its competitors' eliminating competition among themselves, cannot obtain relief under the antitrust laws. Id.; Matsushita Electric Industrial Co. v. Zenith Radio Corp., 475 U.S. 574, 586 (1986). To put it bluntly, you cannot obtain damages without proving injury. (This is a general principle of both common law tort law and statutory tort law, rather than anything special to antitrust.) As a purchaser of emulsified asphalt, JTC could of course be hurt by a producers' cartel, but, to repeat, no producer remains as a defendant.

So what JTC has tried to show is that the applicators enlisted the producers in their conspiracy, assigning them the role of policing the applicators' cartel by refusing to sell to applicators who defied the cartel--such as JTC, which has bid for jobs that the cartel had assigned to other applicators. JTC, a maverick, was a threat to the cartel--but only if it could find a source of supply of emulsified asphalt. The claim is that the applicators got the producers to deny JTC this essential input into its business, and as a result injured it. The producer was the cat's paw; the applicators were the cat.

Matsushita Electric Industrial Co. v. Zenith Radio Corp., supra, 475 U.S. at 587, however, teaches that an antitrust claim which makes no economic sense can on that ground be dismissed on summary judgment. See also In re Brand Name Prescription Drugs Antitrust Litigation, 123 F.3d 599, 614 (7th Cir. 1997). And it might seem to make no sense from the producers' standpoint to shore up a cartel of their customers. Cartels, as we have pointed out, raise price above the competitive level and by doing so reduce the demand for their product. The less asphalt the members of the applicators' cartel sell (perhaps because the higher, cartel price induces municipalities to defer road maintenance), the less they will buy, and so the producers will be hurt. But if the producers have nowhere else to turn to sell their product, as may be the case here because of the specialized character of their plants and the limited radius within which they can ship their product from the plant, the applicator defendants may be able to coerce them into helping to police their cartel by threatening to buy less product from them or pay less for it, as in the well-known case of Eastern States Retail Lumber Dealers' Ass'n v. United States, 234 U.S. 600 (1914); see also Business Electronics Corp. v. Sharp Electronics Corp., 485 U.S. 717, 730 n. 4 (1988); United States v. General Motors Corp., 384 U.S. 127 (1966). . . .

Alternatively, and more plausibly (at least on this record), the cartelists may have been paying the producers to perform the policing function, rather than coercing them, by threats, to do so. In re Brand Name Prescription Drugs Antitrust Litigation, supra, 123 F.3d at 614. If by refusing to sell to mavericks the producers increase the profits of the applicators' cartel, they create a fund out of which the cartel can compensate them, in the form of a higher price for the purchase of the product, for their services to the cartel. The record contains evidence that one of the producers obtained from applicators in the cartel area prices that were 4 to 18 (or maybe even 28) percent higher than the prices it obtained from presumably noncolluding applicators in the adjacent region, though there is no suggestion that the producer's costs were any higher in that region. The evidence is contested by the defendants, but the resolution of the contest is for trial. There is also evidence (again contested, and again this is irrelevant to whether summary judgment was properly granted) that the reasons the producers gave for refusing to sell to JTC were pretextual, as in Eastman Kodak Co. v. Image Technical Services, Inc., 504 U.S. 451, 484 (1992); McDonnell Douglas Corp. v. Green, 411 U.S. 792 (1973)--for example, that JTC was not a good credit risk, even though when JTC offered to pay cash the producers still refused to sell to it. This suggests that the real reason for the refusal was one that the producers didn't want to acknowledge--namely that they were being compensated by the cartel for refusing to sell to a customer whom otherwise they would have been happy to sell to. The combination of the price difference with the evidence of pretext support an inference that the producers were being compensated by the applicators for shoring up the cartel by boycotting an applicator that was competing with the cartel. If so--if the producers were working for the cartel--they were part of the applicators' conspiracy, and for the injury that they inflicted on JTC as agents of the applicators' cartel by denying JTC a source of supply the members of the cartel, three of which are the remaining defendants, would be culpable under elementary principles of both conspiracy law and agency law.

There may be an innocent explanation for why producers would charge lower prices elsewhere or why they refused to sell to JTC. But the only issue for us, in reviewing the grant of summary judgment for these defendants, is whether a rational jury, having before it the evidence developed to date, could conclude (construing the evidence as favorably to the plaintiff as the record permits) that the reason for the producers' refusal to deal with JTC was that they were in cahoots with the cartel to discourage competition in the applicator market. Given the evidence of cartelization at both the applicator and producer level, the suspicious producer price behavior (suggestive of the producers having been "paid off" by the cartel to boycott JTC and other upstarts), and the pretextual character of the reasons the producers gave for the refusal to deal, a rational jury could conclude that JTC was indeed the victim of a producers' boycott organized by the applicator defendants. All the evidence that we have discussed is circumstantial, but of course an inference of conspiracy--of, in this case, an informal agreement among the applicators and the producers to deny supply to firms that tried to break into the applicators' cosily divided market--can be drawn from circumstantial evidence as well as from admissions or other direct testimony of the conspirators' communications with each other. JTC has some direct evidence as well. It strikes us as equivocal, and we have not thought it necessary to discuss it; but we do not mean to suggest that it should not be admitted at the trial to which, we conclude, JTC was entitled.

Section 3. Characterization Questions and Other Issues

Delete Note 3, pages 262-64 and insert after *Brown University*, page 329:

CALIFORNIA DENTAL ASSN. v. FEDERAL TRADE COMMISSION
Supreme Court of the United States, 1999.
526 U.S. 756, 119 S. Ct. 1604, 143 L. Ed. 2d 935.

SOUTER, J. There are two issues in this case: whether the jurisdiction of the Federal Trade Commission extends to the California Dental Association (CDA), a nonprofit professional association, and whether a "quick look" sufficed to justify finding that certain advertising restrictions adopted by the CDA violated the antitrust laws. We hold that the Commission's jurisdiction under the Federal Trade Commission Act (FTC Act) extends to an association that, like the CDA, provides substantial economic benefit to its for-profit members, but that where, as here, any anticompetitive effects of given restraints are far from intuitively obvious, the rule of reason demands a more thorough enquiry into the consequences of those restraints than the Court of Appeals performed.

I

The CDA is a voluntary nonprofit association of local dental societies to which some 19,000 dentists belong, including about three-quarters of those practicing in the State. In re California Dental Assn., 121 F.T.C. 190, 196-197 (1996). The CDA is exempt from federal income tax under 26 U.S.C. § 501(c)(6), covering "business leagues, chambers of commerce, real-estate boards, [and] boards of trade," although it has for-profit subsidiaries that give its members advantageous access to various sorts of insurance, including liability coverage, and to financing for their real estate, equipment, cars, and patients' bills. The CDA lobbies and litigates in its members' interests, and conducts marketing and public relations campaigns for their benefit.

The dentists who belong to the CDA through these associations agree to abide by a Code of Ethics (Code) including the following § 10:

> "Although any dentist may advertise, no dentist shall advertise or solicit patients in any form of communication in a manner that is false or misleading in any material respect. In order to properly serve the public, dentists should represent themselves in a manner that contributes to the esteem of the public. Dentists should not misrepresent their training and competence in any way that would be false or misleading in any material respect."

The CDA has issued a number of advisory opinions interpreting this section, and through separate advertising guidelines intended to help members comply with the Code and with state law the CDA has advised its dentists of disclosures they must make under state law when engaging in discount advertising.[1]

---

[1] The disclosures include:

"1. The dollar amount of the nondiscounted fee for the service[.]

"2. Either the dollar amount of the discount fee or the percentage of the discount for the specific service[.]

"3. The length of time that the discount will be offered[.]

"4. Verifiable fees[.]

"5. [The identity of] specific groups who qualify for the discount or any other terms and conditions or restrictions for qualifying for the discount." *Id., at 724.*

Responsibility for enforcing the Code rests in the first instance with the local dental societies, to which applicants for CDA membership must submit copies of their own advertisements and those of their employers or referral services to assure compliance with the Code. The local societies also actively seek information about potential Code violations by applicants or CDA members. Applicants who refuse to withdraw or revise objectionable advertisements may be denied membership; and members who, after a hearing, remain similarly recalcitrant are subject to censure, suspension, or expulsion from the *CDA. 128 F.3d at 724.*

The Commission brought a complaint against the CDA, alleging that it applied its guidelines so as to restrict truthful, nondeceptive advertising, and so violated § 5 of the FTC Act, 38 Stat. 717, *15 U.S.C. §45.*[2] The complaint alleged that the CDA had unreasonably restricted two types of advertising: price advertising, particularly discounted fees, and advertising relating to the quality of dental services. An Administrative Law Judge (ALJ) held the Commission to have jurisdiction over the CDA, which, the ALJ noted, had itself "stated that a selection of its programs and services has a potential value to members of between $22,739 and $65,127," *121 F.T.C. at 207.* He found that, although there had been no proof that the CDA exerted market power, no such proof was required to establish an antitrust violation under In re Mass. Bd. of Registration in Optometry, 110 F.T.C. 549 (1988), since the CDA had unreasonably prevented members and potential members from using truthful, nondeceptive advertising, all to the detriment of both dentists and consumers of dental services. He accordingly found a violation of § 5 of the FTC Act.

The Commission adopted the factual findings of the ALJ except for his conclusion that the CDA lacked market power, with which the Commission disagreed. The Commission treated the CDA's restrictions on discount advertising as illegal per se. 128 F.3d at 725. In the alternative, the Commission held the price advertising (as well as the nonprice) restrictions to be violations of the Sherman and FTC Acts under an abbreviated rule-of-

---

2 The FTC Act's prohibition of unfair competition and deceptive acts or practices, *15 U.S.C. § 45*(a)(1), overlaps the scope of § 1 of the Sherman Act, *15 U.S.C. § 1,* aimed at prohibiting restraint of trade, *FTC v. Indiana Federation of Dentists, 476 U.S. 447, 454-455 (1986),* and the Commission relied upon Sherman Act law in adjudicating this case, *In re California Dental Assn., 121 F.T.C. 190, 292, n. 5 (1996).*

reason analysis. . . .

The Court of Appeals for the Ninth Circuit affirmed, sustaining the Commission's assertion of jurisdiction over the CDA and its ultimate conclusion on the merits. *Id.* at 730. The court thought it error for the Commission to have applied *per se* analysis to the price advertising restrictions, finding analysis under the rule of reason required for all the restrictions. But the Court of Appeals went on to explain that the Commission had properly

> "applied an abbreviated, or 'quick look,' rule of reason analysis designed for restraints that are not per se unlawful but are sufficiently anticompetitive on their face that they do not require a full-blown rule of reason inquiry. See [*National Collegiate Athletic Assn. v. Board of Regents of Univ. of Okla., 468 U.S. 85 and n. 39 (1984)]* ('The essential point is that the rule of reason can sometimes be applied in the twinkling of an eye.' [Ibid. (citing P. Areeda, The "Rule of Reason" in Antitrust Analysis: General Issues 37-38 (Federal Judicial Center, June 1981) (parenthetical omitted)).] It allows the condemnation of a 'naked restraint' on price or output without an 'elaborate industry analysis.' *Id.* at 109." *Id.*, at 727.

The Court of Appeals thought truncated rule-of-reason analysis to be in order for several reasons. As for the restrictions on discount advertising, they "amounted in practice to a fairly 'naked' restraint on price competition itself," *ibid.* The CDA's procompetitive justification, that the restrictions encouraged disclosure and prevented false and misleading advertising, carried little weight because "it is simply infeasible to disclose all of the information that is required," *id.*, at 728, and "the record provides no evidence that the rule has in fact led to increased disclosure and transparency of dental pricing," ibid. As to non-price advertising restrictions, the court said that

> "[t]hese restrictions are in effect a form of output limitation, as they restrict the supply of information about individual dentists' services. *See* Areeda & Hovenkamp, Antitrust Law ¶1505 at 693-694 (Supp. 1997) . . . . The restrictions may also affect output more directly, as quality and comfort advertising may induce some customers to obtain nonemergency care when they might not otherwise do so . . . . Under these circumstances, we

think that the restriction is a sufficiently naked restraint on output to justify quick look analysis." *Ibid.*

The Court of Appeals went on to hold that the Commission's findings with respect to the CDA's agreement and intent to restrain trade, as well as on the effect of the restrictions and the existence of market power, were all supported by substantial evidence. *Id.*, at 728-730. In dissent, Judge Real took the position that the Commission's jurisdiction did not cover the CDA as a nonprofit professional association engaging in no commercial operations. But even assuming jurisdiction, he argued, full-bore rule-of-reason analysis was called for, since the disclosure requirements were not naked restraints and neither fixed prices nor banned nondeceptive advertising.

We granted certiorari to resolve conflicts among the Circuits on the Commission's jurisdiction over a nonprofit professional association and the occasions for abbreviated rule-of-reason analysis. We now vacate the judgment of the Court of Appeals and remand.

II

The FTC Act gives the Commission authority over "persons, partnerships, or corporations," 15 U.S.C. § 45(a)(2), and defines "corporation" to include "any company . . . or association, incorporated or unincorporated, without shares of capital or capital stock or certificates of interest, except partnerships, which is organized to carry on business for its own profit or that of its members," § 44. Although the Circuits have not agreed on the precise extent of this definition, the Commission has long held that some circumstances give it jurisdiction over an entity that seeks no profit for itself. While the Commission has claimed to have jurisdiction over a nonprofit entity if a substantial part of its total activities provide pecuniary benefits to its members, *see In re American Medical Assn., 94 F.T.C. 701, 983-984 (1980),* respondent now advances the slightly different formulation that the Commission has jurisdiction "over anticompetitive practices by nonprofit associations whose activities provide substantial economic benefits to their for-profit members' businesses." Brief for Respondent 20. . . .

Just as the FTC Act does not require that a supporting organization must devote itself entirely to its members' profits, neither does the Act say anything about how much of the entity's activities must go to raising the members' bottom lines. There is accordingly no apparent reason to let the statute's application turn on meeting some threshold percentage of activity for this purpose, or even satisfying a softer formulation calling for a substantial part of the nonprofit entity's total activities to be aimed at its members' pecuniary benefit. To be sure, proximate relation to lucre must appear; the FTC Act does not cover all membership organizations of profit-making corporations without more, and an organization devoted solely to professional education may lie outside the FTC Act's jurisdictional reach, even though the quality of professional services ultimately affects the profits of those who deliver them.

There is no line drawing exercise in this case, however, where the CDA's contributions to the profits of its individual members are proximate and apparent. Through for-profit subsidiaries, the CDA provides advantageous insurance and preferential financing arrangements for its members, and it engages in lobbying, litigation, marketing, and public relations for the benefit of its members' interests. This congeries of activities confers far more than de minimis or merely presumed economic benefits on CDA members; the economic benefits conferred upon the CDA's profit-seeking professionals plainly fall within the object of enhancing its members' "profit,"[3] which the FTC Act makes the jurisdictional touchstone. There is no difficulty in concluding that the Commission has jurisdiction over the CDA. . . .

III

The Court of Appeals treated as distinct questions the sufficiency of the

---

[3] . . . .(It should go without saying that the FTC Act does not require for Commission jurisdiction that members of an entity turn a profit on their membership, but only that the entity be organized to carry on business for members' profit.) Nonetheless, we do not, and indeed, on the facts here, could not, decide today whether the Commission has jurisdiction over nonprofit organizations that do not confer profit on for-profit members but do, for example, show annual income surpluses, engage in significant commerce, or compete in relevant markets with for-profit players. We therefore do not foreclose the possibility that various paradigms of profit might fall within the ambit of the FTC Act. Nor do we decide whether a purpose of contributing to profit only in a presumed sense, as by enhancing professional educational efforts, would implicate the Commission's jurisdiction.

analysis of anticompetitive effects and the substantiality of the evidence supporting the Commission's conclusions. Because we decide that the Court of Appeals erred when it held as a matter of law that quick-look analysis was appropriate (with the consequence that the Commission's abbreviated analysis and conclusion were sustainable), we do not reach the question of the substantiality of the evidence supporting the Commission's conclusion.[4]

In National Collegiate Athletic Assn. v. Board of Regents of Univ. of Okla., 468 U.S. 85 (1984), we held that a "naked restraint on price and output requires some competitive justification even in the absence of a detailed market analysis." *Id.*, at 110. Elsewhere, we held that "no elaborate industry analysis is required to demonstrate the anticompetitive character of" horizontal agreements among competitors to refuse to discuss prices, National Soc. of Professional Engineers v. United States, 435 U.S. 679, 692 (1978), or to withhold a particular desired service, FTC v. Indiana Federation of Dentists, 476 U.S. 447, 459, (1986) (quoting National Soc. of Professional Engineers, supra, at 692). In each of these cases, which have formed the basis for what has come to be called abbreviated or "quick-look" analysis under the rule of reason, an observer with even a rudimentary understanding of economics could conclude that the arrangements in question would have an anticompetitive effect on customers and markets. In National Collegiate Athletic Assn., the league's television plan expressly limited output (the number of games that could be televised) and fixed a minimum price. 468 U.S. at 99-100. In National Soc. of Professional Engineers, the restraint was "an absolute ban on competitive bidding." 435 U.S. at 692. In Indiana Federation of Dentists, the restraint was "a horizontal agreement among the participating dentists to withhold from their customers a particular service that they desire." 476 U.S. at 459. As in such cases, quick-look analysis carries the day when the great likelihood of anticompetitive effects can easily be ascertained. See Law v. National Collegiate Athletic Assn., 134 F.3d 1010, 1020 (CA10 1998) (explaining that quick-look analysis applies "where a practice has obvious anticompetitive effects"); Chicago Professional Sports Limited Partnership v. National Basketball Assn., 961 F.2d 667, 674-676 (CA7 1992) (finding quick-look analysis adequate after assessing and rejecting logic of proffered

---

[4] We leave to the Court of Appeals the question whether on remand it can effectively assess the Commission's decision for substantial evidence on the record, or whether it must remand to the Commission for a more extensive rule-of-reason analysis on the basis of an enhanced record.

procompetitive justifications); cf. United States v. Brown University, 5 F.3d 658, 677-678 (CA3 1993) (finding full rule-of-reason analysis required where universities sought to provide financial aid to needy students and noting by way of contrast that the agreements in *National Soc. of Professional Engineers and Indiana Federation of Dentists* "embodied a strong economic self-interest of the parties to them").

The case before us, however, fails to present a situation in which the likelihood of anticompetitive effects is comparably obvious. Even on JUSTICE BREYER's view that bars on truthful and verifiable price and quality advertising are prima facie anticompetitive, and place the burden of procompetitive justification on those who agree to adopt them, the very issue at the threshold of this case is whether professional price and quality advertising is sufficiently verifiable in theory and in fact to fall within such a general rule. Ultimately our disagreement with JUSTICE BREYER turns on our different responses to this issue. Whereas he accepts, as the Ninth Circuit seems to have done, that the restrictions here were like restrictions on advertisement of price and quality generally, it seems to us that the CDA's advertising restrictions might plausibly be thought to have a net procompetitive effect, or possibly no effect at all on competition. The restrictions on both discount and nondiscount advertising are, at least on their face, designed to avoid false or deceptive advertising[5] in a market characterized by striking disparities between the information available to the professional and the patient. [6] Cf. Carr & Mathewson, The Economics of Law Firms: A Study in

---

[5] That false or misleading advertising has an anticompetitive effect, as that term is customarily used, has been long established. Cf. FTC v. Algoma Lumber Co., 291 U.S. 67, 79-80 (1934) (finding a false advertisement to be unfair competition).

[6] "The fact that a restraint operates upon a profession as distinguished from a business is, of course, relevant in determining whether that particular restraint violates the Sherman Act. It would be unrealistic to view the practice of professions as interchangeable with other business activities, and automatically to apply to the professions antitrust concepts which originated in other areas. The public service aspect, and other features of the professions, may require that a particular practice, which could properly be viewed as a violation of the Sherman Act in another context, be treated differently." Goldfarb v. Virginia State Bar, 421 U.S. 773, 788-789 and n. 17 (1975).

the Legal Organization of the Firm, 33 J. Law & Econ. 307, 309 (1990) (explaining that in a market for complex professional services, "inherent asymmetry of knowledge about the product" arises because "professionals supplying the good are knowledgeable [whereas] consumers demanding the good are uninformed"); Akerlof, The Market for 'Lemons': Quality Uncertainty and the Market Mechanism, 84 Q. J. Econ. 488 (1970) (pointing out quality problems in market characterized by asymmetrical information). In a market for professional services, in which advertising is relatively rare and the comparability of service packages not easily established, the difficulty for customers or potential competitors to get and verify information about the price and availability of services magnifies the dangers to competition associated with misleading advertising. What is more, the quality of professional services tends to resist either calibration or monitoring by individual patients or clients, partly because of the specialized knowledge required to evaluate the services, and partly because of the difficulty in determining whether, and the degree to which, an outcome is attributable to the quality of services (like a poor job of tooth-filling) or to something else (like a very tough walnut). . . . Patients' attachments to particular professionals, the rationality of which is difficult to assess, complicate the picture even further. Cf. Evans, Professionals and the Production Function: Can Competition Policy Improve Efficiency in the Licensed Professions?, in Occupational Licensure and Regulation 235-236 (S. Rottenberg ed. 1980) (describing long-term relationship between professional and client not as "a series of spot contracts" but rather as "a long-term agreement, often implicit, to deal with each other in a set of future unspecified or incompletely specified circumstances according to certain rules," and adding that "it is not clear how or if these [implicit contracts] can be reconciled with the promotion of effective price competition in individual spot markets for particular services"). The existence of such significant challenges to informed decisionmaking by the customer for professional services immediately suggests that advertising restrictions arguably protecting patients from misleading or irrelevant advertising call for more than cursory treatment as obviously comparable to classic horizontal agreements to limit output or price competition.

The explanation proffered by the Court of Appeals for the likely anticompetitive effect of the CDA's restrictions on discount advertising began with the unexceptionable statements that "price advertising is fundamental to price competition," 128 F.3d at 727, and that "restrictions on the ability to advertise prices normally make it more difficult for consumers to find a lower price and for dentists to compete on the basis of price," *ibid.* (citing Bates v.

State Bar of Ariz., 433 U.S. 350, 364, (1977); Morales v. Trans World Airlines, Inc., 504 U.S. 374, 388 1992)). The court then acknowledged that, according to the CDA, the restrictions nonetheless furthered the "legitimate, indeed procompetitive, goal of preventing false and misleading price advertising." 128 F.3d at 728. The Court of Appeals might, at this juncture, have recognized that the restrictions at issue here are very far from a total ban on price or discount advertising, and might have considered the possibility that the particular restrictions on professional advertising could have different effects from those "normally" found in the commercial world, even to the point of promoting competition by reducing the occurrence of unverifiable and misleading across-the-board discount advertising.[7] Instead, the Court of Appeals confined itself to the brief assertion that the "CDA's disclosure requirements appear to prohibit across-the-board discounts because it is simply infeasible to disclose all of the information that is required," *ibid.*, followed by the observation that "the record provides no evidence that the rule has in fact led to increased disclosure and transparency of dental pricing," *ibid.*

But these observations brush over the professional context and describe no anticompetitive effects. Assuming that the record in fact supports the conclusion that the CDA disclosure rules essentially bar advertisement of across-the-board discounts, it does not obviously follow that such a ban would have a net anticompetitive effect here. Whether advertisements that announced discounts for, say, first-time customers, would be less effective at conveying information relevant to competition if they listed the original and discounted prices for checkups, X-rays, and fillings, than they would be if they simply specified a percentage discount across the board, seems to us a question susceptible to empirical but not a priori analysis. In a suspicious world, the discipline of specific example may well be a necessary condition of plausibility for professional claims that for all practical purposes defy comparison shopping. It is also possible in principle that, even if across-the-board discount advertisements were more effective in drawing customers in the short run, the

---

[7] JUSTICE BREYER claims that "the Court of Appeals did consider the relevant differences." But the language he cites says nothing more than that *per se* analysis is inappropriate here and that "some caution" was appropriate where restrictions purported to restrict false advertising, see *128 F.3d at 726-727.* Caution was of course appropriate, but this statement by the Court of Appeals does not constitute a consideration of the possible differences between these and other advertising restrictions.

recurrence of some measure of intentional or accidental misstatement due to the breadth of their claims might leak out over time to make potential patients skeptical of any such across-the-board advertising, so undercutting the method's effectiveness. . . . It might be, too, that across-the-board discount advertisements would continue to attract business indefinitely, but might work precisely because they were misleading customers, and thus just because their effect would be anticompetitive, not procompetitive. Put another way, the CDA's rule appears to reflect the prediction that any costs to competition associated with the elimination of across-the-board advertising will be outweighed by gains to consumer information (and hence competition) created by discount advertising that is exact, accurate, and more easily verifiable (at least by regulators). As a matter of economics this view may or may not be correct, but it is not implausible, and neither a court nor the Commission may initially dismiss it as presumptively wrong.[8]

In theory, it is true, the Court of Appeals neither ruled out the plausibility of some procompetitive support for the CDA's requirements nor foreclosed the utility of an evidentiary discussion on the point. The court indirectly acknowledged the plausibility of procompetitive justifications for the CDA's position when it stated that "the record provides no evidence that the rule has in fact led to increased disclosure and transparency of dental pricing," 128 F.3d at 728. But because petitioner alone would have had the incentive to introduce such evidence, the statement sounds as though the Court of Appeals may have thought it was justified without further analysis to shift a burden to

---

[8] JUSTICE BREYER suggests that our analysis is "of limited relevance," because "the basic question is whether this . . . theoretically redeeming virtue in fact offsets the restrictions' anticompetitive effects in this case." He thinks that the Commission and the Court of Appeals "adequately answered that question," but the absence of any empirical evidence on this point indicates that the question was not answered, merely avoided by implicit burden-shifting of the kind accepted by JUSTICE BREYER. The point is that before a theoretical claim of anticompetitive effects can justify shifting to a defendant the burden to show empirical evidence of procompetitive effects, as quick-look analysis in effect requires, there must be some indication that the court making the decision has properly identified the theoretical basis for the anticompetitive effects and considered whether the effects actually are anticompetitive. Where, as here, the circumstances of the restriction are somewhat complex, assumption alone will not do.

the CDA to adduce hard evidence of the procompetitive nature of its policy; the court's adversion to empirical evidence at the moment of this implicit burden-shifting underscores the leniency of its enquiry into evidence of the restrictions' anticompetitive effects.

The Court of Appeals was comparably tolerant in accepting the sufficiency of abbreviated rule-of-reason analysis as to the nonprice advertising restrictions. The court began with the argument that "[t]hese restrictions are in effect a form of output limitation, as they restrict the supply of information about individual dentists' services." *Ibid.* (citing P. Areeda & H. Hovenkamp, Antitrust Law ¶1505, pp. 693-694 (1997 Supp.)). Although this sentence does indeed appear as cited, it is puzzling, given that the relevant output for antitrust purposes here is presumably not information or advertising, but dental services themselves. The question is not whether the universe of possible advertisements has been limited (as assuredly it has), but whether the limitation on advertisements obviously tends to limit the total delivery of dental services. The court came closest to addressing this latter question when it went on to assert that limiting advertisements regarding quality and safety "prevents dentists from fully describing the package of services they offer," 128 F.3d at 728, adding that "the restrictions may also affect output more directly, as quality and comfort advertising may induce some customers to obtain nonemergency care when they might not otherwise do so," *ibid.* This suggestion about output is also puzzling. If quality advertising actually induces some patients to obtain more care than they would in its absence, then restricting such advertising would reduce the demand for dental services, not the supply; and it is of course the producers' supply of a good in relation to demand that is normally relevant in determining whether a producer-imposed output limitation has the anticompetitive effect of artificially raising prices, [9]

---

[9] JUSTICE BREYER wonders if we "mea[n] this statement as an argument against the anticompetitive tendencies that flow from an agreement not to advertise service quality." But as the preceding sentence shows, we intend simply to question the logic of the Court of Appeals's suggestion that the restrictions are anticompetitive because they somehow "affect output," 128 F.3d at 728, presumably with the intent to raise prices by limiting supply while demand remains constant. We do not mean to deny that an agreement not to advertise service quality might have anticompetitive effects. We merely mean that, absent further analysis of the kind JUSTICE BREYER undertakes, it is not possible to conclude that the net effect of this particular restriction is

see General Leaseways, Inc. v. National Truck Leasing Assn., 744 F.2d 588, 594-595 (CA7 1984) ("An agreement on output also equates to a price-fixing agreement. If firms raise price, the market's demand for their product will fall, so the amount supplied will fall too — in other words, output will be restricted. If instead the firms restrict output directly, price will as mentioned rise in order to limit demand to the reduced supply. Thus, with exceptions not relevant here, raising price, reducing output, and dividing markets have the same anticompetitive effects").

Although the Court of Appeals acknowledged the CDA's view that "claims about quality are inherently unverifiable and therefore misleading," 128 F.3d at 728, it responded that this concern "does not justify banning all quality claims without regard to whether they are, in fact, false or misleading," *ibid.* As a result, the court said, "the restriction is a sufficiently naked restraint on output to justify quick look analysis." *Ibid.* The court assumed, in these words, that some dental quality claims may escape justifiable censure, because they are both verifiable and true. But its implicit assumption fails to explain why it gave no weight to the countervailing, and at least equally plausible, suggestion that restricting difficult-to-verify claims about quality or patient comfort would have a procompetitive effect by preventing misleading or false claims that distort the market. It is, indeed, entirely possible to understand the CDA's restrictions on unverifiable quality and comfort advertising as nothing more than a procompetitive ban on puffery, cf. Bates, 433 U.S. at 366 (claims relating to the quality of legal services "probably are not susceptible of precise measurement or verification and, under some circumstances, might well be deceptive or misleading to the public, or even false"); *id.* at 383-384 ("[A]dvertising claims as to the quality of services . . . are not susceptible of measurement or verification; accordingly, such claims may be so likely to be misleading as to warrant restriction"), notwithstanding JUSTICE BREYER's citation (to a Commission discussion that never faces the issue of the unverifiability of professional quality claims, raised in Bates), post, at 5.[10]

---

anticompetitive.

[10] The Commission said only that "'mere puffing' deceives no one and has never been subject to regulation.'" *121 F.T.C. at 318.* The question here, of course, is not whether puffery may be subject to governmental regulation, but whether a professional organization may ban it.

The point is not that the CDA's restrictions necessarily have the procompetitive effect claimed by the CDA; it is possible that banning quality claims might have no effect at all on competitiveness if, for example, many dentists made very much the same sort of claims. And it is also of course possible that the restrictions might in the final analysis be anticompetitive. The point, rather, is that the plausibility of competing claims about the effects of the professional advertising restrictions rules out the indulgently abbreviated review to which the Commission's order was treated. The obvious anticompetitive effect that triggers abbreviated analysis has not been shown.

In light of our focus on the adequacy of the Court of Appeals's analysis, JUSTICE BREYER's thorough-going, *de novo* antitrust analysis contains much to impress on its own merits but little to demonstrate the sufficiency of the Court of Appeals's review. The obligation to give a more deliberate look than a quick one does not arise at the door of this Court and should not be satisfied here in the first instance. Had the Court of Appeals engaged in a painstaking discussion in a league with JUSTICE BREYER's (compare his 14 pages with the Ninth Circuit's 8), and had it confronted the comparability of these restrictions to bars on clearly verifiable advertising, its reasoning might have sufficed to justify its conclusion. Certainly JUSTICE BREYER's treatment of the antitrust issues here is no "quick look." Lingering is more like it, and indeed JUSTICE BREYER, not surprisingly, stops short of endorsing the Court of Appeals's discussion as adequate to the task at hand.

Saying here that the Court of Appeals's conclusion at least required a more extended examination of the possible factual underpinnings than it received is not, of course, necessarily to call for the fullest market analysis. Although we have said that a challenge to a "naked restraint on price and output" need not be supported by "a detailed market analysis" in order to "requir[e] some competitive justification," National Collegiate Athletic Assn., 468 U.S. at 110, it does not follow that every case attacking a less obviously anticompetitive restraint (like this one) is a candidate for plenary market examination. The truth is that our categories of analysis of anticompetitive effect are less fixed than terms like "*per se*," "quick look," and "rule of reason" tend to make them appear. We have recognized, for example, that "there is often no bright line separating per se from Rule of Reason analysis," since "considerable inquiry into market conditions" may be required before the application of any so-called "*per se*" condemnation is justified. *Id.*, at 104, n. 26. "[W]hether the ultimate finding is the product of a presumption or actual market analysis, the essential inquiry remains the same —whether or not the challenged restraint enhances competition." *Id.*, at 104. Indeed, the scholar who enriched antitrust law with the metaphor of "the twinkling of an eye" for the most condensed rule-of-reason analysis himself cautioned against the risk of misleading even in speaking of a "spectrum" of adequate reasonableness analysis for passing upon antitrust claims: "There is always something of a sliding scale in appraising reasonableness, but the sliding scale formula deceptively suggests greater precision than we can hope for.... Nevertheless, the quality of proof required should vary with the circumstances." P. Areeda, Antitrust Law ¶1507, p. 402 (1986).[11] At the same time, Professor Areeda also emphasized the necessity, particularly great in the quasi-common law realm of antitrust, that courts explain the logic of their conclusions. "By exposing their reasoning, judges . . . are subjected to others' critical analyses, which in turn can lead to better understanding for the future." *Id.* ¶1500, at 364. As the circumstances here demonstrate, there is generally no categorical line to be drawn between restraints that give rise to an intuitively obvious inference of anticompetitive effect and those that call for more detailed treatment. What is required, rather, is an enquiry meet for the case, looking to the circumstances, details, and logic of a restraint. The object is to see whether the experience of the market has been so clear, or necessarily will be, that a confident conclusion about the principal tendency of a restriction will follow from a quick (or at least quicker) look, in place of a more sedulous one. And of course what we

[11] Other commentators have expressed similar views. See, *e.g.*, Kolasky, Counterpoint: The Department of Justice's "Stepwise" Approach Imposes Too Heavy a Burden on Parties to Horizontal Agreements, Antitrust 41, 43 (Spring 1998) ("[I]n applying the rule of reason, the courts, as with any balancing test, use a sliding scale to determine how much proof to require"); Piraino, Making Sense of the Rule of Reason: A New Standard for Section 1 of the Sherman Act, 47 Vand. L. Rev. 1753, 1771 (1994) ("[C]ourts will have to undertake varying degrees of inquiry depending upon the type of restraint at issue. The legality of certain restraints will be easy to determine because their competitive effects are obvious. Other restrictions will require a more detailed analysis because their competitive impact is more ambiguous"). But see Klein, A "Stepwise" Approach for Analyzing Horizontal Agreements Will Provide a Much Needed Structure for Antitrust Review, Antitrust 41, 42 (Spring 1990) (examination of procompetitive justifications "is by no means a full scrutiny of the proffered efficiency justification. It is, rather, a hard look at the justification to determine if it meets the defendant's burden of coming forward with— but not establishing— a valid efficiency justification").

see may vary over time, if rule-of-reason analyses in case after case reach identical conclusions. For now, at least, a less quick look was required for the initial assessment of the tendency of these professional advertising restrictions. Because the Court of Appeals did not scrutinize the assumption of relative anticompetitive tendencies, we vacate the judgment and remand the case for a fuller consideration of the issue.

BREYER, J., with whom STEVENS, KENNEDY, and GINSBURG, JJ., join, concurring in part and dissenting in part.

I agree with the Court that the Federal Trade Commission has jurisdiction over petitioner, and I join Parts I and II of its opinion. I also agree that in a "rule of reason" antitrust case "the quality of proof required should vary with the circumstances," that "[w]hat is required . . . is an enquiry meet for the case," and that the object is a "confident conclusion about the principal tendency of a restriction." But I do not agree that the Court has properly applied those unobjectionable principles here. In my view, a traditional application of the rule of reason to the facts as found by the Commission requires affirming the Commission — just as the Court of Appeals did below.

I

The Commission's conclusion is lawful if its "factual findings," insofar as they are supported by "substantial evidence," "make out a violation of Sherman Act § 1." FTC v. Indiana Federation of Dentists, 476 U.S. 447, 454-455 (1986). To determine whether that is so, I would not simply ask whether the restraints at issue are anticompetitive overall. Rather, like the Court of Appeals (and the Commission), I would break that question down into four classical, subsidiary antitrust questions: (1) What is the specific restraint at issue? (2) What are its likely anticompetitive effects? (3) Are there offsetting procompetitive justifications? (4) Do the parties have sufficient market power to make a difference?

A

The most important question is the first: What are the specific restraints at issue?... Those restraints do not include merely the agreement to which the California Dental Association's (Dental Association or Association) ethical rule literally refers, namely, a promise to refrain from advertising that is "'false or misleading in any material respect.'" Instead, the Commission found a set of restraints arising out of the way the Dental Association implemented this innocent-sounding ethical rule in practice, through advisory opinions, guidelines, enforcement policies, and review of membership applications. In re California Dental Assn., 121 F.T.C. 190 (1996). As implemented, the ethical rule reached beyond its nominal target, to prevent truthful and nondeceptive advertising. In particular, the Commission determined that the rule, in practice:

(1) "precluded advertising that characterized a dentist's fees as being low, reasonable, or affordable," *Id.*, at 301.

(2) "precluded advertising . . . of across the board discounts," ibid.; and

(3) "prohibited all quality claims," *id.*, at 308.

Whether the Dental Association's basic rule as *implemented* actually restrained the truthful and nondeceptive advertising of low prices, across-the-board discounts, and quality service are questions of fact. The Administrative Law Judge (ALJ) and the Commission may have found those questions difficult ones. But both the ALJ and the Commission ultimately found against the Dental Association in respect to these facts. And the question for us—whether those agency findings are supported by substantial evidence, see Indiana Federation, supra, at 454—455— is not difficult.

The Court of Appeals referred explicitly to some of the evidence that it found adequate to support the Commission's conclusions. It pointed out, for example, that the Dental Association's "advisory opinions and guidelines indicate that . . . descriptions of prices as 'reasonable' or 'low' do not comply" with the Association's rule; that in "numerous cases" the Association "advised members of objections to special offers, senior citizen discounts, and new patient discounts, apparently without regard to their truth"; and that one advisory opinion "expressly states that claims as to the quality of services are inherently likely to be false or misleading," all "without any particular consideration of whether" such statements were "true or false." 128 F.3d 720, 729 (CA9 1997).

The Commission itself had before it far more evidence. It referred to instances in which the Association, without regard for the truthfulness of the statements at issue, recommended denial of membership to dentists wishing to advertise, for example, "reasonable fees quoted in advance," "major savings," or "making teeth cleaning . . . inexpensive." 121 F.T.C. at 301. It referred to testimony that "across-the-board discount advertising in literal compliance with the requirements 'would probably take two pages in the telephone book' and 'nobody is going to really advertise in that fashion.'" *Id.* at 302. And it pointed to many instances in which the Dental Association suppressed such advertising claims as "we guarantee all dental work for 1 year," "latest in cosmetic dentistry," and "gentle dentistry in a caring environment." *Id.* at 308-310.

I need not review the evidence further, for this Court has said that "substantial evidence" is a matter for the courts of appeals, and that it "will intervene only in what ought to be the rare instance when the standard appears to have been misapprehended or grossly misapplied." Universal Camera Corp. v. NLRB, 340 U.S. 474, 490—491 (1951). I have said enough to make clear that this is not a case warranting our intervention. Consequently, we must decide only the basic legal question whether the three restraints described above unreasonably restrict competition.

B

Do each of the three restrictions mentioned have "the potential for genuine adverse effects on competition"? Indiana Federation, 476 U.S. at 460; 7 P. Areeda, Antitrust Law ¶1503a, pp. 372-377 (1986) (hereinafter Areeda). I should have thought that the anticompetitive tendencies of the three restrictions were obvious. An agreement not to advertise that a fee is reasonable, that service is inexpensive, or that a customer will receive a discount makes it more difficult for a dentist to inform customers that he charges a lower price. If the customer does not know about a lower price, he will find it more difficult to buy lower price service. That fact, in turn, makes it less likely that a dentist will obtain more customers by offering lower prices. And that likelihood means that dentists will prove less likely to offer lower prices. But why should I have to spell out the obvious? To restrain truthful advertising about lower prices is likely to restrict competition in respect to price — "the central nervous system of the economy." United States v. Socony-Vacuum Oil Co., 310 U.S. 150, 226, n. 59 (1940); cf., *e.g.*, Bates v. State Bar of Ariz., 433 U.S. 350, 364 (1977) (price advertising plays an "indispensable role in the allocation of resources in a free enterprise system"); Virginia Bd. of Pharmacy v. Virginia Citizens Consumer Council, Inc., 425 U.S. 748, 765 (1976). The Commission thought this fact sufficient to hold (in the alternative) that the price advertising restrictions were unlawful *per se*. See

121 F.T.C. at 307; cf. Socony-Vacuum, *supra*, at 222-228 (finding agreement among competitors to buy "spot-market oil" unlawful per se because of its tendency to restrict price competition). For present purposes, I need not decide whether the Commission was right in applying a per se rule. I need only assume a rule of reason applies, and note the serious anticompetitive tendencies of the price advertising restraints.

The restrictions on the advertising of service quality also have serious anticompetitive tendencies. This is not a case of "mere puffing," as the FTC recognized. The days of my youth, when the billboards near Emeryville, California, home of AAA baseball's Oakland Oaks, displayed the name of "Painless" Parker, Dentist, are long gone -- along with the Oakland Oaks. But some parents may still want to know that a particular dentist makes a point of "gentle care." Others may want to know about 1-year dental work guarantees. To restrict that kind of service quality advertisement is to restrict competition over the quality of service itself, for, unless consumers know, they may not purchase, and dentists may not compete to supply that which will make little difference to the demand for their services. That, at any rate, is the theory of the Sherman Act. And it is rather late in the day for anyone to deny the significant anticompetitive tendencies of an agreement that restricts competition in any legitimate respect, see, *e.g.*, Paramount Famous Lasky Corp. v. United States, 282 U.S. 30, 43 (1930); United States v. First Nat. Pictures, Inc., 282 U.S. 44, 54-55 (1930), let alone one that inhibits customers from learning about the quality of a dentist's service.

Nor did the Commission rely solely on the unobjectionable proposition that a restriction on the ability of dentists to advertise on quality is likely to limit their incentive to compete on quality. Rather, the Commission pointed to record evidence affirmatively establishing that quality-based competition is important to dental consumers in California. Unsurprisingly, these consumers choose dental services based at least in part on "information about the type and quality of service." Similarly, as the Commission noted, the ALJ credited testimony to the effect that "advertising the comfort of services will 'absolutely' bring in more patients," and, conversely, that restraining the ability to advertise based on quality would decrease the number of patients that a dentist could attract. Finally, the Commission looked to the testimony of dentists who themselves had suffered adverse effects on their business when forced by petitioner to discontinue advertising quality of care.

The FTC found that the price advertising restrictions amounted to a "naked attempt to eliminate price competition." *Id.* at 300. It found that the service quality advertising restrictions "deprive consumers of information they value and of healthy competition for their patronage." *Id.*, at 311. It added that the "anticompetitive nature of these restrictions" was "plain." *Ibid.* The Court of Appeals agreed. I do not believe it possible to deny the anticompetitive tendencies I have mentioned.

C

We must also ask whether, despite their anticompetitive tendencies, these restrictions might be justified by other procompetitive tendencies or redeeming virtues. See 7 Areeda, ¶1504, at 377-383. This is a closer question— at least in theory. The Dental Association argues that the three relevant restrictions are inextricably tied to a legitimate Association effort to restrict false or misleading advertising. The Association, the argument goes, had to prevent dentists from engaging in the kind of truthful, nondeceptive advertising that it banned in order effectively to stop dentists from making unverifiable claims about price or service quality, which claims would mislead the consumer.

The problem with this or any similar argument is an empirical one. Notwithstanding its theoretical plausibility, the record does not bear out such a claim. The Commission, which is expert in the area of false and misleading advertising, was uncertain whether petitioner had even *made* the claim. It characterized petitioner's efficiencies argument as rooted in the (unproved) factual assertion that its ethical rule "challenges *only* advertising that is false or misleading." 121 F.T.C. at 316 (emphasis added). Regardless, the Court of Appeals wrote, in respect to the price restrictions, that "the record provides no evidence that the rule has in fact led to increased disclosure and transparency of dental pricing." 128 F.3d at 728. With respect to quality advertising, the Commission stressed that the Association "offered no convincing argument, let alone evidence, that consumers of dental services have been, or are likely to be, harmed by the broad categories of advertising it restricts." 121 F.T.C. at 319. Nor did the Court of Appeals think that the Association's unsubstantiated contention that "claims about quality are inherently unverifiable and therefore misleading" could "justify banning all quality claims without regard to whether they are, in fact, false or misleading." 128 F.3d at 728.

With one exception, my own review of the record reveals no significant evidentiary support for the proposition that the Association's members must agree to ban truthful price and quality advertising in order to stop untruthful claims. The one exception is the obvious fact that one can stop untruthful advertising if one prohibits all advertising. But since the Association made virtually no effort to sift the false from the true, *see* 121 F.T.C. at 316-317, that fact does not make out a valid antitrust defense. See *NCAA*, 468 U.S. at 119; 7 Areeda, ¶1505, at 383-384.

In the usual Sherman Act § 1 case, the defendant bears the burden of establishing a procompetitive justification. See National Soc. of Professional Engineers v. United States, 435 U.S. 679, 695 (1978); 7 Areeda, ¶1507b, at 397; 11 H. Hovenkamp, Antitrust Law ¶1914c, pp. 313-315 (1998); see also Law v. National Collegiate Athletic Assn., 134 F.3d 1010, 1019 (CA10), cert. denied, 525 U.S. ___ (1998); United States v. Brown Univ., 5 F.3d 658, 669 (CA3 1993). . . . And the Court of Appeals was correct when it concluded that no such justification had been established here.

D

I shall assume that the Commission must prove one additional circumstance, namely, that the Association's restraints would likely have made a real difference in the marketplace. See 7 Areeda, ¶1503, at 376-377. The Commission, disagreeing with the ALJ on this single point, found that the Association did possess enough market power to make a difference. In at least one region of California, the mid-Peninsula, its members accounted for more than 90% of the marketplace; on average they accounted for 75%. See 121 F.T.C. at 314. In addition, entry by new dentists into the market place is fairly difficult. Dental education is expensive (leaving graduates of dental school with $50,000-$100,000 of debt), as is opening a new dentistry office (which costs $75,000-$100,000). And Dental Association members believe membership in the Association is important, valuable, and recognized as such by the public.

These facts, in the Court of Appeals' view, were sufficient to show "enough market power to harm competition through [the Association's] standard setting in the area of advertising." 128 F.3d at 730. And that conclusion is correct. Restrictions on advertising price discounts in Palo Alto may make a difference because potential patients may not respond readily to discount advertising by the handful (10%) of dentists who are not members of the Association. And that fact, in turn, means that the remaining 90% will prove less likely to engage in price competition. Facts such as these have previously led this Court to find market power— unless the defendant has overcome the showing with strong contrary evidence. See, e.g., Indiana Federation, 476 U.S. at 456-457; cf. United States v. Loew's Inc., 371 U.S. 38, 45 (1962); Brown Shoe Co. v. United States, 370 U.S. 294, 341-344 (1962); accord, United States v. Aluminum Co. of America, 148 F.2d 416, 424 (CA2 1945). I can find no reason for departing from that precedent here.

II

In the Court's view, the legal analysis conducted by the Court of Appeals was insufficient, and the Court remands the case for a more thorough application of the rule of reason. But in what way did the Court of Appeals fail? I find the Court's answers to this question unsatisfactory — when one divides the overall Sherman Act question into its traditional component parts and adheres to traditional judicial practice for allocating the burdens of persuasion in an antitrust case.

Did the Court of Appeals misconceive the anticompetitive tendencies of the restrictions? After all, the object of the rule of reason is to separate those restraints that "may suppress or even destroy competition" from those that "merely regulat[e] and perhaps thereby promot[e] competition." Board of Trade of Chicago v. United States, 246 U.S. 231, 238 (1918). The majority says that the Association's "advertising restrictions might plausibly be thought to have a net procompetitive effect, or possibly no effect at all on competition." It adds that

> "advertising restrictions arguably protecting patients from misleading or irrelevant advertising call for more than cursory treatment as obviously comparable to classic horizontal agreements to limit output or price competition."

And it criticizes the Court of Appeals for failing to recognize that "the restrictions at issue here are very far from a total ban on price or discount advertising" and that "the particular restrictions on professional advertising could have different effects from those 'normally' found in the commercial world, even to the point of promoting competition . . . ."

The problem with these statements is that the Court of Appeals did consider the relevant differences. It *rejected* the legal "treatment" customarily applied "to classic horizontal agreements to limit output or price competition" — *i.e.*, the FTC's (alternative) *per se* approach. See 128 F.3d at 726-727. It did so because the Association's "policies do not, on their face, ban truthful nondeceptive ads"; instead, they "have been enforced in a way that restricts truthful advertising." *Id.*, at 727. It added that "[t]he value of restricting false advertising . . . counsels some caution in attacking rules that purport to do so but merely sweep too broadly." *Ibid.*

Did the Court of Appeals misunderstand the nature of an anticompetitive effect? The Court says:

> "If quality advertising actually induces some patients to obtain more care than they would in its absence, then restricting such advertising would reduce the demand for dental services, not the supply; and . . . the producers' supply . . . is normally relevant in determining whether a . . . limitation has the anticompetitive effect of artificially raising prices."

But if the Court means this statement as an argument against the anticompetitive tendencies that flow from an agreement not to advertise service quality, I believe it is the majority, and not the Court of Appeals, that is mistaken. An agreement not to advertise, say, "gentle care" is anticompetitive because it imposes an artificial barrier against each dentist's independent decision to advertise gentle care. That barrier, in turn, tends to inhibit those dentists who want to supply gentle care from getting together with those customers who want to buy gentle care. See P. Areeda & H. Hovenkamp, Antitrust Law ¶1505', p. 404 (Supp. 1998). There is adequate reason to believe that tendency present in this case.

Did the Court of Appeals inadequately consider possible procompetitive justifications? The Court seems to think so, for it says:

> "[T]he [Association's] rule appears to reflect the prediction that any costs to competition associated with the elimination of across-the-board advertising will be outweighed by gains to consumer information (and hence competition) created by discount advertising that is exact, accurate, and more easily verifiable (at least by regulators)."

That may or may not be an accurate assessment of the Association's motives in adopting its rule, but it is of limited relevance. Cf. *Chicago Board of Trade, supra*, at 238. The basic question is whether this, or some other, theoretically redeeming virtue in fact offsets the restrictions' anticompetitive effects in this case. Both court and Commission adequately answered that question.

The Commission found that the defendant did not make the necessary showing that a redeeming virtue existed in practice. The Court of Appeals, asking whether the rules, as enforced, "augmented competition and increased market efficiency," found the Commission's conclusion supported by substantial evidence. 128 F.3d at 728. That is why the court said that "the record provides no evidence that the rule has in fact led to increased disclosure and transparency of dental pricing"— which is to say that the record provides no evidence that the effects, though anticompetitive, are nonetheless redeemed or justified. *Ibid.*

The majority correctly points out that "petitioner alone would have had the incentive to introduce such evidence" of procompetitive justification. (Indeed, that is one of the reasons defendants normally bear the burden of persuasion about redeeming virtues.) But despite this incentive, petitioner's brief in this Court offers nothing concrete to counter the Commission's conclusion that the record does not support the claim of justification. Petitioner's failure to produce such evidence itself "explain[s]why [the lower court] gave no weight to the . . . suggestion that restricting difficult-to-verify claims about quality or patient comfort would have a procompetitive effect by preventing misleading or false claims that distort the market."

With respect to the restraint on advertising across-the-board discounts, the majority summarizes its concerns as follows: "Assuming that the record in fact supports the conclusion that the [Association's] disclosure rules essentially bar advertisement of [such] discounts, it does not obviously follow that such a ban would have a net anticompetitive effect here." I accept, rather than assume, the premise: The FTC found that the disclosure rules did bar advertisement of across-the-board discounts, and that finding is supported by substantial evidence. And I accept as *literally* true the conclusion that the Court says follows from that premise, namely, that "net anticompetitive effects" do not "*obviously*" follow from that premise. But obviousness is not the point. With respect to any of the three restraints found by the Commission, whether "net anticompetitive effects" follow is a matter of how the Commission, and, here, the Court of Appeals, have answered the questions I laid out at the beginning. Has the Commission shown that the restriction has anticompetitive tendencies? It has. Has the Association nonetheless shown offsetting virtues? It has not. Has the Commission shown market power sufficient for it to believe that the restrictions will likely make a real world difference? It has.

The upshot, in my view, is that the Court of Appeals, applying ordinary antitrust principles, reached an unexceptional conclusion. It is the same legal conclusion that this Court itself reached in Indiana Federation— a much closer case than this one. There the Court found that an agreement by dentists not to submit dental X rays to insurers violated the rule of reason. The anticompetitive tendency of that agreement was to reduce competition among dentists in respect to their willingness to submit X rays to insurers, see 476 U.S. at 456 — a matter in respect to which consumers are relatively indifferent, as compared to advertising of price discounts and service quality, the matters at issue here. The redeeming virtue in *Indiana Federation* was the alleged undesirability of having insurers consider a range of matters when deciding whether treatment was justified— a virtue no less plausible, and no less proved, than the virtue offered here. See *id.*, at 462—464. The "power" of the dentists to enforce their agreement was no greater than that at issue here (control of 75% to 90% of the relevant markets). See *id., at 460.* It is difficult to see how the two cases can be reconciled.

* * *

I would note that the form of analysis I have followed is not rigid; it admits of some variation according to the circumstances. The important point, however, is that its allocation of the burdens of persuasion reflects a gradual evolution within the courts over a period of many years. That evolution represents an effort carefully to blend the procompetitive objectives of the law of antitrust with administrative necessity. It represents a considerable advance, both from the days when the Commission had to present and/or refute every possible fact and theory, and from antitrust theories so abbreviated as to prevent proper analysis. The former prevented cases from ever reaching a conclusion, cf. Bok, Section 7 of the Clayton Act and the Merging of Law and Economics, 74 Harv. L. Rev. 226, 266 (1960), and the latter called forth the criticism that the "Government always wins," United States v. Von's Grocery Co., 384 U.S. 270, 301 (1966) (Stewart, J., dissenting). I hope that this case does not represent an abandonment of that basic, and important, form of analysis.

For these reasons, I respectfully dissent from Part III of the Court's opinion.

Notes

1. In September 2000, after *California Dental* was remanded, the Ninth Circuit held that the FTC had failed to carry its burden of proving that the restrictions on price and quality advertising had a net anticompetitive effect. The FTC, according to the Ninth Circuit, made a tactical decision to try to win the case on a *per se* or abbreviated rule-of-reason theory, and under these circumstances, the CDA was found correct in arguing that "further factfinding would give the FTC an unwaranted second bite at the apple." California Dental Assn. v. FTC, 224 F.3d 942 (9th Cir. 2000).

2. In Continental Airlines, Inc. v. United Air Lines, Inc., 136 F. Supp. 2d 542 (E.D. Va. 2001), which dealt with an agreement among airlines to restrict the size of carry-on bags at Washington Dulles International Airport, the district court applied an abbreviated rule-of reason analysis and concluded:

> In summary, defendants' agreement to restrict carry-on baggage size for all airlines at Dulles is a horizontal agreement to restrict output meriting an abbreviated Rule of Reason analysis. This analysis shifts the burden to defendants to offer plausible procompetitive justifications for the restraint. An examination of defendants' proffered justifications discloses that they do not enhance and are otherwise not material to, competition. Accordingly, the restriction is an unreasonable restraint of trade that caused plaintiffs antitrust injury.

CHAPTER 5: GROUP REFUSALS TO DEAL AND JOINT VENTURES

Section 1. Refusals To Deal

Insert after *Klors*, page 371:

NYNEX CORP. v. DISCON, INC.
Supreme Court of the United States, 1998.
525 U.S. 128, 119 S. Ct. 493, 142 L. Ed. 2d 510.

BREYER, J. In this case we ask whether the antitrust rule that group boycotts are illegal *per se* as set forth in Klor's, Inc. v. Broadway-Hale Stores, Inc., 359 U.S. 207, 212 (1959), applies to a buyer's decision to buy from one seller rather than another, when that decision cannot be justified in terms of ordinary competitive objectives. We hold that the *per se* group boycott rule does not apply.

I

Before 1984 American Telephone and Telegraph Company (AT&T) supplied most of the Nation's telephone service and, through wholly owned subsidiaries such as Western Electric, it also supplied much of the Nation's telephone equipment. In 1984 an antitrust consent decree took AT&T out of the local telephone service business and left AT&T a *long-distance* telephone service provider, competing with such firms as MCI and Sprint. See M. Kellogg, J. Thorne, & P. Huber, Federal Telecommunications Law § 4.6, p. 221 (1992). The decree transformed AT&T's formerly owned local telephone companies into independent firms. At the same time, the decree insisted that those local firms help assure competitive long-distance service by guaranteeing long-distance companies physical access to their systems and to their local customers. See United States v. American Telephone & Telegraph Co., 552 F. Supp. 131, 225, 227 (DC 1982), aff'd *sub nom.* Maryland v. United States, 460 U.S. 1001 (1983). To guarantee that physical access, some local telephone firms had to install new call-switching equipment; and to install new call-switching equipment, they often had to remove old call-switching equipment. This case involves the business of removing that old switching equipment (and other obsolete telephone equipment)—a business called *"removal services."*

Discon, Inc., the respondent, sold removal services used by New York

Telephone Company, a firm supplying local telephone service in much of New York State and parts of Connecticut. New York Telephone is a subsidiary of NYNEX Corporation. NYNEX also owns Materiel Enterprises Company, a purchasing entity that bought removal services for New York Telephone. Discon, in a lengthy detailed complaint, alleged that the NYNEX defendants (namely, NYNEX, New York Telephone, Materiel Enterprises, and several NYNEX related individuals) engaged in unfair, improper, and anticompetitive activities in order to hurt Discon and to benefit Discon's removal services competitor, AT&T Technologies, a lineal descendant of Western Electric. The Federal District Court dismissed Discon's complaint for failure to state a claim. The Court of Appeals for the Second Circuit affirmed that dismissal with an exception, and that exception is before us for consideration.

The Second Circuit focused on one of Discon's specific claims, a claim that Materiel Enterprises had switched its purchases from Discon to Discon's competitor, AT&T Technologies, as part of an attempt to defraud local telephone service customers by hoodwinking regulators. According to Discon, Materiel Enterprises would pay AT&T Technologies more than Discon would have charged for similar removal services. It did so because it could pass the higher prices on to New York Telephone, which in turn could pass those prices on to telephone consumers in the form of higher regulatory-agency-approved telephone service charges. At the end of the year, Materiel Enterprises would receive a special rebate from AT&T Technologies, which Materiel Enterprises would share with its parent, NYNEX. Discon added that it refused to participate in this fraudulent scheme, with the result that Materiel Enterprises would not buy from Discon, and Discon went out of business.

These allegations, the Second Circuit said, state a cause of action under §1 of the Sherman Act, though under a "different legal theory" from the one articulated by Discon. The Second Circuit conceded that ordinarily "the decision to discriminate in favor of one supplier over another will have a pro-competitive intent and effect." But, it added, in this case, "no such pro-competitive rationale appears on the face of the complaint." Rather, the complaint alleges Materiel Enterprises' decision to buy from AT&T Technologies, rather than from Discon, was intended to be, and was, "anti-competitive." Hence, "Discon has alleged a cause of action under, at least, the rule of reason, and possibly under the *per se* rule applied to group boycotts in *Klor's*, if the restraint of trade '"has no purpose except stifling competition."' " (quoting Oreck Corp. v. Whirlpool Corp., 579 F.2d 126, 131 (CA2) (en banc) (in turn quoting White Motor Co. v. United States, 372 U.S. 253, 263

(1963)), cert. denied, *439 U.S. 946 (1978)).* For somewhat similar reasons the Second Circuit believed the complaint stated a valid claim of conspiracy to monopolize under §2 of the Sherman Act. See 93 F.3d at 1061-1062.

The Second Circuit noted that the Courts of Appeals are uncertain as to whether, or when, the *per se* group boycott rule applies to a decision by a purchaser to favor one supplier over another (which the Second Circuit called a "two-firm group boycott"). Compare Com-Tel, Inc. v. DuKane Corp., 669 F.2d 404, 411-413, and nn. 13, 16 (CA6 1982); Cascade Cabinet Co. v. Western Cabinet & Millwork Inc., 710 F.2d 1366, 1370-1371 (CA9 1983), with Construction Aggregate Transport, Inc. v. Florida Rock Industries, Inc., 710 F.2d 752, 776-778 (CA11 1983). We granted certiorari in order to consider the applicability of the *per se* group boycott rule where a single buyer favors one seller over another, albeit for an improper reason.

II

As this Court has made clear, the Sherman Act's prohibition of "[e]very" agreement in "restraint of trade," prohibits only agreements that *unreasonably* restrain trade. See Business Electronics Corp. v. Sharp Electronics Corp., 485 U.S. 717, 723 (1988) (citing National Collegiate Athletic Assn. v. Board of Regents of Univ. of Okla., 468 U.S. 85, 98 (1984)); Standard Oil Co. of N. J. v. United States, 221 U.S. 1, 59-62 (1911); 2 P. Areeda & H. Hovenkamp, Antitrust Law ¶320b, p. 49 (1995). Yet certain kinds of agreements will so often prove so harmful to competition and so rarely prove justified that the antitrust laws do not require proof that an agreement of that kind is, in fact, anticompetitive in the particular circumstances. See State Oil Co. v. Khan, 522 U.S. 3, 10 (1997); Northwest Wholesale Stationers, Inc. v. Pacific Stationery & Printing Co., 472 U.S. 284, 289-290 (1985); *supra* 2 Areeda & Hovenkamp, ¶320b, at 49-52. An agreement of such a kind is unlawful *per se.* See, *e.g.*, United States v. Socony-Vacuum Oil Co., 310 U.S. 150, 218 (1940) (finding horizontal price-fixing agreement *per se* illegal); Dr. Miles Medical Co. v. John D. Park & Sons Co., 220 U.S. 373, 408 (1911) (finding vertical price-fixing agreement *per se* illegal); Palmer v. BRG of Ga., Inc., 498 U.S. 46, 49-50 (1990) (per curiam) (finding horizontal market division *per se* illegal).

The Court has found the *per se* rule applicable in certain group boycott cases. Thus, in Fashion Originators' Guild of America, Inc. v. FTC, 312 U.S. 457 (1941), this Court considered a group boycott created by an agreement among a group of clothing designers, manufacturers, suppliers, and retailers. The defendant designers, manufacturers, and suppliers had promised not to sell their clothes to retailers who bought clothes from competing manufacturers and suppliers. The defendants wanted to present evidence that would show their agreement was justified because the boycotted competitors used "pira[ted]" fashion designs. But the Court wrote that "it was not error to refuse to hear the evidence offered"—evidence that the agreement was reasonable and necessary to "protect . . . against the devastating evils" of design pirating—for that evidence "is no more material than would be the reasonableness of the prices fixed" by a price-fixing agreement.

In *Klor's* the Court also applied the *per se* rule. The Court considered a boycott created when a retail store, Broadway-Hale, and 10 household appliance manufacturers and their distributors agreed that the distributors would not sell, or would sell only at discriminatory prices, household appliances to Broadway-Hale's small, nearby competitor, namely, *Klor's*. 359 U.S. at 208-209. The defendants had submitted undisputed evidence that their agreement hurt only one competitor (Klor's) and that so many other nearby appliance-selling competitors remained that competition in the marketplace continued to thrive. *Id.* at 209-210. The Court held that this evidence was beside the point. The conspiracy was "not to be tolerated merely because the victim is just one merchant." The Court thereby inferred injury to the competitive process itself from the nature of the boycott agreement. And it forbade, as a matter of law, a defense based upon a claim that only one small firm, not competition itself, had suffered injury.

The case before us involves *Klor's*. The Second Circuit did not forbid the defendants to introduce evidence of "justification." To the contrary, it invited the defendants to do so, for it said that the *"per se* rule*"* would apply only if no "pro-competitive justification" were to be found. 93 F.3d at 1061; cf. 7 P. Areeda & H. Hovenkamp, Antitrust Law ¶1510, p. 416 (1986) ("Boycotts are said to be unlawful *per se* but justifications are routinely considered in defining the forbidden category"). Thus, the specific legal question before us is whether an antitrust court considering an agreement by a buyer to purchase goods or services from one supplier rather than another should (after examining the buyer's reasons or justifications) apply the *per se* rule if it finds no legitimate business reason for that purchasing decision. We conclude no boycott-related *per se* rule applies and that the plaintiff here must allege and prove harm, not just to a single competitor, but to the competitive process, *i.e.*, to competition itself.

Our conclusion rests in large part upon precedent, for precedent limits the *per se* rule in the boycott context to cases involving horizontal agreements among direct competitors. The agreement in *Fashion Originators' Guild* involved what may be called a group boycott in the strongest sense: A group of competitors threatened to withhold business from third parties unless those third parties would help them injure their directly competing rivals. Although *Klor's* involved a threat made by a *single* powerful firm, it also involved a horizontal agreement among those threatened, namely, the appliance suppliers, to hurt a competitor of the retailer who made the threat. See 359 U.S. at 208-209; see also P. Areeda & L. Kaplow, Antitrust Analysis: Problems, Text, and Cases 333 (5th ed. 1997) (defining paradigmatic boycott as "collective action among a group of competitors that may inhibit the competitive vitality of rivals"); 11 H. Hovenkamp, Antitrust Law ¶1901e, pp. 189-190 (1998). This Court emphasized in *Klor's* that the agreement at issue was

> "not a case of a single trader refusing to deal with another, nor even of a manufacturer and a dealer agreeing to an exclusive distributorship. Alleged in this complaint is a wide combination consisting of manufacturers, distributors and a retailer." 359 U.S. at 212-213 (footnote omitted).

This Court subsequently pointed out specifically that *Klor's* was a case involving not simply a "vertical" agreement between supplier and customer, but a case that also involved a "horizontal" agreement among competitors. See Business Electronics, 485 U.S. at 734. And in doing so, the Court held that a "vertical restraint is not illegal *per se* unless it includes some agreement on price or price levels." This precedent makes the *per se* rule inapplicable, for the case before us concerns only a vertical agreement and a vertical restraint, a restraint that takes the form of depriving a supplier of a potential customer. See 11 Hovenkamp, *supra*, ¶1902d, at 198.

Nor have we found any special feature of this case that could distinguish it from the precedent we have just discussed. We concede Discon's claim that the petitioners' behavior hurt consumers by raising telephone service rates. But that consumer injury naturally flowed not so much from a less competitive market for removal services, as from the exercise of market power that is *lawfully* in the hands of a monopolist, namely, New York Telephone, combined with a deception worked upon the regulatory agency that prevented the agency from controlling New York Telephone's exercise of its monopoly power.

To apply the *per se* rule here—where the buyer's decision, though not made for competitive reasons, composes part of a regulatory fraud — would transform cases involving business behavior that is improper for various reasons, say, cases involving nepotism or personal pique, into treble-damages antitrust cases. And that *per se* rule would discourage firms from changing suppliers —even where the competitive process itself does not suffer harm. Cf. Poller v. Columbia Broadcasting System, Inc., 368 U.S. 464, 484 (1962) (Harlan, J., dissenting) (citing Packard Motor Car Co. v. Webster Motor Car Co., 243 F.2d 418, 421 (CADC 1957)).

The freedom to switch suppliers lies close to the heart of the competitive process that the antitrust laws seek to encourage. Cf. *Standard Oil, 221 U.S., at 62* (noting "the freedom of the individual right to contract when not unduly or improperly exercised [is] the most efficient means for the prevention of monopoly"). At the same time, other laws, for example, "unfair competition" laws, business tort laws, or regulatory laws, provide remedies for various "competitive practices thought to be offensive to proper standards of business morality." 3 P. Areeda & H. Hovenkamp, Antitrust Law ¶651d, p. 78 (1996). Thus, this Court has refused to apply *per se* reasoning in cases involving that kind of activity. See Brooke Group Ltd. v. Brown & Williamson Tobacco Corp., 509 U.S. 209, 225 (1993) ("Even an act of pure malice by one business competitor against another does not, without more, state a claim under the federal antitrust laws"); 3 Areeda & Hovenkamp, *supra*, ¶651d, at 80 ("[I]n the presence of substantial market power, some kinds of tortious behavior could anticompetitively create or sustain a monopoly, [but] it is wrong categorically to condemn such practices . . . or categorically to excuse them").

Discon points to another special feature of its complaint, namely, its claim that Materiel Enterprises hoped to drive Discon from the market lest Discon reveal its behavior to New York Telephone or to the relevant regulatory agency. That hope, says Discon, amounts to a special anticompetitive motive.

We do not see how the presence of this special motive, however, could make a significant difference. That motive does not turn Materiel Enterprises' actions into a "boycott" within the meaning of this Court's precedents. Nor, for that matter, do we understand how Discon believes the motive affected Materiel Enterprises' behavior. Why would Discon's demise have made Discon's employees less likely, rather than more likely, to report the overcharge/rebate scheme to telephone regulators? Regardless, a *per se* rule that would turn upon a showing that a defendant not only knew about but also hoped for a firm's demise would create a legal distinction — between corporate knowledge and corporate motive — that does not necessarily correspond to behavioral differences and which would be difficult to prove, making the resolution of already complex antitrust cases yet more difficult. We cannot find a convincing reason why the presence of this special motive should lead to the application of the *per se* rule.

Finally, we shall consider an argument that is related tangentially to Discon's *per se* claims. The complaint alleges that New York Telephone (through Materiel Enterprises) was the largest buyer of removal services in New York State, and that only AT&T Technologies competed for New York Telephone's business. ne might ask whether these accompanying allegations are sufficient to warrant application of a Klor's-type presumption of consequent harm to the competitive process itself.

We believe that these allegations do not do so, for, as we have said, antitrust law does not permit the application of the *per se* rule in the boycott context in the absence of a horizontal agreement. (Though in other contexts, say, vertical price fixing, conduct may fall within the scope of a *per se* rule not at issue here. See, *e.g.*, Dr. Miles Medical Co., 220 U.S. at 408.) The complaint itself explains why any such presumption would be particularly inappropriate here, for it suggests the presence of other potential or actual competitors, which fact, in the circumstances, could argue against the likelihood of anticompetitive harm. The complaint says, for example, that New York Telephone itself was a potential competitor in that New York Telephone considered removing its equipment by itself, and in fact did perform a few jobs itself. The complaint also suggests that other nearby small local telephone companies needing removal services must have worked out some way to supply them. The complaint's description of the removal business suggests that entry was easy, perhaps to the point where other firms, employing workers who knew how to remove a switch and sell it for scrap, might have entered that business almost at will. To that extent, the complaint suggests other actual or potential competitors might have provided roughly similar checks upon "equipment removal" prices and services with or without Discon. At the least, the complaint provides no sound basis for assuming the contrary. Its simple allegation of harm to Discon does not automatically show injury to competition.

III

The Court of Appeals also upheld the complaint's charge of a conspiracy to monopolize in violation of §2 of the Sherman Act. It did so, however, on the understanding that the conspiracy in question consisted of the very same purchasing practices that we have previously discussed. Unless those agreements harmed the competitive process, they did not amount to a conspiracy to monopolize. We do not see, on the basis of the facts alleged, how Discon could succeed on this claim without prevailing on its §1 claim. See 3 Areeda & Hovenkamp, *supra*. Given our conclusion that Discon has not alleged a §1 *per se* violation, we think it prudent to vacate this portion of the Court of Appeals' decision and allow the court to reconsider its finding of a §2 claim.

IV

Petitioners ask us to reach beyond the *"per se"* issues and to hold that Discon's complaint does not allege anywhere that their purchasing decisions harmed the competitive process itself and, for this reason, it should be dismissed. They note that Discon has not pointed to any paragraph of the complaint that alleges harm to the competitive process. This matter, however, lies outside the questions presented for certiorari. Those questions were limited to the application of the *per se* rule. For that reason, we believe petitioners cannot raise that argument in this Court.

V

For these reasons, the judgment of the Court of Appeals is vacated, and the case is remanded for further proceedings consistent with this opinion.

TOYS "R" US, INC. v. FEDERAL TRADE COMMISSION
United States Court of Appeals, Seventh Circuit, 2000.
[Reprinted below, page 112].

Insert after Note 5, page 374:

The area of professional sports continues to supply the courts with cases alleging unlawful group boycotts. How would you evaluate the following two situations?

1. In the United States, professional soccer is organized by Major League Soccer, L.L.C. ("MLS"). MLS in turn is affiliated with the Federation International de Football Association, which World Cup fans know as FIFA. Teams that are members of MLS must comply with its rules, and MLS in turn requires each professional soccer player to sign a Standard Player Agreement that provides that "a player's right to play professional soccer in the United States is subject to rules and regulations promulgated by FIFA."

One of the FIFA rules provides that if a soccer player concludes a contract with a new club, the player's former club shall be entitled to compensation for his training and/or development – in brief, to a transfer fee. If the two clubs cannot agree on the fee, the dispute must be referred to FIFA for final resolution. The transfer fee rule applies whether or not the player is still under contract to his first club, or his contract has expired (making him an "out-of-contract player").

A class of players brought a lawsuit against MLS claiming that its enforcement of the transfer fee amounted to a restraint of trade that was per se illegal under Sherman Act § 1, either as a price-fixing agreement or as a group boycott. Should the district court apply the per se rule or a rule of reason to their claim? How would you evaluate the restriction, either way? Would it make any difference to you if MLS represented to the court that it had never paid or requested a transfer fee for an out-of-contract player? What if MLS had in fact never invoked the rule, but it refused to enter into a binding stipulation assuring the court and the plaintiffs that it would never do so in the future?

See Fraser v. Major League Soccer, L.L.C., 1998 WL 295521 (D. Mass, decided Jan. 28, 1998) (O'Toole, D.J.) (denying summary judgment to both sides).

2. Moving to the area of amateur soccer, now consider the actions of several local soccer associations in Texas. The plaintiff, Eleven Line, Inc., owned and operated a sports facility known as the Permian Basin Sports Center ("PBSC"). PBSC wanted to organize and sponsor indoor soccer leagues. It ran against a stone wall, however, when it discovered that defendants North Texas State Soccer Association, Midland Soccer Association, and Odessa Soccer Association, had a rule (Rule II) that prohibited their registered teams, players, and coaches from playing with

any team or player that is not registered with an affiliate of the United States Soccer Federation (USSF), as all defendants were. If a registered team or player engages in this type of unsanctioned play, it or he is automatically expelled from the defendant organizations. PBSC sued under the Sherman Act, claiming that Rule II operated as an unlawful restraint on competition. The North Texas, Midland, and Odessa organizations, which were the only amateur soccer groups in the area, had combined to persuade or coerce their member players and coaches to refuse to deal with a competitor, PBSC. Should the court approach this claim under the per se rule or the rule of reason? How would you rule on the defendants' motion to dismiss the case for failure to state a claim?

See Eleven Line, Inc. v. North Texas State Soccer Ass'n, 1998 WL 25566 (N.D. Tex., decided Jan. 13, 1998) (Buchmeyer, C.D.J.).

Insert after Note 6, page 376:

The question of non-commercial boycotts and refusals to deal by single firms with significant market power also continues to percolate. Although the following case discusses it more in terms of the "trade or commerce" requirement than the substantive reach of the antitrust laws, it presents interesting questions of both kinds.

HAMILTON CHAPTER OF ALPHA DELTA PHI, INC. v. HAMILTON COLLEGE
United States Court of Appeals, Second Circuit, 1997.
128 F.3d 59.

Before: KEARSE and JACOBS, Circuit Judges, and GLEESON, District Judge.

GLEESON, J. Four Hamilton College fraternities brought this action against Hamilton College ("Hamilton") and its president, Eugene M. Tobin, alleging a violation of Section 2 of the Sherman Act, 15 U.S.C. § 2. The fraternities challenge Hamilton's residential policy, which requires all of its students to live in college housing and participate in a college meal plan. According to plaintiffs, that policy unlawfully monopolizes the market for residential services in Clinton, New York. The United States District Court for the Northern District of New York, Rosemary S. Pooler, Judge, concluded that Hamilton's provision of room and board pursuant to its residential policy is not "trade or commerce" and lacks a substantial nexus to interstate commerce, and dismissed the complaint for lack of subject matter jurisdiction. For the reasons set forth below, we reverse.

BACKGROUND

A. The Facts

Hamilton is a private college located in Clinton, New York. Chartered in 1812 as an all-male college, it became fully co-educational upon its consolidation in 1978 with nearby Kirkland College. It draws more than half of its students from foreign countries and states other than New York. During the 1993-94 school year, for example, only 41% of its 1,668 students were residents of New York State.

For many years, Hamilton required only first-year students to live in college-owned housing and to participate in a college-run meal plan, and permitted students in their second, third and fourth years to room and board in fraternities or other private housing not owned or controlled by the college. In the spring of 1994, however, Hamilton began changing this residential policy by formally restricting the number of students who could live off-campus. Then, on March 3, 1995, Hamilton announced that, effective September 1995, all students would be required to live in college-owned facilities and to purchase college-sponsored meal plans.

In the 1993-94 school year, before the implementation of the new policy, Hamilton received more than $7 million in revenues for providing such services, while the fraternities and other off-campus landlords received approximately $1 million. Plaintiffs contend that Hamilton's new residential plan has a commercial purpose: to eliminate competition in the provision of "residential services" (essentially, room and board) to Hamilton students in order to raise revenues. They further allege that Hamilton, having announced that the private ownership societies that own the fraternity houses will be unable to house Hamilton students, has attempted to exercise monopoly power as the sole available buyer by attempting to purchase the fraternity houses at artificially low prices, intending to use them to provide housing for its students.

On the other hand, Hamilton submitted affidavits and documentary evidence to the district court attempting to demonstrate that the primary purpose of the challenged residential plan was entirely noncommercial.

According to Hamilton, the purpose of the plan is to create an academic environment that is more appealing to female applicants to Hamilton. According to the Chairman of the Board of Trustees,

> fewer than 20% of the current students, self-selected [fraternity] males who have inherited these [fraternity houses,] virtually control social life on [Hamilton's campus]. Women students tell us time and again that, while they are fond of Hamilton, they do not feel they have the same social and residential opportunities as their male classmates. They do not enjoy--and cannot afford to replicate--the privileges of fraternity life. More disturbing is evidence that this disparity is leading many of the most talented prospective female applicants to seek education elsewhere. . . . The most disturbing result, however, has been increasing evidence that Hamilton is in danger of being perceived more for its social life than for its academic rigor. . . .

B. Procedural History

On July 10, 1995, the four plaintiff fraternities--the Psi Chapter of Psi Upsilon, Inc., the Hamilton Chapter of Alpha Delta Phi, Inc., Beta of Sigma Phi Society, Inc., and Delta Kappa Epsilon Society of Hamilton College--brought this action pursuant to Sections 4 and 16 of the Clayton Act (15 U.S.C. §§ 15 and 26), alleging that Hamilton's residential policy violates Section 2 of the Sherman Act, 15 U.S.C. § 2. Plaintiffs seek damages, injunctive relief and attorneys' fees. Simultaneously with the filing of the complaint, the fraternities sought and the district court issued an order directing defendants to show cause why a preliminary injunction should not be entered enjoining the implementation of the residential policy announced on March 3, 1995.

On August 1, 1995, defendants moved to dismiss the complaint pursuant to Rules 12(b)(1) and 12(b)(6) of the Federal Rules of Civil Procedure. Defendants argued that the provision of room and board to Hamilton students is not "trade or commerce" within the meaning of Section 2 of the Sherman Act. They further argued that Hamilton's conduct had an insufficient nexus to interstate commerce to fall within the boundaries of the Sherman Act.

On October 2, 1995, the district court heard oral argument on plaintiffs' motion for a preliminary injunction and defendants' motion to dismiss. In addition to their jurisdictional arguments, defendants urged the court to dismiss the complaint because the relevant product market was not the market for room and board for Hamilton students, as alleged in the complaint, but the market for highly selective liberal arts colleges in which Hamilton competes for students with more than 100 colleges. In support of this claim, defendants submitted the affidavit of Jerry A. Hausman, a professor of economics at the Massachusetts Institute of Technology. Defendants acknowledged that any disposition on this ground would require the court to convert the motion to dismiss into one for summary judgment, as permitted by Rule 12(b) of the Federal Rules of Civil Procedure. At the conclusion of the oral argument, the court took both motions under advisement.

On October 12, 1995, the district court notified counsel by letter that it anticipated relying on the Hausman affidavit. Pursuant to the requirement in Rule 12(b) that the parties be given a reasonable opportunity to present affidavits and other material pertinent to a motion for summary judgment, the court invited any such material, expressing particular interest in plaintiffs' response to the relevant market and market power assertions in the Hausman affidavit. In response to the district court's invitation, plaintiffs submitted, among other things, the affidavit of an economist, William O. Kerr, who asserted that the primary market relevant to plaintiffs' antitrust claim is the market for the sale of residential services to Hamilton's students.

In a written decision dated April 12, 1996, the district court granted the defendants' motion to dismiss. Despite the numerous affidavits submitted by both parties, the court did not convert the motion into one for summary judgment, but rather stated that it based its decision on the complaint alone, and held that it lacked subject matter jurisdiction. Specifically, the court held that the allegations in the complaint failed to establish that the provision of residential services under the challenged residential policy was "trade or commerce," and thus subject to the prohibitions of the Sherman Act. It further held that the complaint failed to establish the requisite nexus between Hamilton's conduct and interstate commerce. The court did not reach the issues of the relevant product market and Hamilton's market power.

DISCUSSION

[The court began by discussing the appropriate standard of review, concluding that the defendants were entitled to dismissal only if the plaintiffs could prove no set of facts that would entitle them to relief. It then addressed the central question whether the Sherman Act applied to the plaintiffs' allegations.]

B. "Trade or Commerce" Under the Sherman Act

Although there is no blanket exemption from the antitrust laws based on an organization's non-profit status or public-service orientation, see National Collegiate Athletic Association v. Board of Regents of the University of Oklahoma, 468 U.S. 85, 100 n. 22 (1984); Goldfarb v. Virginia State Bar, 421 U.S. 773 787-88 95 S.Ct. (1975), the Sherman Act does not apply to all activities of all organizations. Plaintiffs may challenge Hamilton's provision of room and board pursuant to its residential policy under the Act only if that conduct constitutes "trade or commerce." 15 U.S.C. § 2.

Congress intended the antitrust laws to apply to a wide array of commercial conduct . . . so as to foreclose unfair business practices wherever they occur. . . . This broad application serves the Sherman Act's essential purpose: safeguarding consumer welfare. On the other hand, the legislative history of the Sherman Act reveals that it was not intended to reach noncommercial activities that are intended to promote social causes. See generally National Organization for Women v. Scheidler, 968 F.2d 612, 617-21 (7th Cir.1992), rev'd on other grounds, 510 U.S. 249 (1994); Missouri v. National Organization for Women, 620 F.2d 1301, 1304-09 (8th Cir.), cert. denied, 449 U.S. 842 (1980). As stated by the Supreme Court in Apex Hosiery Co. v. Leader, 310 U.S. 469, 493 n. 15 (1940):

> The history of the Sherman Act as contained in the legislative proceedings is emphatic in its support for the conclusion that "business competition" was the problem considered and that the act was designed to prevent restraints of trade which had a significant effect on such competition.

Thus, the Sherman Act prevents "restraints to free competition in business and commercial transactions which tend[ ] to restrict production, raise prices or otherwise control the market to the detriment of purchasers or consumers of goods and services." *Id.* at 493.

Accordingly, the noncommercial activities of certain organizations have been found to be outside the scope of the antitrust laws. For example, in Apex Hosiery, the Court found that a labor union's sit-down strike was not "trade or commerce" under the Sherman Act. *Id.* at 483-84; see also National

Organization for Women v. Scheidler, 968 F.2d at 621 (violent pro-life protests that successfully closed abortion clinics did not constitute trade or commerce under the Sherman Act); Missouri v. National Organization for Women, 620 F.2d at 1319 (organization's boycott of states for failing to ratify the ERA did not constitute trade or commerce).

Although the Sherman Act applies "only to a very limited extent to organizations, like labor unions," which normally act with noncommercial objectives, . . . the Supreme Court has since made clear that an organization's status alone does not prevent antitrust scrutiny. Rather, in determining whether particular conduct is "commerce," a court's principal focus must be on the nature of the activity, rather than the form or objectives of the organization.

In the context of higher education, certain activities have been held to be so central to the educational mission, and so far removed from the "business competition" regulated by the Sherman Act, that they are not "trade or commerce." The most prominent such decision is Marjorie Webster Junior College, Inc. v. Middle States Association of Colleges and Secondary Schools, Inc., 432 F.2d 650 (D.C. Cir.), cert. denied, 400 U.S. 965 (1970). . . . Building on [the rationale of *Marjorie Webster*], admissions criteria have also been found to be "noncommercial in nature" and beyond the scope of the Sherman Act. See Selman v. Harvard Medical School, 494 F. Supp. 603, 621 (S.D.N.Y.), aff'd, 636 F.2d 1204 (2d Cir.1980).

At the other end of the spectrum, certain activities in higher education are so proprietary in nature that the applicability of the Sherman Act is not even questioned. In National Collegiate Athletic Association v. Board of Regents of the University of Oklahoma, 468 U.S. 85 (1984), two universities challenged the National Collegiate Athletic Association's (the "NCAA's") college football television plan, which limited the number of games that could be broadcast. The NCAA, a non-profit educational association, did not rely on its non-profit character as a basis to avoid antitrust jurisdiction, *id.* at 100 n. 22, and the Court upheld a judgment against the NCAA despite noting that its role in maintaining amateurism in college sports and preserving the student-athlete in higher education is entirely consistent with the Sherman Act. *Id.* at 120.

Similarly, when a private bookseller charged that Temple University's bookstore engaged in predatory pricing in violation of Section 2, there was no suggestion that the university was not engaged in "trade or commerce." See Sunshine Books, Ltd. v. Temple University, 697 F.2d 90 (3d Cir.1982). Indeed, in the only reported case involving an antitrust challenge to a university housing policy requiring certain students to live in university residence halls, the parties and the court appear to have assumed that a private landlord's Sherman Act claims satisfied the "trade or commerce" requirement. American Nat'l. Bank and Trust Co. of Chicago v. Board of Regents for Regency Universities, 607 F. Supp. 845 (N.D. Ill.1984).

In between these two extremes are closer cases, including the Third Circuit's decision in United States v. Brown University, 5 F.3d 658 (3d Cir.1993). In that case, the Massachusetts Institute of Technology ("MIT") and eight Ivy League colleges and universities agreed that, through shared information and the use of the same criteria, any commonly-admitted student would be offered a comparable financial aid package from each school. The effect of the schools' agreement was to collectively set the amount of financial aid extended to each commonly-admitted student. The Justice Department brought suit, alleging that this arrangement restrained trade in violation of Section 1 of the Sherman Act. *Id.* at 661-63.

MIT argued that the conduct challenged by the government was not trade or commerce. Specifically, it contended that the financial aid agreement increased access to the member schools by widening the pool of applicants that could afford to attend them and enhanced the quality of education by promoting the socio-economic diversity of the student bodies. In light of these goals, and relying heavily on Marjorie Webster, MIT argued that the agreement at issue was a "noncommercial aspect[ ] of the liberal arts" and thus beyond the reach of the Sherman Act. *Id.* at 667.

The Third Circuit rejected MIT's argument. It drew a distinction between the "distinctly noncommercial" accreditation activity in Marjorie Webster and the "commercial process of setting tuition." *Id.* at 666-67. Because the challenged conduct bore directly on the price charged to students, an essentially commercial transaction, it fell within the realm of trade or commerce. *Id.* at 668.

The case law thus recognizes that institutions of higher learning engage in a wide spectrum of conduct, ranging from the distinctly noncommercial to the purely proprietary. It also reflects some disagreement, particularly in the context of college sports, as to whether an asserted noncommercial objective of a challenged restraint affects the "trade or commerce" inquiry, the substantive antitrust analysis, or both. Compare Jones v. National Collegiate

Athletic Association, 392 F. Supp. 295, 303 (D. Mass. 1975) (denying preliminary injunction because NCAA's "no-compensation" rule, which strips college athletes who played for compensation of eligibility, likely has no nexus to trade or commerce) and Gaines v. National Collegiate Athletic Association, 746 F. Supp. 738, 743 (M.D. Tenn. 1990) (applying Jones to the NCAA's "no-draft" and "no-agent" rules) with Banks v. National Collegiate Athletic Association, 746 F. Supp. 850, 858-62 (N.D. Ind. 1990) (refusing to exempt the "no-draft" and "no-agent" rules from antitrust scrutiny, but holding that they likely survive "Rule of Reason" analysis); see also Brown University, 5 F.3d at 665-68 (even where noncommercial social welfare goals do not remove a defendant's conduct from the realm of trade or commerce, they will influence the merits of the Sherman Act claim).

The fraternities argue that anything a college or university does to enhance its reputation is, as a matter of law, commercial activity subject to antitrust scrutiny. We disagree. Some conduct, such as determining the content of curricula, for example, is distinctly noncommercial in character, and the Sherman Act does not apply to these aspects of higher education. See Brown, 5 F.3d at 667; Marjorie Webster, 432 F.2d at 654.

This analysis may lead to some difficult decisions, including ones that cannot be made without providing the plaintiff an opportunity for discovery. As the D.C. Circuit recognized in *Marjorie Webster*, even superficially noncommercial activity could conceivably have a commercial motive that would subject it to the antitrust laws. *Id.* at 654-55 & n. 21 ("[f]or example, if accreditation were denied any institution purchasing textbooks from a supplier who did not provide special discounts to association members, it would be hard to imagine other than a commercial motive for the action").

In this case, the district court concluded that Hamilton's residential policy was not trade or commerce because it could not be extricated from Hamilton's academic mission. The court noted that Hamilton had responded to evidence that the fraternities' dominance of social life on campus was leading the most talented of Hamilton's prospective female students to enroll elsewhere and had begun to drive away top male applicants as well. The residential policy, the court held, was no different than admissions criteria--both are academic decisions by which Hamilton seeks to shape its unique learning environment--and thus concerns neither trade nor commerce.

As a preliminary matter, the district court incorrectly characterized the "trade or commerce" inquiry as jurisdictional. Whether or not a challenged activity constitutes "trade or commerce" within the meaning of the Sherman Act is not a jurisdictional question. Congress's enactment of the Sherman Act was an exercise of its power to regulate interstate and foreign commerce. See, e.g., Summit Health, Ltd. v. Pinhas, 500 U.S. 322, 329 n. 10 (1991). In the absence of a sufficient nexus to such commerce, federal courts lack subject matter jurisdiction over an antitrust claim. However, assuming such a nexus exists, the inquiry into whether the impact of the challenged activity is merely incidental to a noncommercial purpose, or is distinctly noncommercial in character, is a question that goes to the substantive reach of the Sherman Act, not to the jurisdiction of the court. . . .

[The district court also erred on the substantive question.] Although the district court stated that it accepted as true all of the factual allegations in the complaint, its opinion accepts and relies upon Hamilton's assertion that its "decision regarding residential services concerns education rather than commercial gain." . . . The plaintiffs have alleged otherwise. They allege that Hamilton adopted the residential policy for the commercial purpose of raising revenues by (1) forcing all Hamilton students to purchase residential services from Hamilton; (2) allowing Hamilton to raise its prices for such services; and (3) attempting to purchase the fraternity houses at below-market prices. They further allege that Hamilton's stated purpose for the new policy is a pretext designed to obfuscate this purely commercial purpose. In the procedural posture of this case, these allegations must be accepted as true. The district court's failure to do so was error.

[The Second Circuit declined to reach the question whether a failure to prove such a commercial motive would be fatal to plaintiffs' claim. In the final section of the opinion, it concluded that the plaintiffs had adequately alleged a nexus with interstate commerce. It therefore reversed the district court's judgment and remanded the case for further proceedings.]

Section 2. Joint Ventures Revisited

Insert after *Associated Press*, page 423:

PADDOCK PUBLICATIONS, INC. v. CHICAGO TRIBUNE CO.
United States Court of Appeals, Seventh Circuit, 1997.
103 F.3d 42.

Before: EASTERBROOK, MANION and ROVNER, Circuit Judges.

EASTERBROOK, J. Newspapers' content has many sources. To the work of their own staff, papers add dispatches from syndicated news services such as the Associated Press and Reuters that station reporters or stringers across the globe. Leading newspapers such as the New York Times, the Los Angeles Times, the Washington Post, the Chicago Tribune, and the Wall Street Journal have set up supplemental news services. The New York Times News Service carries that paper's stories; the Los Angeles Times/Washington Post News Service combines stories from those papers; the Knight-Ridder/Tribune Information Service pools stories from the Tribune and the Knight-Ridder chain's papers. Subscribers can reprint the originating paper's stories (and those of other papers that contribute to the supplemental service) in the subscribers' home markets. Cartoons, op-ed pieces, book reviews, chess columns, puzzles, and other features are available from syndicators such as United Press Syndicate, United Features Syndicate, King Features Syndicate, Creators Syndicate, and Tribune Media Services.

Supplemental news services and features syndicators offer exclusive contracts to subscribers in each metropolitan area. Because the Chicago Tribune subscribes to the New York Times News Service, stories from the Times are unavailable to the Chicago Sun-Times and smaller newspapers in the Chicago area; the Sun-Times subscribes to the Los Angeles Times/Washington Post News Service, which therefore is unavailable to the Tribune and smaller papers. News services and features syndicates charge by the circulation of the subscribing paper, and they therefore strive to sign up the largest paper in each market. Exclusivity is one valuable feature the service offers, for a paper with exclusive rights to a service or feature is both more attractive to readers and more distinctive from its rivals. When selling to smaller papers, however, the supplemental news services and features syndicates generally do not offer exclusivity--for they still hope to interest the larger, and therefore more lucrative, papers in the market (which can sign up later with exclusive rights against all but the original customer).

As a rule, the larger papers subscribe to the more popular services and features; or perhaps it is the very fact that a feature runs in a market's larger papers that makes it "more popular." Causation need not concern us. No matter which way it runs, smaller papers perceive that they get the crumbs. This suit, by the Daily Herald, the number three general-interest paper in the Chicago area (with 6.7 percent of average weekly readership), contends that the pattern of exclusive distribution rights violates § 1 of the Sherman Antitrust Act, 15 U.S.C. § 1, by making it harder for small papers to grow. Like the district court, we assume without deciding that "general-interest-newspaper readership in the Chicago SMSA" is a market. According to the complaint, the Chicago Tribune and the Chicago Sun-Times have locked up the "most popular" or "best" supplemental services and features, injuring consumers by frustrating competition. (We assume that "the best" services and features can constitute a market, although it sounds more like an aesthetic judgment; no one would say that "the best film of 1996" has a monopoly of any market just because there can be only one "best" film.) The Daily Herald views the Knight-Ridder/Tribune Information Service as a distant third to the supplemental news services the Tribune and Sun-Times use, and even it is unavailable because the Tribune will not license its stories to a competitor in its home market. The Herald concedes that the Associated Press, Reuters, and many quality comics and features are available to it (for example, it publishes Dilbert, one of today's most-followed comic strips) but insists that the best ones are committed to its larger rivals. After assuming that all of the Herald's allegations are true, the district court dismissed the complaint for failure to state a claim on which relief may be granted.

The Herald does not contend that the Tribune has conspired with the Sun-Times to bring about this state of affairs. Compare Associated Press v. United States, 326 U.S. 1 (1945) (holding that the Associated Press, a consortium of newspapers, must eliminate an exclusivity feature that could be traced to agreement among horizontal rivals). Nor does it contend that the supplemental news services and features syndicators (or their contributing papers and authors) have agreed among themselves. It concedes that each has adopted its method of doing business independently; they take the same approach to distribution because each has discovered that it is the most profitable way to do business. All of the contracts between services and newspapers are terminable at will or on short notice (usually 30 days, although some features require a year's notice). Instead of seeing whether money could persuade a supplemental news service to cut off one of the larger papers--the Herald has never tried to outbid the Tribune or Sun-Times, either on a total compensation basis or a per-subscriber basis--it asked the district court to declare that the antitrust laws entitle it to receive the leading supplemental news services and features without regard to the contractual exclusivity that the Tribune and Sun-Times currently enjoy. At times the Herald suggests that it would be happy with rights to articles from the New York Times, Los Angeles Times, and Washington Post that the Tribune and Sun-Times do not reprint; "there's plenty for all" is a theme of its brief. But this won't work well for news (must the Tribune give the Herald advance notice of its contents?) or at all for features, which are sold one at a time. For example, King Features Syndicate does not sell its entire portfolio to one paper per market; the Tribune, Sun-Times, and Herald each publish some of its comics and columns. So the Herald necessarily argues that it is entitled to run Peanuts and Dick Tracy even though these comic strips also appear in the Tribune.

This is fundamentally an "essential facilities" claim--but without any essential facility. There are three supplemental news services that the Herald is willing to acknowledge as major competitors (and others besides, though the Herald denigrates them). There are hundreds, if not thousands, of opinion and entertainment features; a newspaper deprived of access to the New York Times crossword puzzles can find others, even if the Times has the best known one. Unlike United States v. Terminal Railroad Ass'n, 224 U.S. 383 (1912), the granddaddy of these cases, in which the Court held that a bottleneck facility that could not feasibly be duplicated must be shared among rivals, this case does not involve a single facility that monopolizes one level of production and creates a potential to extend the monopoly to others. We have, instead, competition at each level of production; no one can "take over" another level of production by withholding access from disfavored rivals. Flip Side Productions, Inc. v. Jam Productions, Ltd., 843 F.2d 1024, 1032-34 (7th Cir.1988), holds that the existence of three competing facilities not only means that none is an "essential facility" but also means that each of the three is entitled to sign an exclusive contract with a favored user. Other firms that want to enter the market can do so by competing at intervals for these contracts.

Competition-for-the-contract is a form of competition that antitrust laws protect rather than proscribe, and it is common. Every year or two, General Motors, Ford, and Chrysler invite tire manufacturers to bid for exclusive rights to have their tires used in the manufacturers' cars. Exclusive contracts make the market hard to enter in mid-year but cannot stifle competition over the longer run, and competition of this kind drives down the price of tires, to the ultimate benefit of consumers. Just so in the news business--if smaller newspapers are willing to bid with cash rather than legal talent. In the meantime, exclusive stories and features help the newspapers differentiate themselves, the better to compete with one another. A market in which every newspaper carried the same stories, columns, and cartoons would be a less vigorous market than the existing one. And a market in which the creators of intellectual property (such as the New York Times) could not decide how best to market it for maximum profit would be a market with less (or less interesting) intellectual property created in the first place. No one can take the supply of well researched and written news as a given; legal rulings that diminish the incentive to find and explicate the news (by reducing the return from that business) have little to commend them.

In what way could the news services' practices harm consumers? Tacit collusion (economists' term for "shared monopoly") could be a source of monopoly profits and injury to consumers even if none of the stages of production is monopolized. Some distribution arrangements might be objectionable because they facilitate tacit collusion. But collusion, tacit or express, requires some horizontal cooperation, or at least forbearance from vigorous competition among rivals. . . . Although the newspaper market is concentrated on the readers' side, the inputs to newspaper production are unconcentrated and therefore do not facilitate tacit collusion in the more concentrated market. The New York Times News Service competes for column inches of ink not only with other supplemental news services but also with the Associated Press, Reuters, and the reporters of the subscribing papers. Markets here are less concentrated, and use fewer of the devices that facilitate oligopolistic interdependence, than the markets in E.I. Du Pont de Nemours & Co. v. FTC, 729 F.2d 128 (2d Cir.1984), where an antitrust claim was nonetheless rejected. The Herald does not argue that the practices at hand facilitate tacit collusion.

What the Herald does argue is that a mixture of fewness of firms, exclusive contracts, and relations between suppliers and users of news that endure despite short contract terms, hampers the growth of small rivals even though each market is competitive. Such an argument does not come within any of the economic approaches to tacit collusion--but it does, the Herald insists, come within the holding of FTC v. Motion Picture Advertising Service Co., 344 U.S. 392 (1953) [and similar cases].

[In *Motion Picture Advertising Service,* the Supreme Court affirmed a finding of the FTC that exclusive dealing contracts for in-theater advertisements between four companies and approximately 75 percent of the nation's motion picture theaters violated § 5 of the Federal Trade Commission Act, 15 U.S.C. § 45, because they stifled competition by firms that wanted to enter the business of furnishing ads to movie theaters.] According to the Herald, the same kind of thing now has occurred in the news industry, making it equally appropriate to aggregate the market shares of the firms without proof of horizontal collaboration (for there was none in *Motion Picture Advertising Service*). The district court was not impressed, for the approach of *Motion Picture Advertising Service*--which depends on "foreclosure" of sales to competitors without proof of injury to consumers--reflects a bygone day in antitrust analysis. But the district court properly did not rely entirely on a belief that the opinion is a derelict. See Khan v. State Oil Co., 93 F.3d 1358, 1362-64 (7th Cir.1996) (implementing another antique antitrust opinion that is unlikely to be reaffirmed if the Supreme Court revisits the subject). It held that *Motion Picture Advertising Service* is not controlling even if it remains authoritative.

First, *Motion Picture Advertising Service* was decided under § 5 of the FTC Act. The Commission has the authority under that provision to forbid practices that pose risks to effective competition, even when they do not violate the Sherman Act. The Court remarked on this in *Motion Picture Advertising Service*: "The 'unfair methods of competition,' which are condemned by § 5(a) of the Act, are not confined to those that were illegal at common law or that were condemned by the Sherman Act." 344 U.S. at 394. A district court lacks the FTC's power to go beyond the limits of the Sherman Act. Similarly, Standard Stations was decided under § 3 of the Clayton Act, 15 U.S.C. § 14, and does not assist the plaintiff in a Sherman Act case that cannot be characterized as involving tie-in sales. Granted, the Court remarked in *Motion Picture Advertising Service* that "a device which has sewed up a market so tightly for the benefit of a few falls within the prohibitions of the Sherman Act," 344 U.S. at 395, but this bald and unreasoned assertion is not conclusive. Poorly reasoned holdings bind the inferior courts; unreasoned dictum does not--and this statement was obiter dictum, for the Court had emphasized only a paragraph before that it was deferring to the FTC's findings as § 5 of the FTC Act requires. No subsequent case has read *Motion Picture Advertising Service* to abolish the requirement of concerted action under § 1 of the Sherman Act.

Second, *Motion Picture Advertising Service* involved exclusive dealing, while this case involves exclusive distributorships. Despite the similarity in nomenclature, there is a difference--one vital to the theory of *Motion Picture Advertising Service* itself. See generally Hovenkamp, Federal Antitrust Policy § 10.8. An exclusive dealing contract obliges a firm to obtain its inputs from a single source. Each of the theaters was committed to one distributor for all of its ads. This was the genesis of the concern about foreclosure. A new advertising distributor could not find outlets. An exclusive distributorship, by contrast, does not restrict entry at either level. None of the newspapers in Chicago (or anywhere else) has promised by contract to obtain all of its news from a single source--and the sources have not locked all of their output together (unlike the "block booking" involved in *Loew's*). A new entrant to the supplemental news service business could sell to every newspaper in the United States, if it chose to do so. Existing features syndicates sell to multiple firms in the same market (although most features go to one paper per city; this is the exclusive distribution aspect of the contracts). So vendors can and do sell news and features to multiple customers, and customers can and do buy news and features from multiple vendors. "Foreclosure" of the kind about which *Motion Picture Advertising Service* was concerned does not occur under exclusive distribution contracts.

Third, the FTC and the Supreme Court concluded that even exclusive dealing contracts are lawful if limited to a year's duration. 344 U.S. at 395-96. The Commission saw that exclusivity can promote competition by making it feasible for firms to invest in promoting their products--for these costs would not be recoverable if the contracts were of very short terms, or if rivals could exhibit the same films and obtain the benefit of this promotional activity. Moreover, with year-long contracts, the entire market is up for grabs. A new entrant can sell to a twelfth of the theaters in the first month, a sixth of all theaters by the end of the second month, and so on; competition for the contract makes it possible to have the benefits of exclusivity and rivalry simultaneously. Things work similarly in the newspaper business. Contract terms are short, so competition for the contract can flourish. Meanwhile, exclusive distribution of news or features through a single paper in a city helps the paper distinguish itself from, and compete with, its rivals. The SunTimes will not promote a readership for a particular columnist if the Tribune and the Herald carry the same column; free-riding would spoil the investment and thwart this aspect of competition.

Contracts in the news business, unlike those in the motion picture advertising business, are of indefinite duration, and either side may terminate after giving the required advance notice. According to the Herald, this makes all the difference, but we don't see why. A termination clause works just like a stated time limit in facilitating competition for the contract. The FTC did not insist that dealings between a distributor and a theater cease after a year; the parties were free to renew their arrangement for successive years; it was enough that there be an option to change distributors or renegotiate once a year. That option exists in the newspaper business. Both sides to these contracts enjoy an annual (or more frequent) right to negotiate new terms or change partners. To this the Herald responds, in essence: The contracts aren't terminated in fact, so the legal terms do not matter; the contracts should be treated as perpetual. Yet for all we can tell renewal was (and remains) the norm in the motion picture business. As long as arrangements serve the interests of both parties, they will continue, whether that means signing another in a series of one-year contracts or declining to exercise an annual option to cancel a contract. Enduring exclusive distribution contracts characterize markets that are recognized as competitive: for example, Babylon 5 appears exclusively on WPWR-TV (Channel 50) in Chicago, and almost all other shows are exhibited exclusively on one channel per locale, sticking with that station for their entire original production run, even though no one thinks that individual stations or producers have market power. Cf. Schurz Communications, Inc. v. FCC, 982 F.2d 1043 (7th Cir.1992); Capital Cities/ABC, Inc. v. FCC, 29 F.3d 309 (7th Cir.1994). The FTC and the Supreme Court in Motion Picture Advertising Service wanted to ensure that dealings continued only while they remained in the interests of both distributors and theaters--which meant that someone else could come along with a better deal and get the business. Likewise someone with a better offer can get or sell news on short notice. The Herald has never tried to make a better offer, and we conclude that it has come to the wrong forum. It should try to outbid the Tribune and Sun-Times in the marketplace, rather than to outmaneuver them in court.

AFFIRMED.

Insert after *Berkey Photo*, page 445:

U.S. Department of Justice and FTC Antitrust Guidelines for Collaborations Among Competitors, 2000

[Introduction: In recent years, the antitrust enforcement agencies issued guidelines with respect to enforcement intentions involving joint ventures in particular sectors of the economy such as health care (see Casebook, page 300, note 2) and the licensing of intellectual property, but not an across-the-board statement of the Agencies' analytical approach to competitor collaborations. In April 2000, a broad general statement offering a comprehensive analytical approach to all horizontal collaborations was issued. Important excerpts from those guidelines are set forth below.]

SECTION 1: PURPOSE, DEFINITIONS, AND OVERVIEW

1.1 Purpose and Definitions

These Guidelines state the antitrust enforcement policy of the Agencies with respect to competitor collaborations. By stating their general policy, the Agencies hope to assist businesses in assessing whether the Agencies will challenge a competitor collaboration or any of the agreements of which it is comprised. However, these Guidelines cannot remove judgment and discretion in antitrust law enforcement. The Agencies evaluate each case in light of its own facts and apply the analytical framework set forth in these Guidelines reasonably and flexibly.[1]

A "competitor collaboration" comprises a set of one or more agreements, other than merger agreements, between or among competitors to engage in economic activity, and the economic activity resulting therefrom. "Competitors" encompasses both actual and potential competitors. Competitor collaborations involve one or more business activities, such as research and development ("R&D"), production, marketing, distribution, sales or purchasing. Information sharing and various trade association activities also may take place through competitor collaborations.

These Guidelines use the terms "anticompetitive harm," "procompetitive benefit," and "overall competitive effect" in analyzing the competitive effects of agreements among competitors. All of these terms include actual and likely competitive effects. The Guidelines use the term "anticompetitive harm" to refer to an agreement's adverse competitive

---

[1] The analytical framework set forth in these Guidelines is consistent with the analytical frameworks in the *Health Care Statements* and the *Intellectual Property Guidelines*, which remain in effect to address issues in their special contexts.

consequences, without taking account of offsetting procompetitive benefits. Conversely, the term "procompetitive benefit" refers to an agreement's favorable competitive consequences, without taking account of its anticompetitive harm. The terms "overall competitive effect" or "competitive effect" are used in discussing the combination of an agreement's anticompetitive harm and procompetitive benefit.

1.2 Overview of Analytical Framework

Two types of analysis are used by the Supreme Court to determine the lawfulness of an agreement among competitors: per se and rule of reason.[2] Certain types of agreements are so likely to harm competition and to have no significant procompetitive benefit that they do not warrant the time and expense required for particularized inquiry into their effects. Once identified, such agreements are challenged as per se unlawful.[3] All other agreements are evaluated under the rule of reason, which involves a factual inquiry into an agreement's overall competitive effect. As the Supreme Court has explained, rule of reason analysis entails a flexible inquiry and varies in focus and detail depending on the nature of the agreement and market circumstances.[4]

This overview briefly sets forth questions and factors that the Agencies assess in analyzing an agreement among competitors. The rest of the Guidelines should be consulted for the detailed definitions and discussion that underlie this analysis.

Agreements Challenged as Per Se Illegal. Agreements of a type that always or almost always tends to raise price or to reduce output are per se illegal. The Agencies challenge such agreements, once identified, as per se

---

[2] *See* National Soc'y of Prof'l. Eng'rs v. United States, 435 U.S. 679, 692 (1978).

[3] *See* FTC v. Superior Court Trial Lawyers Ass'n, 493 U.S. 411, 432-36 (1990).

[4] *See* California Dental Ass'n v. FTC, 119 S. Ct. 1604, 1617-18 (1999); FTC v. Indiana Fed'n of Dentists, 476 U.S. 447, 459-61 (1986); National Collegiate Athletic Ass'n v. Board of Regents of the Univ. of Okla., 468 U.S. 85, 104-13 (1984).

illegal. Types of agreements that have been held per se illegal include agreements among competitors to fix prices or output, rig bids, or share or divide markets by allocating customers, suppliers, territories, or lines of commerce. The courts conclusively presume such agreements, once identified, to be illegal, without inquiring into their claimed business purposes, anticompetitive harms, procompetitive benefits, or overall competitive effects. The Department of Justice prosecutes participants in hard-core cartel agreements criminally.

Agreements Analyzed under the Rule of Reason. Agreements not challenged as per se illegal are analyzed under the rule of reason to determine their overall competitive effect. These include agreements of a type that otherwise might be considered per se illegal, provided they are reasonably related to, and reasonably necessary to achieve procompetitive benefits from, an efficiency-enhancing integration of economic activity.

Rule of reason analysis focuses on the state of competition with, as compared to without, the relevant agreement. The central question is whether the relevant agreement likely harms competition by increasing the ability or incentive profitably to raise price above or reduce output, quality, service, or innovation below what likely would prevail in the absence of the relevant agreement.

Rule of reason analysis entails a flexible inquiry and varies in focus and detail depending on the nature of the agreement and market circumstances. The Agencies focus on only those factors, and undertake only that factual inquiry, necessary to make a sound determination of the overall competitive effect of the relevant agreement. Ordinarily, however, no one factor is dispositive in the analysis.

The Agencies' analysis begins with an examination of the nature of the relevant agreement. As part of this examination, the Agencies ask about the business purpose of the agreement and examine whether the agreement, if already in operation, has caused anticompetitive harm. In some cases, the nature of the agreement and the absence of market power together may demonstrate the absence of anticompetitive harm. In such cases, the Agencies do not challenge the agreement. Alternatively, where the likelihood of anticompetitive harm is evident from the nature of the agreement, or anticompetitive harm has resulted from an agreement already in operation, then, absent overriding benefits that could offset the anticompetitive harm, the Agencies challenge such agreements without a detailed market analysis.

If the initial examination of the nature of the agreement indicates possible competitive concerns, but the agreement is not one that would be challenged without a detailed market analysis, the Agencies analyze the agreement in greater depth. The Agencies typically define relevant markets and calculate market shares and concentration as an initial step in assessing whether the agreement may create or increase market power or facilitate its exercise. The Agencies examine the extent to which the participants and the collaboration have the ability and incentive to compete independently. The Agencies also evaluate other market circumstances, e.g. entry, that may foster or prevent anticompetitive harms.

If the examination of these factors indicates no potential for anticompetitive harm, the Agencies end the investigation without considering procompetitive benefits. If investigation indicates anticompetitive harm, the Agencies examine whether the relevant agreement is reasonably necessary to achieve procompetitive benefits that likely would offset anticompetitive harms.

. . .

SECTION 2: GENERAL PRINCIPLES FOR EVALUATING AGREEMENTS AMONG COMPETITORS. . . .

2.2 Potential Anticompetitive Harms

Competitor collaborations may harm competition and consumers by increasing the ability or incentive profitably to raise price above or reduce output, quality, service, or innovation below what likely would prevail in the absence of the relevant agreement. Such effects may arise through a variety of mechanisms. Among other things, agreements may limit independent decision making or combine the control of or financial interests in production, key assets, or decisions regarding price, output, or other competitively sensitive variables, or may otherwise reduce the participants' ability or incentive to compete independently.

Competitor collaborations also may facilitate explicit or tacit collusion through facilitating practices such as the exchange or disclosure of competitively sensitive information or through increased market concentration. Such collusion may involve the relevant market in which the collaboration operates or another market in which the participants in the collaboration are actual or potential competitors.

2.3 Analysis of the Overall Collaboration and the Agreements of Which It Consists

A competitor collaboration comprises a set of one or more agreements, other than merger agreements, between or among competitors to engage in economic activity, and the economic activity resulting therefrom. In general, the Agencies assess the competitive effects of the overall collaboration and any individual agreement or set of agreements within the collaboration that may harm competition. For purposes of these Guidelines, the phrase "relevant agreement" refers to whichever of these three – the overall collaboration, an individual agreement, or a set of agreements – the evaluating Agency is assessing. Two or more agreements are assessed together if their procompetitive benefits or anticompetitive harms are so intertwined that they cannot meaningfully be isolated and attributed to any individual agreement. . . .

2.4 Competitive Effects Are Assessed as of the Time of Possible Harm to Competition

The competitive effects of a relevant agreement may change over time, depending on changes in circumstances such as internal reorganization, adoption of new agreements as part of the collaboration, addition or departure of participants, new market conditions, or changes in market share. The Agencies assess the competitive effects of a relevant agreement as of the time of possible harm to competition, whether at formation of the collaboration or at a later time, as appropriate. . . . However, an assessment after a collaboration has been formed is sensitive to the reasonable expectations of participants whose significant sunk cost investments in reliance on the relevant agreement were made before it became anticompetitive.

SECTION 3: ANALYTICAL FRAMEWORK FOR EVALUATING AGREEMENTS AMONG COMPETITORS. . . .

3.2 Agreements Challenged as Per Se Illegal

Agreements of a type that always or almost always tends to raise price or reduce output are per se illegal.[5] The Agencies challenge such agreements, once identified, as per se illegal. Typically these are agreements not to compete on price or output. Types of agreements that have been held per se illegal include agreements among competitors to fix prices or output, rig bids, or share or divide markets by allocating customers, suppliers, territories or lines of commerce.[6] The courts conclusively presume such agreements, once identified, to be illegal, without inquiring into their claimed business purposes, anticompetitive harms, procompetitive benefits, or overall competitive effects. The Department of Justice prosecutes participants in hard-core cartel agreements criminally.

If, however, participants in an efficiency-enhancing integration of economic activity enter into an agreement that is reasonably related to the integration and reasonably necessary to achieve its procompetitive benefits, the Agencies analyze the agreement under the rule of reason, even if it is of a type that might otherwise be considered per se illegal.[7] . . . In an efficiency-enhancing integration, participants collaborate to perform or cause to be performed (by a joint venture entity created by the collaboration or by one or more participants or by a third party acting on behalf of other participants) one or more business functions, such as production, distribution, marketing, purchasing or R&D, and thereby benefit, or potentially benefit, consumers by expanding output, reducing price, or enhancing quality, service, or innovation. Participants in an efficiency-enhancing integration typically combine, by contract or otherwise, significant capital, technology, or other complementary assets to achieve procompetitive benefits that the participants could not achieve separately. The mere coordination of decisions on price, output, customers, territories, and the like is not integration, and cost savings without integration are not a basis for avoiding per se condemnation. The integration must be of a type that plausibly would generate procompetitive benefits cognizable under

---

[5] *See* Broadcast Music, Inc. v. Columbia Broadcasting Sys., 441 U.S. 1, 19-20 (1979).

[6] *See, e.g.*, Palmer v. BRG of Georgia, Inc., 498 U.S. 46 (1990) (market allocation); United States v. Trenton Potteries Co., 273 U.S. 392 (1927) (price fixing).

[7] *See* Arizona v. Maricopa County Medical Soc'y, 457 U.S. 332, 339 n.7, 356-57 (1982) (finding no integration).

the efficiencies analysis set forth in Section 3.36 below. Such procompetitive benefits may enhance the participants' ability or incentives to compete and thus may offset an agreement's anticompetitive tendencies. . . .

An agreement may be "reasonably necessary" without being essential. However, if the participants could achieve an equivalent or comparable efficiency-enhancing integration through practical, significantly less restrictive means, then the Agencies conclude that the agreement is not reasonably necessary.[8] In making this assessment, except in unusual circumstances, the Agencies consider whether practical, significantly less restrictive means were reasonably available when the agreement was entered into, but do not search for a theoretically less restrictive alternative that was not practical given the business realities.

Before accepting a claim that an agreement is reasonably necessary to achieve procompetitive benefits from an integration of economic activity, the Agencies undertake a limited factual inquiry to evaluate the claim.[9] Such an inquiry may reveal that efficiencies from an agreement that are possible in theory are not plausible in the context of the particular collaboration. Some claims – such as those premised on the notion that competition itself is unreasonable – are insufficient as a matter of law,[10] and others may be implausible on their face. In any case, labeling an arrangement a "joint venture" will not protect what is merely a device to raise price or restrict

---

[8] *See id.* at 352-53 (observing that even if a maximum fee schedule for physicians' services were desirable, it was not necessary that the schedule be established by physicians rather than by insurers); *Broadcast Music*, 441 U.S. at 20-21 (setting of price "necessary" for the blanket license).

[9] *See Maricopa*, 457 U.S. at 352-53, 356-57 (scrutinizing the defendant medical foundations for indicia of integration and evaluating the record evidence regarding less restrictive alternatives).

[10] *See Indiana Fed'n of Dentists*, 476 U.S. at 463-64; *NCAA*, 468 U.S. at 116-17; *Prof'l. Eng'rs*, 435 U.S. at 693-96. Other claims, such as an absence of market power, are no defense to per se illegality. *See Superior Court Trial Lawyers Ass'n*, 493 U.S. at 434-36; United States v. Socony-Vacuum Oil Co., 310 U.S. 150, 224-26 & n.59 (1940).

output;[11] the nature of the conduct, not its designation, is determinative.

3.3 Agreements Analyzed under the Rule of Reason

Agreements not challenged as per se illegal are analyzed under the rule of reason to determine their overall competitive effect. Rule of reason analysis focuses on the state of competition with, as compared to without, the relevant agreement. The central question is whether the relevant agreement likely harms competition by increasing the ability or incentive profitably to raise price above or reduce output, quality, service, or innovation below what likely would prevail in the absence of the relevant agreement.[12]

Rule of reason analysis entails a flexible inquiry and varies in focus and detail depending on the nature of the agreement and market circumstances.[13] The Agencies focus on only those factors, and undertake only that factual inquiry, necessary to make a sound determination of the overall competitive effect of the relevant agreement. Ordinarily, however, no one factor is dispositive in the analysis.

Under the rule of reason, the Agencies' analysis begins with an examination of the nature of the relevant agreement, since the nature of the agreement determines the types of anticompetitive harms that may be of concern. As part of this examination, the Agencies ask about the business purpose of the agreement and examine whether the agreement, if already in operation, has caused anticompetitive harm.[14] If the nature of the agreement

---

[11] *See* Timken Roller Bearing Co. v. United States, 341 U.S. 593, 598 (1951).

[12] In addition, concerns may arise where an agreement increases the ability or incentive of buyers to exercise monopsony power.

[13] *See California Dental Ass'n* , 119 S. Ct. at 1612-13, 1617 ("What is required . . . is an enquiry meet for the case, looking to the circumstances, details, and logic of a restraint."); *NCAA*, 468 U.S. 109 n.39 ("the rule of reason can sometimes be applied in the twinkling of an eye") (quoting Phillip E. Areeda, *The "Rule of Reason" in Antitrust Analysis: General Issues* 37-38 (Federal Judicial Center, June 1981)).

[14] *See* Board of Trade of the City of Chicago v. United States, 246 U.S. 231, 238 (1918).

and the absence of market power[15] together demonstrate the absence of anticompetitive harm, the Agencies do not challenge the agreement. . . . Alternatively, where the likelihood of anticompetitive harm is evident from the nature of the agreement,[16] or anticompetitive harm has resulted from an agreement already in operation,[17] then, absent overriding benefits that could offset the anticompetitive harm, the Agencies challenge such agreements without a detailed market analysis.[18]

If the initial examination of the nature of the agreement indicates possible competitive concerns, but the agreement is not one that would be challenged without a detailed market analysis, the Agencies analyze the agreement in greater depth. The Agencies typically define relcvant markets and calculate market shares and concentration as an initial step in assessing whether the agreement may create or increase market power[19] or facilitate its

---

[15] That market power is absent may be determined without defining a relevant market. For example, if no market power is likely under any plausible market definition, it does not matter which one is correct. Alternatively, easy entry may indicate an absence of market power.

[16] *See California Dental Ass'n*, 119 S. Ct. at 1612-13, 1617 (an "obvious anticompetitive effect" would warrant quick condemnation); *Indiana Fed'n of Dentists*, 476 U.S. at 459; *NCAA*, 468 U.S. at 104, 106-10.

[17] *See Indiana Fed'n of Dentists*, 476 U.S. at 460-61 ("Since the purpose of the inquiries into market definition and market power is to determine whether an arrangement has the potential for genuine adverse effects on competition, 'proof of actual detrimental effects, such as a reduction of output,' can obviate the need for an inquiry into market power, which is but a 'surrogate for detrimental effects.'") (quoting 7 Phillip E. Areeda, *Antitrust Law* ¶ 1511, at 424 (1986)); *NCAA*, 468 U.S. at 104-08, 110 n.42.

[18] *See Indiana Fed'n of Dentists*, 476 U.S. at 459-60 (condemning without "detailed market analysis" an agreement to limit competition by withholding x-rays from patients' insurers after finding no competitive justification).

[19] Market power to a seller is the ability profitably to maintain prices above competitive levels for a significant period of time. Sellers also may exercise market power with respect to significant competitive dimensions other than price, such as quality, service, or innovation. Market power to a buyer is the

exercise and thus poses risks to competition.[20] The Agencies examine factors relevant to the extent to which the participants and the collaboration have the ability and incentive to compete independently, such as whether an agreement is exclusive or non-exclusive and its duration.[21] The Agencies also evaluate whether entry would be timely, likely, and sufficient to deter or counteract any anticompetitive harms. In addition, the Agencies assess any other market circumstances that may foster or impede anticompetitive harms.

If the examination of these factors indicates no potential for anticompetitive harm, the Agencies end the investigation without considering procompetitive benefits. If investigation indicates anticompetitive harm, the Agencies examine whether the relevant agreement is reasonably necessary to achieve procompetitive benefits that likely would offset anticompetitive harms.[22]. . .

3.34 Factors Relevant to the Ability and Incentive of the Participants and the Collaboration to Compete

Competitor collaborations sometimes do not end competition among the participants and the collaboration. Participants may continue to compete against each other and their collaboration, either through separate, independent business operations or through membership in other collaborations. Collaborations may be managed by decision makers independent of the individual participants. Control over key competitive variables may remain

---

ability profitably to depress the price paid for a product below the competitive level for a significant period of time and thereby depress output.

[20] *See* Eastman Kodak Co. v. Image Technical Services, Inc., 504 U.S. 451, 464 (1992).

[21] *Compare NCAA*, 468 U.S. at 113-15, 119-20 (noting that colleges were not permitted to televise their own games without restraint), *with Broadcast Music*, 441 U.S. at 23-24 (finding no legal or practical impediment to individual licenses).

[22] *See NCAA*, 468 U.S. at 113-15 (rejecting efficiency claims when production was limited, not enhanced); *Prof'l. Eng'rs*, 435 U.S. at 696 (dictum) (distinguishing restraints that promote competition from those that eliminate competition); *Chicago Bd. of Trade*, 246 U.S. at 238 (same).

outside the collaboration, such as where participants independently market and set prices for the collaboration's output.

Sometimes, however, competition among the participants and the collaboration may be restrained through explicit contractual terms or through financial or other provisions that reduce or eliminate the incentive to compete. The Agencies look to the competitive benefits and harms of the relevant agreement, not merely the formal terms of agreements among the participants.

Where the nature of the agreement and market share and market concentration data reveal a likelihood of anticompetitive harm, the Agencies more closely examine the extent to which the participants and the collaboration have the ability and incentive to compete independent of each other. The Agencies are likely to focus on six factors: (a) the extent to which the relevant agreement is non-exclusive in that participants are likely to continue to compete independently outside the collaboration in the market in which the collaboration operates; (b) the extent to which participants retain independent control of assets necessary to compete; (c) the nature and extent of participants' financial interests in the collaboration or in each other; (d) the control of the collaboration's competitively significant decision making; (e) the likelihood of anticompetitive information sharing; and (f) the duration of the collaboration.

Each of these factors is discussed in further detail below. Consideration of these factors may reduce or increase competitive concern. The analysis necessarily is flexible: the relevance and significance of each factor depends upon the facts and circumstances of each case, and any additional factors pertinent under the circumstances are considered. For example, when an agreement is examined subsequent to formation of the collaboration, the Agencies also examine factual evidence concerning participants' actual conduct.

3.34(a) Exclusivity

The Agencies consider whether, to what extent, and in what manner the relevant agreement permits participants to continue to compete against each other and their collaboration, either through separate, independent business operations or through membership in other collaborations. The Agencies inquire whether a collaboration is non-exclusive in fact as well as in name and consider any costs or other impediments to competing with the collaboration.

In assessing exclusivity when an agreement already is in operation, the Agencies examine whether, to what extent, and in what manner participants actually have continued to compete against each other and the collaboration. In general, competitive concern likely is reduced to the extent that participants actually have continued to compete, either through separate, independent business operations or through membership in other collaborations, or are permitted to do so.

3.34(b) Control over Assets

The Agencies ask whether the relevant agreement requires participants to contribute to the collaboration significant assets that previously have enabled or likely would enable participants to be effective independent competitors in markets affected by the collaboration. If such resources must be contributed to the collaboration and are specialized in that they cannot readily be replaced, the participants may have lost all or some of their ability to compete against each other and their collaboration, even if they retain the contractual right to do so.[23] In general, the greater the contribution of specialized assets to the collaboration that is required, the less the participants may be relied upon to provide independent competition.

3.34(c) Financial Interests in the Collaboration or in Other Participants

The Agencies assess each participant's financial interest in the collaboration and its potential impact on the participant's incentive to compete independently with the collaboration. The potential impact may vary depending on the size and nature of the financial interest (e.g., whether the financial interest is debt or equity). In general, the greater the financial interest in the collaboration, the less likely is the participant to compete with the collaboration.[24] The Agencies also assess direct equity investments between

---

[23] For example, if participants in a production collaboration must contribute most of their productive capacity to the collaboration, the collaboration may impair the ability of its participants to remain effective independent competitors regardless of the terms of the agreement.

[24] Similarly, a collaboration's financial interest in a participant may diminish the collaboration's incentive to compete with that participant.

or among the participants. Such investments may reduce the incentives of the participants to compete with each other. In either case, the analysis is sensitive to the level of financial interest in the collaboration or in another participant relative to the level of the participant's investment in its independent business operations in the markets affected by the collaboration.

3.34(d) Control of the Collaboration's Competitively Significant Decision Making

The Agencies consider the manner in which a collaboration is organized and governed in assessing the extent to which participants and their collaboration have the ability and incentive to compete independently. Thus, the Agencies consider the extent to which the collaboration's governance structure enables the collaboration to act as an independent decision maker. For example, the Agencies ask whether participants are allowed to appoint members of a board of directors for the collaboration, if incorporated, or otherwise to exercise significant control over the operations of the collaboration. In general, the collaboration is less likely to compete independently as participants gain greater control over the collaboration's price, output, and other competitively significant decisions.[25]

To the extent that the collaboration's decision making is subject to the participants' control, the Agencies consider whether that control could be exercised jointly. Joint control over the collaboration's price and output levels could create or increase market power and raise competitive concerns. Depending on the nature of the collaboration, competitive concern also may arise due to joint control over other competitively significant decisions, such as the level and scope of R&D efforts and investment. In contrast, to the extent that participants independently set the price and quantity of their share of a collaboration's output and independently control other competitively significant decisions, an agreement's likely anticompetitive harm is reduced.

3.34(e) Likelihood of Anticompetitive Information Sharing

---

[25] Control may diverge from financial interests. For example, a small equity investment may be coupled with a right to veto large capital expenditures and, thereby, to effectively limit output. The Agencies examine a collaboration's actual governance structure in assessing issues of control.

The Agencies evaluate the extent to which competitively sensitive information concerning markets affected by the collaboration likely would be disclosed. This likelihood depends on, among other things, the nature of the collaboration, its organization and governance, and safeguards implemented to prevent or minimize such disclosure. For example, participants might refrain from assigning marketing personnel to an R&D collaboration, or, in a marketing collaboration, participants might limit access to competitively sensitive information regarding their respective operations to only certain individuals or to an independent third party. Similarly, a buying collaboration might use an independent third party to handle negotiations in which its participants' input requirements or other competitively sensitive information could be revealed. In general, it is less likely that the collaboration will facilitate collusion on competitively sensitive variables if appropriate safeguards governing information sharing are in place.

3.34(f) Duration of the Collaboration

The Agencies consider the duration of the collaboration in assessing whether participants retain the ability and incentive to compete against each other and their collaboration. In general, the shorter the duration, the more likely participants are to compete against each other and their collaboration. . . .

Notes

1. Not long after the Guidelines for Collaborations Among Competitors were issued, the Federal Trade Commission hosted a public workshop on the topic of "Competition Policy in the World of B2B Electronic Marketplaces," on June 29 and 30, 2000. The term "B2B" refers to business-to-business electronic marketplaces that use the Internet to connect businesses to one another electronically. Their growth can only be described as explosive, from practically nothing in the mid-1990s to billions of dollars at present. The results of the workshop were summarized and discussed in a report prepared by the staff of the FTC in October 2000, entitled "Entering the 21st Century: Competition Policy in the World of B2B Electronic Marketplaces." The report touches on subjects including the potential efficiencies that B2B marketplaces may generate, the kinds of antitrust issues B2Bs may raise (both in the markets for goods and services traded on B2Bs at both the seller and buyer level, and in the market for the marketplaces themselves), and the particular issues posed by information-sharing agreements, joint purchasing agreements, and new forms of exclusionary practices that can occur in the B2B world. The overall

message of the report, which is also reflected in many public statements both from FTC members and from Department of Justice enforcers, is that the forms of business arrangements may be new, but the antitrust principles and analysis that have evolved over the years remain pertinent and adequate to the task of policing these new markets.

2. On January 6, 2001, the Commission of the European Union issued a comparable set of guidelines, to those issued by Department of Justice and FTC, on horizontal arrangements, entitled the "Guidelines on the applicability of Article 81 of the EC Treaty to horizontal cooperation agreements." See Official Journal C 3/02, 6.1.2001. These guidelines cover agreements on research and development, production, marketing, purchasing, standardization, and environmental matters. The introductory section describes the purpose and scope of the guidelines. It is followed by a discussion of the basic principles for the assessment of these kinds of arrangements first under Article 81(1) (which prohibits agreements with the object or effect of preventing, restricting, or distorting competition) and then under Article 81(3) (which allows for exemptions of agreements with potentially beneficial effects). Particular attention is paid to the way in which market power and market structure are analyzed and how economic benefits are assessed. After this initial section, the remainder of the guidelines are devoted more particular discussion of different kinds of agreements, with brief case examples that are analyzed.

Section 3. Efforts to Influence Government Action

Insert after Note 1, page 471:

MASSACHUSETTS SCHOOL OF LAW AT ANDOVER, INC. v. AMERICAN BAR ASSOCIATION

United States Court of Appeals, Third Circuit, 1997.
107 F.3d 1026.

Before: BECKER, MANSMANN and GREENBERG, Circuit Judges.

GREENBERG, J. This case is before this court on appeal from an order of the district court granting summary judgment on all counts to the appellees in this antitrust action brought against them by the Massachusetts School of Law at Andover, Inc. ("MSL"). . . .

I. FACTUAL AND PROCEDURAL HISTORY

A. The Parties

MSL has been operating a law school in Massachusetts since 1988. The Board of Regents of Massachusetts authorized MSL to grant the J.D. degree in 1990. This authority allowed MSL's graduates to take several bar examinations, including that in Massachusetts. MSL has the stated policy of providing low-cost but high quality legal education and attracting mid-life, working class, and minority students. MSL facilitates this policy with its admissions procedure and a tuition of $9,000 per year. Many of MSL's policies and practices conflict with American Bar Association ("ABA") accreditation standards, and MSL aggressively has sought changes in those standards.

The ABA, a national professional organization of attorneys whose membership is open to members of any bar in the United States, has been concerned with legal education and bar admissions throughout its history. In 1921, through its Section of Legal Education and Admissions to the Bar (the "Section"), the ABA first developed standards of accreditation for legal education programs. The ABA petitioned state supreme courts to rely on its accreditation decisions in connection with bar admission decisions. Now, all 50 states and the District of Columbia consider graduation from an ABA-accredited law school sufficient for the legal education requirement of bar admission. The United States Secretary of Education considers the Council of the Section to be the national agency for accreditation of professional schools of law and a reliable authority concerning the quality of legal education. The ABA informs the states of its accreditation decisions and annually sends them the Review of Legal Education in the United States, the ABA accreditation standards, and any proposed revisions of the standards. During the period at issue, there were 177 ABA-accredited law schools in the United States and over 50 unaccredited schools with some form of state approval such as MSL enjoys. The ABA consistently has opposed attempts to change or waive bar admission rules to allow graduates of schools not accredited by the ABA to take the bar examination.

Many states have methods of satisfying the legal education requirement other than graduation from an ABA-accredited school. These methods include legal apprenticeship, practice in another state, and graduation from a school approved by the American Association of Law Schools ("AALS") or a state agency. The AALS is an association of 160 law schools which serves as a learned society for law schools and legal faculty and as a representative of the law school community with the federal government and other education organizations. Furthermore, in every state, a bar applicant or law school can petition the bar admission authority for revision or waiver of the rules. MSL won a waiver of New Hampshire's rules to allow its graduates to take the bar in 1995, and has filed petitions seeking similar relief in Connecticut, Maine, New York, and Rhode Island. Maryland and Washington, D.C. have granted petitions of graduates of MSL to take the bar. MSL graduates can take the bar examination immediately after graduation in California, Massachusetts, New Hampshire, Vermont and West Virginia, and in 12 other states after practicing in another state first.

The ABA allows graduates of non-accredited schools to join the ABA once they are admitted to a bar and does not prohibit its members from hiring or otherwise dealing with graduates of such schools. The ABA does not prevent its members from teaching at non-ABA-accredited schools, but it does not allow its accredited schools to let students transfer credits from unaccredited schools or to accept graduates of unaccredited schools into graduate programs.

ABA accreditation is open to any law school that applies and meets the ABA standards. The ABA grants provisional accreditation to schools that substantially comply with its standards and promise to comply fully within three years. An Accreditation Committee makes an initial evaluation of a school for provisional accreditation and gives a recommendation to the Council of the Section. The Council then makes a recommendation to the ABA House of Delegates, which has the ultimate decisionmaking authority.

A law school must have been teaching students for five years and graduated three classes to be eligible for AALS membership. The AALS holds an annual meeting, professional conferences and workshops, and publishes the Journal of Legal Education. All of its current members are ABA-accredited, but accreditation is neither necessary nor sufficient for membership approval. The AALS accredits schools in the sense that it determines whether a school meets its membership requirements, but it has accreditation standards and procedures separate from those of the ABA. The AALS conducts a site visit, independently of the ABA, when a school applies for membership, and it conducts periodic visits after membership, usually jointly with the ABA if the school is ABA- accredited. The AALS is not involved with site inspections for provisional ABA accreditation, such as the one the ABA undertook at MSL.

The Law School Admissions Council, Inc. ("LSAC") is the successor organization to the Law School Admission Council and Law School Admission Services, Inc. The LSAC, as have its predecessors, administers the Law School Admissions Test ("LSAT"). The LSAC is not affiliated formally with either the ABA or the AALS and does not participate in the ABA accreditation process. Membership in the LSAC is open to any United States law school that (1) requires that "substantially all of its applicants for admission take the Law School Admission Test," and (2) is ABA-accredited or an AALS member. MSL does not require the LSAT, never has applied for AALS membership, and is not ABA-accredited, so thus is not eligible for LSAC membership.

In addition to administering the LSAT, the LSAC performs a number of other services. The Candidate Referral Service ("CRS") provides lists of names and addresses of people who have taken the LSAT. Use of the CRS is open to any school which has degree granting authority from a state, regardless of LSAC membership or ABA accreditation, and MSL has made use of this service. The Law School Data Assembly Service ("LSDAS") provides a summary of a law school applicant's college record and LSAT score. LSDAS is also open to all schools and has been used by MSL. The LSAC publishes a handbook, The Official Guide to U.S. Law Schools, with a two-page description of each United States LSAC member school, and two appendices with the names and addresses of Canadian LSAC members and unaccredited United States law schools, including MSL, known to the LSAC. The LSAC also sponsors regional recruiting forums for law school applicants and conferences of pre-law advisors which are only open to LSAC members.

B. The Complaint

MSL applied for provisional ABA accreditation during the fall of 1992 and early 1993. MSL never claimed it was or would be in compliance with ABA standards, but instead asked for a waiver under Standard 802 which allows the Council to grant variances from the standards. Following the established process, a seven-member site evaluation team appointed by and representing only the ABA visited MSL and then prepared a 76-page report which was sent to MSL. MSL sent a 90-page response to the site team report.

The Accreditation Committee, after reviewing the site report and the MSL materials, and hearing a presentation from six MSL representatives, recommended denial of MSL's accreditation application because it did not meet the ABA requirements. The Committee also recommended denial of the waiver request. In a letter to MSL explaining its denial recommendation, the Committee listed 11 areas where MSL failed to comply with ABA standards. These areas included the high student/faculty ratio, over reliance on part-time faculty, the heavy teaching load of full-time faculty, the lack of adequate sabbaticals for faculty, the use of a for-credit bar review class, the failure to limit the hours students may be employed, and the failure to use the LSAT or give evidence validating its own admission test. [MSL took issue with these criticisms.] The body of the letter discussed the inadequacy of MSL's law library, but the letter did not cite that inadequacy as one of the reasons for the denial recommendation. The letter did not discuss the salaries of MSL's faculty. Invoking ABA procedures, MSL appealed but, after a full review at which MSL had the opportunity to make a presentation, the denial of accreditation was upheld on February 8, 1994.

MSL filed this action on November 23, 1993, alleging that the ABA, AALS, LSAC, and 22 individuals combined and conspired to organize and enforce a group boycott in violation of Section 1 of the Sherman Act and conspired to monopolize legal education, law school accreditation, and the licensing of lawyers, in violation of Section 2 of the Sherman Act. 15 U.S.C. §§ 1- 2. The complaint basically alleged that the appellees conspired to enforce the ABA's anticompetitive accreditation standards by: (1) fixing the price of faculty salaries; (2) requiring reduced teaching hours and non-teaching duties; (3) requiring paid sabbaticals; (4) forcing the hiring of more professors in order to lower student/faculty ratios; (5) limiting the use of adjunct professors; (6) prohibiting the use of required or for-credit bar review courses; (7) forcing schools to limit the number of hours students could work; (8) prohibiting ABA-accredited schools from accepting credit transfers from unaccredited schools and from enrolling graduates of unaccredited schools in graduate programs; (9) requiring more expensive and elaborate physical and library facilities; and (10) requiring schools to use the LSAT. MSL alleged that enforcement of these anticompetitive criteria led to the denial of its application for provisional accreditation and caused MSL to suffer a "loss of prestige" and direct economic damage in the form of declining enrollments and tuition revenue. [Enrollments allegedly declined to 40% of the level they had attained prior to the denial of accreditation.]

After MSL filed its complaint, the Antitrust Division of the United States Department of Justice ("DOJ") began an investigation of the ABA's accreditation process and on June 27, 1995, filed suit against the ABA in the United States District Court for the District of Columbia alleging violations of Section 1 of the Sherman Act. The ABA entered into a consent decree with the DOJ on June 25, 1996, settling that case.

[The district court granted summary judgment for the appellees. MSL appealed from that order.]

II. DISCUSSION

* * *

C. Summary Judgment

MSL asserts three types of injury resulting from the ABA's allegedly anticompetitive conduct. The first is that MSL is at a competitive disadvantage in recruiting students because graduates of unaccredited schools cannot take the bar examination in most states. Second, MSL says that denial of accreditation creates a stigma, independent of the bar examination issue. Finally, MSL contends that the ABA's enforcement of its accreditation standards injures it directly by increasing the cost of faculty salaries and creating a boycott of unaccredited schools.

In granting summary judgment to the appellees, the district court held that they were not subject to antitrust liability for MSL's principal alleged injury, a competitive disadvantage in recruiting students, to the extent that the decisions of the individual states to prohibit graduates of unaccredited schools from taking their bar examinations caused the injury. The court based this holding on the principles of Noerr, 365 U.S. 127. MSL argues on appeal that the Noerr principles do not apply here because private anti-competitive conduct is immunized only where it is (1) clearly and affirmatively authorized by state policy, and (2) actively supervised by the state. California Retail Liquor Dealers Ass'n v. Midcal Aluminum, Inc., 445 U.S. 97, 105 (1980). See also FTC v. Ticor Title Ins. Co., 504 U.S. 621 (1992); Patrick v. Burget, 486 U.S. 94 (1988). . . .

In Parker v. Brown the Supreme Court held that the Sherman Act does not prohibit an anticompetitive restraint imposed by a state as an act of government. 317 U.S. 341, 352, 63 S.Ct. 307, 314, 87 L.Ed. 315 (1943). The decision in Noerr reaffirmed the Parker doctrine in stating "where a restraint upon trade or monopolization is the result of valid governmental action, as opposed to private action, no violation of the Act can be made out." 365 U.S. at 136, 81 S.Ct. at 529. Noerr went on to hold that any attempt to petition or influence the government to impose an anticompetitive restraint is immune from antitrust action. *Id.* Further, even if the anticompetitive restraint results directly from private action, it is still immune if it is an "incidental effect" of a legitimate attempt to influence governmental action. *Id.* at 143-44. As the Supreme Court put it, "Parker and Noerr are complementary expressions of the principle that the antitrust laws regulate business, not politics; the former decision protects the States' acts of governing, and the latter the citizens' participation in government." City of Columbia v. Omni Outdoor Advertising, Inc., 499 U.S. 365, 383 (1991). Thus, the initial substantive issues on this appeal are whether state or private conduct caused the injury MSL alleges it suffered because its graduates could not take the bar examination in most states, and whether, if MSL suffered an injury as a result of the ABA's conduct, the injury was an incidental effect of the ABA's attempt to influence the states with respect to establishing criteria for bar admission. We will discuss each alleged injury separately.

1. Injury from bar examination requirements

Each state retains the authority to decide what applicants may take its bar examination and may be admitted to the bar. Accordingly, MSL's argument that the ABA received "carte-blanche delegated authority to decide who can take bar exams," . . . is simply wrong. Many, but not all, states consider the accreditation decisions of the ABA in their legal education requirement (one of many requirements) for taking the bar examination. Yet, every state retains the final authority to set all the bar admission rules, and individual applicants or law schools can petition the states for waivers or changes.

To the extent that MSL's alleged injury arises from the inability of its graduates to take the bar examination in most states, the injury is the result of state action and thus is immune from antitrust action under the doctrine of Parker v. Brown, 317 U.S. at 352. The ABA does not decide who can take the bar examinations. Rather, it makes an accreditation decision which it conveys to the states, but the states make the decisions as to bar admissions. Without state action, the ABA's accreditation decisions would not affect state bar admissions requirements. Because the states are sovereign in imposing the bar admission requirements, the clear articulation and active supervision requirements urged by MSL are inapplicable. . . . In short, this case does not involve a delegation of state authority. To the contrary, the states use the ABA to assist them in their decision-making processes. Thus, we have here a government action case.

Our holding is consistent with current antitrust jurisprudence. The Supreme Court held in a challenge to Arizona's bar admissions policies that the conduct in question "was in reality that of the Arizona Supreme Court," and thus immune under Parker. Hoover v. Ronwin, 466 U.S. 558, 573-74 (1984). Further, the Supreme Court has held that when a state supreme court adopts a state bar rule banning legal advertising, and retains final enforcement authority over it, Parker immunity applies. Bates v. State Bar of Arizona, 433 U.S. 350, 361 (1977) ("The Arizona Supreme Court is the real party in interest; it adopted the rules, and it is the ultimate trier of fact and law in the enforcement process."). This case is entirely analogous. The states do not adopt the ABA's accreditation processes, but they do adopt and give effect to the results. Thus, the cases cited by MSL (Midcal, Patrick, and Ticor) are inapplicable because they dealt with situations where private parties were engaging in conduct, whether price-fixing (Midcal and Ticor) or denying hospital privileges (Patrick), which led directly to the alleged antitrust injury.

Here, the state action setting the bar examination requirements led to the alleged injury.

[The court distinguished the Supreme Court's opinion in Allied Tube & Conduit Corp. v. Indian Head, Inc., 486 U.S. 492 (1988), because that case specifically did not reach the question of any injury caused by the adoption of the challenged standards by a governmental body. It then discussed several additional lower court decisions applying the principles of Noerr and rejected MSL's claim that the ABA's conduct injured it because its graduates could not take the bar examination in most states.]

2. Stigma injury

MSL also alleges that independent of any bar examination requirements, it was injured by the stigmatic effect in the market place of the denial of accreditation. MSL claims that the ABA has conducted a campaign to convey the idea that ABA accreditation is the sine qua non of quality and that the ABA is the most, or only, competent organization to judge law schools. There is enough evidence to create a genuine dispute of material fact on this issue. Nevertheless, the district court ruled that this injury could not form the basis for antitrust liability because it was "incidental to the primary, protected injury," and thus immune under Noerr. MSL challenges this holding on the grounds that there was no petitioning of government here, and therefore Noerr does not apply. . . . We hold that there was sufficient petitioning to invoke Noerr immunity.

MSL relies extensively on the Supreme Court's decision in Allied Tube & Conduit Corp. v. Indian Head, Inc., 486 U.S. 492 (1988). . . . [After further describing Allied Tube, the court applied it to MSL's claim.]

The conduct of which MSL complains here is basically the ABA's justification of its accreditation decisions and MSL is asserting a loss of prestige resulting from it. This conduct is neither normal commercial activity nor the type of restraint of trade involved in Allied Tube, and thus that case is not controlling. A loss of prestige resulting from a refusal to approve a product or service does not alone make out an antitrust claim.

Noerr immunity is proper in this case because the ABA engaged in petitioning activity, and the stigma injury which MSL suffered was incidental to that activity. [Citing Omni Outdoor Advertising, the court flatly rejected the concept of a "conspiracy" exception to either Noerr or Parker immunity.] MSL admits that in the past, "from the 1920's to approximately the mid 1970's," the ABA petitioned the states in a campaign to prohibit graduates from unaccredited schools from taking bar examinations. This campaign was obviously successful as now most states require graduation from an ABA-accredited school for admission to the bar. The ABA's current conduct surely would be considered petitioning if it took place during the past campaign. The fact that the ABA was successful in lobbying the states does not weaken its position. The ABA continues to communicate its accreditation decisions to the states, and it desires that they continue to give them credence. Discussing the quality and competence of its decisions is a legitimate, although somewhat indirect, way of petitioning the states to continue to follow its guidance. Yet, such activity is no more indirect than the public relations campaign held to be petitioning in Noerr.

There is an exception to Noerr immunity that would apply if the ABA "attempted directly to persuade anyone not to deal with" MSL.... There is no evidence that the ABA made such an attempt (there was such evidence in Allied Tube), nor is there any other evidence suggesting that Noerr immunity should not apply here. In a supplemental filing of information after oral argument, MSL produced two instances where it claims the ABA directly mentioned MSL. The first is a Boston Globe article about the denial of accreditation to MSL in which an ABA governor defended the ABA standards as providing "a minimum level of quality and consumer protection assurance to the public." John H. Kennedy, "Andover Law School Loses Appeal for Accreditation," Boston Globe, February 9, 1994, at 42. The second proffered piece of evidence is a transcript of the ABA House of Delegates debate of MSL's accreditation application, where one member urged the denial of MSL's application and stated that the standards with which MSL did not comply "lie at the heart of a quality institution."

Both of these statements do nothing more than defend the ABA standards. As we discuss above, this is valid, if indirect, petitioning activity. The ABA is not saying directly that MSL is a bad institution, or that a particular student should not go there. MSL's attempts to characterize all the ABA's comments about the quality of its accreditation process as direct attacks on MSL does not make them direct attacks. We also point out that if a claim for stigma injury could be advanced in circumstances like those here, Noerr immunity would be confined severely; a petitioner for governmental action is likely to urge that the action is needed to ensure that standards are met, thereby suggesting that some entities do not meet appropriate standards.

3. Direct injury from ABA standards

MSL alleges a third injury which occurs directly from the ABA's enforcement of its standards, independent of both the bar examination and stigma issues. The challenged standards relate to faculty salaries (MSL charges price-fixing) and limitations on accredited schools accepting transfers or graduate students from unaccredited schools (MSL charges a boycott). Although the ABA is immune from liability attributable to the state action in requiring applicants for the bar examination to have graduated from an ABA-accredited law school and from any stigma injury resulting from the denial of accreditation under the Noerr petitioning doctrine, the ABA is not immune in the actual enforcement of its standards. The state action relates to the use of the results of the accreditation process, not the process itself. The process is entirely private conduct which has not been approved or supervised explicitly by any state. Thus, the ABA's enforcement of an anticompetitive standard which injures MSL would not be immune from possible antitrust liability. Extending Noerr immunity to this type of private activity would run counter to Allied Tube.

. . . MSL failed to show sufficient evidence that it was denied accreditation because it did not comply with the salary standard. . . . MSL alleges that the faculty salary standards injured it in two ways. First, MSL asserts that it raised its salaries in an attempt to get accreditation. This claim is in direct conflict to its consistent assertion that it refused to comply with the ABA's anticompetitive standards and for that reason was denied accreditation. The claim also is remarkable because MSL made it clear that it would not comply with ABA standards to obtain certification. . . . The only other related evidence shows that MSL acted independently to increase its salaries, and then later found that this action might help it get accreditation. . . . There has not been sufficient explanation of the contradiction to create a genuine issue of material fact and justify reversing the summary judgment.

MSL's second contention that the ABA's salary standards injured it is that the standards inflated the market cost of law professors, thereby increasing the salaries MSL must pay its faculty. This market price argument is equally unavailing. MSL's stated policy was to rely on adjunct faculty. MSL did not produce evidence that any of its faculty other than its dean ever had been employed at another law school. In effect, MSL was hiring faculty from a different market, one unaffected by the ABA's conduct, or at least a different provider in the same market (teachers who never taught at ABA-accredited schools).

* * *

MSL also alleges a boycott in that the ABA prevented its accredited schools from accepting transfers or graduate students from unaccredited schools. The district court held that MSL had not produced any evidence that it was injured by either of these rules. This holding is correct. MSL has done nothing more than state the standards and allege that they injured MSL. There is no factual support for these allegations. Further, the evidence shows that MSL actively opposed its students transferring, both in policy and practice. MSL therefore cannot claim that the ABA's prohibition on transfers with credit injured it.

MSL also alleges that the AALS boycotted MSL by refusing membership and that the LSAC boycotted MSL by refusing to allow it to attend certain recruiting conferences. The allegations regarding the AALS are simply incorrect. AALS membership is independent of ABA accreditation, and MSL never has applied for such membership. Even though it is not a member, MSL can attend AALS conferences and has done so. Therefore MSL has not suffered any injury at the hands of the AALS.

The LSAC's failure to invite MSL to its conferences does not constitute a boycott. Under the fact-pattern here, to demonstrate a boycott MSL has to show that these conferences are an essential facility for recruiting students, as there is no other potential basis for the boycott claim. Such an essential facility or claim fails whenever a plaintiff (1) cannot show that the defendant has a monopoly over the alleged essential facility; (2) the facility cannot be duplicated in a reasonable manner; and (3) the plaintiff has been denied its use. Ideal Dairy Farms, Inc. v. John Labatt, Ltd., 90 F.3d 737, 748 (3d Cir.1996). MSL has shown only that the LSAC denies it participation. There is no evidence suggesting that the LSAC has a monopoly over access to law students or pre-law advisors, or even over recruiting fairs. The LSAC does not hinder MSL's recruiting in any way, it just does not aid it by allowing MSL to attend its conferences. Such activity is not required by the antitrust laws, and its absence does not constitute antitrust injury.

Further, MSL has not shown that the LSAC injured it. . . . .

*   *   *

III. CONCLUSION

The order of the district court entered August 29, 1996, granting the appellees summary judgment and the other orders on appeal will be affirmed.

CHAPTER 6: MARKET CONCENTRATION, CONSPIRACY, AND THE ANTITRUST LAWS

Insert before the Note on Summary Disposition in Antitrust Cases, page 513:

Twice in recent years the Supreme Court has commented briefly on the problem of conscious parallelism. First, in *Brooke Group v. Brown & Williamson Tobacco Corp.*, 509 U.S. 209 (1993), it addressed a plaintiff's argument that its rival, Brown & Williamson, was engaged in a predatory campaign designed to pressure Liggett to raise prices on its generic cigarettes, through tactics that enlisted the tacit assistance of other cigarette companies. The Supreme Court rejected the point in part II.B. of its opinion, reprinted in the casebook at pages 683-685. Second, in *Brown v. Pro Football, Inc.*, 518 U.S. 231 (1996), in which the Court clarified the reach of the nonstatutory labor exemption to the antitrust laws, it identified the following antitrust risks to members of a multiple employer bargaining unit if the exemption did not apply:

> . . . [T]o subject [multiple employer bargaining] to antitrust law is to require antitrust courts to answer a host of important practical questions about how collective bargaining over wages, hours and working conditions is to proceed—the very result that the implicit labor exemption seeks to avoid. And it is to place in jeopardy some of the potentially beneficial labor-related effects that multiemployer bargaining can achieve. That is because unlike labor law, which sometimes welcomes anticompetitive agreements conducive to industrial harmony, antitrust law forbids all agreements among competitors (such as competing employers) that unreasonably lessen competition among or between them in virtually any respect whatsoever. See, e.g., Paramount Famous Lasky Corp. v. United States, 282 U.S. 30 (1930) (agreement to insert arbitration provisions in motion picture licensing contracts). Antitrust law also sometimes

> permits judges or juries to premise antitrust liability upon little more than uniform behavior among competitors, preceded by conversations implying that later uniformity might prove desirable, . . . or accompanied by other conduct that in context suggests that each competitor failed to make an independent decision . . . .
>
> If the antitrust laws apply, what are employers to do once impasse is reached? If all impose terms similar to their last offer, they invite an antitrust action premised upon identical behavior (along with prior or accompanying conversations) as tending to show a common understanding or agreement. If any, or all, of them individually impose terms that differ significantly from that offer, they invite an unfair labor practice charge. Indeed, how can employers safely discuss their offers together even before a bargaining impasse occurs? A preimpasse discussion about, say, the practical advantages or disadvantages of a particular proposal, invites a later antitrust claim that they agreed to limit the kinds of action each would later take should an impasse occur. The same is true of postimpasse discussions aimed at renewed negotiations with the union. Nor would adherence to the terms of an expired collective-bargaining agreement eliminate a potentially plausible antitrust claim charging that they had "conspired" or tacitly "agreed" to do so, particularly if maintaining the status quo were not in the immediate economic self-interest of some. Cf. Interstate Circuit, supra, at 222-223, ... All this is to say that to permit antitrust liability here threatens to introduce instability and uncertainty into the collective-bargaining process, for antitrust law often forbids or discourages the kinds of joint discussions and behavior that the collective-bargaining process invites or requires.

518 U.S. at 240-242.

With respect to horizontal agreement issues, see *Toys "R" Us*, Inc., page 112 infra.

Insert after note 6, page 578:

7. In Eleven Line, Inc. v. North Texas States Soccer Ass'n, 1997 WL 135684 (N.D. Tex., decided Mar. 12, 1997) (Buchmeyer, C.D.J.), interrelated amateur soccer organizations were found to be a single entity.

Plaintiff Eleven Line sued Defendants North Texas State Soccer Association ("NTSSA"), Midland Soccer Association ("MSA"), and Odessa Soccer Association ("OSA") for alleged antitrust violations and tortious interference with contract arising out of Defendant's enforcement of NTSSA Rule II in order to prevent its registered players from playing indoor soccer in leagues and facilities operated by Plaintiff. . . .

Plaintiff Eleven Line was a Texas corporation which operated, during the relevant time period, an indoor soccer facility in Midland, Texas. This facility, Permian Basin Sports Center, provided the only indoor soccer arena and the only amateur youth and adult indoor soccer leagues in the Midland/Odessa area. The Defendants are all affiliated with the United States Soccer Federation ("USSF"), which is the "national governing body" ("NGB") of soccer in the United States. Defendant NTSSA is a "National State Association" ("NSA") member of the USSF, established as a non-profit corporation with a primary purpose "to foster and advance the cause of soccer" within its North Texas geographic region. It sponsors and oversees USSF-affiliated soccer activities within North Texas. Defendants MSA and OSA are non-profit corporations and members of NTSSA, and they provide the only outdoor soccer leagues in the Midland/Odessa area.

There are NSAs for every geographical region in the United States, and they are the organizations through which USSF organizes soccer on the regional and local level. USSF's Rule Book sets forth several duties for NSAs, one of which is registration of all players on teams sponsored, financed, coached, or administered by NSA member organizations. USSF Rule 4011 § 1(b)(3). Purportedly pursuant to these duties, NTSSA has established several rules regarding player registration. One of these rules states that "[o]nly registered players shall be permitted to play in competitions under the auspices of [the NTSSA] or its affiliated members." NTSA Rule I. Further, NTSSA's rules set forth Rule II regarding unregistered/non-sanctioned play. . . .

The net result of enforcement of Rules I and II is revocation of any player's or team's registration if that player or team participates in soccer games not organized under the auspices of NTSSA or USSF. PBSC, on the other hand, is not a member or an affiliate of NTSSA, and it does not require or recommend that the players or teams that play in its leagues and use its facility be members of NTSSA or any USSF affiliate. . . .

Prior to December, 1995, PBSC was contacted by representatives of NTSSA and MSA and informed that it would be in the best interest of PBSC to become a member of NTSSA and provide leagues for indoor soccer sanctioned by NTSSA. Eleven Line elected not to pursue membership. As PBSC was signing teams for the December 1995 season, NTSSA, MSA and OSA began contacting coaches and players informing them that NTSSA, MSA and OSA would begin enforcing Rule II. As a result, any team or player electing to participate in the indoor soccer season would automatically have his or her registration with NTSSA, MSA and OSA voided and would no longer be eligible to play in an outdoor soccer league.

Many teams withdrew from the indoor leagues rather than forfeit their NTSSA registration. The indoor leagues were decimated, as the number of teams decreased from the previous year by over eighty percent. On the opening weekend of the indoor season, only two youth games could be played, due to a shortage of participants. PBSC lost profits, and many children who had wanted to play indoor soccer were unable to do so.

Eleven Line sued NTSSA, MSA, and OSA, alleging that (1) the three organizations violated Section 1 of the Sherman Act, 15 U.S.C. § 1, (2) the three organizations violated Section 2 of the Sherman Act, 15 U.S.C. § 2, (3) the three organizations tortiously interfered with Eleven Line's existing contractual relationship with its customers by enforcing Rule II, (4) NTSSA alone violated Section 2 of the Sherman Act, and (5) NTSSA alone tortiously interfered with Eleven Line's existing contractual relationship for the acquisition of Soccer Indoors. . . .

C. Section 1 Antitrust Claims

Plaintiff asserts that Defendants conspired to restrain competition among businesses and facilities which provide soccer play in the Midland/Odessa area in violation of Section 1 of the Sherman Act, 15 U.S.C. § 1. Defendants argue that they cannot have violated Section 1 of the Sherman Act because they are not sufficiently separate entities to be capable of concerted activity. Here their argument is based on the Supreme Court's opinion in Copperweld Corp. v. Independence Tube Corp., 467 U.S. 752 (1984), in which the Court concluded that "the coordinated activity of a parent and its wholly owned subsidiary must be viewed as that of a single enterprise for purposes of § 1 of the Sherman Act." 467 U.S. at 771.

* * *

Perhaps most relevant is the court's opinion in [Seabury Management, Inc. v. PGA, 878 F. Supp. 771 (D. Md. 1994)], which, as here, involved Section 1 claims against a national sports organization, the Professional Golfers' Association of America ("PGA"), and one of its geographical member sections, the Middle Atlantic Section PGA ("MAPGA"). 878 F. Supp. at 777. The MAPGA was not a wholly-owned subsidiary of the PGA, and the two entities were separately incorporated. The court noted the apparent separate character of the entities, pointing out that member sections maintained their own revenues, had their own by-laws, elected their own officers, and often conducted programs for the benefit of the members of only one section. However, despite these differences, the court held that the PGA and its member sections functioned as a single economic unit with the PGA possessing ultimate control over the actions of individual sections. The individual sections were all governed by the PGA constitution and by policies adopted by the PGA Board or at the PGA annual meetings. Further, any section's actions were subject to the approval of the PGA to ensure that they were in the best interest of the organization as a whole. *Id.* at 777-78.

The relationship between NTSSA and OSA and MSA is very similar to the relationship between the PGA and the MAPGA. The three entities are separately incorporated and managed, and they associate only voluntarily. Yet, NTSSA maintains a great deal of control over OSA and MSA. To become a member association requires compliance with rules regarding territory and numbers of teams. NTSSA Rule 2.2.1. Once accepted, NTSSA member associations must, "at all times, recognize the authority, rules, rulings, constitution and bylaws of [NTSSA]." NTSSA Rule 2.2.3.6. NTSSA has the authority to investigate alleged violations of its rules and determine sanctions. NTSSA Rule 2.3.6. Specifically, failure to comply with

NTSSA rules results in that member association's players and teams being prohibited from playing in any NTSSA-sanctioned event or league and ultimately leads to a loss of its NTSSA association and voting rights. NTSSA Rule 2.2.3.7-8. There is no economic competition between NTSSA and OSA and MSA, as the organizations exist together to pursue the goals of the national organization.

Here, as in Seabury, the "parent" organization exercises ultimate control over its "subsidiary" organizations. Therefore, though the NTSSA and its member associations are separate in form, in substance they constitute a single economic unit, incapable of conspiring for purposes of Section 1 of the Sherman Act. Accordingly, Defendants are entitled to summary judgment as to Plaintiff's Section 1 claims.

* * *

In Eleven Line, Inc. v. North Texas State Soccer Ass'n, Inc., 213 F.3d 198 (5th Cir. 2000), the Fifth Circuit found that the facts did not support any implied exemption from the antitrust laws, which NTSSA had argued was available to it in the Amateur Sports Act, 36 U.S.C. §§ 220501 *et seq.* Analyzing the merits, it noted that *Copperweld* "renders infeasible any claim of conspiracy" among the various participants in the league, unless the "moms and dads" were seen as the co-conspirators. 213 F.3d at 205. Implicitly rejecting that approach, the court went on to analyze the case as a Section 2 monopolization claim. As such, it commented that the soccer organizations had no economic motive for violating the antitrust laws, because of their non-profit, volunteer status. It did not resolve the merits of the liability claim, however, because it found that the plaintiff had suffered no compensable injuries. It therefore reversed a damage judgment in favor of plaintiff.

Insert after Note 8, page 593:

STATE OIL CO. v. KHAN
Supreme Court of the United States, 1997.
522 U.S. 3, 118 S. Ct. 275, 139 L. Ed. 2d 199.

O'CONNOR, J. Under § 1 of the Sherman Act, 26 Stat. 209, as amended, 15 U.S.C. § 1, "[e]very contract, combination ..., or conspiracy, in restraint of trade" is illegal. In Albrecht v. Herald Co., 390 U.S. 145, 88 S.Ct. 869, 19 L.Ed.2d 998 (1968), this Court held that vertical maximum price fixing is a per se violation of that statute. In this case, we are asked to reconsider that decision in light of subsequent decisions of this Court. We conclude that Albrecht should be overruled.

I

Respondents, Barkat U. Khan and his corporation, entered into an agreement with petitioner, State Oil Company, to lease and operate a gas station and convenience store owned by State Oil. The agreement provided that respondents would obtain the station's gasoline supply from State Oil at a price equal to a suggested retail price set by State Oil, less a margin of 3.25 cents per gallon. Under the agreement, respondents could charge any amount for gasoline sold to the station's customers, but if the price charged was higher than State Oil's suggested retail price, the excess was to be rebated to State Oil. Respondents could sell gasoline for less than State Oil's suggested retail price, but any such decrease would reduce their 3.25 cents-per-gallon margin.

About a year after respondents began operating the gas station, they fell behind in lease payments. State Oil then gave notice of its intent to terminate the agreement and commenced a state court proceeding to evict respondents. At State Oil's request, the state court appointed a receiver to operate the gas station. The receiver operated the station for several months without being subject to the price restraints in respondents' agreement with State Oil. According to respondents, the receiver obtained an overall profit margin in excess of 3.25 cents per gallon by lowering the price of regular-grade gasoline and raising the price of premium grades.

Respondents sued State Oil in the United States District Court for the

Northern District of Illinois, alleging in part that State Oil had engaged in price fixing in violation of § 1 of the Sherman Act by preventing respondents from raising or lowering retail gas prices. According to the complaint, but for the agreement with State Oil, respondents could have charged different prices based on the grades of gasoline, in the same way that the receiver had, thereby achieving increased sales and profits. State Oil responded that the agreement did not actually prevent respondents from setting gasoline prices, and that, in substance, respondents did not allege a violation of antitrust laws by their claim that State Oil's suggested retail price was not optimal.

The District Court found that the allegations in the complaint did not state a per se violation of the Sherman Act because they did not establish the sort of "manifestly anticompetitive implications or pernicious effect on competition" that would justify per se prohibition of State Oil's conduct. Subsequently, in ruling on cross-motions for summary judgment, the District Court concluded that respondents had failed to demonstrate antitrust injury or harm to competition. The District Court held that respondents had not shown that a difference in gasoline pricing would have increased the station's sales; nor had they shown that State Oil had market power or that its pricing provisions affected competition in a relevant market. Accordingly, the District Court entered summary judgment for State Oil on respondents' Sherman Act claim.

The Court of Appeals for the Seventh Circuit reversed. 93 F.3d 1358 (1996). The court first noted that the agreement between respondents and State Oil did indeed fix maximum gasoline prices by making it "worthless" for respondents to exceed the suggested retail prices. *Id.*, at 1360. After reviewing legal and economic aspects of price fixing, the court concluded that State Oil's pricing scheme was a per se antitrust violation under Albrecht v. Herald Co., supra. Although the Court of Appeals characterized Albrecht as "unsound when decided" and "inconsistent with later decisions" of this Court, it felt constrained to follow that decision. 93 F.3d, at 1363. In light of Albrecht and Atlantic Richfield Co. v. USA Petroleum Co., 495 U.S. 328 (1990) (ARCO), the court found that respondents could have suffered antitrust injury from not being able to adjust gasoline prices.

We granted certiorari to consider two questions, whether State Oil's conduct constitutes a per se violation of the Sherman Act and whether respondents are entitled to recover damages based on that conduct. 519 U.S. ----, 117 S.Ct. 941 (1997).

II

A

Although the Sherman Act, by its terms, prohibits every agreement "in restraint of trade," this Court has long recognized that Congress intended to outlaw only unreasonable restraints. See, e.g., Arizona v. Maricopa County Medical Soc., 457 U.S. 332, 342-343 (1982) (citing United States v. Joint Traffic Assn., 171 U.S. 505 (1898)). As a consequence, most antitrust claims are analyzed under a "rule of reason," according to which the finder of fact must decide whether the questioned practice imposes an unreasonable restraint on competition, taking into account a variety of factors, including specific information about the relevant business, its condition before and after the restraint was imposed, and the restraint's history, nature, and effect. 457 U.S., at 343, and n. 13 (citing Board of Trade of Chicago v. United States, 246 U.S. 231, 238 (1918)).

Some types of restraints, however, have such predictable and pernicious anticompetitive effect, and such limited potential for procompetitive benefit, that they are deemed unlawful per se. Northern Pacific R. Co. v. United States, 356 U.S. 1, 5 (1958). Per se treatment is appropriate "[o]nce experience with a particular kind of restraint enables the Court to predict with confidence that the rule of reason will condemn it." Maricopa County, supra, at 344; see also Broadcast Music, Inc. v. Columbia Broadcasting System, Inc., 441 U.S. 1, 19, n. 33 (1979). Thus, we have expressed reluctance to adopt per se rules with regard to "restraints imposed in the context of business relationships where the economic impact of certain practices is not immediately obvious." FTC v. Indiana Federation of Dentists, 476 U.S. 447, 458-459 (1986).

A review of this Court's decisions leading up to and beyond Albrecht is relevant to our assessment of the continuing validity of the per se rule established in Albrecht. Beginning with Dr. Miles Medical Co. v. John D. Park & Sons Co., 220 U.S. 373 (1911), the Court recognized the illegality of agreements under which manufacturers or suppliers set the minimum resale prices to be charged by their distributors. By 1940, the Court broadly declared all business combinations "formed for the purpose and with the effect of raising, depressing, fixing, pegging, or stabilizing the price of a commodity in interstate or foreign commerce" illegal per se. United States v. Socony-Vacuum Oil Co., 310 U.S. 150, 223 (1940). Accordingly, the Court condemned an agreement between two affiliated liquor distillers to limit the maximum price charged by retailers in Kiefer-Stewart Co. v. Joseph E.

Seagram & Sons, Inc., 340 U.S. 211 (1951), noting that agreements to fix maximum prices, "no less than those to fix minimum prices, cripple the freedom of traders and thereby restrain their ability to sell in accordance with their own judgment." *Id.*, at 213.

In subsequent cases, the Court's attention turned to arrangements through which suppliers imposed restrictions on dealers with respect to matters other than resale price. In White Motor Co. v. United States, 372 U.S. 253 (1963), the Court considered the validity of a manufacturer's assignment of exclusive territories to its distributors and dealers. The Court determined that too little was known about the competitive impact of such vertical limitations to warrant treating them as per se unlawful. *Id.*, at 263, 83 S.Ct., at 702. Four years later, in United States v. Arnold, Schwinn & Co., 388 U.S. 365 (1967), the Court reconsidered the status of exclusive dealer territories and held that, upon the transfer of title to goods to a distributor, a supplier's imposition of territorial restrictions on the distributor was "so obviously destructive of competition" as to constitute a per se violation of the Sherman Act. *Id.*, at 379. In Schwinn, the Court acknowledged that some vertical restrictions, such as the conferral of territorial rights or franchises, could have procompetitive benefits by allowing smaller enterprises to compete, and that such restrictions might avert vertical integration in the distribution process. *Id.*, at 379-380. The Court drew the line, however, at permitting manufacturers to control product marketing once dominion over the goods had passed to dealers. *Id.*, at 380.

Albrecht, decided the following Term, involved a newspaper publisher who had granted exclusive territories to independent carriers subject to their adherence to a maximum price on resale of the newspapers to the public. Influenced by its decisions in Socony-Vacuum, Kiefer-Stewart, and Schwinn, the Court concluded that it was per se unlawful for the publisher to fix the maximum resale price of its newspapers. 390 U.S., at 152-154. The Court acknowledged that "[m]aximum and minimum price fixing may have different consequences in many situations," but nonetheless condemned maximum price fixing for "substituting the perhaps erroneous judgment of a seller for the forces of the competitive market." *Id.*, at 152.

Albrecht was animated in part by the fear that vertical maximum price fixing could allow suppliers to discriminate against certain dealers, restrict the services that dealers could afford to offer customers, or disguise minimum price fixing schemes. *Id.*, at 152-153. The Court rejected the notion (both on the record of that case and in the abstract) that, because the newspaper publisher "granted exclusive territories, a price ceiling was necessary to protect the public from price gouging by dealers who had monopoly power in their own territories." *Id.*, at 153.

In a vigorous dissent, Justice Harlan asserted that the majority had erred in equating the effects of maximum and minimum price fixing. *Id.*, at 156-168 (Harlan, J., dissenting). Justice Harlan pointed out that, because the majority was establishing a per se rule, the proper inquiry was "not whether dictation of maximum prices is ever illegal, but whether it is always illegal." *Id.*, at 165-166. He also faulted the majority for conclusively listing "certain unfortunate consequences that maximum price dictation might have in other cases," even as it rejected evidence that the publisher's practice of fixing maximum prices counteracted potentially anticompetitive actions by its distributors. *Id.*, at 165. Justice Stewart also dissented, asserting that the publisher's maximum price fixing scheme should be properly viewed as promoting competition, because it protected consumers from dealers such as Albrecht, who, as "the only person who could sell for home delivery the city's only daily morning newspaper," was "a monopolist within his own territory." *Id.*, at 168 (Stewart, J., dissenting).

Nine years later, in Continental T.V., Inc. v. GTE Sylvania Inc., 433 U.S. 36 (1977), the Court overruled Schwinn, thereby rejecting application of a per se rule in the context of vertical nonprice restrictions. The Court acknowledged the principle of stare decisis, but explained that the need for clarification in the law justified reconsideration of Schwinn:

> Since its announcement, Schwinn has been the subject of continuing controversy and confusion, both in the scholarly journals and in the federal courts. The great weight of scholarly opinion has been critical of the decision, and a number of the federal courts confronted with analogous vertical restrictions have sought to limit its reach. In our view, the experience of the past 10 years should be brought to bear on this subject of considerable commercial importance. 433 U.S., at 47-49 (footnotes omitted).

The Court considered the historical context of Schwinn, noting that Schwinn's per se rule against vertical nonprice restrictions came only four years after the Court had refused to endorse a similar rule in White Motor Co., and that the decision neither explained the "sudden change in position," nor referred to the accepted requirements for per se violations set forth in Northern

Pacific R. Co., 433 U.S., at 51-52. The Court then reviewed scholarly works supporting the economic utility of vertical nonprice restraints. See *id.*, at 54-57 (citing, e.g., Posner, Antitrust Policy and the Supreme Court: An Analysis of the Restricted Distribution, Horizontal Merger and Potential Competition Decisions, 75 Colum. L. Rev. 282 (1975); Preston, Restrictive Distribution Arrangements: Economic Analysis and Public Policy Standards, 30 Law & Contemp. Prob. 506 (1965)). The Court concluded that, because "departure from the rule of reason standard must be based upon demonstrable economic effect rather than as in Schwinn upon formalistic line drawing," the appropriate course would be "to return to the rule of reason that governed vertical restrictions prior to Schwinn." GTE Sylvania, supra, at 58-59.

In GTE Sylvania, the Court declined to comment on Albrecht's per se treatment of vertical maximum price restrictions, noting that the issue "involve[d] significantly different questions of analysis and policy." 433 U.S., at 51, n. 18. Subsequent decisions of the Court, however, have hinted that the analytical underpinnings of Albrecht were substantially weakened by GTE Sylvania. We noted in Maricopa County that vertical restraints are generally more defensible than horizontal restraints. See 457 U.S., at 348, n. 18. And we explained in 324 Liquor Corp. v. Duffy, 479 U.S. 335, 341-342 (1987), that decisions such as GTE Sylvania "recognize the possibility that a vertical restraint imposed by a single manufacturer or wholesaler may stimulate interbrand competition even as it reduces intrabrand competition."

Most recently, in ARCO, 495 U.S. 328 (1990), although Albrecht's continuing validity was not squarely before the Court, some disfavor with that decision was signaled by our statement that we would "assume, arguendo, that Albrecht correctly held that vertical, maximum price fixing is subject to the per se rule." 495 U.S., at 335, n. 5. More significantly, we specifically acknowledged that vertical maximum price fixing "may have procompetitive interbrand effects," and pointed out that, in the wake of GTE Sylvania, "[t]he procompetitive potential of a vertical maximum price restraint is more evident ... than it was when Albrecht was decided, because exclusive territorial arrangements and other nonprice restrictions were unlawful per se in 1968." 495 U.S., at 344, n. 13 (citing several commentators identifying procompetitive effects of vertical maximum price fixing, including, e.g., P. Areeda & H. Hovenkamp, Antitrust Law ¶ 340.30b, p. 378, n. 24 (1988 Supp.); Blair & Harrison, Rethinking Antitrust Injury, 42 Vand. L.Rev. 1539, 1553 (1989); Easterbrook, Maximum Price Fixing, 48 U. Chi. L.Rev. 886, 887-890 (1981)).

B

Thus, our reconsideration of Albrecht's continuing validity is informed by several of our decisions, as well as a considerable body of scholarship discussing the effects of vertical restraints. Our analysis is also guided by our general view that the primary purpose of the antitrust laws is to protect interbrand competition. See, e.g., Business Electronics Corp. v. Sharp Electronics Corp., 485 U.S. 717, 726 (1988). "Low prices," we have explained, "benefit consumers regardless of how those prices are set, and so long as they are above predatory levels, they do not threaten competition." ARCO, supra, at 340. Our interpretation of the Sherman Act also incorporates the notion that condemnation of practiccs rcsulting in lower prices to consumers is "especially costly" because "cutting prices in order to increase business often is the very essence of competition." Matsushita Elec. Industrial Co. v. Zenith Radio Corp., 475 U.S. 574, 594 (1986).

So informed, we find it difficult to maintain that vertically-imposed maximum prices could harm consumers or competition to the extent necessary to justify their per se invalidation. As Chief Judge Posner wrote for the Court of Appeals in this case:

> As for maximum resale price fixing, unless the supplier is a monopsonist he cannot squeeze his dealers' margins below a competitive level; the attempt to do so would just drive the dealers into the arms of a competing supplier. A supplier might, however, fix a maximum resale price in order to prevent his dealers from exploiting a monopoly position. . . . [S]uppose that State Oil, perhaps to encourage ... dealer services ... has spaced its dealers sufficiently far apart to limit competition among them (or even given each of them an exclusive territory); and suppose further that Union 76 is a sufficiently distinctive and popular brand to give the dealers in it at least a modicum of monopoly power. Then State Oil might want to place a ceiling on the dealers' resale prices in order to prevent them from exploiting that monopoly power fully. It would do this not out of disinterested malice, but in its commercial self-interest. The higher the price at which gasoline is resold, the smaller the volume sold, and so the lower the profit to the supplier if the higher profit per gallon at the higher price is being snared by the dealer. 93 F.3d, at 1362.

See also R. Bork, The Antitrust Paradox 281-282 (1978) ("There could, of course, be no anticonsumer effect from [the type of price fixing considered in Albrecht], and one suspects that the paper has a legitimate interest in keeping subscriber prices down in order to increase circulation and maximize revenues from advertising").

We recognize that the Albrecht decision presented a number of theoretical justifications for a per se rule against vertical maximum price fixing. But criticism of those premises abounds. The Albrecht decision was grounded in the fear that maximum price fixing by suppliers could interfere with dealer freedom. 390 U.S., at 152. In response, as one commentator has pointed out, "the ban on maximum resale price limitations declared in Albrecht in the name of 'dealer freedom' has actually prompted many suppliers to integrate forward into distribution, thus eliminating the very independent trader for whom Albrecht professed solicitude." 7 P. Areeda, Antitrust Law, ¶ 1635, p. 395 (1989). For example, integration in the newspaper industry since Albrecht has given rise to litigation between independent distributors and publishers. See P. Areeda & H. Hovenkamp, Antitrust Law ¶ 729.7, pp. 599-614 (1996 Supp.).

The Albrecht Court also expressed the concern that maximum prices may be set too low for dealers to offer consumers essential or desired services. 390 U.S., at 152-153. But such conduct, by driving away customers, would seem likely to harm manufacturers as well as dealers and consumers, making it unlikely that a supplier would set such a price as a matter of business judgment. See, e.g., Lopatka, Stephen Breyer and Modern Antitrust: A Snug Fit, 40 Antitrust Bull. 1, 60 (1995); Blair & Lang, Albrecht After ARCO : Maximum Resale Price Fixing Moves Toward the Rule of Reason, 44 Vand. L.Rev. 1007, 1034 (1991). In addition, Albrecht noted that vertical maximum price fixing could effectively channel distribution through large or specially-advantaged dealers. 390 U.S., at 153. It is unclear, however, that a supplier would profit from limiting its market by excluding potential dealers. See, e.g., Easterbrook, supra, at 905-908. Further, although vertical maximum price fixing might limit the viability of inefficient dealers, that consequence is not necessarily harmful to competition and consumers. See, e.g., Easterbrook, supra, at 907; Lopatka, supra, at 60.

Finally, Albrecht reflected the Court's fear that maximum price fixing could be used to disguise arrangements to fix minimum prices, 390 U.S., at 153, which remain illegal per se. Although we have acknowledged the possibility that maximum pricing might mask minimum pricing, see Maricopa

County, 457 U.S., at 348, we believe that such conduct as with the other concerns articulated in Albrecht can be appropriately recognized and punished under the rule of reason. See, e.g., Easterbrook, 48 U. Chi. L.Rev., at 901-904; see also Pitofsky, In Defense of Discounters: The No-Frills Case for a Per Se Rule Against Vertical Price Fixing, 71 Geo. L.J. 1487, 1490, n. 17 (1983).

Not only are the potential injuries cited in Albrecht less serious than the Court imagined, the per se rule established therein could in fact exacerbate problems related to the unrestrained exercise of market power by monopolist-dealers. Indeed, both courts and antitrust scholars have noted that Albrecht's rule may actually harm consumers and manufacturers. See, e.g., Caribe BMW, Inc. v. Bayerische Motoren Werke Aktiengesellschaft, 19 F.3d 745, 753 (C.A.1 1994) (Breyer, C. J.); Areeda, supra, ¶ 1636a, at 395; G. Mathewson & R. Winter, Competition Policy and Vertical Exchange 13-14 (1985). Other commentators have also explained that Albrecht's per se rule has even more potential for deleterious effect on competition after our decision in GTE Sylvania, because, now that vertical nonprice restrictions are not unlawful per se, the likelihood of dealer monopoly power is increased. See, e.g., Easterbrook, supra, at 890, n. 20; see also ARCO, 495 U.S., at 343, n. 13. We do not intend to suggest that dealers generally possess sufficient market power to exploit a monopoly situation. Such retail market power may in fact be uncommon. See, e.g., Business Electronics, 485 U.S., at 727, n. 2; GTE Sylvania, 433 U.S., at 54. Nor do we hold that a ban on vertical maximum price fixing inevitably has anticompetitive consequences in the exclusive dealer context.

After reconsidering Albrecht's rationale and the substantial criticism the decision has received, however, we conclude that there is insufficient economic justification for per se invalidation of vertical maximum price fixing. That is so not only because it is difficult to accept the assumptions underlying Albrecht, but also because Albrecht has little or no relevance to ongoing enforcement of the Sherman Act. See Copperweld Corp. v. Independence Tube Corp., 467 U.S. 752, 777, and n. 25 (1984). Moreover, neither the parties nor any of the amici curiae have called our attention to any cases in which enforcement efforts have been directed solely against the conduct encompassed by Albrecht's per se rule.

Respondents argue that reconsideration of Albrecht should require "persuasive, expert testimony establishing that the per se rule has distorted the market." Their reasoning ignores the fact that Albrecht itself relied solely upon hypothetical effects of vertical maximum price fixing. Further, Albrecht's dire predictions have not been borne out, even though manufacturers and suppliers appear to have fashioned schemes to get around the per se rule against vertical maximum price fixing. In these circumstances, it is the retention of the rule of Albrecht, and not, as respondents would have it, the rule's elimination, that lacks adequate justification. See, e.g., GTE Sylvania, supra, at 58-59.

Respondents' reliance on Toolson v. New York Yankees, Inc., 346 U.S. 356 (1953) (per curiam), and Flood v. Kuhn, 407 U.S. 258 (1972), is similarly misplaced, because those decisions are clearly inapposite, having to do with the antitrust exemption for professional baseball, which this Court has described as "an aberration ... rest[ing] on a recognition and an acceptance of baseball's unique characteristics and needs," *id.*, at 282. In the context of this case, we infer little meaning from the fact that Congress has not reacted legislatively to Albrecht. In any event, the history of various legislative proposals regarding price fixing seems neither clearly to support nor to denounce the per se rule of Albrecht. Respondents are of course free to seek legislative protection from gasoline suppliers of the sort embodied in the Petroleum Marketing Practices Act, 92 Stat. 322, 15 U.S.C. § 2801 et seq. For the reasons we have noted, however, the remedy for respondents' dispute with State Oil should not come in the form of a per se rule affecting the conduct of the entire marketplace.

C

Despite what Chief Judge Posner aptly described as Albrecht's "infirmities, [and] its increasingly wobbly, moth-eaten foundations," 93 F.3d, at 1363, there remains the question whether Albrecht deserves continuing respect under the doctrine of stare decisis. The Court of Appeals was correct in applying that principle despite disagreement with Albrecht, for it is this Court's prerogative alone to overrule one of its precedents.

We approach the reconsideration of decisions of this Court with the utmost caution. Stare decisis reflects "a policy judgment that 'in most matters it is more important that the applicable rule of law be settled than that it be settled right.'" Agostini v. Felton, 117 S.Ct. 1997, 2016 (1997) (quoting Burnet v. Coronado Oil & Gas Co., 285 U.S. 393, 406 (1932) (Brandeis, J., dissenting)). It "is the preferred course because it promotes the evenhanded, predictable, and consistent development of legal principles, fosters reliance on judicial decisions, and contributes to the actual and perceived integrity of the judicial process." Payne v. Tennessee, 501 U.S. 808, 827 (1991). This Court has expressed its reluctance to overrule decisions involving statutory interpretation, see, e.g., Illinois Brick Co. v. Illinois, 431 U.S. 720, 736 (1977), and has acknowledged that stare decisis concerns are at their acme in cases involving property and contract rights, see, e.g., Payne, 501 U.S., at 828. Both of those concerns are arguably relevant in this case.

But "[s]tare decisis is not an inexorable command." *Ibid.* In the area of antitrust law, there is a competing interest, well-represented in this Court's decisions, in recognizing and adapting to changed circumstances and the lessons of accumulated experience. Thus, the general presumption that legislative changes should be left to Congress has less force with respect to the Sherman Act in light of the accepted view that Congress "expected the courts to give shape to the statute's broad mandate by drawing on common-law tradition." National Soc. of Professional Engineers v. United States, 435 U.S. 679, 688 (1978). As we have explained, the term "restraint of trade," as used in § 1, also "invokes the common law itself, and not merely the static content that the common law had assigned to the term in 1890." Business Electronics, 485 U.S., at 732; see also GTE Sylvania, 433 U.S., at 53, n. 21; McNally v. United States, 483 U.S. 350, 372-373 (1987) (STEVENS, J., dissenting). Accordingly, this Court has reconsidered its decisions construing the Sherman Act when the theoretical underpinnings of those decisions are called into serious question. See, e.g., Copperweld Corp., supra, at 777; GTE Sylvania, supra, at 47-49; Tigner v. Texas, 310 U.S. 141, 147 (1940).

Although we do not "lightly assume that the economic realities underlying earlier decisions have changed, or that earlier judicial perceptions of those realities were in error," we have noted that "different sorts of agreements" may amount to restraints of trade "in varying times and circumstances," and "[i]t would make no sense to create out of the single term 'restraint of trade' a chronologically schizoid statute, in which a 'rule of reason' evolves with new circumstances and new wisdom, but a line of per se illegality remains forever fixed where it was." Business Electronics, supra, at 731-732. Just as Schwinn was "the subject of continuing controversy and confusion" under the "great weight" of scholarly criticism, GTE Sylvania, supra, at 47-48, Albrecht has been widely criticized since its inception. With the views underlying Albrecht eroded by this Court's precedent, there is not much of that decision to salvage. See, e.g., Neal v. United States, 516 U.S. 284, 295 (1996); Patterson v. McLean Credit Union, 491 U.S. 164, 173 (1989); Rodriguez de Quijas v. Shearson/ American Express, Inc., 490 U.S. 477, 480- 481 (1989).

Although the rule of Albrecht has been in effect for some time, the inquiry we must undertake requires considering "'the effect of the antitrust laws upon vertical distributional restraints in the American economy today.'" GTE Sylvania, supra, at 53, n. 21, (quoting Schwinn, 388 U.S., at 392 (Stewart, J., concurring in part and dissenting in part)). As the Court noted in ARCO, 495 U.S., at 336, n. 6, there has not been another case since Albrecht in which this Court has "confronted an unadulterated vertical, maximum-price-fixing arrangement." Now that we confront Albrecht directly, we find its conceptual foundations gravely weakened.

In overruling Albrecht, we of course do not hold that all vertical maximum price fixing is per se lawful. Instead, vertical maximum price fixing, like the majority of commercial arrangements subject to the antitrust laws, should be evaluated under the rule of reason. In our view, rule-of-reason analysis will effectively identify those situations in which vertical maximum price fixing amounts to anticompetitive conduct.

There remains the question whether respondents are entitled to recover damages based on State Oil's conduct. Although the Court of Appeals noted that "the district judge was right to conclude that if the rule of reason is applicable, Khan loses," 93 F.3d, at 1362, its consideration of this case was necessarily premised on Albrecht's per se rule. Under the circumstances, the matter should be reviewed by the Court of Appeals in the first instance. We therefore vacate the judgment of the Court of Appeals and remand the case for further proceedings consistent with this opinion.

It is so ordered.

Insert after Comparative Note on Resale Price Maintenance, page 597:

Current materials from the European Commission can be found on its website, which is <http://europa.eu.int/comm/competition/index_en.html>. Important developments have occurred with respect to the law of vertical restraints in general, which are described in detail in the Commissions's new Guidelines on Vertical Restraints, now available in a preliminary version in English on the website. The Guidelines set forth the way the Commission will implement its new Commission Regulation (EC) No. 2790/1999 of 22 December 1999 on the Application of Article 81(3) of the Treaty to categories of vertical agreements and market practices. See OJ L 336, 29.12.1999, p. 21. The new block exemption regulation, or BER, defines vertical agreements in

Article 2(1) as "agreements or concerted practices entered into between two or more undertakings each of which operates, for the purposes of the agreement, at a different level of the production or distribution chain, and relating to the conditions under which the parties may purchase, sell or resell certain goods or services."

Perhaps the most important change the new BER makes is its explicitly economic approach to the analysis of these restrictions. Paragraph 7 of the Guidelines puts the point as follows:

> The protection of competition is the primary objective of EC competition policy, as this enhances consumer welfare and creates an efficient allocation of resources. In applying the EC competition rules, the Commission will adopt an economic approach which is based on the effects on the market; vertical agreements have to be analysed in their legal and economic context. However, in the case of restrictions by object as listed in Article 4 of the BER, the Commission is not required to assess the actual effects on the market. Market integration is an additional goal of EC competition policy. Market integration enhances competition in the Community. Companies should not be allowed to recreate private barriers between Member States where State barriers have been successfully abolished.

The "restrictions by object" in Article 4 to which this refers are the blacklisted clauses that will lead the entire agreement to be excluded from the scope of the BER. The Commission further warns that individual exemption of such agreements is also unlikely. The prohibited clauses include things like the fixing of minimum resale prices, either directly or indirectly, and agreements that have as their direct or indirect object the restriction of sales by the buyer, insofar as those restrictions relate to the territory in which the customers are located (maintaining the Community's traditional distinction between active and passive sales for this purpose). The Commission does not, however, apply these rules to arrangements that will have a *de minimis* effect in the Community. It defines that term for vertical agreements to include those "agreements entered into by undertakings whose market share on the relevant market does not exceed 10%." The Commission reserves the right to apply Article 81(1) to the "hardcore" restrictions of firms below that 10% threshold, if the arrangement nonetheless has an appreciable effect on trade between Member States and on competition. It also indicates that agreements between small and medium-sized enterprises will rarely be of concern.

The last point to make about the BER is that it is more comprehensive than prior block exemptions in the vertical restraints area. Instead of treating separately the question of vertical restraints in intellectual property licenses, franchises, distribution agreements, etc., the Commission has put forth a single block exemption that applies across-the-board. Having said that, however, it is important to note that specific block exemptions continue to exist in certain areas, including technology transfer, car distribution, and certain vertical agreements concluded in connection with horizontal agreements.

Insert after Note 2, page 670:

Although cases in which vertical price-fixing claims are recognized are relatively rare, consider the following decision from the Third Circuit. Do you think it is consistent with *Business Electronics* and *Monsanto*?

PACE ELECTRONICS, INC. v. CANON COMPUTER SYSTEMS, INC.
United States Court of Appeals, Third Circuit, 2000.
213 F.3d 118.

Before: McKEE, RENDELL, and ROSENN, Circuit Judges.

ROSENN, J. The issue in this appeal is whether the termination of a wholesale dealer's contract for its refusal to acquiesce in an alleged vertical minimum price fixing conspiracy constitutes an antitrust injury that will support an action for damages under section 4 of the Clayton Act. The United States District Court for the District of New Jersey reasoned that a dealer terminated under these circumstances does not suffer an antitrust injury unless it can demonstrate that its termination had an actual, adverse economic effect on a relevant market. After concluding that the plaintiff's complaint in the instant case failed to allege such an effect, the District Court dismissed the complaint for failure to state a claim upon which relief may be granted. Because we believe the court misconstrued the antitrust injury requirement, we will reverse.

I

The plaintiff, Pace Electronics, Inc. ("Pace"), a New Jersey corporation, is engaged in the business of distributing various electronic products, including computer printers and related accessories. Pace purchases these products from manufacturers and wholesale distributors and then resells them to smaller retailers, who operate in the New Jersey and New York region.

In April of 1996, Pace entered into a nonexclusive dealer agreement with defendant Canon Computer Systems, Inc. ("Canon"), a California corporation. Under this agreement, Pace obtained the right to purchase Canon-brand ink-jet printers and related accessories from Canon at "dealer prices." In consideration for the right to purchase these products at "dealer prices," Pace agreed to purchase certain minimum quantities of the products.

The dealer agreement between Pace and Canon remained in effect for approximately one year and three months. Thereafter, on July 1, 1997, Canon terminated the agreement with Pace on the stated ground that Pace failed to purchase the minimum quantities of Canon-brand products required of it under the dealer agreement. Although Pace concedes that it did not purchase the amount of Canon-brand products called for under the dealer agreement, Pace contends that it was unable to do so because Canon ignored its purchase orders. Pace further contends that Canon ignored its purchase orders because Pace refused to acquiesce in a vertical minimum price fixing agreement designed and implemented by Canon and defendant Laguna Corporation ("Laguna"), Pace's direct competitor in the New Jersey and New York region.

In this connection, Pace alleges that, prior to the time it entered its dealer agreement with Canon, Laguna had entered into a similar dealer agreement with Canon. Additionally, Pace alleges that the agreement between Canon and Laguna contemplated the maintenance of a minimum resale price below which Laguna would not sell Canon-brand ink-jet printers. In support of its allegation, Pace asserts that after it entered into its dealer agreement with Canon, the president of Canon repeatedly instructed Pace's president not to sell to past or existing customers of Laguna and not to sell Canon brand ink-jet printers at prices less than those at which Laguna was selling its products.

Pace alleges that it has suffered financial losses as a result of its termination as an authorized Canon-brand dealer. Specifically, Pace avers that "[a]s a direct and proximate result of the actions of Defendants ... Pace has suffered significant financial detriment, consisting of, but not necessarily limited to, lost profits. Pace's losses result directly and proximately from the efforts of Canon and Laguna to limit price competition in the market ... for which both Laguna and Pace were competing." . . . Although these allegations of loss appear somewhat vague and conclusory, we accept them as true, as we must, for the purposes of this appeal.

Pace also alleges that its termination as an authorized dealer of Canon-brand products has harmed competition in two respects. First, it contends that its termination as a dealer has reduced price competition in the wholesale market for Canon-brand ink-jet printers (an intrabrand market) because Laguna no longer faces price competition from Pace in selling these products to smaller retailers. Second, Pace asserts that its termination as a dealer has reduced price competition in the wholesale market for all brands of ink-jet printers (an interbrand market). In this connection, Pace alleges that: (1) Canon- brand ink-jet printers enjoy an inherent competitive price advantage over the ink-jet printers of other manufacturers; (2) until Canon permits its distributors to take advantage of this price advantage, other manufacturers will not attempt to reduce their production costs; and, (3) until an unrestrained free competitive market requires other manufacturers to reduce their production costs, the price of all brands of ink-jet printers will remain at an artificially high level.

II

To state a claim for damages under section 4 of the Clayton Act, 15 U.S.C. § 15, a plaintiff must allege more than that it has suffered an injury causally linked to a violation of the antitrust laws. *See Brunswick Corp. v. Pueblo Bowl-O-Mat, Inc.*, 429 U.S. 477, 489 (1977). In addition, it must allege antitrust injury, "which is to say injury of the type the antitrust laws were intended to prevent and that flows from that which makes defendants' acts unlawful." *Id.* This is so even where, as in the instant case, the alleged acts of the defendants constitute a per se violation of the antitrust laws. *See also Atlantic Richfield Co. v. USA Petroleum Co.,* 495 U.S. 328, 341 (1990). In applying the antitrust injury requirement, the Supreme Court has inquired whether the injury alleged by the plaintiff "resembles any of the potential dangers" which led the Court to label the defendants' alleged conduct violative of the antitrust laws in the first instance. *Id.* at 336 . . . .

For example, in *Atlantic Richfield,* the plaintiff, an independent retail marketer of gasoline, brought suit against ARCO, an integrated oil company which sold gasoline to consumers through its own stations and indirectly through ARCO-brand dealers, claiming that ARCO violated section 1 of the Sherman Act by conspiring with its dealers to fix the maximum resale price of gasoline at an artificially low level. *Id.* at 331. Although the plaintiff conceded that the fixed prices were not predatory, it nevertheless maintained that it suffered antitrust injury, in the form of lost profits, as a result of the vertical maximum price fixing agreement between ARCO and its dealers. *See id.* at 334-35. The Supreme Court disagreed, noting that the plaintiff's alleged injury did not resemble any of the dangers which caused the Court to label vertical maximum price fixing *per se* illegal in *Albrecht v. Herald Co.,* 390 U.S. 145 (1968).[1] *See id.* at 336.

In this connection, the Court identified four potential adverse effects of vertical maximum price fixing agreements which led it to label those agreements *per se* illegal in the *Albrecht* decision. First, it noted that a vertical maximum price fixing agreement might intrude on the ability of dealers to compete and survive "'by substituting the perhaps erroneous judgment of a [supplier] for the forces of the competitive market.' " *Id.* at 335. (quoting *Albrecht,* 390 U.S. at 152, 88 S.Ct. 869). Additionally, the Court observed that " '[m]aximum prices may be fixed too low for the dealer to furnish services essential to the value which goods have for the consumer or to furnish services and conveniences which consumers desire and for which they are willing to pay.' " *Id.* at 335-36. Next, the Court explained that "[b]y limiting the ability of small dealers to engage in nonprice competition, a maximum-price-fixing agreement might 'channel distribution through a few large or specifically advantaged dealers.' " *Id.* at 336. Finally, the Court noted that " 'if the actual price charged under a maximum price scheme is nearly always the fixed maximum price, which is increasingly likely as the maximum price approaches the actual cost of the dealer, the scheme tends to acquire all the attributes of an arrangement fixing minimum prices.' " *Id.*

Having identified the potential dangers which led it to condemn categorically vertical maximum price fixing agreements, the Supreme Court had little difficulty determining that the plaintiff in *Atlantic Richfield* had not

---

[1] *Albrecht's* specific holding--that vertical maximum price fixing is *per se* illegal -- has since been overruled. *See State Oil Co. v. Khan,* 522 U.S. 3, 7 (1997). However, *Atlantic Richfield's* approach--i.e. discerning the reasons that led the Supreme Court to label certain conduct a *per se* violation, and determining whether the harm suffered by the plaintiff is consistent with the rationale for labeling the defendant's conduct *per se* illegitimate--remains valid and is clearly applicable to the case before us.

suffered an antitrust injury. The Court noted that the dangers identified in the *Albrecht* decision focused on the potential adverse effects of vertical maximum pricefixing agreements on *dealers and consumers,* not competitors of dealers subject to such agreements. *See id.* The Court explained: "[i]ndeed, the gravamen of [the plaintiff's] complaint--that the price fixing scheme between[the defendant] and its dealers enabled those dealers to increase their sales--amounts to an assertion that the dangers with which we were concerned in *Albrecht* have not materialized in the instant case." *Id.* at 337. In sum, the Court concluded that the plaintiff had not suffered antitrust injury because its losses did not flow from those aspects of vertical maximum pricing that rendered it illegal. *Id.* at 337.

Turning now to the instant case, we think it appropriate to ask whether Pace's alleged injury resembles any of the dangers which have led the Supreme Court to condemn vertical minimum price fixing agreements under the antitrust laws. Pace alleges that it has suffered antitrust injury because it was terminated as a wholesale dealer after it sold Canon-brand products at prices below the minimum resale price allegedly fixed by Canon and Laguna. Pace further alleges that its termination as a wholesale dealer has caused it to suffer lost profits because it may no longer obtain profits from selling Canon-brand products at "dealer prices." Under the Supreme Court's jurisprudence, these allegations suffice to establish antitrust injury.

On this point, *Simpson v. Union Oil,* 377 U.S. 13 (1964) is instructive. In *Simpson,* the plaintiff entered into a year-to-year "consignment" agreement with Union Oil. *See id.* at 14. Under the agreement, which was terminable by either party at the end of any one-year term, Union Oil required the plaintiff to charge a minimum retail price for gasoline. *See id.* Contrary to the terms of the agreement with Union Oil, the plaintiff sold gasoline below the minimum retail price. *See id.* at 15. Because he did so, Union Oil terminated its "consignment" agreement with the plaintiff at the end of the first one-year term. *See id.*

Sometime thereafter, the plaintiff brought suit against Union Oil seeking damages under section 4 of the Clayton Act. *See id.* After two pretrial hearings, the District Court granted summary judgment in favor of Union Oil, holding that the plaintiff failed to establish a violation of section 1 of the Sherman Act and that, even assuming the plaintiff had established a violation, the plaintiff suffered no actionable damage. *See id.* at 15-16. The Court of Appeals affirmed on the ground that the plaintiff suffered no actionable wrong or damage. *See id.* at 16. The Supreme Court granted certiorari and reversed.

In reversing, the Court placed primary focus on the consignment agreement's restriction on the ability of dealers such as the plaintiff to make independent, competitive pricing decisions. For example, the Court explained:

> We disagree with the Court of Appeals that there is no actionable wrong or damage if a Sherman Act violation is assumed. If the "consignment" agreement achieves resale price maintenance in violation of the Sherman Act, it and the lease are being used to injure interstate commerce *by depriving independent dealers of the exercise of free judgment* whether to become consignees at all, or remain consignees, and, in any event, to sell at competitive prices. *Id.* (emphasis added).

The Court also stated:

> Dealers, like [the plaintiff], are independent businessmen; and they have all or most of the indicia of entrepreneurs, except for price fixing.... Their return is affected by the rise and fall in the market price, their commissions declining as retail prices drop. *Practically the only power they have to be wholly independent businessmen, whose service depends on their own initiative and enterprise, is taken from them by the proviso that they must sell their gasoline at prices fixed by Union Oil....* The evil of the resale price maintenance program ... is its inexorable potentiality for and even certainty in destroying competition in retail sales of gasoline by these nominal 'consignees' who are in reality small struggling competitors seeking retail gas customers.

Id. at 21 (emphasis added) (footnote and citations omitted).

Thus, the Supreme Court considered a restriction on dealer independence with respect to pricing decisions to be an anticompetitive aspect of vertical minimum pricefixing agreements, and one that the antitrust laws have an interest in forestalling. . . . Accordingly, we think that a maverick dealer, such as Pace, which is terminated for charging prices less than those set under a vertical minimum price fixing agreement, suffers the type of injury which the antitrust laws are designed to prevent and may recover damages, such as lost profits, which flow from that termination. . . .

Naturally, the defendants argue that the above analysis misses the mark. In essence, they contend that *Simpson* is no longer good law in light of the Supreme Court's decision in *Atlantic Richfield.* Furthermore, they urge, and the district court agreed, that a terminated dealer seeking to establish that it has suffered antitrust injury must allege facts demonstrating that its termination as an authorized dealer resulted in an actual, adverse economic effect on competition in a relevant interbrand market. In support of their position, the defendants primarily rely on the Supreme Court's statement in *Atlantic Richfield* that a plaintiff can recover damages under section 4 of the Clayton Act "only if [its] loss[es] stem[ ] from a competition-reducing aspect or effect of the defendant's behavior." *Atlantic Richfield,* 495 U.S. at 344. On the basis of this brief statement, the defendants then argue that to be "competition-reducing" a defendant's challenged conduct must have had an actual adverse effect on a relevant interbrand market. Although the defendants' syllogism may have some allure, we decline to construe the antitrust injury requirement as suggested by the defendants for the following reasons.

First, we believe that requiring a plaintiff to demonstrate that an injury stemming from a *per se* violation of the antitrust laws caused an actual, adverse effect on a relevant market in order to satisfy the antitrust injury requirement comes dangerously close to transforming a *per se* violation into a case to be judged under the rule of reason. The *per se* standard is reserved for certain categories of conduct which experience has shown to be "manifestly anticompetitive." *Continental T.V., Inc. v. GTE Sylvania Inc.,* 433 U.S. 36, 39 (1977). That standard, which is based on considerations of "business certainty and litigation efficiency," *Arizona v. Maricopa County Med. Society,* 457 U.S. 332, 344 (1982), allows a court to presume that certain limited classes of conduct have an anticompetitive effect without engaging in the type of involved, market- specific analysis ordinarily necessary to reach such a conclusion. *See Business Electronics Corp. v. Sharp Electronics Corp.,* 485 U.S. 717, 723 (1988) ("Certain categories of agreements, however, have been held to be *per se* illegal, dispensing with the need for case-by-case evaluation."). Were we to accept the defendants' construction of the antitrust injury requirement, we would, in substance, be removing the presumption of anticompetitive effect implicit in the *per se* standard under the guise of the antitrust injury requirement.[2]

---

[2] We recognize that various scholars have taken issue with the Supreme Court's *per se* treatment of vertical minimum price fixing agreements and argued that

Second, we do not believe that the Supreme Court's statement in *Atlantic Richfield* that a plaintiff can recover for losses only if they stem "from a competition-reducing aspect or effect of the defendant's behavior," *Atlantic Richfield,* 495 U.S. at 344, when viewed in the context of the Court's entire opinion, can be fairly read to require a terminated dealer to prove that its termination caused an actual, adverse economic effect on a relevant market. In this connection, we note that in determining that the plaintiff in *Atlantic Richfield* failed to satisfy the antitrust injury requirement, the Supreme Court simply did not focus on whether the challenged conduct of the defendant had an actual, adverse economic effect on a relevant market. Rather, as outlined above, the Court focused on whether the plaintiff's injury stemmed from any of the potential anticompetitive dangers which led the Court to label vertical maximum price fixing unlawful in the first instance. Implicit in the Court's approach is that a plaintiff who had suffered loss as a result of an anticompetitive aspect of a *per se* restraint of trade agreement would have suffered antitrust injury, without demonstrating that the challenged practice had an actual, adverse economic effect on a relevant market. . . . The issue, thus, is not whether the plaintiff's alleged injury produced an anticompetitive result, but, rather, whether the injury claimed resulted from the anticompetitive aspect of the challenged conduct.

Finally, we point out that our holding--that a dealer terminated for its refusal to abide by a vertical minimum price fixing agreement suffers antitrust injury and may recover losses flowing from that termination--is consistent with the decisions of those courts which have explored the issue thus far. *See, e.g., Sterling Interiors Group, Inc. v. Haworth, Inc.,* No. 94-9216, 1996 WL 426379 at *18-*19 (S.D.N.Y. July 30, 1996) ("The anti- competitive dangers of minimum price arrangements flow to both customers who purchase at prices set higher than competitive levels, and to dealers who are effectively foreclosed from competing in the marketplace.").

---

these agreements may have significant, procompetitive attributes. *See, e.g., Antitrust Policy,* 75 Colum. L.Rev. at 283. But, academic commentary, even if persuasive, does not permit us to expand the antitrust injury requirement to a point which undermines the Court's categorical disapproval of vertical minimum price fixing.

III

For the reasons set forth above, the district court's order dismissing Pace's complaint will be reversed and the case remanded to the district court for further proceedings consistent with this opinion. Costs taxed against the appellees.

Insert after Note 4, page 671:

TOYS "R" US, INC. V. FEDERAL TRADE COMMISSION
United States Court of Appeals, Seventh Circuit, 2000.
221 F. 3d 928.

Before: COFFEY, KANNE and DIANE P. WOOD, Circuit Judges.

WOOD, J. The antitrust laws, which aim to preserve and protect competition in economically sensible markets, have long drawn a sharp distinction between contractual restrictions that occur up and down a distribution chain--so-called vertical restraints--and restrictions that come about as a result of agreements among competitors, or horizontal restraints. Sometimes, however, it can be hard as a matter of fact to be sure what kind of agreement is at issue. This was the problem facing the Federal Trade Commission ("the Commission") when it brought under its antitrust microscope the large toy retailer Toys "R" Us (more properly Toys "R" Us, but to avoid debate we will abbreviate the company's name as TRU, in keeping with the parties' usage).

The Commission concluded, upon an extensive administrative record, that TRU had acted as the coordinator of a horizontal agreement among a number of toy manufacturers. The agreements took the form of a network of vertical agreements between TRU and the individual manufacturers, in each of which the manufacturer promised to restrict the distribution of its products to low-priced warehouse club stores, on the condition that other manufacturers would do the same. This practice, the Commission found, violated § 5 of the Federal Trade Commission Act, *15 U.S.C. § 45.* It also found that TRU had entered into a series of vertical agreements that flunked scrutiny under antitrust's rule of reason. TRU appealed that decision to us. It attacks both the sufficiency of the evidence supporting the Commission's conclusions and the scope of the Commission's remedial order. It is hard to prevail on either type of challenge: the former is fact-intensive and faces the hurdle of the substantial evidence standard of review, while the latter calls into question the Commission's exercise of its discretion to remedy an established violation of the law. We conclude that, while reasonable people could differ on the facts in this voluminous record, the Commission's decisions pass muster, and we therefore affirm.

I

TRU is a giant in the toy retailing industry. The Commission found that it sells approximately 20% of all the toys sold in the United States, and that in some metropolitan areas its share of toy sales ranges between 35% and 49%. The variety of toys it sells is staggering: over the course of a year, it offers about 11,000 individual toy items, far more than any of its competitors. As one might suspect from these figures alone, TRU is a critical outlet for toy manufacturers. It buys about 30% of the large, traditional toy companies' total output and it is usually their most important customer. According to evidence before the Commission's administrative law judge, or ALJ, even a company as large as Hasbro felt that it could not find other retailers to replace TRU--and Hasbro, along with Mattel, is one of the two largest toy manufacturers in the country, accounting for approximately 12% of the market for traditional toys and 10% of a market that includes video games. Similar opinions were offered by Mattel and smaller manufacturers.

Toys are sold in a number of different kinds of stores. At the high end are traditional toy stores and department stores, both of which typically sell toys for 40 to 50% above their cost. Next are the specialized discount stores--a category virtually monopolized by TRU today--that sell at an average 30% mark-up. General discounters like Wal-Mart, K-Mart, and Target are next, with a 22% mark-up, and last are the stores that are the focus of this case, the warehouse clubs like Costco and Pace. The clubs sell toys at a slender mark-up of 9% or so.

The toys customers seek in all these stores are highly differentiated products. The little girl who wants Malibu Barbie is not likely to be satisfied with My First Barbie, and she certainly does not want Ken or Skipper. The boy who has his heart set on a figure of Anakin Skywalker will be disappointed if he receives Jar-Jar Binks, or a truck, or a baseball bat instead. Toy retailers naturally want to have available for their customers the season's hottest items, because toys are also a very faddish product, as those old enough to recall the mania over Cabbage Patch kids or Tickle Me Elmo dolls will attest.

What happened in this case, according to the Commission, was fairly simple. For a long time, TRU had enjoyed a strong position at the low price end for toy sales, because its only competition came from traditional toy stores who could not or did not wish to meet its prices, or from general discounters like Wal-Mart or K-Mart, which could not offer anything like the variety of items TRU had and whose prices were not too far off TRU's mark.

The advent of the warehouse clubs changed all that. They were a retail innovation of the late 1970s: the first one opened in 1976, and by 1992 there were some 600 individual club stores around the country. Rather than earning all of their money from their mark-up on products, the clubs sell only to their members, and they charge a modest annual membership fee, often about $30. As the word "warehouse" in the name suggests, the clubs emphasize price competition over service amenities. Nevertheless, the Commission found that the clubs seek to offer name-brand merchandise, including toys. During the late 1980s and early 1990s, warehouse clubs selected and purchased from the toy manufacturers' full array of products, just like everyone else. In some instances they bought specialized packs assembled for the "club" trade, but they normally preferred stocking conventional products so that their customers could readily compare the price of an item at the club against the price of the same item at a competing store.

To the extent this strategy was successful, however, TRU did not welcome it. By 1989, its senior executives were concerned that the clubs were a threat to TRU's low-price image and, more importantly, to its profits. A little legwork revealed that as of that year the clubs carried approximately 120-240 items in direct competition with TRU, priced as much as 25 to 30% below TRU's own price levels.

TRU put its President of Merchandising, a Mr. Goddu, to work to see what could be done. The response Goddu and other TRU executives formulated to beat back the challenge from the clubs began with TRU's decision to contact some of its suppliers, including toy manufacturing heavyweights Mattel, Hasbro, and Fisher Price. At the Toy Fair in 1992 (a major event at which the next Christmas season's orders are placed), Goddu informed the manufacturers of a new TRU policy, which was reflected in a memo of January 29, 1992. The policy set forth the following conditions and privileges for TRU:

- The clubs could have no new or promoted product

unless they carried the entire line.

- All specials and exclusives to be sold to the clubs had to be shown first to TRU to see if TRU wanted the item.

- Old and basic product had to be in special packs.

- Clearance and closeout items were permissible provided that TRU was given the first opportunity to buy the product.

- There would be no discussion about prices.

TRU was careful to meet individually with each of its suppliers to explain its new policy. Afterwards, it then asked each one what it intended to do. Negotiations between TRU and the manufacturers followed, as a result of which each manufacturer eventually agreed that it would sell to the clubs only highly-differentiated products (either unique individual items or combo packs) that were not offered to anything but a club (and thus of course not to TRU). As the Commission put it, "through its announced policy and the related agreements discussed below, TRU sought to eliminate the competitive threat the clubs posed by denying them merchandise, forcing the clubs' customers to buy products they did not want, and frustrating customers' ability to make direct price comparisons of club prices and TRU prices." FTC opinion at 14.

The agreements between TRU and the various manufacturers were, of course, vertical agreements, because they ran individually from the supplier/manufacturer to the purchaser/retailer. The Commission found that TRU reached about 10 of these agreements. After the agreements were concluded, TRU then supervised and enforced each toy company's compliance with its commitment.

But TRU was not content to stop with vertical agreements. Instead, the Commission found, it decided to go further. It worked for over a year and a half to put the vertical agreements in place, but "the biggest hindrance TRU had to overcome was the major toy companies' reluctance to give up a new, fast-growing, and profitable channel of distribution." FTC opinion at 28. The manufacturers were also concerned that any of their rivals who broke ranks and sold to the clubs might gain sales at their expense, given the widespread and increasing popularity of the club format. To address this problem, the Commission found, TRU orchestrated a horizontal agreement among its key suppliers to boycott the clubs. The evidence on which the Commission relied showed that, at a minimum, Mattel, Hasbro, Fisher Price, Tyco, Little Tikes, Today's Kids, and Tiger Electronics agreed to join in the boycott "*on the condition that their competitors would do the same.*" FTC opinion at 28 (emphasis added).

The Commission first noted that internal documents from the manufacturers revealed that they were trying to expand, not to restrict, the number of their major retail outlets and to reduce their dependence on TRU. They were specifically interested in cultivating a relationship with the warehouse clubs and increasing sales there. Thus, the sudden adoption of measures under which they decreased sales to the clubs ran against their independent economic self-interest. Second, the Commission cited evidence that the manufacturers were unwilling to limit sales to the clubs without assurances that their competitors would do likewise. FTC opinion at 29. Goddu himself testified that TRU communicated the message "I'll stop if they stop" from manufacturer to competing manufacturer. FTC opinion at 30. He specifically mentioned having such conversations with Mattel and Hasbro, and he said more generally "We communicated to our vendors that we were communicating with all our key suppliers, and we did that I believe at Toy Fair 1992. We made a point to tell each of the vendors that we spoke to that we would be talking to our other key suppliers." *Id.* at 31.

Evidence from the manufacturers corroborated Goddu's account. A Mattel executive said that it would not sell the clubs the same items it was selling to TRU, and that this decision was "based on the fact that competition would do the same." *Id.* at 32. A Hasbro executive said much the same thing: "because our competitors had agreed not to sell loaded [that is, promoted] product to the clubs, that we would . . . go along with this." *Id.* TRU went so far as to assure individual manufacturers that no one would be singled out.

Once the special warehouse club policy (or, in the Commission's more pejorative language, boycott) was underway, TRU served as the central clearinghouse for complaints about breaches in the agreement. The Commission gave numerous examples of this conduct in its opinion. See *id.* at 33-37.

Last, the Commission found that TRU's policies had bite. In the year before the boycott began, the clubs' share of all toy sales in the United States grew from 1.5% in 1991 to 1.9% in 1992. After the boycott took hold, that percentage slipped back by 1995 to 1.4%. Local numbers were more impressive. Costco, for example, experienced overall growth on sales of all products during the period 1991 to 1993 of 25%. Its toy sales increased during same period by 51%. But, after the boycott took hold in 1993, its toy sales decreased by 1.6% even while its overall sales were still growing by 19.5%. The evidence indicated that this was because TRU had succeeded in cutting off its access to the popular toys it needed. In 1989, over 90% of the Mattel toys Costco and other clubs purchased were regular (i.e. easily comparable) items, but by 1993 that percentage was zero. Once again, the Commission's opinion is chock full of similar statistics.

The Commission also considered the question whether TRU might have been trying to protect itself against free riding, at least with respect to its vertical agreements. It acknowledged that TRU provided several services that might be important to consumers, including "advertising, carrying an inventory of goods early in the year, and supporting a full line of products." FTC opinion at 41-42. Nevertheless, it found that the manufacturers compensated TRU directly for advertising toys, storing toys made early in the year, and stocking a broad line of each manufacturer's toys under one roof. A 1993 TRU memorandum confirms that advertising is manufacturer-funded and is "essentially free." FTC opinion at 42. In 1994, TRU's net cost of advertising was a tiny 0.02% of sales, or $750,000, out of a total of $199 million it spent on advertising that year. As the Commission saw it, "advertising . . . was a service the toy manufacturers provided for TRU and not the other way around." *Id.* (emphasis in original). TRU records also showed that manufacturers routinely paid TRU credits for warehousing services, and that they compensated it for full line stocking. In short, the Commission found, there was no evidence that club competition without comparable services threatened to drive TRU services out of the market or to harm customers. Manufacturers paid each retailer directly for the services they wanted the retailer to furnish.

Based on this record, the Commission drew three central conclusions of law: (1) the TRU-led manufacturer boycott of the warehouse clubs was illegal per se under the rule enunciated in *Northwest Wholesale Stationers, Inc. v. Pacific Stationery & Printing Co., 472 U.S. 284 (1985);* (2) the boycott was illegal under a full rule of reason analysis because its anticompetitive effects "clearly outweighed any possible business justification"; and (3) the vertical agreements between TRU and the individual toy manufacturers, "entered into seriatim with clear anticompetitive effect, violate section 1 of the Sherman Act." FTC opinion at 46. These antitrust violations in turn were enough to prove a violation of FTC Act § 5, which for present purposes tracks the prohibitions of the Sherman and Clayton Acts. After offering a detailed explanation of these conclusions (spanning 42 pages in its slip opinion), it turned to the question of remedy and affirmed the order the ALJ had entered.

In the Commission's words, its order:

> . . . prohibits TRU from continuing, entering into, or attempting to enter into, vertical agreements with its suppliers to limit the supply of, or refuse to sell, toys to a toy discounter. See ¶ II.A. The order also prohibits TRU from facilitating, or attempting to facilitate, an agreement between or among its suppliers relating to the sale of toys to any retailer. See ¶ II.D. Additionally, TRU is enjoined from requesting information from suppliers about their sales to any toy discounter, and from urging or coercing suppliers to restrict sales to any toy discounter. See ¶¶ II.B, C. These four elements of relief are narrowly tailored to stop, and prevent the repetition of, TRU's illegal conduct.

FTC opinion at 88. TRU complained that the order trampled on its ability to exercise its rights under *United States v. Colgate & Co., 250 U.S. 300 (1919),* to choose unilaterally the companies with which it wanted to deal. The Commission rejected the point, because it found that TRU had repeatedly crossed the line from unilateral to concerted behavior in illegal ways, and that it was entitled to include remedial provisions that were necessary to prevent recurrence of the illegal behavior, citing *FTC v. National Lead Co., 352 U.S. 419, 430 (1957).*

Commissioner Swindle concurred in part and dissented in part. He agreed with the majority's determination that TRU had engaged in a series of anticompetitive vertical agreements, and he thus agreed with the remedial provisions designed to proscribe those practices and their effects. He was unconvinced, however, that TRU had orchestrated a horizontal combination as well, believing that the evidence was too thin to support that conclusion. TRU appealed from the Commission's final order of October 13, 1998, to this court, under *15 U.S.C. § 45*(c), as it carries on business in this circuit (as well as every other circuit, to the best of our knowledge).

II

On appeal, TRU makes four principal arguments: (1) the Commission's finding of a horizontal conspiracy is contrary to the facts and impermissibly confuses the law of vertical restraints with the law of horizontal restraints; (2) whether the restrictions were vertical or horizontal, they were not unlawful because TRU has no market power, and thus the conduct can have no significant anticompetitive effect; (3) the TRU policy was a legitimate response to free riding; and (4) the relief ordered by the Commission goes too far. We review the Commission's legal conclusions de novo, but we must accept its findings of fact if they are supported by such relevant evidence as a reasonable mind might accept as adequate to support a conclusion. *FTC v. Indiana Fed'n of Dentists, 476 U.S. 447, 454 (1986).*

A. Horizontal Conspiracy

As TRU correctly points out, the critical question here is whether substantial evidence supported the Commission's finding that there was a horizontal agreement among the toy manufacturers, with TRU in the center as the ringmaster, to boycott the warehouse clubs. It acknowledges that such an agreement may be proved by either direct or circumstantial evidence, under cases such as *Matsushita Electric Indus. Co. v. Zenith Radio Corp., 475 U.S. 574 (1986)* (horizontal agreements), *Monsanto Co. v. Spray-Rite Service Corp., 465 U.S. 752 (1984)* (vertical agreements), and *Interstate Circuit, Inc. v. United States, 306 U.S. 208 (1939).* When circumstantial evidence is used, there must be some evidence that "tends to exclude the possibility" that the alleged conspirators acted independently. *Monsanto, 465 U.S. at 764,* quoted in *Matsushita, 475 U.S. at 588.* This does not mean, however, that the Commission had to exclude all possibility that the manufacturers acted independently. As we pointed out in *In re Brand Name Prescription Drugs Antitrust Litigation, 186 F.3d 781 (7th Cir. 1999),* that would amount to an absurd and legally unfounded burden to prove with 100% certainty that an antitrust violation occurred. *Id.* at 787. The test states only that there must be some evidence which, if believed, would support a finding of concerted behavior. In the context of an appeal from the Commission, the question is whether substantial evidence supports its conclusion that it is more likely than not that the manufacturers acted collusively.

In TRU's opinion, this record shows nothing more than a series of separate, similar vertical agreements between itself and various toy manufacturers. It believes that each manufacturer in its independent self-interest had an incentive to limit sales to the clubs, because TRU's policy provided strong unilateral incentives for the manufacturer to reduce its sales to the clubs. Why gain a few sales at the clubs, it asks, when it would have much more to gain by maintaining a good relationship with the 100-pound gorilla of the industry, TRU, and make far more sales?

We do not disagree that there was some evidence in the record that would bear TRU's interpretation. But that is not the standard we apply when we review decisions of the Federal Trade Commission. Instead, we apply the substantial evidence test, which we described as follows in another case in which the Commission's decision to stop a hospital merger was at issue:

> Our only function is to determine whether the Commission's analysis of the probable effects of these acquisitions on hospital competition in Chattanooga is so implausible, so feebly supported by the record, that it flunks even the deferential test of substantial evidence.

Hospital Corp. of America v. F.T.C., 807 F.2d 1381, 1385 (7th Cir. 1986). There, as here, the Commission painstakingly explained in a long opinion exactly what evidence in the record supported its conclusion. We need only decide whether the inference the Commission drew of horizontal agreement was a permissible one from that evidence, not if it was the only possible one.

The Commission's theory, stripped to its essentials, is that this case is a modern equivalent of the old Interstate Circuit decision. That case too involved actors at two levels of the distribution chain, distributors of motion pictures and exhibitors. Interstate Circuit was one of the exhibitors; it had a stranglehold on the exhibition of movies in a number of Texas cities. The antitrust violation occurred when Interstate's manager, O'Donnell, sent an identical letter to the eight branch managers of the distributor companies, with each letter naming all eight as addressees, in which he asked them to comply with two demands: a minimum price for first-run theaters, and a policy against double features at night. The trial court there drew an inference of agreement from the nature of the proposals, from the manner in which they were made, from the substantial unanimity of action taken, and from the lack of evidence of a benign motive; the Supreme Court affirmed. The new policies represented a radical shift from the industry's prior business practices, and the Court rejected as beyond the range of probability that such unanimity of action was explainable only by chance.

The Commission is right. Indeed, as it argues in its brief, the TRU case if anything presents a more compelling case for inferring horizontal agreement than did Interstate Circuit, because not only was the manufacturers' decision to stop dealing with the warehouse clubs an abrupt shift from the past, and not only is it suspicious for a manufacturer to deprive itself of a profitable sales outlet, but the record here included the direct evidence of communications that was missing in Interstate Circuit. Just as in Interstate Circuit, TRU tries to avoid this result by hypothesizing independent motives. *306 U.S. at 223-24.* If there were no evidence in the record tending to support concerted behavior, then we agree that Matsushita would require a ruling in TRU's favor. But there is. The evidence showed that the companies wanted to diversify from TRU, not to become more dependent upon it; it showed that each manufacturer was afraid to curb its sales to the warehouse clubs alone, because it was afraid its rivals would cheat and gain a special advantage in that popular new market niche. The Commission was not required to disbelieve the testimony of the different toy company executives and TRU itself to the effect that the only condition on which each toy manufacturer would agree to TRU's demands was if it could be sure its competitors were doing the same thing.

That is a horizontal agreement. As we explain further below in discussing TRU's free rider argument, it has nothing to do with enhancing efficiencies of distribution from the manufacturer's point of view. The typical story of a legitimate vertical transaction would have the manufacturer going to TRU and asking it to be the exclusive carrier of the manufacturer's goods; in exchange for that exclusivity, the manufacturer would hope to receive more effective promotion of its goods, and TRU would have a large enough profit margin to do the job well. But not all manufacturers think that exclusive dealing arrangements will maximize their profits. Some think, and are entitled to think, that using the greatest number of retailers possible is a better strategy.

These manufacturers were in effect being asked by TRU to reduce their output (especially of the popular toys), and as is classically true in such cartels, they were willing to do so only if TRU could protect them against cheaters.

Northwest Stationers also demonstrates why the facts the Commission found support its conclusion that the essence of the agreement network TRU supervised was horizontal. There the Court described the cases that had condemned boycotts as *"per se"* illegal as those involving "joint efforts by a firm or firms to disadvantage competitors by either directly denying or persuading or coercing suppliers or customers to deny relationships the competitors need in the competitive struggle." *472 U.S. at 294* (internal citations omitted). The boycotters had to have some market power, though the Court did not suggest that the level had to be as high as it would require in a case under Sherman Act § 2. Here, TRU was trying to disadvantage the warehouse clubs, its competitors, by coercing suppliers to deny the clubs the products they needed. It accomplished this goal by inducing the suppliers to collude, rather than to compete independently for shelf space in the different toy retail stores. See also *NYNEX Corp. v. Discon, Inc., 525 U.S. 128 (1998); Klor's, Inc. v. Broadway-Hale Stores, Inc., 359 U.S. 207 (1959).*

B. Degree of TRU's Market Power

TRU's efforts to deflate the Commission's finding of market power are pertinent only if we had agreed with its argument that the Commission's finding of a horizontal agreement was without support. Horizontal agreements among competitors, including group boycotts, remain illegal per se in the sense the Court used the term in Northwest Stationers. We have found that this case satisfies the criteria the Court used in Northwest Stationers for condemnation without an extensive inquiry into market power and economic pros and cons: (1) the boycotting firm has cut off access to a supply, facility or market necessary for the boycotted firm (i.e. the clubs) to compete; (2) the boycotting firm possesses a "dominant" position in the market (where "dominant" is an undefined term, but plainly chosen to stand for something different from antitrust's term of art "monopoly"); and (3) the boycott, as we explain further below, cannot be justified by plausible arguments that it was designed to enhance overall efficiency. *472 U.S. at 294.* We address the market power point here, therefore, only in the alternative.

TRU seems to think that anticompetitive effects in a market cannot be shown unless the plaintiff, or here the Commission, first proves that it has a large market share. This, however, has things backwards. As we have explained elsewhere, the share a firm has in a properly defined relevant market is only a way of estimating market power, which is the ultimate consideration. *Ball Memorial Hospital, Inc. v. Mutual Hospital Insurance, 784 F.2d 1325, 1336 (7th Cir. 1986).* The Supreme Court has made it clear that there are two ways of proving market power. One is through direct evidence of anticompetitive effects. See *FTC v. Indiana Fed'n of Dentists, 476 U.S. 447, 460-61 (1986)* ("the finding of actual, sustained adverse effects on competition in those areas where IFD dentists predominated, viewed in light of the reality that markets for dental services tend to be relatively localized, is legally sufficient to support a finding that the challenged restraint was unreasonable even in the absence of elaborate market analysis."). The other, more conventional way, is by proving relevant product and geographic markets and by showing that the defendant's share exceeds whatever threshold is important for the practice in the case. See, e.g., *United States v. E.I. du Pont de Nemours & Co., 351 U.S. 377 (1956); United States v. Grinnell Corp., 384 U.S. 563 (1966); United States v. Aluminum Co. of America, 148 F.2d 416 (2d Cir. 1945)* (suggesting that more than 90% is enough to constitute a monopoly for purposes of Sherman Act § 2 and 33% is not); *Jefferson Parish Hospital Dist. No. 2 v. Hyde, 466 U.S. 2 (1984)* (indicating that something more than 30% would be needed to show the kind of power over a tying product necessary for a violation of Sherman Act § 1).

The Commission found here that, however TRU's market power as a toy retailer was measured, it was clear that its boycott was having an effect in the market. It was remarkably successful in causing the 10 major toy manufacturers to reduce output of toys to the warehouse clubs, and that reduction in output protected TRU from having to lower its prices to meet the clubs' price levels. Price competition from conventional discounters like Wal-Mart and K-Mart, in contrast, imposed no such constraint on it, or so the Commission found. In addition, the Commission showed that the affected manufacturers accounted for some 40% of the traditional toy market, and that TRU had 20% of the national wholesale market and up to 49% of some local wholesale markets. Taking steps to prevent a price collapse through coordination of action among competitors has been illegal at least since *United States v. Socony-Vacuum Oil Co., 310 U.S. 150 (1940).* Proof that this is what TRU was doing is sufficient proof of actual anticompetitive effects that no more elaborate market analysis was necessary.

C. Free Riding Explanation

TRU next urges that its policy was a legitimate business response to combat free riding by the warehouse clubs. We think, however, that it has fundamentally misunderstood the theory of free riding. Briefly, that theory is as follows. The manufacturer of a product, say widgets, has an incentive to distribute as many widgets as it can, while keeping its costs of distribution down as low as possible. In many instances, this means that the manufacturer will want to sell its widgets for a particular wholesale price and it will want its retailer to apply as low a mark-up as possible (i.e. put the product on the market for as little extra expense as possible). Sometimes, however, the manufacturer will want the retailer to provide special services or amenities that cost money, such as attractive premises, trained salespeople, long business hours, full-line stocking, or fast warranty service. But the costs of providing some of those amenities (usually pre-sale services) are hard to pass on to customers unless some form of restricted distribution is available. What the manufacturer does not want is for the shopper to visit the attractive store with highly paid, intelligent sales help, learn all about the product, and then go home and order it from a discount warehouse or (today) on-line discounters. The shopper in that situation has taken a "free ride" on the retailer's efforts; the retailer never gets paid for them, and eventually it stops offering the services. If those services were genuinely useful, in the sense that the product plus service package resulted in greater sales for the manufacturer than the product alone would have enjoyed, there is a loss both for the manufacturer and the consumer. Hence, antitrust law permits nonprice vertical restraints that are designed to facilitate the provision of extra services, recognizing that a manufacturer in a competitive market who has guessed wrong will eventually be forced by the market to abandon the restrictions. See *Business Electronics Corp. v. Sharp Electronics Corp., 485 U.S. 717, 724 (1988),* quoting *Continental T.V., Inc. v. GTE Sylvania Inc., 433 U.S. 36, 52 n.19 (1977).*

Here, the evidence shows that the free-riding story is inverted. The manufacturers wanted a business strategy under which they distributed their toys to as many different kinds of outlets as would accept them: exclusive toy shops, TRU, discount department stores, and warehouse clubs. Rightly or wrongly, this was the distribution strategy that each one believed would maximize its individual output and profits. The manufacturers did not think that the alleged "extra services" TRU might have been providing were necessary. This is crucial, because the most important insight behind the free rider concept is the fact that, with respect to the cost of distribution services, the interests of the manufacturer and the consumer are aligned, and are basically adverse to the interests of the retailer (who would presumably like to charge as much as possible for its part in the process). See *Premier Electrical Construction Co. v. Nat'l Electrical Contractors Ass'n, 814 F.2d 358, 369-70 (7th Cir. 1987)* ("[the rationale for permitting restricted distribution policies] depends on the alignment of interests between consumers and manufacturers. Destroy that alignment and you destroy the power of the argument.").

What TRU wanted or did not want is neither here nor there for purposes of the free rider argument. Its economic interest was in maximizing its own profits, not in keeping down its suppliers' cost of doing business. Furthermore, we note that the Commission made a plausible argument for the proposition that there was little or no opportunity to "free" ride on anything here in any event. The consumer is not taking a free ride if the cost of the service can be captured in the price of the item. As our earlier review of the facts demonstrated, the manufacturers were paying for the services TRU furnished, such as advertising, full-line product stocking, and extensive inventories. These expenses, we may assume, were folded into the price of the goods the manufacturers charged to TRU, and thus these services were not susceptible to free riding. On this record, in short, TRU cannot prevail on the basis that its practices were designed to combat free riding.

D. Remedy

Last, we consider TRU's challenge to the remedial provisions the Commission ordered. TRU's basic point here is that the Commission has commanded it to do things that it would have been free to refuse, and conversely to refrain from actions it would have been free to take, in the absence of its violation of FTC Act § 5. So that its arguments can be fully understood, we set forth Section II of the decree in its entirety here:

> IT IS ORDERED that respondent, directly or indirectly, through any corporation, subsidiary, division or other device, in connection with the actual or potential purchase or distribution of toys and related products, in or affecting commerce, as "commerce" is defined in the Federal Trade Commission Act, forthwith cease and desist from:
>
> A. Continuing, maintaining, entering into, and attempting to enter into any agreement or understanding with any supplier to limit supply or to refuse to sell toys and related products to any toy

discounter.

B. Urging, inducing, coercing, or pressuring, or attempting to urge, induce, coerce, or pressure, any supplier to limit supply or to refuse to sell toys and related products to any toy discounter.

C. Requiring, soliciting, requesting or encouraging any supplier to furnish information to respondent relating to any supplier's sales or actual or intended shipments to any toy discounter.

D. Facilitating or attempting to facilitate agreements or understandings between or among suppliers relating to limiting the sale of toys and related products to any retailer(s) by, among other things, transmitting or conveying complaints, intentions, plans, actions, or other similar information from one supplier to another supplier relating to sales to such retailer(s).

E. For a period of five years, (1) announcing or communicating that respondent will or may discontinue purchasing or refuse to purchase toys and related products from any supplier because that supplier intends to sell or sells toys and related products to any toy discounter, or (2) refusing to purchase toys and related products from a supplier because, in whole or in part, that supplier offered to sell or sold toys and related products to any toy discounter.

PROVIDED, however, that nothing in this order shall prevent respondent from seeking or entering into exclusive arrangements with suppliers with respect to particular toys.

TRU makes a perfunctory, one-paragraph argument that paragraphs II(B), II(C), II(D), and II(E)(1) impose a "gag order" that contravenes the Supreme Court's recognition in *Monsanto Co. v. Spray-Rite Corp., supra,* that manufacturers and distributors have a legitimate need for a free flow of information between them. This order, they claim, will create an irrational dislocation in the market to the detriment of toy suppliers, retailers, and consumers. With respect to paragraph II(E)(2), it argues that the five-year restriction on refusals to deal impermissibly cabins its Colgate rights to choose the suppliers with which it wants to deal. In effect, it claims, the decree will force it to purchase all toys that are offered to anyone, unless it can somehow prove that its refusal was because of a safety defect or other similar flaw.

We consider first TRU's challenges to parts II(B) through II(D) of the order. (It has not mentioned II(A) in its brief, and thus it has waived any challenge to that part of the order.) In general, if a retailer had some kind of restricted distribution arrangement with a manufacturer, Monsanto holds that it is permissible for the retailer to urge the manufacturer to respect the limits of that agreement. The retailer may communicate complaints about the provision of product to discounters, if that runs afoul of the promises in the distribution agreement. Colgate indicates that the retailer would also be within its rights to tell the manufacturer that it will no longer stock the manufacturer's product, if it is unhappy with the company it is keeping (i.e. if the manufacturer is sending too many goods to discounters, stores with a reputation for rude and sloppy service, or other undesirables).

Two facts distinguish these general rules from the situation in which TRU finds itself. First, unilateral actions of the sort protected by Monsanto and Colgate are not the same thing as a retailer's request to the manufacturer to change the latter's business practice. Under paragraph II(B) of the decree, TRU must not tell the manufacturer what to do; it is still permitted to decide which toys it wants to carry and which ones to drop, based on busincss considerations such as the expected popularity of the item. Second, to the extent paragraph II(B) might indirectly inhibit TRU from exercising its unilateral judgment, TRU must confront the fact that the FTC is not limited to restating the law in its remedial orders. Such orders can restrict the options for a company that has violated § 5, to ensure that the violation will cease and competition will be restored. See *National Lead Co., supra, 352 U.S. at 430; FTC v. Cement Institute, 333 U.S. 683, 726-27 (1948); Corning Glass Works v. FTC, 509 F.2d 293, 303 (7th Cir. 1975).* See also *FTC v. Colgate-Palmolive Co., 380 U.S. 374, 392 (1965)* (making the same point, in context of the Commission's deceptive practices authority).

The second point also applies to TRU's objections to paragraphs II(C) and II(D). In addition, we note that the retailer should not have any reason to obtain its suppliers' business records about shipments to the retailer's competitors. That is the supplier's concern. TRU is protected as long as it can ensure that it receives what was promised to it. Also, of course, the decree preserves TRU's right to enter into exclusive arrangements with respect to particular toys. In so doing, it also implicitly allows TRU to engage in communications that are necessary for the implementation and enforcement of such agreements. Paragraph II(D) directly addresses the Commission's finding of a horizontal agreement, and it orders TRU not to go out and create a new one. The Commission was certainly acting within the bounds of its discretion when it included these provisions.

Paragraph II(E) appears to be the one that causes the greatest concern to TRU. This strikes us as a closer call, but in this connection the standard of review becomes important. The Commission has represented in its brief to this court that the decree "leaves [TRU] free to make stocking decisions based on a wide range of business reasons; it must simply make those decisions--for a period of five years--independent of whether clubs or other discounters are carrying the same item." FTC Brief at 58. The attempt to use its market clout to harm the warehouse clubs lies at the heart of this case, and so it is easy to see why the Commission chose to prohibit reliance on the supplier's practices vis ... vis the clubs as a reason for TRU's own purchasing decisions. At bottom, TRU is really just worried that it will be difficult to prove that any particular purchasing decision was free from the prohibited taint. It will be easy to refrain from announcements or communications about refusals to deal, which is what II(E)(1) prohibits. With respect to II(E)(2), if TRU implements adequate internal procedural safeguards, it should be possible to demonstrate that its buying decisions were not influenced by anything the manufacturers were doing with discounters like the clubs. These refusals to deal were the means TRU used to accomplish the unlawful result, and as such, they are subject to regulation by the Commission. See *National Lead, 352 U.S. at 425.* Under the abuse of discretion standard that governs our review of the Commission's choice of remedy, see *Siegel Co. v. FTC, 327 U.S. 608, 612-13 (1946),* this does not appear to be a remedy that "has no reasonable relation to the unlawful practices found to exist." We therefore have no warrant to set it aside. If, however, it becomes clear in practice that this provision is unworkable, TRU is free to return to the Commission to petition for a modification of the order.

III

We conclude that the Commission's decision is supported by substantial evidence on the record, and that its remedial decree falls within the broad discretion it has been granted under the FTC Act. The decision is hereby Affirmed.

CHAPTER 8: ADDITIONAL LIMITATIONS ON A SINGLE FIRM EXERCISING MARKET POWER

Section 1. Predatory Price Cutting

Insert after Note 8, page 701:

Note on the *American Airlines* Case

In United States v. AMR Corp., American Airlines, Inc., 140 F. Supp. 2d 1141 (D. Kan. 2001), American Airlines, the dominant airline on routes into and out of Dallas-Fort Worth, during the period from 1995-97, was often challenged by small carriers charging substantially lower fares. The government charged that American Airlines violated Section 2 of the Sherman Act when it responded by cutting fares below its costs to the level of its challengers and adding to the number of its flights per day, thereby taking passenger business away from challengers. The result, intended according to American Airlines' documents, was that the low-price carriers abandoned their challenges on these particular routes or went out of business altogether.

The Antitrust Division charged that American Airlines priced below cost to drive low-price carriers out of business and with the intent subsequently to recoup its investment through higher airline prices. It further claimed that even on routes where American Airlines was not directly challenged, American Airlines' aggressive behavior earned the company a "reputation for predation" which deterred other challengers on other routes from taking on the company.

The district court granted American Airlines motion for summary judgment. It followed those courts and commentators that have adopted the rule that predatory pricing requires pricing below average variable costs, and found that American Airlines' pricing never reached so low a level. It also found that American's prices were not predatory because it met but did not beat prices offered by smaller challengers, and that it was implausible that American Airlines could recoup its lower prices through subsequent high prices, a requirement to show predation, because there continued to be a substantial number of competitors into and out of Dallas-Fort Worth.

With respect to predation by reputation, the court found that the theory was unprecedented, and was dependent on a finding of underlying predatory pricing behavior which the court concluded was not present. In any event, any such reputation is almost an inevitable consequence of hard-nosed competition which the law does not preclude.

The district court's approach on the central policy question of what constitutes predation is summarized in the following italicized portion of its opinion:

> *Antitrust begins with the premise that all firms, even dominant firms, are permitted to compete aggressively, and that hard competition is a desideratum rather than an evil. Thus prices above the relevant measure of costs become an absolute safe harbor.*

Section 2. Tying Arrangements

Insert after Note 7, page 751:

UNITED STATES v. MICROSOFT CORP.
United States Court of Appeals, District of Columbia Circuit, 2001.
2001 U.S. App. Lexis 14324.

Section 4. Section 2 Revisited: Special Limits on Single Firm Market Power by Monopolists and Would-Be Monopolists

Insert after Note 3, page 814:

UNITED STATES v. MICROSOFT CORP.
United States Court of Appeals, District of Columbia Circuit, 2001.
2001 U.S. App. Lexis 14324.

Before: EDWARDS, Chief Judge, WILLIAMS, GINSBURG, SENTELLE, RANDOLPH, ROGERS, and TATEL, Circuit Judges.

PER CURIAM. Microsoft Corporation appeals from judgments of the District Court finding the company in violation of §§ 1 and 2 of the Sherman Act and ordering various remedies.

The action against Microsoft arose pursuant to a complaint filed by the United States and separate complaints filed by individual States. The District Court determined that Microsoft had maintained a monopoly in the market for

Intel-compatible PC operating systems in violation of § 2; attempted to gain a monopoly in the market for internet browsers in violation of § 2; and illegally tied two purportedly separate products, Windows and Internet Explorer ("IE"), in violation of § 1. *United States v. Microsoft Corp., 87 F. Supp. 2d 30 (D.D.C. 2000)* ("Conclusions of Law"). The District Court then found that the same facts that established liability under §§ 1 and 2 of the Sherman Act mandated findings of liability under analogous state law antitrust provisions. Id. To remedy the Sherman Act violations, the District Court issued a Final Judgment requiring Microsoft to submit a proposed plan of divestiture, with the company to be split into an operating systems business and an applications business. *United States v. Microsoft Corp., 97 F. Supp. 2d 59, 64-65 (D.D.C. 2000)* ("Final Judgment"). The District Court's remedial order also contains a number of interim restrictions on Microsoft's conduct. *Id. at 66-69.*

Microsoft's appeal contests both the legal conclusions and the resulting remedial order. There are three principal aspects of this appeal. First, Microsoft challenges the District Court's legal conclusions as to all three alleged antitrust violations and also a number of the procedural and factual foundations on which they rest. Second, Microsoft argues that the remedial order must be set aside, because the District Court failed to afford the company an evidentiary hearing on disputed facts and, also, because the substantive provisions of the order are flawed. Finally, Microsoft asserts that the trial judge committed ethical violations by engaging in impermissible ex parte contacts and making inappropriate public comments on the merits of the case while it was pending. Microsoft argues that these ethical violations compromised the District Judge's appearance of impartiality, thereby necessitating his disqualification and vacatur of his Findings of Fact, Conclusions of Law, and Final Judgment.

After carefully considering the voluminous record on appeal--including the District Court's Findings of Fact and Conclusions of Law, the testimony and exhibits submitted at trial, the parties' briefs, and the oral arguments before this court--we find that some but not all of Microsoft's liability challenges have merit. Accordingly, we affirm in part and reverse in part the District Court's judgment that Microsoft violated § 2 of the Sherman Act by employing anticompetitive means to maintain a monopoly in the operating system market; we reverse the District Court's determination that Microsoft violated § 2 of the Sherman Act by illegally attempting to monopolize the internet browser market; and we remand the District Court's finding that Microsoft violated § 1 of the Sherman Act by unlawfully tying its browser to its operating system. Our judgment extends to the District Court's findings with respect to the state law counterparts of the plaintiffs' Sherman Act claims.

We also find merit in Microsoft's challenge to the Final Judgment embracing the District Court's remedial order. There are several reasons supporting this conclusion. First, the District Court's Final Judgment rests on a number of liability determinations that do not survive appellate review; therefore, the remedial order as currently fashioned cannot stand. Furthermore, we would vacate and remand the remedial order even were we to uphold the District Court's liability determinations in their entirety, because the District Court failed to hold an evidentiary hearing to address remedies-specific factual disputes.

Finally, we vacate the Final Judgment on remedies, because the trial judge engaged in impermissible ex parte contacts by holding secret interviews with members of the media and made numerous offensive comments about Microsoft officials in public statements outside of the courtroom, giving rise to an appearance of partiality. Although we find no evidence of actual bias, we hold that the actions of the trial judge seriously tainted the proceedings before the District Court and called into question the integrity of the judicial process. We are therefore constrained to vacate the Final Judgment on remedies, remand the case for reconsideration of the remedial order, and require that the case be assigned to a different trial judge on remand. We believe that this disposition will be adequate to cure the cited improprieties.

In sum, for reasons more fully explained below, we affirm in part, reverse in part, and remand in part the District Court's judgment assessing liability. We vacate in full the Final Judgment embodying the remedial order and remand the case to a different trial judge for further proceedings consistent with this opinion.

I. INTRODUCTION

A. Background

In July 1994, officials at the Department of Justice ("DOJ"), on behalf of the United States, filed suit against Microsoft, charging the company with, among other things, unlawfully maintaining a monopoly in the operating system market through anticompetitive terms in its licensing and software developer agreements. The parties subsequently entered into a consent decree, thus avoiding a trial on the merits. See *United States v. Microsoft Corp., 56*

F.3d 1448 (D.C. Cir. 1995) ("Microsoft I"). Three years later, the Justice Department filed a civil contempt action against Microsoft for allegedly violating one of the decree's provisions. On appeal from a grant of a preliminary injunction, this court held that Microsoft's technological bundling of IE 3.0 and 4.0 with Windows 95 did not violate the relevant provision of the consent decree. *United States v. Microsoft Corp., 147 F.3d 935 (D.C. Cir. 1998)* ("Microsoft II"). We expressly reserved the question whether such bundling might independently violate §§ 1 or 2 of the *Sherman Act. 147 F.3d at 950 n.14.*

On May 18, 1998, shortly before issuance of the Microsoft II decision, the United States and a group of State plaintiffs filed separate (and soon thereafter consolidated) complaints, asserting antitrust violations by Microsoft and seeking preliminary and permanent injunctions against the company's allegedly unlawful conduct. The complaints also sought any "other preliminary and permanent relief as is necessary and appropriate to restore competitive conditions in the markets affected by Microsoft's unlawful conduct." Gov't's Compl. at 53, *United States v. Microsoft Corp., 84 F. Supp. 2d 9, 19 (D.D.C. 1999).* Relying almost exclusively on Microsoft's varied efforts to unseat Netscape Navigator as the preeminent internet browser, plaintiffs charged four distinct violations of the Sherman Act: (1) unlawful exclusive dealing arrangements in violation of § 1; (2) unlawful tying of IE to Windows 95 and Windows 98 in violation of § 1; (3) unlawful maintenance of a monopoly in the PC operating system market in violation of § 2; and (4) unlawful attempted monopolization of the internet browser market in violation of § 2. The States also brought pendent claims charging Microsoft with violations of various State antitrust laws.

The District Court scheduled the case on a "fast track." The hearing on the preliminary injunction and the trial on the merits were consolidated pursuant to FED. R. CIV. P. 65(a)(2). The trial was then scheduled to commence on September 8, 1998, less than four months after the complaints had been filed. In a series of pretrial orders, the District Court limited each side to a maximum of 12 trial witnesses plus two rebuttal witnesses. It required that all trial witnesses' direct testimony be submitted to the court in the form of written declarations. The District Court also made allowances for the use of deposition testimony at trial to prove subordinate or predicate issues. Following the grant of three brief continuances, the trial started on October 19, 1998.

After a 76-day bench trial, the District Court issued its Findings of Fact. *United States v. Microsoft Corp., 84 F. Supp. 2d 9 (D.D.C. 1999)* ("Findings of Fact"). This triggered two independent courses of action. First, the District Court established a schedule for briefing on possible legal conclusions, inviting Professor Lawrence Lessig to participate as amicus curiae. Second, the District Court referred the case to mediation to afford the parties an opportunity to settle their differences. The Honorable Richard A. Posner, Chief Judge of the United States Court of Appeals for the Seventh Circuit, was appointed to serve as mediator. The parties concurred in the referral to mediation and in the choice of mediator.

Mediation failed after nearly four months of settlement talks between the parties. On April 3, 2000, with the parties' briefs having been submitted and considered, the District Court issued its conclusions of law. The District Court found Microsoft liable on the § 1 tying and § 2 monopoly maintenance and attempted monopolization claims, Conclusions of Law, at 35-51, while ruling that there was insufficient evidence to support a § 1 exclusive dealing violation, *id . at 51-54.* As to the pendent State actions, the District Court found the State antitrust laws conterminous with §§ 1 and 2 of the Sherman Act, thereby obviating the need for further State specific analysis. *Id. at 54-56.* In those few cases where a State's law required an additional showing of intrastate impact on competition, the District Court found the requirement easily satisfied on the evidence at hand. *Id. at 55.*

Having found Microsoft liable on all but one count, the District Court then asked plaintiffs to submit a proposed remedy. Plaintiffs' proposal for a remedial order was subsequently filed within four weeks, along with six supplemental declarations and over 50 new exhibits. In their proposal, plaintiffs sought specific conduct remedies, plus structural relief that would split Microsoft into an applications company and an operating systems company. The District Court rejected Microsoft's request for further evidentiary proceedings and, following a single hearing on the merits of the remedy question, issued its Final Judgment on June 7, 2000. The District Court adopted plaintiffs' proposed remedy without substantive change.

Microsoft filed a notice of appeal within a week after the District Court issued its Final Judgment. This court then ordered that any proceedings before it be heard by the court sitting en banc. Before any substantive matters were addressed by this court, however, the District Court certified appeal of the case brought by the United States directly to the Supreme Court pursuant to *15*

U.S.C. § 29 (b), while staying the final judgment order in the federal and state cases pending appeal. The States thereafter petitioned the Supreme Court for a writ of certiorari in their case. The Supreme Court declined to hear the appeal of the Government's case and remanded the matter to this court; the Court likewise denied the States' petition for writ of certiorari. *Microsoft Corp. v. United States, 530 U.S. 1301 (2000).* This consolidated appeal followed.

B. Overview

Before turning to the merits of Microsoft's various arguments, we pause to reflect briefly on two matters of note, one practical and one theoretical.

The practical matter relates to the temporal dimension of this case. The litigation timeline in this case is hardly problematic. Indeed, it is noteworthy that a case of this magnitude and complexity has proceeded from the filing of complaints through trial to appellate decision in a mere three years. See, e.g., *Data Gen. Corp. v. Grumman Sys. Support Corp., 36 F.3d 1147, 1155 (1st Cir. 1994)* (six years from filing of complaint to appellate decision); *Transamerica Computer Co., Inc. v. IBM, 698 F.2d 1377, 1381 (9th Cir. 1983)* (over four years from start of trial to appellate decision); *United States v. United Shoe Mach. Corp., 110 F. Supp. 295, 298 (D. Mass. 1953)* (over five years from filing of complaint to trial court decision).

What is somewhat problematic, however, is that just over six years have passed since Microsoft engaged in the first conduct plaintiffs allege to be anticompetitive. As the record in this case indicates, six years seems like an eternity in the computer industry. By the time a court can assess liability, firms, products, and the marketplace are likely to have changed dramatically. This, in turn, threatens enormous practical difficulties for courts considering the appropriate measure of relief in equitable enforcement actions, both in crafting injunctive remedies in the first instance and reviewing those remedies in the second. Conduct remedies may be unavailing in such cases, because innovation to a large degree has already rendered the anticompetitive conduct obsolete (although by no means harmless). And broader structural remedies present their own set of problems, including how a court goes about restoring competition to a dramatically changed, and constantly changing, marketplace. That is just one reason why we find the District Court's refusal in the present case to hold an evidentiary hearing on remedies--to update and flesh out the available information before seriously entertaining the possibility of dramatic structural relief--so problematic. See infra Section V.

We do not mean to say that enforcement actions will no longer play an important role in curbing infringements of the antitrust laws in technologically dynamic markets, nor do we assume this in assessing the merits of this case. Even in those cases where forward-looking remedies appear limited, the Government will continue to have an interest in defining the contours of the antitrust laws so that law-abiding firms will have a clear sense of what is permissible and what is not. And the threat of private damage actions will remain to deter those firms inclined to test the limits of the law.

The second matter of note is more theoretical in nature. We decide this case against a backdrop of significant debate amongst academics and practitioners over the extent to which "old economy" § 2 monopolization doctrines should apply to firms competing in dynamic technological markets characterized by network effects. In markets characterized by network effects, one product or standard tends towards dominance, because "the utility that a user derives from consumption of the good increases with the number of other agents consuming the good." Michael L. Katz & Carl Shapiro, Network Externalities, Competition, and Compatibility, *75 AM. ECON. REV. 424, 424 (1985).* For example, "an individual consumer's demand to use (and hence her benefit from) the telephone network ... increases with the number of other users on the network whom she can call or from whom she can receive calls." Howard A. Shelanski & J. Gregory Sidak, Antitrust Divestiture in Network Industries, *68 U. CHI. L. REV. 1, 8 (2001).* Once a product or standard achieves wide acceptance, it becomes more or less entrenched. Competition in such industries is "for the field" rather than "within the field." See Harold Demsetz, Why Regulate Utilities?, *11 J.L. & ECON. 55, 57 & n.7 (1968)* (emphasis omitted).

In technologically dynamic markets, however, such entrenchment may be temporary, because innovation may alter the field altogether. See JOSEPH A. SCHUMPETER, CAPITALISM, SOCIALISM AND DEMOCRACY 81-90 (Harper Perennial 1976) (1942). Rapid technological change leads to markets in which "firms compete through innovation for temporary market dominance, from which they may be displaced by the next wave of product advancements." Shelanski & Sidak, at 11-12 (discussing Schumpeterian competition, which proceeds "sequentially over time rather than simultaneously across a market"). Microsoft argues that the operating system market is just such a market.

Whether or not Microsoft's characterization of the operating system market is correct does not appreciably alter our mission in assessing the alleged antitrust violations in the present case. As an initial matter, we note that there is no consensus among commentators on the question of whether, and to what extent, current monopolization doctrine should be amended to account for competition in technologically dynamic markets characterized by network effects. Compare Steven C. Salop & R. Craig Romaine, Preserving Monopoly: Economic Analysis, Legal Standards, and Microsoft, *7 GEO. MASON L. REV. 617, 654-55, 663-64 (1999)* (arguing that exclusionary conduct in high-tech networked industries deserves heightened antitrust scrutiny in part because it may threaten to deter innovation), with Ronald A. Cass & Keith N. Hylton, Preserving Competition: Economic Analysis, Legal Standards and Microsoft, *8 GEO. MASON L. REV. 1, 36-39 (1999)* (equivocating on the antitrust implications of network effects and noting that the presence of network externalities may actually encourage innovation by guaranteeing more durable monopolies to innovating winners). Indeed, there is some suggestion that the economic consequences of network effects and technological dynamism act to offset one another, thereby making it difficult to formulate categorical antitrust rules absent a particularized analysis of a given market. See Shelanski & Sidak, at 6-7 ("High profit margins might appear to be the benign and necessary recovery of legitimate investment returns in a Schumpeterian framework, but they might represent exploitation of customer lock-in and monopoly power when viewed through the lens of network economics.... The issue is particularly complex because, in network industries characterized by rapid innovation, both forces may be operating and can be difficult to isolate.").

Moreover, it should be clear that Microsoft makes no claim that anticompetitive conduct should be assessed differently in technologically dynamic markets. It claims only that the measure of monopoly power should be different. For reasons fully discussed below, we reject Microsoft's monopoly power argument. See infra Section II.A.

With this backdrop in mind, we turn to the specific challenges raised in Microsoft's appeal.

II. MONOPOLIZATION

Section 2 of the Sherman Act makes it unlawful for a firm to "monopolize." *15 U.S.C. § 2.* The offense of monopolization has two elements: "(1) the possession of monopoly power in the relevant market and

(2) the willful acquisition or maintenance of that power as distinguished from growth or development as a consequence of a superior product, business acumen, or historic accident." *United States v. Grinnell Corp., 384 U.S. 563, 570-71 (1966).* The District Court applied this test and found that Microsoft possesses monopoly power in the market for Intel-compatible PC operating systems. Focusing primarily on Microsoft's efforts to suppress Netscape Navigator's threat to its operating system monopoly, the court also found that Microsoft maintained its power not through competition on the merits, but through unlawful means. Microsoft challenges both conclusions. We defer to the District Court's findings of fact, setting them aside only if clearly erroneous. We review legal questions de novo.

We begin by considering whether Microsoft possesses monopoly power, see infra Section II.A, and finding that it does, we turn to the question whether it maintained this power through anticompetitive means. Agreeing with the District Court that the company behaved anticompetitively, see infra Section II.B, and that these actions contributed to the maintenance of its monopoly power, see infra Section II.C, we affirm the court's finding of liability for monopolization.

A. Monopoly Power

While merely possessing monopoly power is not itself an antitrust violation, see *Northeastern Tel. Co. v. AT & T, 651 F.2d 76, 84-85 (2d Cir. 1981),* it is a necessary element of a monopolization charge, see *Grinnell, 384 U.S. at 570.* The Supreme Court defines monopoly power as "the power to control prices or exclude competition." *United States v. E.I. du Pont de Nemours & Co., 351 U.S. 377, 391 (1956).* More precisely, a firm is a monopolist if it can profitably raise prices substantially above the competitive level.... Where evidence indicates that a firm has in fact profitably done so, the existence of monopoly power is clear. See *Rebel Oil Co. v. Atl. Richfield Co., 51 F.3d 1421, 1434 (9th Cir. 1995);* see also *FTC v. Indiana Fed'n of Dentists, 476 U.S. 447 (1986)* (using direct proof to show market power in Sherman Act § 1 unreasonable restraint of trade action). Because such direct proof is only rarely available, courts more typically examine market structure in search of circumstantial evidence of monopoly power. Under this structural approach, monopoly power may be inferred from a firm's possession of a dominant share of a relevant market that is protected by entry barriers. See *Rebel Oil, 51 F.3d at 1434.* "Entry barriers" are factors (such as certain regulatory requirements) that prevent new rivals from timely responding to an increase in price above the competitive level.

The District Court considered these structural factors and concluded that Microsoft possesses monopoly power in a relevant market. Defining the market as Intel-compatible PC operating systems, the District Court found that Microsoft has a greater than 95% share. It also found the company's market position protected by a substantial entry barrier. Conclusions of Law, at 36.

Microsoft argues that the District Court incorrectly defined the relevant market. It also claims that there is no barrier to entry in that market. Alternatively, Microsoft argues that because the software industry is uniquely dynamic, direct proof, rather than circumstantial evidence, more appropriately indicates whether it possesses monopoly power. Rejecting each argument, we uphold the District Court's finding of monopoly power in its entirety.

1. Market Structure

a. Market definition

"Because the ability of consumers to turn to other suppliers restrains a firm from raising prices above the competitive level," *Rothery Storage & Van Co. v. Atlas Van Lines, Inc., 792 F.2d 210, 218 (D.C. Cir. 1986),* the relevant market must include all products "reasonably interchangeable by consumers for the same purposes." *du Pont, 351 U.S. at 395.* In this case, the District Court defined the market as "the licensing of all Intel-compatible PC operating systems worldwide," finding that there are "currently no products--and ... there are not likely to be any in the near future--that a significant percentage of computer users worldwide could substitute for [these operating systems] without incurring substantial costs." Conclusions of Law, at 36. Calling this market definition "far too narrow," Microsoft argues that the District Court improperly excluded three types of products: non-Intel compatible operating systems (primarily Apple's Macintosh operating system, Mac OS), operating systems for non-PC devices (such as handheld computers and portal websites), and "middleware" products, which are not operating systems at all.

We begin with Mac OS. Microsoft's argument that Mac OS should have been included in the relevant market suffers from a flaw that infects many of the company's monopoly power claims: the company fails to challenge the District Court's factual findings, or to argue that these findings do not support the court's conclusions. The District Court found that consumers would not switch from Windows to Mac OS in response to a substantial price increase because of the costs of acquiring the new hardware needed to run Mac OS (an Apple computer and peripherals) and compatible software applications, as well as because of the effort involved in learning the new system and transferring files to its format. Findings of Fact P 20. The court also found the Apple system less appealing to consumers because it costs considerably more and supports fewer applications. Id. P 21. Microsoft responds only by saying: "the district court's market definition is so narrow that it excludes Apple's Mac OS, which has competed with Windows for years, simply because the Mac OS runs on a different microprocessor." This general, conclusory statement falls far short of what is required to challenge findings as clearly erroneous....

Microsoft's challenge to the District Court's exclusion of non-PC based competitors, such as information appliances (handheld devices, etc.) and portal websites that host serverbased software applications, suffers from the same defect: the company fails to challenge the District Court's key factual findings. In particular, the District Court found that because information appliances fall far short of performing all of the functions of a PC, most consumers will buy them only as a supplement to their PCs. Findings of Fact P 23. The District Court also found that portal websites do not presently host enough applications to induce consumers to switch, nor are they likely to do so in the near future. Id. P 27....

This brings us to Microsoft's main challenge to the District Court's market definition: the exclusion of middleware. Because of the importance of middleware to this case, we pause to explain what it is and how it relates to the issue before us.

Operating systems perform many functions, including allocating computer memory and controlling peripherals such as printers and keyboards. Operating systems also function as platforms for software applications. They do this by "exposing"--i.e., making available to software developers--routines or protocols that perform certain widely-used functions. These are known as Application Programming Interfaces, or "APIs." For example, Windows contains an API that enables users to draw a box on the screen. Software developers wishing to include that function in an application need not duplicate it in their own code. Instead, they can "call"--i.e., use--the Windows API. See Direct Testimony of James Barksdale P P 70-71, reprinted in 5 J.A. at 2895-97. Windows contains thousands of APIs, controlling everything from data storage to font display.

Every operating system has different APIs. Accordingly, a developer who writes an application for one operating system and wishes to sell the application to users of another must modify, or "port," the application to the second operating system. Findings of Fact P 4. This process is both time consuming and expensive. Id. P 30.

"Middleware" refers to software products that expose their own APIs.... Because of this, a middleware product written for Windows could take over some or all of Windows's valuable platform functions--that is, developers might begin to rely upon APIs exposed by the middleware for basic routines rather than relying upon the API set included in Windows. If middleware were written for multiple operating systems, its impact could be even greater. The more developers could rely upon APIs exposed by such middleware, the less expensive porting to different operating systems would be. Ultimately, if developers could write applications relying exclusively on APIs exposed by middleware, their applications would run on any operating system on which the middleware was also present. Netscape Navigator and Java--both at issue in this case--are middleware products written for multiple operating systems. Findings of Fact P 28.

Microsoft argues that, because middleware could usurp the operating system's platform function and might eventually take over other operating system functions (for instance, by controlling peripherals), the District Court erred in excluding Navigator and Java from the relevant market. The District Court found, however, that neither Navigator, Java, nor any other middleware product could now, or would soon, expose enough APIs to serve as a platform for popular applications, much less take over all operating system functions. Id. P P 28-29. Again, Microsoft fails to challenge these findings, instead simply asserting middleware's "potential" as a competitor. The test of reasonable interchangeability, however, required the District Court to consider only substitutes that constrain pricing in the reasonably foreseeable future, and only products that can enter the market in a relatively short time can perform this function. See *Rothery, 792 F.2d at 218* ("Because the ability of consumers to turn to other suppliers restrains a firm from raising prices above the competitive level, the definition of the 'relevant market' rests on a determination of available substitutes."); see also Findings of Fact P 29 ("It would take several years for middleware ... to evolve" into a product that can constrain operating system pricing.). Whatever middleware's ultimate potential, the District Court found that consumers could not now abandon their operating systems and switch to middleware in response to a sustained price for Windows above the competitive level. Findings of Fact P P 28, 29. Nor is middleware likely to overtake the operating system as the primary platform for software development any time in the near future. Id.

Alternatively, Microsoft argues that the District Court should not have excluded middleware from the relevant market because the primary focus of the plaintiffs' § 2 charge is on Microsoft's attempts to suppress middleware's threat to its operating system monopoly. According to Microsoft, it is "contradictory," 2/26/2001 Ct. Appeals Tr. at 20, to define the relevant market to exclude the "very competitive threats that gave rise" to the action. Appellant's Opening Br. at 84. The purported contradiction lies between plaintiffs' § 2 theory, under which Microsoft preserved its monopoly against middleware technologies that threatened to become viable substitutes for Windows, and its theory of the relevant market, under which middleware is not presently a viable substitute for Windows. Because middleware's threat is only nascent, however, no contradiction exists. Nothing in § 2 of the Sherman Act limits its prohibition to actions taken against threats that are already well-developed enough to serve as present substitutes. See infra Section II.C. Because market definition is meant to identify products "reasonably interchangeable by consumers," *du Pont, 351 U.S. at 395,* and because middleware is not now interchangeable with Windows, the District Court had good reason for excluding middleware from the relevant market.

b. Market power

Having thus properly defined the relevant market, the District Court found that Windows accounts for a greater than 95% share. Findings of Fact P 35. The court also found that even if Mac OS were included, Microsoft's share would exceed 80%. Id. Microsoft challenges neither finding, nor does it argue that such a market share is not predominant. Cf. *Grinnell, 384 U.S. at 571* (87% is predominant); *Eastman Kodak Co. v. Image Technical Servs., Inc., 504 U.S. 451 (1992)* (80%); *du Pont, 351 U.S. at 379, 391* (75%).

Instead, Microsoft claims that even a predominant market share does not by itself indicate monopoly power. Although the "existence of [monopoly] power ordinarily may be inferred from the predominant share of the market," *Grinnell, 384 U.S. at 571,* we agree with Microsoft that because of the possibility of competition from new entrants, see *Ball Mem'l Hosp., Inc., 784 F.2d at 1336,* looking to current market share alone can be "misleading." *Hunt-Wesson Foods, Inc. v. Ragu Foods, Inc., 627 F.2d 919, 924 (9th Cir. 1980);*

see also *Ball Mem'l Hosp., Inc., 784 F.2d at 1336* ("Market share reflects current sales, but today's sales do not always indicate power over sales and price tomorrow.") In this case, however, the District Court was not misled. Considering the possibility of new rivals, the court focused not only on Microsoft's present market share, but also on the structural barrier that protects the company's future position. Conclusions of Law, at 36. That barrier--the "applications barrier to entry"--stems from two characteristics of the software market: (1) most consumers prefer operating systems for which a large number of applications have already been written; and (2) most developers prefer to write for operating systems that already have a substantial consumer base. See Findings of Fact P P 30, 36. This "chicken-and-egg" situation ensures that applications will continue to be written for the already dominant Windows, which in turn ensures that consumers will continue to prefer it over other operating systems. Id.

Challenging the existence of the applications barrier to entry, Microsoft observes that software developers do write applications for other operating systems, pointing out that at its peak IBM's OS/2 supported approximately 2,500 applications. Id. P 46. This misses the point. That some developers write applications for other operating systems is not at all inconsistent with the finding that the applications barrier to entry discourages many from writing for these less popular platforms. Indeed, the District Court found that IBM's difficulty in attracting a larger number of software developers to write for its platform seriously impeded OS/2's success. Id. P 46.

Microsoft does not dispute that Windows supports many more applications than any other operating system. It argues instead that "it defies common sense" to suggest that an operating system must support as many applications as Windows does (more than 70,000, according to the District Court, id. P 40) to be competitive. Appellant's Opening Br. at 96. Consumers, Microsoft points out, can only use a very small percentage of these applications. Id. As the District Court explained, however, the applications barrier to entry gives consumers reason to prefer the dominant operating system even if they have no need to use all applications written for it:

The consumer wants an operating system that runs not only types of applications that he knows he will want to use, but also those types in which he might develop an interest later. Also, the consumer knows that if he chooses an operating system with enough demand to support multiple applications in each product category, he will be less likely to find himself straitened later by having to use an application whose features disappoint him. Finally, the average user knows that, generally speaking, applications improve through successive versions. He thus wants an operating system for which successive generations of his favorite applications will be released--promptly at that. The fact that a vastly larger number of applications are written for Windows than for other PC operating systems attracts consumers to Windows, because it reassures them that their interests will be met as long as they use Microsoft's product.

Findings of Fact P 37. Thus, despite the limited success of its rivals, Microsoft benefits from the applications barrier to entry.

Of course, were middleware to succeed, it would erode the applications barrier to entry. Because applications written for multiple operating systems could run on any operating system on which the middleware product was present with little, if any, porting, the operating system market would become competitive. Id. P P 29, 72. But as the District Court found, middleware will not expose a sufficient number of APIs to erode the applications barrier to entry in the foreseeable future. See id. PP 28-29.

Microsoft next argues that the applications barrier to entry is not an entry barrier at all, but a reflection of Windows' popularity. It is certainly true that Windows may have gained its initial dominance in the operating system market competitively--through superior foresight or quality. But this case is not about Microsoft's initial acquisition of monopoly power. It is about Microsoft's efforts to maintain this position through means other than competition on the merits. Because the applications barrier to entry protects a dominant operating system irrespective of quality, it gives Microsoft power to stave off even superior new rivals. The barrier is thus a characteristic of the operating system market, not of Microsoft's popularity, or, as asserted by a Microsoft witness, the company's efficiency. See Direct Testimony of Richard Schmalensee P 115, reprinted in 25 J.A. at 16153-14.

Finally, Microsoft argues that the District Court should not have considered the applications barrier to entry because it reflects not a cost borne disproportionately by new entrants, but one borne by all participants in the operating system market. According to Microsoft, it had to make major investments to convince software developers to write for its new operating system, and it continues to "evangelize" the Windows platform today. Whether costs borne by all market participants should be considered entry barriers is the subject of much debate.... We need not resolve this issue, however, for even under the more narrow definition it is clear that there are barriers. When Microsoft entered the operating system market with MS-DOS and the first version of Windows, it did not confront a dominant rival operating system with as massive an installed base and as vast an existing array of applications as the Windows operating systems have since enjoyed. Findings of Fact P P 6, 7, 43. Moreover, when Microsoft introduced Windows 95 and 98, it was able to bypass the applications barrier to entry that protected the incumbent Windows by including APIs from the earlier version in the new operating systems. See id. P 44. This made porting existing Windows applications to the new version of Windows much less costly than porting them to the operating systems of other entrants who could not freely include APIs from the incumbent Windows with their own.

2. Direct Proof

Having sustained the District Court's conclusion that circumstantial evidence proves that Microsoft possesses monopoly power, we turn to Microsoft's alternative argument that it does not behave like a monopolist. Claiming that software competition is uniquely "dynamic," Appellant's Opening Br. at 84 (quoting Findings of Fact P 59), the company suggests a new rule: that monopoly power in the software industry should be proven directly, that is, by examining a company's actual behavior to determine if it reveals the existence of monopoly power. According to Microsoft, not only does no such proof of its power exist, but record evidence demonstrates the absence of monopoly power. The company claims that it invests heavily in research and development, id. at 88-89 (citing Direct Testimony of Paul Maritz P 155, reprinted in 6 J.A. at 3698 (testifying that Microsoft invests approximately 17% of its revenue in R&D)), and charges a low price for Windows (a small percentage of the price of an Intel-compatible PC system and less than the price of its rivals, id. at 90 (citing Findings of Fact P P 19, 21, 46)).

Microsoft's argument fails because, even assuming that the software market is uniquely dynamic in the long term, the District Court correctly applied the structural approach to determine if the company faces competition in the short term. Structural market power analyses are meant to determine whether potential substitutes constrain a firm's ability to raise prices above the competitive level; only threats that are likely to materialize in the relatively near future perform this function to any significant degree.... The District Court expressly considered and rejected Microsoft's claims that innovations such as handheld devices and portal websites would soon expand the relevant market beyond Intel-compatible PC operating systems. Because the company does not challenge these findings, we have no reason to believe that prompt substitutes are available. The structural approach, as applied by the District Court, is thus capable of fulfilling its purpose even in a changing market. Microsoft cites no case, nor are we aware of one, requiring direct evidence to show monopoly power in any market. We decline to adopt such a rule now.

Even if we were to require direct proof, moreover, Microsoft's behavior may well be sufficient to show the existence of monopoly power. Certainly, none of the conduct Microsoft points to--its investment in R&D and the relatively low price of Windows--is inconsistent with the possession of such power. Conclusions of Law, at 37. The R&D expenditures Microsoft points to are not simply for Windows, but for its entire company, which most likely does not possess a monopoly for all of its products. Moreover, because innovation can increase an already dominant market share and further delay the emergence of competition, even monopolists have reason to invest in R&D. Findings of Fact P 61. Microsoft's pricing behavior is similarly equivocal. The company claims only that it never charged the short-term profit-maximizing price for Windows. Faced with conflicting expert testimony, the District Court found that it could not accurately determine what this price would be. Id. P 65. In any event, the court found, a price lower than the short-term profit-maximizing price is not inconsistent with possession or improper use of monopoly power. Id. P P 65-66. Cf. *Berkey Photo, Inc. v. Eastman Kodak Co., 603 F.2d 263, 274 (2d Cir. 1979)* ("If monopoly power has been acquired or maintained through improper means, the fact that the power has not been used to extract [a monopoly price] provides no succor to the monopolist."). Microsoft never claims that it did not charge the longterm monopoly price. Micosoft does argue that the price of Windows is a fraction of the price of an Intel-compatible PC system and lower than that of rival operating systems, but these facts are not inconsistent with the District Court's finding that Microsoft has monopoly power. See Findings of Fact P 36 ("Intel-compatible PC operating systems other than Windows [would not] attract[ ] significant demand ... even if Micosoft held its prices substantially above the competitive level.").

More telling, the District Court found that some aspects of Microsoft's behavior are difficult to explain unless Windows is a monopoly product. For instance, according to the District Court, the company set the price of Windows without considering rivals' prices, Findings of Fact P 62, something a firm without a monopoly would have been unable to do. The District Court also found that Microsoft's pattern of exclusionary conduct could only be rational "if the firm knew that it possessed monopoly power." Conclusions of Law, at 37. It is to that conduct that we now turn.

B. Anticompetitive Conduct

As discussed above, having a monopoly does not by itself violate § 2. A firm violates § 2 only when it acquires or maintains, or attempts to acquire or maintain, a monopoly by engaging in exclusionary conduct "as distinguished from growth or development as a consequence of a superior product, business acumen, or historic accident." *Grinnell, 384 U.S. at 571;* see also *United States v. Aluminum Co. of Am., 148 F.2d 416, 430 (2d Cir. 1945)* (Hand, J.) ("The successful competitor, having been urged to compete, must not be turned upon when he wins.").

In this case, after concluding that Microsoft had monopoly power, the District Court held that Microsoft had violated § 2 by engaging in a variety of exclusionary acts (not including predatory pricing), to maintain its monopoly by preventing the effective distribution and use of products that might threaten that monopoly. Specifically, the District Court held Microsoft liable for: (1) the way in which it integrated IE into Windows; (2) its various dealings with Original Equipment Manufacturers ("OEMs"), Internet Access Providers ("IAPs"), Internet Content Providers ("ICPs"), Independent Software Vendors ("ISVs"), and Apple Computer; (3) its efforts to contain and to subvert Java technologies; and (4) its course of conduct as a whole. Upon appeal, Microsoft argues that it did not engage in any exclusionary conduct.

Whether any particular act of a monopolist is exclusionary, rather than merely a form of vigorous competition, can be difficult to discern: the means of illicit exclusion, like the means of legitimate competition, are myriad. The challenge for an antitrust court lies in stating a general rule for distinguishing between exclusionary acts, which reduce social welfare, and competitive acts, which increase it.

From a century of case law on monopolization under § 2, however, several principles do emerge. First, to be condemned as exclusionary, a monopolist's act must have an "anticompetitive effect." That is, it must harm the competitive process and thereby harm consumers. In contrast, harm to one or more competitors will not suffice. "The [Sherman Act] directs itself not against conduct which is competitive, even severely so, but against conduct which unfairly tends to destroy competition itself." *Spectrum Sports, Inc. v. McQuillan, 506 U.S. 447, (1993);* see also *Brooke Group Ltd. v. Brown & Williamson Tobacco Corp., 509 U.S. 209, 225 (1993)* ("Even an act of pure malice by one business competitor against another does not, without more, state a claim under the federal antitrust laws....").

Second, the plaintiff, on whom the burden of proof of course rests, must demonstrate that the monopolist's conduct indeed has the requisite anticompetitive effect. See generally *Brooke Group, 509 U.S. at 225-26.* In a case brought by a private plaintiff, the plaintiff must show that its injury is "of 'the type that the statute was intended to forestall,'" *Brunswick Corp. v. Pueblo Bowl-O-Mat, Inc., 429 U.S. 477, 487-88 (1977)*; no less in a case brought by the Government, it must demonstrate that the monopolist's conduct harmed competition, not just a competitor.

Third, if a plaintiff successfully establishes a prima facie case under § 2 by demonstrating anticompetitive effect, then the monopolist may proffer a "procompetitive justification" for its conduct. See *Eastman Kodak, 504 U.S. at 483.* If the monopolist asserts a procompetitive justification--a nonpretextual claim that its conduct is indeed a form of competition on the merits because it involves, for example, greater efficiency or enhanced consumer appeal--then the burden shifts back to the plaintiff to rebut that claim. Cf. *Capital Imaging Assocs., P.C. v. Mohawk Valley Med. Assocs., Inc., 996 F.2d 537, 543 (2d Cir. 1993).*

Fourth, if the monopolist's procompetitive justification stands unrebutted, then the plaintiff must demonstrate that the anticompetitive harm of the conduct outweighs the procompetitive benefit. In cases arising under § 1 of the Sherman Act, the courts routinely apply a similar balancing approach under the rubric of the "rule of reason." The source of the rule of reason is *Standard Oil Co. v. United States, 221 U.S. 1 (1911),* in which the Supreme Court used that term to describe the proper inquiry under both sections of the Act. See *id. at 61-62* ("When the second section [of the Sherman Act] is thus harmonized with ... the first, it becomes obvious that the criteria to be resorted to in any given case for the purpose of ascertaining whether violations of the section have been committed, is the rule of reason guided by the established law...."). As the Fifth Circuit more recently explained, "it is clear ... that the analysis under section 2 is similar to that under section 1 regardless whether the rule of reason label is applied...." *Mid-Texas Communications Sys., Inc. v. AT & T, 615 F.2d 1372, 1389 n.13 (5th Cir. 1980)* (citing *Byars v. Bluff City*

News Co., 609 F.2d 843, 860 (6th Cir. 1979)); see also *Cal. Computer Prods., Inc. v. IBM Corp., 613 F.2d 727, 737 (9th Cir. 1979).*

Finally, in considering whether the monopolist's conduct on balance harms competition and is therefore condemned as exclusionary for purposes of § 2, our focus is upon the effect of that conduct, not upon the intent behind it. Evidence of the intent behind the conduct of a monopolist is relevant only to the extent it helps us understand the likely effect of the monopolist's conduct. See, e.g., *Chicago Bd. of Trade v. United States, 246 U.S. 231, 238 (1918)* ("knowledge of intent may help the court to interpret facts and to predict consequences"); *Aspen Skiing Co. v. Aspen Highlands Skiing Corp., 472 U.S. 585, 603 (1985).*

With these principles in mind, we now consider Microsoft's objections to the District Court's holding that Microsoft violated § 2 of the Sherman Act in a variety of ways.

1. Licenses Issued to Original Equipment Manufacturers

The District Court condemned a number of provisions in Microsoft's agreements licensing Windows to OEMs, because it found that Microsoft's imposition of those provisions (like many of Microsoft's other actions at issue in this case) serves to reduce usage share of Netscape's browser and, hence, protect Microsoft's operating system monopoly. The reason market share in the browser market affects market power in the operating system market is complex, and warrants some explanation.

Browser usage share is important because, as we explained in Section II.A above, a browser (or any middleware product, for that matter) must have a critical mass of users in order to attract software developers to write applications relying upon the APIs it exposes, and away from the APIs exposed by Windows. Applications written to a particular browser's APIs, however, would run on any computer with that browser, regardless of the underlying operating system. "The overwhelming majority of consumers will only use a PC operating system for which there already exists a large and varied set of ... applications, and for which it seems relatively certain that new types of applications and new versions of existing applications will continue to be marketed...." Findings of Fact P 30. If a consumer could have access to the applications he desired--regardless of the operating system he uses--simply by installing a particular browser on his computer, then he would no longer feel compelled to select Windows in order to have access to those applications; he could select an operating system other than Windows based solely upon its quality and price. In other words, the market for operating systems would be competitive.

Therefore, Microsoft's efforts to gain market share in one market (browsers) served to meet the threat to Microsoft's monopoly in another market (operating systems) by keeping rival browsers from gaining the critical mass of users necessary to attract developer attention away from Windows as the platform for software development. Plaintiffs also argue that Microsoft's actions injured competition in the browser market--an argument we will examine below in relation to their specific claims that Microsoft attempted to monopolize the browser market and unlawfully tied its browser to its operating system so as to foreclose competition in the browser market. In evaluating the § 2 monopoly maintenance claim, however, our immediate concern is with the anticompetitive effect of Microsoft's conduct in preserving its monopoly in the operating system market.

In evaluating the restrictions in Microsoft's agreements licensing Windows to OEMs, we first consider whether plaintiffs have made out a prima facie case by demonstrating that the restrictions have an anticompetitive effect. In the next subsection, we conclude that plaintiffs have met this burden as to all the restrictions. We then consider Microsoft's proffered justifications for the restrictions and, for the most part, hold those justifications insufficient.

a. Anticompetitive effect of the license restrictions

The restrictions Microsoft places upon Original Equipment Manufacturers are of particular importance in determining browser usage share because having an OEM pre-install a browser on a computer is one of the two most cost-effective methods by far of distributing browsing software. (The other is bundling the browser with internet access software distributed by an IAP.) Findings of Fact P 145. The District Court found that the restrictions Microsoft imposed in licensing Windows to OEMs prevented many OEMs from distributing browsers other than IE. Conclusions of Law, at 39-40. In particular, the District Court condemned the license provisions prohibiting the OEMs from: (1) removing any desktop icons, folders, or "Start" menu entries; (2) altering the initial boot sequence; and (3) otherwise altering the appearance of the Windows desktop. Findings of Fact P 213.

The District Court concluded that the first license restriction--the prohibition upon the removal of desktop icons, folders, and Start menu entries--thwarts the distribution of a rival browser by preventing OEMs from removing visible means of user access to IE. Id. P 203. The OEMs cannot practically install a second browser in addition to IE, the court found, in part because "pre-installing more than one product in a given category ... can significantly increase an OEM's support costs, for the redundancy can lead to confusion among novice users." Id. P 159; see also id. P 217. That is, a certain number of novice computer users, seeing two browser icons, will wonder which to use when and will call the OEM's support line. Support calls are extremely expensive and, in the highly competitive original equipment market, firms have a strong incentive to minimize costs. Id. P 210.

Microsoft denies the "consumer confusion" story; it observes that some OEMs do install multiple browsers and that executives from two OEMs that do so denied any knowledge of consumers being confused by multiple icons....

Other testimony, however, supports the District Court's finding that fear of such confusion deters many OEMs from pre-installing multiple browsers.... Most telling, in presentations to OEMs, Microsoft itself represented that having only one icon in a particular category would be "less confusing for endusers." See Government's Trial Exhibit ("GX") 319 at MS98 0109453. Accordingly, we reject Microsoft's argument that we should vacate the District Court's Finding of Fact 159 as it relates to consumer confusion.

As noted above, the OEM channel is one of the two primary channels for distribution of browsers. By preventing OEMs from removing visible means of user access to IE, the license restriction prevents many OEMs from pre-installing a rival browser and, therefore, protects Microsoft's monopoly from the competition that middleware might otherwise present. Therefore, we conclude that the license restriction at issue is anticompetitive. We defer for the moment the question whether that anticompetitive effect is outweighed by Microsoft's proffered justifications.

The second license provision at issue prohibits OEMs from modifying the initial boot sequence--the process that occurs the first time a consumer turns on the computer. Prior to the imposition of that restriction, "among the programs that many OEMs inserted into the boot sequence were Internet sign-up procedures that encouraged users to choose from a list of IAPs assembled by the OEM." Findings of Fact P 210. Microsoft's prohibition on any alteration of the boot sequence thus prevents OEMs from using that process to promote the services of IAPs, many of which--at least at the time Microsoft imposed the restriction--used Navigator rather than IE in their internet access software. See id. P 212; GX 295, reprinted in 12 J.A. at 14533 (Upon learning of OEM practices including boot sequence modification, Microsoft's Chairman, Bill Gates, wrote: "Apparently a lot of OEMs are bundling non-Microsoft browsers and coming up with offerings together with [IAPs] that get displayed on their machines in a FAR more prominent way than MSN or our Internet browser."). Microsoft does not deny that the prohibition on modifying the boot sequence has the effect of decreasing competition against IE by preventing OEMs from promoting rivals' browsers. Because this prohibition has a substantial effect in protecting Microsoft's market power, and does so through a means other than competition on the merits, it is anticompetitive. Again the question whether the provision is nonetheless justified awaits later treatment.

Finally, Microsoft imposes several additional provisions that, like the prohibition on removal of icons, prevent OEMs from making various alterations to the desktop: Microsoft prohibits OEMs from causing any user interface other than the Windows desktop to launch automatically, from adding icons or folders different in size or shape from those supplied by Microsoft, and from using the "Active Desktop" feature to promote third-party brands. These restrictions impose significant costs upon the OEMs; prior to Microsoft's prohibiting the practice, many OEMs would change the appearance of the desktop in ways they found beneficial....

The dissatisfaction of the OEM customers does not, of course, mean the restrictions are anticompetitive. The anticompetitive effect of the license restrictions is, as Microsoft itself recognizes, that OEMs are not able to promote rival browsers, which keeps developers focused upon the APIs in Windows. Findings of Fact P 212 (quoting Microsoft's Gates as writing, "winning Internet browser share is a very very important goal for us," and emphasizing the need to prevent OEMs from promoting both rival browsers and IAPs that might use rivals' browsers); see also 01/13/99 Tr. at 305-06 (excerpts from deposition of James Von Holle of Gateway) (prior to restriction Gateway had pre-installed non-IE internet registration icon that was larger than other desktop icons). This kind of promotion is not a zero-sum game; but for the restrictions in their licenses to use Windows, OEMs could promote multiple IAPs and browsers. By preventing the OEMs from doing so, this type of license restriction, like the first two restrictions, is anticompetitive: Microsoft reduced rival browsers' usage share not by improving its own product but, rather, by preventing OEMs from taking actions that could increase rivals' share of usage.

b. Microsoft's justifications for the license restrictions

Microsoft argues that the license restrictions are legally justified because, in imposing them, Microsoft is simply "exercising its rights as the holder of valid copyrights." Appellant's Opening Br. at 102. Microsoft also argues that the licenses "do not unduly restrict the opportunities of Netscape to distribute Navigator in any event." Id.

Microsoft's primary copyright argument borders upon the frivolous. The company claims an absolute and unfettered right to use its intellectual property as it wishes: "If intellectual property rights have been lawfully acquired," it says, then "their subsequent exercise cannot give rise to antitrust liability. Appellant's Opening Br. at 105. That is no more correct than the proposition that use of one's personal property, such as a baseball bat, cannot give rise to tort liability. As the Federal Circuit succinctly stated: "Intellectual property rights do not confer a privilege to violate the antitrust laws." *In re Indep. Serv. Orgs. Antitrust Litig., 203 F.3d 1322, 1325 (Fed. Cir. 2000).*

Although Microsoft never overtly retreats from its bold and incorrect position on the law, it also makes two arguments to the effect that it is not exercising its copyright in an unreasonable manner, despite the anticompetitive consequences of the license restrictions discussed above. In the first variation upon its unqualified copyright defense, Microsoft cites two cases indicating that a copyright holder may limit a licensee's ability to engage in significant and deleterious alterations of a copyrighted work. See *Gilliam v. ABC, 538 F.2d 14, 21 (2d Cir. 1976); WGN Cont'l Broad. Co. v. United Video, Inc., 693 F.2d 622, 625 (7th Cir. 1982).* The relevance of those two cases for the present one is limited, however, both because those cases involved substantial alterations of a copyrighted work, see *Gilliam, 538 F.2d at 18,* and because in neither case was there any claim that the copyright holder was, in asserting its rights, violating the antitrust laws, see *WGN Cont'l Broad., 693 F.2d at 626;* see also *Cmty. for Creative Non-Violence v. Reid, 846 F.2d 1485, 1498 (D.C. Cir. 1988)* (noting, again in a context free of any antitrust concern, that "an author [ ] may have rights against" a licensee that "excessively mutilated or altered" the copyrighted work).

The only license restriction Microsoft seriously defends as necessary to prevent a "substantial alteration" of its copyrighted work is the prohibition on OEMs automatically launching a substitute user interface upon completion of the boot process. See Findings of Fact P 211 ("[A] few large OEMs developed programs that ran automatically at the conclusion of a new PC system's first boot sequence. These programs replaced the Windows desktop either with a user interface designed by the OEM or with Navigator's user interface."). We agree that a shell that automatically prevents the Windows desktop from ever being seen by the user is a drastic alteration of Microsoft's copyrighted work, and outweighs the marginal anticompetitive effect of prohibiting the OEMs from substituting a different interface automatically upon completion of the initial boot process. We therefore hold that this particular restriction is not an exclusionary practice that violates § 2 of the Sherman Act.

In a second variation upon its copyright defense, Microsoft argues that the license restrictions merely prevent OEMs from taking actions that would reduce substantially the value of Microsoft's copyrighted work: that is, Microsoft claims each license restriction in question is necessary to prevent OEMs from so altering Windows as to undermine "the principal value of Windows as a stable and consistent platform that supports a broad range of applications and that is familiar to users." Appellant's Opening Br. at 102. Microsoft, however, never substantiates this claim, and, because an OEM's altering the appearance of the desktop or promoting programs in the boot sequence does not affect the code already in the product, the practice does not self-evidently affect either the "stability" or the "consistency" of the platform. See Conclusions of Law, at 41; Findings of Fact P 227. Microsoft cites only one item of evidence in support of its claim that the OEMs' alterations were decreasing the value of Windows. Defendant's Trial Exhibit ("DX") 2395 at MSV0009378A, reprinted in 19 J.A. at 12575. That document, prepared by Microsoft itself, states: "there are quality issues created by OEMs who are too liberal with the pre-install process," referring to the OEMs' installation of Windows and additional software on their PCs, which the document says may result in "user concerns and confusion." To the extent the OEMs' modifications cause consumer confusion, of course, the OEMs bear the additional support costs. See Findings of Fact P 159. Therefore, we conclude Microsoft has not shown that the OEMs' liberality reduces the value of Windows except in the sense that their promotion of rival browsers undermines Microsoft's monopoly--and that is not a permissible justification for the license restrictions.

Apart from copyright, Microsoft raises one other defense of the OEM license agreements: It argues that, despite the restrictions in the OEM license, Netscape is not completely blocked from distributing its product. That claim is insufficient to shield Microsoft from liability for those restrictions because, although Microsoft did not bar its rivals from all means of distribution, it did bar them from the cost-efficient ones.

In sum, we hold that with the exception of the one restriction prohibiting automatically launched alternative interfaces, all the OEM license restrictions at issue represent uses of Microsoft's market power to protect its monopoly, unredeemed by any legitimate justification. The restrictions therefore violate § 2 of the Sherman Act.

2. Integration of IE and Windows

Although Microsoft's license restrictions have a significant effect in closing rival browsers out of one of the two primary channels of distribution, the District Court found that "Microsoft's executives believed ... its contractual restrictions placed on OEMs would not be sufficient in themselves to reverse the direction of Navigator's usage share. Consequently, in late 1995 or early 1996, Microsoft set out to bind [IE] more tightly to Windows 95 as a technical matter." Findings of Fact P 160.

Technologically binding IE to Windows, the District Court found, both prevented OEMs from pre-installing other browsers and deterred consumers from using them. In particular, having the IE software code as an irremovable part of Windows meant that pre-installing a second browser would "increase an OEM's product testing costs," because an OEM must test and train its support staff to answer calls related to every software product preinstalled on the machine; moreover, pre-installing a browser in addition to IE would to many OEMs be "a questionable use of the scarce and valuable space on a PC's hard drive." Id. P 159.

Although the District Court, in its Conclusions of Law, broadly condemned Microsoft's decision to bind "Internet Explorer to Windows with ... technological shackles," Conclusions of Law, at 39, its findings of fact in support of that conclusion center upon three specific actions Microsoft took to weld IE to Windows: excluding IE from the "Add/Remove Programs" utility; designing Windows so as in certain circumstances to override the user's choice of a default browser other than IE; and commingling code related to browsing and other code in the same files, so that any attempt to delete the files containing IE would, at the same time, cripple the operating system. As with the license restrictions, we consider first whether the suspect actions had an anticompetitive effect, and then whether Microsoft has provided a procompetitive justification for them.

a. Anticompetitive effect of integration

As a general rule, courts are properly very skeptical about claims that competition has been harmed by a dominant firm's product design changes. See, e.g., *Foremost Pro Color, Inc. v. Eastman Kodak Co., 703 F.2d 534, 544-45 (9th Cir. 1983).* In a competitive market, firms routinely innovate in the hope of appealing to consumers, sometimes in the process making their products incompatible with those of rivals; the imposition of liability when a monopolist does the same thing will inevitably deter a certain amount of innovation. This is all the more true in a market, such as this one, in which the product itself is rapidly changing. See Findings of Fact P 59. Judicial deference to product innovation, however, does not mean that a monopolist's product design decisions are per se lawful. See *Foremost Pro Color, 703 F.2d at 545;* see also *Cal. Computer Prods., 613 F.2d at 739, 744; In re IBM Peripheral EDP Devices Antitrust Litig., 481 F. Supp. 965, 1007-08 (N.D. Cal. 1979).*

The District Court first condemned as anticompetitive Microsoft's decision to exclude IE from the "Add/Remove Programs" utility in Windows 98. Findings of Fact P 170. Microsoft had included IE in the Add/Remove Programs utility in Windows 95, see id. P P 175-76, but when it modified Windows 95 to produce Windows 98, it took IE out of the Add/Remove Programs utility. This change reduces the usage share of rival browsers not by making Microsoft's own browser more attractive to consumers but, rather, by discouraging OEMs from distributing rival products. See id. P 159. Because Microsoft's conduct, through something other than competition on the merits, has the effect of significantly reducing usage of rivals' products and hence protecting its own operating system monopoly, it is anticompetitive; we defer for the moment the question whether it is nonetheless justified.

Second, the District Court found that Microsoft designed Windows 98 "so that using Navigator on Windows 98 would have unpleasant consequences for users" by, in some circumstances, overriding the user's choice of a browser other than IE as his or her default browser. Id. PP 171-72. Plaintiffs argue that this override harms the competitive process by deterring consumers from using a browser other than IE even though they might prefer to do so, thereby reducing rival browsers' usage share and, hence, the ability of rival browsers to draw developer attention away from the APIs exposed by Windows. Microsoft does not deny, of course, that overriding the user's preference prevents some people from using other browsers. Because the override reduces rivals' usage share and protects Microsoft's monopoly, it too is anticompetitive.

Finally, the District Court condemned Microsoft's decision to bind IE to Windows 98 "by placing code specific to Web browsing in the same files as code that provided operating system functions." Id. P 161; see also id. P P 174, 192. Putting code supplying browsing functionality into a file with code supplying operating system functionality "ensures that the deletion of any file containing browsing-specific routines would also delete vital operating system routines and thus cripple Windows...." Id. P 164. As noted above, preventing an OEM from removing IE deters it from installing a second browser because doing so increases the OEM's product testing and support costs; by contrast, had OEMs been able to remove IE, they might have chosen to pre-install Navigator alone. See id. P 159.

Microsoft denies, as a factual matter, that it commingled browsing and non-browsing code, and it maintains the District Court's findings to the contrary are clearly erroneous. According to Microsoft, its expert "testified without contradiction that 'the very same code in Windows 98 that provides Web browsing functionality' also performs essential operating system functions--not code in the same files, but the very same software code." Appellant's Opening Br. at 79 (citing 5 J.A. 3291-92).

Microsoft's expert did not testify to that effect "without contradiction," however. A Government expert, Glenn Weadock, testified that Microsoft "designed [IE] so that some of the code that it uses co-resides in the same library files as other code needed for Windows." Direct Testimony P 30. Another Government expert likewise testified that one library file, SHDOCVW.DLL, "is really a bundle of separate functions. It contains some functions that have to do specifically with Web browsing, and it contains some general user interface functions as well." 12/14/98 am Tr. at 60-61 (trial testimony of Edward Felten), reprinted in 11 J.A. at 6953-54. One of Microsoft's own documents suggests as much. See Plaintiffs' Proposed Findings of Fact P 131.2.vii (citing GX 1686 (under seal) (Microsoft document indicating some functions in SHDOCVW.DLL can be described as "IE only," others can be described as "shell only" and still others can be described as providing both "IE" and "shell" functions)).

In view of the contradictory testimony in the record, some of which supports the District Court's finding that Microsoft commingled browsing and non-browsing code, we cannot conclude that the finding was clearly erroneous. See *Anderson v. City of Bessemer City, 470 U.S. 564, 573-74 (1985)* ("If the district court's account of the evidence is plausible in light of the record viewed in its entirety, the court of appeals may not reverse it even though convinced that had it been sitting as the trier of fact, it would have weighed the evidence differently."). Accordingly, we reject Microsoft's argument that we should vacate Finding of Fact 159 as it relates to the commingling of code, and we conclude that such commingling has an anticompetitive effect; as noted above, the commingling deters OEMs from pre-installing rival browsers, thereby reducing the rivals' usage share and, hence, developers' interest in rivals' APIs as an alternative to the API set exposed by Microsoft's operating system.

b. Microsoft's justifications for integration

Microsoft proffers no justification for two of the three challenged actions that it took in integrating IE into Windows--excluding IE from the Add/Remove Programs utility and commingling browser and operating system code. Although Microsoft does make some general claims regarding the benefits of integrating the browser and the operating system, see, e.g., Direct Testimony of James Allchin P 94, reprinted in 5 J.A. at 3321 ("Our vision of deeper levels of technical integration is highly efficient and provides substantial benefits to customers and developers."), it neither specifies nor substantiates those claims. Nor does it argue that either excluding IE from the Add/Remove Programs utility or commingling code achieves any integrative benefit. Plaintiffs plainly made out a prima facie case of harm to competition in the operating system market by demonstrating that Microsoft's actions increased its browser usage share and thus protected its operating system monopoly from a middleware threat and, for its part, Microsoft failed to meet its burden of showing that its conduct serves a purpose other than protecting its operating system monopoly. Accordingly, we hold that Microsoft's exclusion of IE from the Add/Remove Programs utility and its commingling of browser and operating system code constitute exclusionary conduct, in violation of § 2.

As for the other challenged act that Microsoft took in integrating IE into Windows--causing Windows to override the user's choice of a default browser in certain circumstances--Microsoft argues that it has "valid technical reasons." Specifically, Microsoft claims that it was necessary to design Windows to override the user's preferences when he or she invokes one of "a few" out "of the nearly 30 means of accessing the Internet." Appellant's Opening Br. at 82. According to Microsoft:

The Windows 98 Help system and Windows Update feature depend on ActiveX controls not supported by Navigator, and the now-discontinued Channel Bar utilized Microsoft's Channel Definition Format, which Navigator also did not support. Lastly, Windows 98 does not invoke Navigator if a user accesses the Internet through "My Computer" or "Windows Explorer" because doing so would defeat one of the purposes of those features--enabling users to move seamlessly from local storage devices to the Web in the same browsing window. Id. (internal citations omitted). The plaintiff bears the burden not only of rebutting a proffered justification but also of demonstrating that the anticompetitive effect of the challenged action outweighs it. In the District Court, plaintiffs appear to have done neither, let alone both; in any event, upon appeal, plaintiffs offer no rebuttal whatsoever. Accordingly, Microsoft may not be held liable for this aspect of its product design.

3. Agreements with Internet Access Providers

The District Court also condemned as exclusionary Microsoft's agreements with various IAPs. The IAPs include both Internet Service Providers, which offer consumers internet access, and Online Services ("OLSs") such as America Online ("AOL"), which offer proprietary content in addition to internet access and other services. Findings of Fact P 15. The District Court deemed Microsoft's agreements with the IAPs unlawful because:

> Microsoft licensed [IE] and the [IE] Access Kit [(of which, more below)] to hundreds of IAPs for no charge. [Findings of Fact] P P 250-51. Then, Microsoft extended valuable promotional treatment to the ten most important IAPs in exchange for their commitment to promote and distribute [IE] and to exile Navigator from the desktop. Id. P P 255-58, 261, 272, 288-90, 305-06. Finally, in exchange for efforts to upgrade existing subscribers to client software that came bundled with

[IE] instead of Navigator, Microsoft granted rebates--and in some cases made outright payments--to those same IAPs. Id. P P 259-60, 295. Conclusions of Law, at 41.

The District Court condemned Microsoft's actions in (1) offering IE free of charge to IAPs and (2) offering IAPs a bounty for each customer the IAP signs up for service using the IE browser. In effect, the court concluded that Microsoft is acting to preserve its monopoly by offering IE to IAPs at an attractive price. Similarly, the District Court held Microsoft liable for (3) developing the IE Access Kit ("IEAK"), a software package that allows an IAP to "create a distinctive identity for its service in as little as a few hours by customizing the [IE] title bar, icon, start and search pages," Findings of Fact P 249, and (4) offering the IEAK to IAPs free of charge, on the ground that those acts, too, helped Microsoft preserve its monopoly. Conclusions of Law, at 41-42. Finally, the District Court found that (5) Microsoft agreed to provide easy access to IAPs' services from the Windows desktop in return for the IAPs' agreement to promote IE exclusively and to keep shipments of internet access software using Navigator under a specific percentage, typically 25%. See Conclusions of Law, at 42 (citing Findings of Fact P P 258, 262, 289). We address the first four items--Microsoft's inducements--and then its exclusive agreements with IAPs.

Although offering a customer an attractive deal is the hallmark of competition, the Supreme Court has indicated that in very rare circumstances a price may be unlawfully low, or "predatory." See generally *Brooke Group, 509 U.S. at 220-27*. Plaintiffs argued before the District Court that Microsoft's pricing was indeed predatory; but instead of making the usual predatory pricing argument--that the predator would drive out its rivals by pricing below cost on a particular product and then, sometime in the future, raise its prices on that product above the competitive level in order to recoup its earlier losses--plaintiffs argued that by pricing below cost on IE (indeed, even paying people to take it), Microsoft was able simultaneously to preserve its stream of monopoly profits on Windows, thereby more than recouping its investment in below-cost pricing on IE. The District Court did not assign liability for predatory pricing, however, and plaintiffs do not press this theory on appeal.

The rare case of price predation aside, the antitrust laws do not condemn even a monopolist for offering its product at an attractive price, and we therefore have no warrant to condemn Microsoft for offering either IE or the IEAK free of charge or even at a negative price. Likewise, as we said above, a monopolist does not violate the Sherman Act simply by developing an attractive product. See *Grinnell, 384 U.S. at 571* ("Growth or development as a consequence of a superior product [or] business acumen" is no violation.). Therefore, Microsoft's development of the IEAK does not violate the Sherman Act.

We turn now to Microsoft's deals with IAPs concerning desktop placement. Microsoft concluded these exclusive agreements with all "the leading IAPs," Findings of Fact P 244, including the major OLSs. Id. P 245; see also id. P P 305, 306. The most significant of the OLS deals is with AOL, which, when the deal was reached, "accounted for a substantial portion of all existing Internet access subscriptions and ... attracted a very large percentage of new IAP subscribers." Id. P 272. Under that agreement Microsoft puts the AOL icon in the OLS folder on the Windows desktop and AOL does not promote any non-Microsoft browser, nor provide software using any non-Microsoft browser except at the customer's request, and even then AOL will not supply more than 15% of its subscribers with a browser other than IE. Id. P 289.

The Supreme Court most recently considered an antitrust challenge to an exclusive contract in *Tampa Electric Co. v. Nashville Coal Co., 365 U.S. 320 (1961).* That case, which involved a challenge to a requirements contract, was brought under § 3 of the Clayton Act and §§ 1 and 2 of the Sherman Act. The Court held that an exclusive contract does not violate the Clayton Act unless its probable effect is to "foreclose competition in a substantial share of the line of commerce affected." *Id. at 327.* The share of the market foreclosed is important because, for the contract to have an adverse effect upon competition, "the opportunities for other traders to enter into or remain in that market must be significantly limited." *Id. at 328.* Although "neither the Court of Appeals nor the District Court [had] considered in detail the question of the relevant market," *id. at 330,* the Court in Tampa Electric examined the record and, after defining the relevant market, determined that the contract affected less than one percent of that market. *Id. at 333.* After concluding, under the Clayton Act, that this share was "conservatively speaking, quite insubstantial," id., the Court went on summarily to reject the Sherman Act claims. *Id. at 335* ("If [the contract] does not fall within the broader prescription of § 3 of the Clayton Act it follows that it is not forbidden by those of the [Sherman Act].").

Following Tampa Electric, courts considering antitrust challenges to exclusive contracts have taken care to identify the share of the market foreclosed. Some courts have indicated that § 3 of the Clayton Act and § 1 of the Sherman Act require an equal degree of foreclosure before prohibiting exclusive contracts. See, e.g., *Roland Mach. Co. v. Dresser Indus., Inc., 749 F.2d 380, 393 (7th Cir. 1984)* (Posner, J.). Other courts, however, have held that a higher market share must be foreclosed in order to establish a violation of the Sherman Act as compared to the Clayton Act. See, e.g., *Barr Labs. v. Abbott Labs., 978 F.2d 98, 110 (3d Cir. 1992);* 11 HERBERT HOVENKAMP, ANTITRUST LAW P 1800c4 (1998) ("The cases are divided, with a likely majority stating that the Clayton Act requires a smaller showing of anticompetitive effects.").

Though what is "significant" may vary depending upon the antitrust provision under which an exclusive deal is challenged, it is clear that in all cases the plaintiff must both define the relevant market and prove the degree of foreclosure. This is a prudential requirement; exclusivity provisions in contracts may serve many useful purposes. See, e.g., *Omega Envtl., Inc. v. Gilbarco, Inc., 127 F.3d 1157, 1162 (9th Cir. 1997)* ("There are, however, well-recognized economic benefits to exclusive dealing arrangements, including the enhancement of interbrand competition."); *Barry Wright Corp. v. ITT Grinnell Corp., 724 F.2d 227, 236 (1st Cir. 1983)* (Breyer, J.) ("Virtually every contract to buy 'forecloses' or 'excludes' alternative sellers from some portion of the market, namely the portion consisting of what was bought."). Permitting an antitrust action to proceed any time a firm enters into an exclusive deal would both discourage a presumptively legitimate business practice and encourage costly antitrust actions. Because an exclusive deal affecting a small fraction of a market clearly cannot have the requisite harmful effect upon competition, the requirement of a significant degree of foreclosure serves a useful screening function. Cf. Frank H. Easterbrook, The Limits of Antitrust, *63 TEX. L. REV. 1, 21-23 (1984)* (discussing use of presumptions in antitrust law to screen out cases in which loss to consumers and economy is likely outweighed by cost of inquiry and risk of deterring procompetitive behavior).

In this case, plaintiffs challenged Microsoft's exclusive dealing arrangements with the IAPs under both §§ 1 and 2 of the Sherman Act. The District Court, in analyzing the § 1 claim, stated, "unless the evidence demonstrates that Microsoft's agreements excluded Netscape altogether from access to roughly forty percent of the browser market, the Court should decline to find such agreements in violation of § 1." Conclusions of Law, at 52. The court recognized that Microsoft had substantially excluded Netscape from "the most efficient channels for Navigator to achieve browser usage share," *id. at 53;* see also Findings of Fact P 145 ("No other distribution channel for browsing software even approaches the efficiency of OEM pre-installation and IAP bundling."), and had relegated it to more costly and less effective methods (such as mass mailing its browser on a disk or offering it for download over the internet); but because Microsoft has not "completely excluded Netscape" from reaching any potential user by some means of distribution, however ineffective, the court concluded the agreements do not violate § 1. Conclusions of Law, at 53. Plaintiffs did not cross-appeal this holding.

Turning to § 2, the court stated: "the fact that Microsoft's arrangements with various [IAPs and other] firms did not foreclose enough of the relevant market to constitute a § 1 violation in no way detracts from the Court's assignment of liability for the same arrangements under § 2.... All of Microsoft's agreements, including the non-exclusive ones, severely restricted Netscape's access to those distribution channels leading most efficiently to the acquisition of browser usage share." Conclusions of Law, at 53.

On appeal Microsoft argues that "courts have applied the same standard to alleged exclusive dealing agreements under both Section 1 and Section 2," Appellant's Opening Br. at 109, and it argues that the District Court's holding of no liability under § 1 necessarily precludes holding it liable under § 2. The District Court appears to have based its holding with respect to § 1 upon a "total exclusion test" rather than the 40% standard drawn from the caselaw. Even assuming the holding is correct, however, we nonetheless reject Microsoft's contention.

The basic prudential concerns relevant to §§ 1 and 2 are admittedly the same: exclusive contracts are commonplace-particularly in the field of distribution--in our competitive, market economy, and imposing upon a firm with market power the risk of an antitrust suit every time it enters into such a contract, no matter how small the effect, would create an unacceptable and unjustified burden upon any such firm. At the same time, however, we agree with plaintiffs that a monopolist's use of exclusive contracts, in certain circumstances, may give rise to a § 2 violation even though the contracts foreclose less than the roughly 40% or 50% share usually required in order to establish a § 1 violation. See generally Dennis W. Carlton, A General Analysis of Exclusionary Conduct and Refusal to Deal--Why Aspen and Kodak Are Misguided, *68 ANTITRUST L.J. 659 (2001)* (explaining various scenarios under which exclusive dealing, particularly by a dominant firm, may raise legitimate concerns about harm to competition).

In this case, plaintiffs allege that, by closing to rivals a substantial percentage of the available opportunities for browser distribution, Microsoft managed to preserve its monopoly in the market for operating systems. The IAPs constitute one of the two major channels by which browsers can be distributed. Findings of Fact P 242. Microsoft has exclusive deals with "fourteen of the top fifteen access providers in North America[, which] account for a large majority of all Internet access subscriptions in this part of the world." Id. P 308. By ensuring that the "majority" of all IAP subscribers are offered IE either as the default browser or as the only browser, Microsoft's deals with the IAPs clearly have a significant effect in preserving its monopoly; they help keep usage of Navigator below the critical level necessary for Navigator or any other rival to pose a real threat to Microsoft's monopoly. See, e.g., id. P 143 (Microsoft sought to "divert enough browser usage from Navigator to neutralize it as a platform."); see also Carlton, at 670.

Plaintiffs having demonstrated a harm to competition, the burden falls upon Microsoft to defend its exclusive dealing contracts with IAPs by providing a procompetitive justification for them. Significantly, Microsoft's only explanation for its exclusive dealing is that it wants to keep developers focused upon its APIs--which is to say, it wants to preserve its power in the operating system market. 02/26/01 Ct. Appeals Tr. at 45-47. That is not an unlawful end, but neither is it a procompetitive justification for the specific means here in question, namely exclusive dealing contracts with IAPs. Accordingly, we affirm the District Court's decision holding that Microsoft's exclusive contracts with IAPs are exclusionary devices, in violation of § 2 of the Sherman Act.

4. Dealings with Internet Content Providers, Independent Software Vendors, and Apple Computer

The District Court held that Microsoft engages in exclusionary conduct in its dealings with ICPs, which develop websites; ISVs, which develop software; and Apple, which is both an OEM and a software developer. See Conclusions of Law, at 42-43 (deals with ICPs, ISVs, and Apple "supplemented Microsoft's efforts in the OEM and IAP channels"). The District Court condemned Microsoft's deals with ICPs and ISVs, stating: "By granting ICPs and ISVs free licenses to bundle [IE] with their offerings, and by exchanging other valuable inducements for their agreement to distribute, promote[,] and rely on [IE] rather than Navigator, Microsoft directly induced developers to focus on its own APIs rather than ones exposed by Navigator." Id. (citing Findings of Fact P P 334-35, 340).

With respect to the deals with ICPs, the District Court's findings do not support liability. After reviewing the ICP agreements, the District Court specifically stated that "there is not sufficient evidence to support a finding that Microsoft's promotional restrictions actually had a substantial, deleterious impact on Navigator's usage share." Findings of Fact P 332. Because plaintiffs failed to demonstrate that Microsoft's deals with the ICPs have a substantial effect upon competition, they have not proved the violation of the Sherman Act.

As for Microsoft's ISV agreements, however, the District Court did not enter a similar finding of no substantial effect. The District Court described Microsoft's deals with ISVs as follows:

> In dozens of "First Wave" agreements signed between the fall of 1997 and the spring of 1998, Microsoft has promised to give preferential support, in the form of early Windows 98 and Windows NT betas, other technical information, and the right to use certain Microsoft seals of approval, to important ISVs that agree to certain conditions. One of these conditions is that the ISVs use Internet Explorer as the default browsing software for any software they develop with a hypertext-based user interface. Another condition is that the ISVs use Microsoft's "HTML Help," which is accessible only with Internet Explorer, to implement their applications' help systems.

Id. P 339. The District Court further found that the effect of these deals is to "ensure [ ] that many of the most popular Web-centric applications will rely on browsing technologies found only in Windows," id. P 340, and that Microsoft's deals with ISVs therefore "increase[ ] the likelihood that the millions of consumers using [applications designed by ISVs that entered into agreements with Microsoft] will use Internet Explorer rather than Navigator." Id. P 340.

The District Court did not specifically identify what share of the market for browser distribution the exclusive deals with the ISVs foreclose. Although the ISVs are a relatively small channel for browser distribution, they take on greater significance because, as discussed above, Microsoft] had largely foreclosed the two primary channels to its rivals. In that light, one can tell from the record that by affecting the applications used by "millions" of consumers, Microsoft's exclusive deals with the ISVs had a substantial effect in further foreclosing rival browsers from the market. (Data introduced by Microsoft, see Direct Testimony of Cameron Myhrvold P 84, reprinted in 6 J.A. at 3922-23, and subsequently relied upon by the District Court in its findings, see, e.g., Findings of Fact P 270, indicate that over the two-year period 1997-98, when Microsoft entered into the First Wave agreements, there were 40 million new users of the internet.) Because, by keeping rival browsers from gaining widespread distribution (and potentially attracting the attention of developers away from the APIs in Windows), the deals have a substantial effect in preserving Microsoft's monopoly, we hold that plaintiffs have made a prima facie showing that the deals have an anticompetitive effect.

Of course, that Microsoft's exclusive deals have the anticompetitive effect of preserving Microsoft's monopoly does not, in itself, make them unlawful. A monopolist, like a competitive firm, may have a perfectly legitimate reason for wanting an exclusive arrangement with its distributors. Accordingly, Microsoft had an opportunity to, but did not, present the District Court with evidence demonstrating that the exclusivity provisions have some such procompetitive justification. See Conclusions of Law, at 43 (citing Findings of Fact P P 339-40) ("With respect to the ISV agreements, Microsoft has put forward no procompetitive business ends whatsoever to justify their exclusionary terms."). On appeal Microsoft likewise does not claim that the exclusivity required by the deals serves any legitimate purpose; instead, it states only that its ISV agreements reflect an attempt "to persuade ISVs to utilize Internet-related system services in Windows rather than Navigator." Appellant's Opening Br. at 114. As we explained before, however, keeping developers focused upon Windows--that is, preserving the Windows monopoly-is a competitively neutral goal. Microsoft having offered no procompetitive justification for its exclusive dealing arrangements with the ISVs, we hold that those arrangements violate § 2 of the Sherman Act.

Finally, the District Court held that Microsoft's dealings with Apple violated the Sherman Act. See Conclusions of Law, at 42-43. Apple is vertically integrated: it makes both software (including an operating system, Mac OS), and hardware (the Macintosh line of computers). Microsoft primarily makes software, including, in addition to its operating system, a number of popular applications. One, called "Office," is a suite of business productivity applications that Microsoft has ported to Mac OS. The District Court found that "ninety percent of Mac OS users running a suite of office productivity applications [use] Microsoft's Mac Office." Findings of Fact P 344. Further, the District Court found that:

> In 1997, Apple's business was in steep decline, and many doubted that the company would survive much longer.... Many ISVs questioned the wisdom of continuing to spend time and money developing applications for the Mac OS. Had Microsoft announced in the midst of this atmosphere that it was ceasing to develop new versions of Mac Office, a great number of ISVs, customers, developers, and investors would have interpreted the announcement as Apple's death notice.

Id. P 344. Microsoft recognized the importance to Apple of its continued support of Mac Office. See id. P 347 (quoting internal Microsoft e-mail) ("[We] need a way to push these guys[, i.e., Apple] and [threatening to cancel Mac Office] is the only one that seems to make them move."); see also id. ("[Microsoft Chairman Bill] Gates asked whether Microsoft could conceal from Apple in the coming month the fact that Microsoft was almost finished developing Mac Office 97."); id. at P 354 ("I think ... Apple should be using [IE] everywhere and if they don't do it, then we can use Office as a club.").

In June 1997 Microsoft Chairman Bill Gates determined that the company's negotiations with Apple " 'have not been going well at all.... Apple let us down on the browser by making Netscape the standard install.' Gates then reported that he had already called Apple's CEO ... to ask 'how we should announce the cancellation of Mac Office....' " Id. at P 349. The District Court further found that, within a month of Gates' call, Apple and Microsoft had reached an agreement pursuant to which

> Microsoft's primary obligation is to continue releasing up-to-date versions of Mac Office for at least five years.... [and] Apple has agreed ... to "bundle the most current version of [IE] ... with [Mac OS]"... [and to] "make [IE] the default [browser]".... Navigator is not installed on the computer hard drive during the default installation, which is the type of installation most users elect to employ.... [The] Agreement further provides that ... Apple may not position icons for non-Microsoft browsing software on the desktop of new Macintosh

PC systems or Mac OS upgrades.

Id. P P 350-52. The agreement also prohibits Apple from encouraging users to substitute another browser for IE, and states that Apple will "encourage its employees to use [IE]." Id. P 352.

This exclusive deal between Microsoft and Apple has a substantial effect upon the distribution of rival browsers. If a browser developer ports its product to a second operating system, such as the Mac OS, it can continue to display a common set of APIs. Thus, usage share, not the underlying operating system, is the primary determinant of the platform challenge a browser may pose. Pre-installation of a browser (which can be accomplished either by including the browser with the operating system or by the OEM installing] the browser) is one of the two most important methods of browser distribution, and Apple had a not insignificant share of worldwide sales of operating systems. See id. P 35 (Microsoft has 95% of the market not counting Apple and "well above" 80% with Apple included in the relevant market). Because Microsoft's exclusive contract with Apple has a substantial effect in restricting distribution of rival browsers, and because (as we have described several times above) reducing usage share of rival browsers serves to protect Microsoft's monopoly, its deal with Apple must be regarded as anticompetitive. See Conclusions of Law, at 42 (citing Findings of Fact P 356) ("By extracting from Apple terms that significantly diminished the usage of Navigator on the Mac OS, Microsoft helped to ensure that developers would not view Navigator as truly cross-platform middleware.").

Microsoft offers no procompetitive justification for the exclusive dealing arrangement. It makes only the irrelevant claim that the IE-for-Mac Office deal is part of a multifaceted set of agreements between itself and Apple, see Appellant's Opening Br. at 61 ("Apple's 'browsing software' obligation was [not] the quid pro quo for Microsoft's Mac Office obligation[;] ... all of the various obligations ... were part of one 'overall agreement' between the two companies."); that does not mean it has any procompetitive justification. Accordingly, we hold that the exclusive deal with Apple is exclusionary, in violation of § 2 of the Sherman Act.

5. Java

Java, a set of technologies* developed by Sun Microsystems, is another type of middleware posing a potential threat to Windows' position as the ubiquitous platform for software development. Findings of Fact P 28. The Java technologies include: (1) a programming language; (2) a set of programs written in that language, called the "Java class libraries," which expose APIs; (3) a compiler, which translates code written by a developer into "bytecode"; and (4) a Java Virtual Machine ("JVM"), which translates bytecode into instructions to the operating system. Id. P 73. Programs calling upon the Java APIs will run on any machine with a "Java runtime environment," that is, Java class libraries and a JVM. Id. P P 73, 74.

In May 1995 Netscape agreed with Sun to distribute a copy of the Java runtime environment with every copy of Navigator, and "Navigator quickly became the principal vehicle by which Sun placed copies of its Java runtime environment on the PC systems of Windows users." Id. P 76. Microsoft, too, agreed to promote the Java technologies--or so it seemed. For at the same time, Microsoft took steps "to maximize the difficulty with which applications written in Java could be ported from Windows to other platforms, and vice versa." Conclusions of Law, at 43. Specifically, the District Court found that Microsoft took four steps to exclude Java from developing as a viable cross-platform threat: (a) designing a JVM incompatible with the one developed by Sun; (b) entering into contracts, the so-called "First Wave Agreements," requiring major ISVs to promote Microsoft's JVM exclusively; (c) deceiving Java developers about the Windows-specific nature of the tools it distributed to them; and (d) coercing Intel to stop aiding Sun in improving the Java technologies.

a. The incompatible JVM

The District Court held that Microsoft engaged in exclusionary conduct by developing and promoting its own JVM. Conclusions of Law, at 43-44. Sun had already developed a JVM for the Windows operating system when Microsoft began work on its version. The JVM developed by Microsoft allows Java applications to run faster on Windows than does Sun's JVM, Findings of Fact P 389, but a Java application designed to work with Microsoft's JVM does not work with Sun's JVM and vice versa. Id. P 390. The District Court found that Microsoft "made a large investment of engineering resources to develop a high-performance Windows JVM," id. P 396, and, "by bundling its ... JVM with every copy of [IE] ... Microsoft endowed its Java runtime environment with the unique attribute of guaranteed, enduring ubiquity across the enormous Windows installed base," id. P 397. As explained above, however, a monopolist does not violate the antitrust laws simply by developing a product that is incompatible with those of its rivals. See supra Section II.B.1. In order to violate the antitrust laws, the incompatible product must have an anticompetitive effect that outweighs any procompetitive justification for the design. Microsoft's JVM is not only incompatible with Sun's, it allows Java applications to run faster on Windows than does Sun's JVM. Microsoft's faster JVM lured Java developers into using Microsoft's developer tools, and Microsoft offered those tools deceptively, as we discuss below. The JVM, however, does allow applications to run more swiftly and does not itself have any anticompetitive effect. Therefore, we reverse the District Court's imposition of liability for Microsoft's development and promotion of its JVM.

b. The First Wave Agreements

The District Court also found that Microsoft entered into First Wave Agreements with dozens of ISVs to use Microsoft's JVM. See Findings of Fact P 401 ("In exchange for costly technical support and other blandishments, Microsoft induced dozens of important ISVs to make their Java applications reliant on Windows-specific technologies and to refrain from distributing to Windows users JVMs that complied with Sun's standards."). Again, we reject the District Court's condemnation of low but non-predatory pricing by Microsoft.

To the extent Microsoft's First Wave Agreements with the ISVs conditioned receipt of Windows technical information upon the ISVs' agreement to promote Microsoft's JVM exclusively, they raise a different competitive concern. The District Court found that, although not literally exclusive, the deals were exclusive in practice because they required developers to make Microsoft's JVM the default in the software they developed. Id. P 401.

While the District Court did not enter precise findings as to the effect of the First Wave Agreements upon the overall distribution of rival JVMs, the record indicates that Microsoft's deals with the major ISVs had a significant effect upon JVM promotion. As discussed above, the products of First Wave ISVs reached millions of consumers. Id. P 340. The First Wave ISVs included such prominent developers as Rational Software, see GX 970, reprinted in 15 J.A. at 9994-10000, "a world leader" in software development tools, see Direct Testimony of Michael Devlin P 2, reprinted in 5 J.A. at 3520, and Symantec, see GX 2071, reprinted in 22 J.A. at 14960-66 (sealed), which, according to Microsoft itself, is "the leading supplier of utilities such as anti-virus software," Defendant's Proposed Findings of Fact P 276, reprinted in 3 J.A. at 1689. Moreover, Microsoft's exclusive deals with the leading ISVs took place against a backdrop of foreclosure: the District Court found that "when Netscape announced in May 1995] [prior to Microsoft's execution of the First Wave Agreements] that it would include with every copy of Navigator a copy of a Windows JVM that complied with Sun's standards, it appeared that Sun's Java implementation would achieve the necessary ubiquity on Windows." Findings of Fact P 394. As discussed above, however, Microsoft undertook a number of anticompetitive actions that seriously reduced the distribution of Navigator, and the District Court found that those actions thereby seriously impeded distribution of Sun's JVM. Conclusions of Law, at 43-44. Because Microsoft's agreements foreclosed a substantial portion of thc field for JVM distribution and because, in so doing, they protected Microsoft's monopoly from a middleware threat, they are anticompetitive.

Microsoft offered no procompetitive justification for the default clause that made the First Wave Agreements exclusive as a practical matter. See Findings of Fact P 401. Because the cumulative effect of the deals is anticompetitive and because Microsoft has no procompetitive justification for them, we hold that the provisions in the First Wave Agreements requiring use of Microsoft's JVM as the default are exclusionary, in violation of the Sherman Act.

c. Deception of Java developers

Microsoft's "Java implementation" included, in addition to a JVM, a set of software development tools it created to assist ISVs in designing Java applications. The District Court found that, not only were these tools incompatible with Sun's cross-platform aspirations for Java--no violation, to be sure-but Microsoft deceived Java developers regarding the Windows-specific nature of the tools. Microsoft's tools included "certain 'keywords' and 'compiler directives' that could only be executed properly by Microsoft's version of the Java runtime environment for Windows." Id. P 394; see also Direct Testimony of James Gosling P 58, reprinted in 21 J.A. at 13959 (Microsoft added "programming instructions ... that alter the behavior of the code."). As a result, even Java "developers who were opting for portability over performance ... unwittingly [wrote] Java applications that [ran] only on Windows." Conclusions of Law, at 43. That is, developers who relied upon Microsoft's public commitment to cooperate with Sun and who used Microsoft's tools to develop what Microsoft led them to believe were cross-platform] applications ended up producing applications that would run only on the Windows operating system.

When specifically accused by a PC Week reporter of fragmenting Java standards so as to prevent cross-platform uses, Microsoft denied the accusation and indicated it was only "adding rich platform support" to what remained a crossplatform implementation. An e-mail message internal to Microsoft, written shortly after the conversation with the reporter, shows otherwise:

> Ok, i just did a followup call.... [The reporter] liked that i kept pointing customers to w3c standards [(commonly observed internet protocols)].... [but] he accused us of being schizo with this vs. our java approach, i said he misunderstood [--] that [with Java] we are merely trying to add rich platform support to an interop layer.... this plays well.... at this point its [sic] not good to create MORE noise around our win32 java classes. instead we should just quietly grow j [(Microsoft's development tools)] share and assume that people will take more advantage of our classes without ever realizing they are building win 32-only java apps.

GX 1332, reprinted in 22 J.A. at 14922-23.

Finally, other Microsoft documents confirm that Microsoft intended to deceive Java developers, and predicted that the effect of its actions would be to generate Windows-dependent Java applications that their developers believed would be cross-platform; these documents also indicate that Microsoft's ultimate objective was to thwart Java's threat to Microsoft's monopoly in the market for operating systems. One Microsoft document, for example, states as a strategic goal: "Kill cross-platform Java by growing the polluted Java market." GX 259, reprinted in 22 J.A. at 14514; see also id. ("Cross-platform capability is by far the number one reason for choosing/using Java.") (emphasis in original).

Microsoft's conduct related to its Java developer tools served to protect its monopoly of the operating system in a manner not attributable either to the superiority of the operating system or to the acumen of its makers, and therefore was anticompetitive. Unsurprisingly, Microsoft offers no procompetitive explanation for its campaign to deceive developers. Accordingly, we conclude this conduct is exclusionary, in violation of § 2 of the Sherman Act.

d. The threat to Intel

The District Court held that Microsoft also acted unlawfully with respect to Java by using its "monopoly power to prevent firms such as Intel from aiding in the creation of cross-platform interfaces." Conclusions of Law, at 43. In 1995 Intel was in the process of developing a highperformance, Windows-compatible JVM. Microsoft wanted Intel to abandon that effort because a fast, cross-platform JVM would threaten Microsoft's monopoly in the operating system market. At an August 1995 meeting, Microsoft's Gates told Intel that its "cooperation with Sun and Netscape to develop a Java runtime environment ... was one of the issues threatening to undermine cooperation between Intel and Microsoft." Findings of Fact P 396. Three months later, "Microsoft's Paul Maritz told a senior Intel executive that Intel's [adaptation of its multimedia software to comply with] Sun's Java standards was as inimical to Microsoft as Microsoft's support for non-Intel microprocessors would be to Intel." Id. P 405.

Intel nonetheless continued to undertake initiatives related to Java. By 1996 "Intel had developed a JVM designed to run well ... while complying with Sun's cross-platform standards." Id. P 396. In April of that year, Microsoft again urged Intel not to help Sun by distributing Intel's fast, Suncompliant JVM. Id. And Microsoft threatened Intel that if it did not stop aiding Sun on the multimedia front, then Microsoft would refuse to distribute Intel technologies bundled with Windows. Id. P 404.

Intel finally capitulated in 1997, after Microsoft delivered the coup de grace.

One of Intel's competitors, called AMD, solicited support from Microsoft for its "3DX" technology.... Microsoft's Allchin asked Gates whether Microsoft should support 3DX, despite the fact that Intel would oppose it. Gates responded: "If Intel has a real problem with us supporting this then they will have to stop supporting Java Multimedia the way they are. I would gladly give up supporting this if they would back off from their work on JAVA." Id. P 406.

Microsoft's internal documents and deposition testimony confirm both the anticompetitive effect and intent of its actions. See, e.g., GX 235, reprinted in 22 J.A. at 14502 (Microsoft executive, Eric Engstrom, included among Microsoft's goals for Intel: "Intel to stop helping Sun create Java Multimedia APIs, especially ones that run well ... on Windows."); Deposition of Eric Engstrom at 179 ("We were successful [in convincing Intel to stop aiding Sun] for some period of time.").

Microsoft does not deny the facts found by the District Court, nor does it offer any procompetitive justification for pressuring Intel not to support cross-platform Java. Microsoft lamely characterizes its threat to Intel as "advice." The District Court, however, found that Microsoft's "advice" to Intel to stop aiding cross-platform Java was backed by the threat of retaliation, and this conclusion is supported by the evidence cited above. Therefore we affirm the conclusion that Microsoft's threats to Intel were exclusionary, in violation of § 2 of the Sherman Act.

6. Course of Conduct

The District Court held that, apart from Microsoft's specific acts, Microsoft was liable under § 2 based upon its general "course of conduct." In reaching this conclusion the court relied upon *Continental Ore Co. v. Union Carbide & Carbon Corp., 370 U.S. 690, 699 (1962),* where the Supreme Court stated, "in [Sherman Act cases], plaintiffs should be given the full benefit of their proof without tightly compartmentalizing the various factual components and wiping the slate clean after scrutiny of each."

Microsoft points out that Continental Ore and the other cases cited by plaintiffs in support of "course of conduct" liability all involve conspiracies among multiple firms, not the conduct of a single firm; in that setting the "course of conduct" is the conspiracy itself, for which all the participants may be held liable. Plaintiffs respond that, as a policy matter, a monopolist's unilateral "campaign of [acts intended to exclude a rival] that in the aggregate has the requisite impact" warrants liability even if the acts viewed individually would be lawful for want of a significant effect upon competition.

We need not pass upon plaintiffs' argument, however, because the District Court did not point to any series of acts, each of which harms competition only slightly but the cumulative effect of which is significant enough to form an independent basis for liability. The "course of conduct" section of the District Court's opinion contains, with one exception, only broad, summarizing conclusions. See, e.g., Conclusions of Law, at 44

("Microsoft placed an oppressive thumb on the scale of competitive fortune...."). The only specific acts to which the court refers are Microsoft's expenditures in promoting its browser, see id. ("Microsoft has expended wealth and foresworn opportunities to realize more...."), which we have explained are not in themselves unlawful. Because the District Court identifies no other specific acts as a basis for "course of conduct" liability, we reverse its conclusion that Microsoft's course of conduct separately violates § 2 of the Sherman Act.

C. Causation

As a final parry, Microsoft urges this court to reverse on the monopoly maintenance claim, because plaintiffs never established a causal link between Microsoft's anticompetitive conduct, in particular its foreclosure of Netscape's and Java's distribution channels, and the maintenance of Microsoft's operating system monopoly. See Findings of Fact P 411 ("There is insufficient evidence to find that, absent Microsoft's actions, Navigator and Java already would have ignited genuine competition in the market for Intel-compatible PC operating systems."). This is the flip side of Microsoft's earlier argument that the District Court should have included middleware in the relevant market. According to Microsoft, the District Court cannot simultaneously find that middleware is not a reasonable substitute and that Microsoft's exclusionary conduct contributed to the maintenance of monopoly power in the operating system market. Microsoft claims that the first finding depended on the court's view that middleware does not pose a serious threat to Windows, see supra Section II.A, while the second finding required the court to find that Navigator and Java would have developed into serious enough cross-platform threats to erode the applications barrier to entry. We disagree.

Microsoft points to no case, and we can find none, standing for the proposition that, as to § 2 liability in an equitable enforcement action, plaintiffs must present direct proof that a defendant's continued monopoly power is precisely attributable to its anticompetitive conduct. As its lone authority, Microsoft cites the following passage from Professor Areeda's antitrust treatise: "The plaintiff has the burden of pleading, introducing evidence, and presumably proving by a preponderance of the evidence that reprehensible behavior has contributed significantly to the ... maintenance of the monopoly." 3 PHILLIP E. AREEDA & HERBERT HOVENKAMP, ANTITRUST LAW P 650c, at 69 (1996) (emphasis added).

But, with respect to actions seeking injunctive relief, the authors of that treatise also recognize the need for courts to infer "causation" from the fact that a defendant has engaged in anticompetitive conduct that "reasonably appears capable of making a significant contribution to ... maintaining monopoly power." Id. P 651c, at 78; see also *Morgan v. Ponder, 892 F.2d 1355, 1363 (8th Cir. 1989); Barry Wright, 724 F.2d at 230.* To require that § 2 liability turn on a plaintiff's ability or inability to reconstruct the hypothetical marketplace absent a defendant's anticompetitive conduct would only encourage monopolists to take more and earlier anticompetitive action.

We may infer causation when exclusionary conduct is aimed at producers of nascent competitive technologies as well as when it is aimed at producers of established substitutes. Admittedly, in the former case there is added uncertainty, inasmuch as nascent threats are merely potential substitutes. But the underlying proof problem is the same--neither plaintiffs nor the court can confidently reconstruct a product's hypothetical technological development in a world absent the defendant's exclusionary conduct. To some degree, "the defendant is made to suffer the uncertain consequences of its own undesirable conduct." 3 AREEDA & HOVENKAMP, ANTITRUST LAW P 651c, at 78.

Given this rather edentulous test for causation, the question in this case is not whether Java or Navigator would actually have developed into viable platform substitutes, but (1) whether as a general matter the exclusion of nascent threats is the type of conduct that is reasonably capable of contributing significantly to a defendant's continued monopoly power and (2) whether Java and Navigator reasonably constituted nascent threats at the time Microsoft engaged in the anticompetitive conduct at issue. As to the first, suffice it to say that it would be inimical to the purpose of the Sherman Act to allow monopolists free reign to squash nascent, albeit unproven, competitors at will--particularly in industries marked by rapid technological advance and frequent paradigm shifts. Findings of Fact P P 59-60. As to the second, the District Court made ample findings that both Navigator and Java showed potential as middleware platform threats. Findings of Fact P P 68-77. Counsel for Microsoft admitted as much at oral argument. 02/26/01 Ct. Appeals Tr. at 27 ("There are no constraints on output. Marginal costs are essentially zero. And there are to some extent network effects. So a company like Netscape founded in 1994 can be by the middle of 1995 clearly a potentially lethal competitor to Windows because it can supplant its position in the market because of the characteristics of these markets.").

Microsoft's concerns over causation have more purchase in connection with the appropriate remedy issue, i.e., whether the court should impose a structural remedy or merely enjoin the offensive conduct at issue. As we point out later in this opinion, divestiture is a remedy that is imposed only with great caution, in part because its long-term efficacy is rarely certain. See infra Section V.E. Absent some measure of confidence that there has been an actual loss to competition that needs to be restored, wisdom counsels against adopting radical structural relief. See 3 AREEDA & HOVENKAMP, ANTITRUST LAW P 653b, at 91-92 ("More extensive equitable relief, particularly remedies such as divestiture designed to eliminate the monopoly altogether, raise more serious questions and require a clearer indication of a significant causal connection between the conduct and creation or maintenance of the market power."). But these queries go to questions of remedy, not liability. In short, causation affords Microsoft no defense to liability for its unlawful actions undertaken to maintain its monopoly in the operating system market.

III. ATTEMPTED MONOPOLIZATION

Microsoft further challenges the District Court's determination of liability for "attempting to monopolize ... any part of the trade or commerce among the several States." *15 U.S.C. § 2* (1997). To establish a § 2 violation for attempted monopolization, "a plaintiff must prove (1) that the defendant has engaged in predatory or anticompetitive conduct with (2) a specific intent to monopolize and (3) a dangerous probability of achieving monopoly power." *Spectrum Sports, Inc. v. McQuillan, 506 U.S. 447, 456 (1993).* Because a deficiency on any one of the three will defeat plaintiffs' claim, we look no further than plaintiffs' failure to prove a dangerous probability of achieving monopoly power in the putative browser market.

The determination whether a dangerous probability of success exists is a particularly fact-intensive inquiry. Because the Sherman Act does not identify the activities that constitute the offense of attempted monopolization, the court "must examine the facts of each case, mindful that the determination of what constitutes an attempt, as Justice Holmes explained, 'is a question of proximity and degree.' " *United States v. Am. Airlines, Inc., 743 F.2d 1114, 1118 (5th Cir. 1984)* (quoting *Swift & Co. v. United States, 196 U.S. 375, 402 (1904)).* The District Court determined that "the evidence supports the conclusion that Microsoft's actions did pose such a danger." Conclusions of Law, at 45. Specifically, the District Court concluded that "Netscape's assent to Microsoft's market division proposal would have, instanter, resulted in

Microsoft's attainment of monopoly power in a second market," and that "the proposal itself created a dangerous probability of that result." Conclusions of Law, at 46 (citation omitted). The District Court further concluded that "the predatory course of conduct Microsoft has pursued since June of 1995 has revived the dangerous probability that Microsoft will attain monopoly power in a second market." Id.

At the outset we note a pervasive flaw in the District Court's and plaintiffs' discussion of attempted monopolization. Simply put, plaintiffs have made the same argument under two different headings--monopoly maintenance and attempted monopolization. They have relied upon Microsoft's § 2 liability for monopolization of the operating system market as a presumptive indicator of attempted monopolization of an entirely different market. The District Court implicitly accepted this approach: It agreed with plaintiffs that the events that formed the basis for the § 2 monopolization claim "warranted additional liability as an illegal attempt to amass monopoly power in 'the browser market.' " Id. at 45 (emphasis added). Thus, plaintiffs and the District Court failed to recognize the need for an analysis wholly independent of the conclusions and findings on monopoly maintenance.

To establish a dangerous probability of success, plaintiffs must as a threshold matter show that the browser market can be monopolized, i.e., that a hypothetical monopolist in that market could enjoy market power. This, in turn, requires plaintiffs (1) to define the relevant market and (2) to demonstrate that substantial barriers to entry protect that market. Because plaintiffs have not carried their burden on either prong, we reverse without remand.

A. Relevant Market....

Defining a market for an attempted monopolization claim involves the same steps as defining a market for a monopoly maintenance claim, namely a detailed description of the purpose of a browser--what functions may be included and what are not--and an examination of the substitutes that are part of the market and those that are not. See also supra Section II.A. The District Court never engaged in such an analysis nor entered detailed findings defining what a browser is or what products might constitute substitutes. In the Findings of Fact, the District Court (in a section on whether IE and Windows are separate products) stated only that "a Web browser provides the ability for the end user to select, retrieve, and perceive resources on the Web." Findings of Fact P 150. Furthermore, in discussing attempted monopolization in its

Conclusions of Law, the District Court failed to demonstrate analytical rigor when it employed varying and imprecise references to the "market for browsing technology for Windows," "the browser market," and "platform-level browsing software." Conclusions of Law, at 45....

B. Barriers to Entry

Because a firm cannot possess monopoly power in a market unless that market is also protected by significant barriers to entry, see supra Section II.A, it follows that a firm cannot threaten to achieve monopoly power in a market unless that market is, or will be, similarly protected. See *Spectrum Sports, 506 U.S. at 456....*

Giving plaintiffs and the District Court the benefit of the doubt, we might remand if the possible existence of entry barriers resulting from the possible creation and exploitation of network effects in the browser market were the only concern. That is not enough to carry the day, however, because the District Court did not make two key findings: (1) that network effects were a necessary or even probable, rather than merely possible, consequence of high market share in the browser market and (2) that a barrier to entry resulting from network effects would be "significant" enough to confer monopoly power. Again, these deficiencies are in large part traceable to plaintiffs' own failings....

IV. TYING

Microsoft also contests the District Court's determination of liability under § 1 of the Sherman Act. The District Court concluded that Microsoft's contractual and technological bundling of the IE web browser (the "tied" product) with its Windows operating system ("OS") (the "tying" product) resulted in a tying arrangement that was per se unlawful. Conclusions of Law, at 47-51. We hold that the rule of reason, rather than per se analysis, should govern the legality of tying arrangements involving platform software products. The Supreme Court has warned that " 'it is only after considerable experience with certain business relationships that courts classify them as per se violations....' " *Broad. Music, Inc. v. CBS, 441 U.S. 1, 9, (1979)* (quoting *United States v. Topco Assocs., 405 U.S. 596, 607-08 (1972))* While every "business relationship" will in some sense have unique features, some represent entire, novel categories of dealings. As we shall explain, the arrangement before us is an example of the latter, offering the first up-close look at the technological integration of added functionality into software that serves as a platform for third-party applications. There being no close parallel in prior antitrust cases, simplistic application of per se tying rules carries a serious risk of harm. Accordingly, we vacate the District Court's finding of a per se tying violation and remand the case. Plaintiffs may on remand pursue their tying claim under the rule of reason.

The facts underlying the tying allegation substantially overlap with those set forth in Section II.B in connection with the § 2 monopoly maintenance claim. The key District Court findings are that (1) Microsoft required licensees of Windows 95 and 98 also to license IE as a bundle at a single price, Findings of Fact P P 137, 155, 158; (2) Microsoft refused to allow OEMs to uninstall or remove IE from the Windows desktop, id. P P 158, 203, 213; (3) Microsoft designed Windows 98 in a way that withheld from consumers the ability to remove IE by use of the Add/Remove Programs utility, id. P 170; cf. id. P 165 (stating that IE was subject to Add/Remove Programs utility in Windows 95); and (4) Microsoft designed Windows 98 to override the user's choice of default web browser in certain circumstances, id. P P 171, 172. The court found that these acts constituted a per se tying violation. Conclusions of Law, at 47-51. Although the District Court also found that Microsoft commingled operating system-only and browser-only routines in the same library files, Findings of Fact P P 161, 164, it did not include this as a basis for tying liability despite plaintiffs' request that it do so, Plaintiffs' Proposed Findings of Fact, P P 131-32, reprinted in 2 J.A. at 941-47.

There are four elements to a per se tying violation: (1) the tying and tied goods are two separate products; (2) the defendant has market power in the tying product market; (3) the defendant affords consumers no choice but to purchase the tied product from it; and (4) the tying arrangement forecloses a substantial volume of commerce. See *Eastman Kodak Co. v. Image Tech. Servs., Inc., 504 U.S. 451, 461-62 (1992); Jefferson Parish Hosp. Dist. No. 2 v. Hyde, 466 U.S. 2, 12-18 (1984).*

Microsoft does not dispute that it bound Windows and IE in the four ways the District Court cited. Instead it argues that Windows (the tying good) and IE browsers (the tied good) are not "separate products," Appellant's Opening Br. at 69-79, and that it did not substantially foreclose competing browsers from the tied product market, *id. at 79-83.* (Microsoft also contends that it does not have monopoly power in the tying product market, *id. at 84-96,* but, for reasons given in Section II.A, we uphold the District Court's finding to the contrary.)

We first address the separate-products inquiry, a source of much argument between the parties and of confusion in the cases. Our purpose is to highlight the poor fit between the separate-products test and the facts of this case. We then offer further reasons for carving an exception to the per se rule when the tying product is platform software. In the final section we discuss the District Court's inquiry if plaintiffs pursue a rule of reason claim on remand.

A. Separate-Products Inquiry Under the Per Se Test

The requirement that a practice involve two separate products before being condemned as an illegal tie started as a purely linguistic requirement: unless products are separate, one cannot be "tied" to the other. Indeed, the nature of the products involved in early tying cases--intuitively distinct items such as a movie projector and a film, *Motion Picture Patents Co. v. Universal Film Mfg. Co., 243 U.S. 502 (1917)*-led courts either to disregard the separate-products question.... It was not until *Times-Picayune Publishing Co. v. United States, 345 U.S. 594 (1953)*, that the separate-products issue became a distinct element of the test for an illegal tie. *Id. at 614.* Even that case engaged in a rather cursory inquiry into whether ads sold in the morning edition of a paper were a separate product from ads sold in the evening edition.

The first case to give content to the separate-products test was *Jefferson Parish, 466 U.S. 2.* That case addressed a tying arrangement in which a hospital conditioned surgical care at its facility on the purchase of anesthesiological services from an affiliated medical group. The facts were a challenge for casual separate-products analysis because the tied service--anesthesia--was neither intuitively distinct from nor intuitively contained within the tying service--surgical care. A further complication was that, soon after the Court enunciated the per se rule for tying liability in *International Salt Co. v. United States, 332 U.S. 392, 396 (1947)*, new economic research began to cast doubt on the assumption, voiced by the Court when it established the rule, that " 'tying agreements serve hardly any purpose beyond the suppression of competition....'"

The Jefferson Parish Court resolved the matter in two steps. First, it clarified that "the answer to the question whether one or two products are involved" does not turn "on the functional relation between them...." *Jefferson Parish, 466 U.S. at 19;* see also *466 U.S. at 19 n.30.* In other words, the mere fact that two items are complements, that "one ... is useless without the other," id., does not make them a single "product" for purposes of tying law. Accord

Eastman Kodak, 504 U.S. at 463. Second, reasoning that the "definitional question [whether two distinguishable products are involved] depends on whether the arrangement may have the type of competitive consequences addressed by the rule [against tying]," *Jefferson Parish, 466 U.S. at 21,* the Court decreed that "no tying arrangement can exist unless there is a sufficient demand for the purchase of anesthesiological services separate from hospital services to identify a distinct product market in which it is efficient to offer anesthesiological services separately from hospital service," *id. at 21-22* (emphasis added); accord *Eastman Kodak, 504 U.S. at 462....*

To understand the logic behind the Court's consumer demand test, consider first the postulated harms from tying. The core concern is that tying prevents goods from competing directly for consumer choice on their merits, i.e., being selected as a result of "buyers' independent judgment," *id. at 13* (internal quotes omitted). With a tie, a buyer's "freedom to select the best bargain in the second market [could be] impaired by his need to purchase the tying product, and perhaps by an inability to evaluate the true cost of either product...." *Id. at 15.* Direct competition on the merits of the tied product is foreclosed when the tying product either is sold only in a bundle with the tied product or, though offered separately, is sold at a bundled price, so that the buyer pays the same price whether he takes the tied product or not. In both cases, a consumer buying the tying product becomes entitled to the tied product; he will therefore likely be unwilling to buy a competitor's version of the tied product even if, making his own price/quality assessment, that is what he would prefer.

But not all ties are bad. Bundling obviously saves distribution and consumer transaction costs. 9 PHILLIP E. AREEDA, ANTITRUST LAW P 1703g2, at 51-52 (1991). This is likely to be true, to take some examples from the computer industry, with the integration of math co-processors and memory into microprocessor chips and the inclusion of spell checkers in word processors.... Bundling can also capitalize on certain economies of scope. A possible example is the "shared" library files that perform OS and browser functions with the very same lines of code and thus may save drive space from the clutter of redundant routines and memory when consumers use both the OS and browser simultaneously.... Indeed, if there were no efficiencies from a tie (including economizing on consumer transaction costs such as the time and effort involved in choice), we would expect distinct consumer demand for each individual component of every good. In a competitive market with zero transaction costs, the computers on which this opinion was written would only be sold piecemeal--keyboard, monitor, mouse, central processing unit, disk drive, and memory all sold in separate transactions and likely by different manufacturers.

Recognizing the potential benefits from tying, see *Jefferson Parish , 466 U.S. at 21 n.33,* the Court in Jefferson Parish forged a separate-products test that, like those of market power and substantial foreclosure, attempts to screen out false positives under per se analysis. The consumer demand test is a rough proxy for whether a tying arrangement may, on balance, be welfare-enhancing, and unsuited to per se condemnation. In the abstract, of course, there is always direct separate demand for products: assuming choice is available at zero cost, consumers will prefer it to no choicc. Only when the efficiencies from bundling are dominated by the benefits to choice for enough consumers, however, will we actually observe consumers making independent purchases. In other words, perceptible separate demand is inversely proportional to net efficiencies. On the supply side, firms without market power will bundle two goods only when the cost savings from joint sale outweigh the value consumers place on separate choice. So bundling by all competitive firms implies strong net efficiencies. If a court finds either that there is no noticeable separate demand for the tied product or, there being no convincing direct evidence of separate demand, that the entire "competitive fringe" engages in the same behavior as the defendant, 10 AREEDA ET AL., ANTITRUST LAW P 1744c4, at 200, then the tying and tied products should be declared one product and per se liability should be rejected.

Before concluding our exegesis of Jefferson Parish's separate-products test, we should clarify two things. First, Jefferson Parish does not endorse a direct inquiry into the efficiencies of a bundle. Rather, it proposes easy-to administer proxies for net efficiency. In describing the separate-products test we discuss efficiencies only to explain the rationale behind the consumer demand inquiry. To allow the separate-products test to become a detailed inquiry into possible welfare consequences would turn a screening test into the very process it is expected to render unnecessary. 10 AREEDA ET AL., ANTITRUST LAW P P 1741b & c, at 180-85; see also *Jefferson Parish, 466 U.S. at 34-35* (O'Connor, J., concurring).

Second, the separate-products test is not a one-sided inquiry into the cost savings from a bundle. Although Jefferson Parish acknowledged that prior lower court cases looked at cost-savings to decide separate products, see *id . at 22 n.35,* the Court conspicuously did not adopt that approach in its disposition of tying arrangement before it. Instead it chose proxies that balance costs savings against reduction in consumer choice.

With this background, we now turn to the separate products inquiry before us. The District Court found that many consumers, if given the option, would choose their browser separately from the OS. Findings of Fact P 151 (noting that "corporate consumers ... prefer to standardize on the same browser across different [OSs]" at the workplace). Turning to industry custom, the court found that, although all major OS vendors bundled browsers with their OSs, these companies either sold versions without a browser, or allowed OEMs or end-users either not to install the bundled browser or in any event to "uninstall" it. Id. P 153. The court did not discuss the record evidence as to whether OS vendors other than Microsoft sold at a bundled price, with no discount for a browserless OS, perhaps because the record evidence on the issue was in conflict. Compare, e.g., Direct Testimony of Richard Schmalensee P 241, reprinted in 7 J.A. at 4315 ("All major operating system vendors do in fact include Web-browsing software with the operating system at no extra charge.") (emphasis added), with, e.g., 1/6/99 pm Tr. at 42 (trial testimony of Franklin Fisher of MIT) (suggesting all OSs but Microsoft offer discounts).

Microsoft does not dispute that many consumers demand alternative browsers. But on industry custom Microsoft contends that no other firm requires non-removal because no other firm has invested the resources to integrate web browsing as deeply into its OS as Microsoft has.... Microsoft contends not only that its integration of IE into Windows is innovative and beneficial but also that it requires non-removal of IE. In our discussion of monopoly maintenance we find that these claims fail the efficiency balancing applicable in that context. But the separate-products analysis is supposed to perform its function as a proxy without embarking on any direct analysis of efficiency. Accordingly, Microsoft's implicit argument--that in this case looking to a competitive fringe is inadequate to evaluate fully its potentially innovative technological integration, that such a comparison is between apples and oranges--poses a legitimate objection to the operation of Jefferson Parish's separate-products test for the per se rule.

In fact there is merit to Microsoft's broader argument that Jefferson Parish's consumer demand test would "chill innovation to the detriment of consumers by preventing firms from integrating into their products new functionality previously provided by standalone products--and hence, by definition, subject to separate consumer demand." Appellant's Opening Br. at

69. The per se rule's direct consumer demand and indirect industry custom inquiries are, as a general matter, backward-looking and therefore systematically poor proxies for overall efficiency in the presence of new and innovative integration. See 10 AREEDA ET AL., ANTITRUST LAW P 1746, at 224-29; Amicus Brief of Lawrence Lessig at 24-25, and sources cited therein (brief submitted regarding Conclusions of Law). The direct consumer demand test focuses on historic consumer behavior, likely before integration, and the indirect industry custom test looks at firms that, unlike the defendant, may not have integrated the tying and tied goods. Both tests compare incomparables--the defendant's decision to bundle in the presence of integration, on the one hand, and consumer and competitor calculations in its absence, on the other. If integration has efficiency benefits, these may be ignored by the Jefferson Parish proxies. Because one cannot be sure beneficial integration will be protected by the other elements of the per se rule, simple application of that rule's separate-products test may make consumers worse off.

In light of the monopoly maintenance section, obviously, we do not find that Microsoft's integration is welfare-enhancing or that it should be absolved of tying liability. Rather, we heed Microsoft's warning that the separate-products element of the per se rule may not give newly integrated products a fair shake.

B. Per Se Analysis Inappropriate for this Case.

We now address directly the larger question as we see it: whether standard per se analysis should be applied "off the shelf" to evaluate the defendant's tying arrangement, one which involves software that serves as a platform for thirdparty applications. There is no doubt that "it is far too late in the history of our antitrust jurisprudence to question the proposition that certain tying arrangements pose an unacceptable risk of stifling competition and therefore are unreasonable 'per se.'" *Jefferson Parish, 466 U.S. at 9* (emphasis added). But there are strong reasons to doubt that the integration of additional software functionality into an OS falls among these arrangements. Applying per se analysis to such an amalgamation creates undue risks of error and of deterring welfare-enhancing innovation....

In none of these [Supreme Court] cases was the tied good physically and technologically integrated with the tying good. Nor did the defendants ever argue that their tie improved the value of the tying product to users and to makers of complementary goods. In those cases where the defendant claimed that use of the tied good made the tying good more valuable to users, the Court ruled that the same result could be achieved via quality standards for substitutes of the tied good. See, e.g., *Int'l Salt, 332 U.S. at 397-98; IBM, 298 U.S. at 138-40.* Here Microsoft argues that IE and Windows are an integrated physical product and that the bundling of IE APIs with Windows makes the latter a better applications platform for third-party software. It is unclear how the benefits from IE APIs could be achieved by quality standards for different browser manufacturers. We do not pass judgment on Microsoft's claims regarding the benefits from integration of its APIs. We merely note that these and other novel, purported efficiencies suggest that judicial "experience" provides little basis for believing that, "because of their pernicious effect on competition and lack of any redeeming virtue," a software firm's decisions to sell multiple functionalities as a package should be "conclusively presumed to be unreasonable and therefore illegal without elaborate inquiry as to the precise harm they have caused or the business excuse for their use." *N. Pac. Ry., 356 U.S. at 5* (emphasis added). Nor have we found much insight into software integration among the decisions of lower federal courts....

The software case that bears the greatest resemblance to that at bar is, not surprisingly, *Microsoft II, 147 F.3d 935,* where we examined the bundling of IE with Windows 95. But the issue there was whether the bundle constituted an "integrated product" as the term was used in a 1994 consent decree between the *Department of Justice and Microsoft. 147 F.3d at 939.* We did not consider whether Microsoft's bundling should be condemned as per se illegal. We certainly did not make any finding that bundling IE with Windows had "no purpose except stifling of competition," *White Motor, 372 U.S. at 263,* an important consideration in defining the scope of any of antitrust law's per se rules, see *Cont'l T.V., 433 U.S. at 57-59.* While we believed our interpretation of the term "integrated product" was consistent with the test for separate products under tying law, we made clear that the "antitrust question is of course distinct." *Microsoft II, 147 F.3d at 950 n.14.* We even cautioned that our conclusion that IE and Windows 95 were integrated was "subject to reexamination on a more complete record." Id. at 952. To the extent that the decision completely disclaimed judicial capacity to evaluate "high-tech product design," id., it cannot be said to conform to prevailing antitrust doctrine (as opposed to resolution of the decree-interpretation issue then before us). In any case, mere review of asserted breaches of a consent decree hardly constitutes enough "experience" to warrant application of per se analysis. See *Broad. Music, 441 U.S. at 10-16* (refusing to apply per se analysis to defendant's blanket licenses even though those licenses had been thoroughly investigated by the Department of Justice and were the subject of a consent decree that had been reviewed by numerous courts).

While the paucity of cases examining software bundling suggests a high risk that per se analysis may produce inaccurate results, the nature of the platform software market affirmatively suggests that per se rules might stunt valuable innovation. We have in mind two reasons.

First, as we explained in the previous section, the separate products test is a poor proxy for net efficiency from newly integrated products. Under per se analysis the first firm to merge previously distinct functionalities (e.g., the inclusion of starter motors in automobiles) or to eliminate entirely the need for a second function (e.g., the invention of the stain resistant carpet) risks being condemned as having tied two separate products because at the moment of integration there will appear to be a robust "distinct" market for the tied product. Rule of reason analysis, however, affords the first mover an opportunity to demonstrate that an efficiency gain from its "tie" adequately offsets any distortion of consumer choice....

The failure of the separate-products test to screen out certain cases of productive integration is particularly troubling in platform software markets such as that in which the defendant competes. Not only is integration common in such markets, but it is common among firms without market power. We have already reviewed evidence that nearly all competitive OS vendors also bundle browsers. Moreover, plaintiffs do not dispute that OS vendors can and do incorporate basic internet plumbing and other useful functionality into their OSs.... Firms without market power have no incentive to package different pieces of software together unless there are efficiency gains from doing so. The ubiquity of bundling in competitive platform software markets should give courts reason to pause before condemning such behavior in less competitive markets.

Second, because of the pervasively innovative character of platform software markets, tying in such markets may produce efficiencies that courts have not previously encountered and thus the Supreme Court had not factored into the per se rule as originally conceived. For example, the bundling of a browser with OSs enables an independent software developer to count on the presence of the browser's APIs, if any, on consumers' machines and thus to omit them from its own package.... It is true that software developers can bundle the browser APIs they need with their own products, see id. P 193, but that may force consumers to pay twice for the same API if it is bundled with two different software programs. It is also true that OEMs can include APIs with the computers they sell, id., but diffusion of uniform APIs by that route may be inferior....

These arguments all point to one conclusion: we cannot comfortably say that bundling in platform software markets has so little "redeeming virtue," *N. Pac. Ry., 356 U.S. at 5,* and that there would be so "very little loss to society" from its ban, that "an inquiry into its costs in the individual case [can be] considered [ ] unnecessary." *Jefferson Parish, 466 U.S. at 33-34* (O'Connor, J., concurring). We do not have enough empirical evidence regarding the effect of Microsoft's practice on the amount of consumer surplus created or consumer choice foreclosed by the integration of added functionality into platform software to exercise sensible judgment regarding that entire class of behavior. (For some issues we have no data.) "We need to know more than we do about the actual impact of these arrangements on competition to decide whether they ... should be classified as per se violations of the Sherman Act." *White Motor, 372 U.S. at 263.* Until then, we will heed the wisdom that "easy labels do not always supply ready answers," *Broad. Music, 441 U.S. at 8,* and vacate the District Court's finding of per se tying liability under Sherman Act § 1. We remand the case for evaluation of Microsoft's tying arrangements under the rule of reason....

Our judgment regarding the comparative merits of the per se rule and the rule of reason is confined to the tying arrangement before us, where the tying product is software whose major purpose is to serve as a platform for third-party applications and the tied product is complementary software functionality. While our reasoning may at times appear to have broader force, we do not have the confidence to speak to facts outside the record, which contains scant discussion of software integration generally. Microsoft's primary justification for bundling IE APIs is that their inclusion with Windows increases the value of third-party software (and Windows) to consumers. See Appellant's Opening Br. at 41-43. Because this claim applies with distinct force when the tying product is platform software, we have no present basis for finding the per se rule inapplicable to software markets generally. Nor should we be interpreted as setting a precedent for switching to the rule of reason every time a court identifies an efficiency justification for a tying arrangement. Our reading of the record suggests merely that integration of new functionality into platform software is a common practice and that wooden application of per se rules in this litigation may cast a cloud over platform innovation in the market for PCs, network computers and information appliances....

V. TRIAL PROCEEDINGS AND REMEDY

Microsoft additionally challenges the District Court's procedural rulings on two fronts. First, with respect to the trial phase, Microsoft proposes that the court mismanaged its docket by adopting an expedited trial schedule and receiving evidence through summary witnesses. Second, with respect to the remedies decree, Microsoft argues that the court improperly ordered that it be divided into two separate companies. Only the latter claim will long detain us. The District Court's trial-phase procedures were comfortably within the bounds of its broad discretion to conduct trials as it sees fit. We conclude, however, that the District Court's remedies decree must be vacated for three independent reasons: (1) the court failed to hold a remedies-specific evidentiary hearing when there were disputed facts; (2) the court failed to provide adequate reasons for its decreed remedies; and (3) this Court has revised the scope of Microsoft's liability and it is impossible to determine to what extent that should affect the remedies provisions.

A. Factual Background

On April 3, 2000, the District Court concluded the liability phase of the proceedings by the filing of its Conclusions of Law holding that Microsoft had violated §§ 1 and 2 of the Sherman Act. The court and the parties then began discussions of the procedures to be followed in the imposition of remedies. Initially, the District Court signaled that it would enter relief only after conducting a new round of proceedings. In its Conclusions of Law, the court stated that it would issue a remedies order "following proceedings to be established by further Order of the Court." Conclusions of Law, at 57. And, when during a post-trial conference, Microsoft's counsel asked whether the court "contemplated further proceedings," the judge replied, "Yes. Yes. I assume that there would be further proceedings." 4/4/00 Tr. at 8-9, 11, reprinted in 4 J.A. at 2445-46, 2448. The District Court further speculated that those proceedings might "replicate the procedure at trial with testimony in written form subject to crossexamination." Id. at 11, reprinted in 4 J.A. at 2448.

On April 28, 2000, plaintiffs submitted their proposed final judgment, accompanied by six new supporting affidavits and several exhibits. In addition to a series of temporary conduct restrictions, plaintiffs proposed that Microsoft be split into two independent corporations, with one continuing Microsoft's operating systems business and the other undertaking the balance of Microsoft's operations. Microsoft filed a "summary response" on May 10, contending both that the proposed decree was too severe and that it would be impossible to resolve certain remedies-specific factual disputes "on a highly expedited basis." Defendant's Summary Response at 6-7, reprinted in 4 J.A. at 2587-88. Another May 10 submission argued that if the District Court considered imposing plaintiffs' proposed remedy, "then substantial discovery, adequate time for preparation and a full trial on relief will be required." Defendant's Position as to Future Proceedings at 2, reprinted in 4 J.A. at 2646.

After the District Court revealed during a May 24 hearing that it was prepared to enter a decree without conducting "any further process," 5/24/00 pm Tr. at 33, reprinted in 14 J.A. at 9866, Microsoft renewed its argument that the underlying factual disputes between the parties necessitated a remedies-specific evidentiary hearing. In two separate offers of proof, Microsoft offered to produce a number of pieces of evidence....

B. Trial Proceedings

Microsoft's first contention--that the District Court erred by adopting an expedited trial schedule and receiving evidence through summary witnesses--is easily disposed of. Trial courts have extraordinarily broad discretion to determine the manner in which they will conduct trials.... Although the company claims that setting an early trial date inhibited its ability to conduct discovery, it never identified a specific deposition or document it was unable to obtain. And while Microsoft now argues that the use of summary witnesses made inevitable the improper introduction of hearsay evidence, the company actually agreed to the District Court's proposal to limit each side to 12 summary witnesses.... Even absent Microsoft's agreement, the company's challenge fails to show that this use of summary witnesses falls outside the trial court's wide latitude to receive evidence as it sees fit....

C. Failure to Hold an Evidentiary Hearing

The District Court's remedies-phase proceedings are a different matter. It is a cardinal principle of our system of justice that factual disputes must be heard in open court and resolved through trial-like evidentiary proceedings. Any other course would be contrary "to the spirit which imbues our judicial tribunals prohibiting decision without hearing." *Sims v. Greene, 161 F.2d 87, 88 (3d Cir. 1947).*

A party has the right to judicial resolution of disputed facts not just as to the liability phase, but also as to appropriate relief. "Normally, an evidentiary hearing is required before an injunction may be granted." *United States v. McGee, 714 F.2d 607, 613 (6th Cir. 1983)....* Other than a temporary restraining order, no injunctive relief may be entered without a hearing. See generally FED. R. CIV. P. 65. A hearing on the merits-- i.e., a trial on liability--does not substitute for a relief-specific evidentiary hearing unless the matter of relief was part of the trial on liability, or unless there are no disputed factual issues regarding the matter of relief....

Despite plaintiffs' protestations, there can be no serious doubt that the parties disputed a number of facts during the remedies phase. In two separate offers of proof, Microsoft identified 23 witnesses who, had they been permitted to testify, would have challenged a wide range of plaintiffs' factual representations, including the feasibility of dividing Microsoft, the likely impact on consumers, and the effect of divestiture on shareholders. To take but two examples, where plaintiffs' economists testified that splitting Microsoft in two would be socially beneficial, the company offered to prove that the proposed remedy would "cause substantial social harm by raising software prices, lowering rates of innovation and disrupting the evolution of Windows as a software development platform." Defendant's Offer of Proof at 6, reprinted in 4 J.A. at 2747. And where plaintiffs' investment banking experts proposed that divestiture might actually increase shareholder value, Microsoft proffered evidence that structural relief "would inevitably result in a significant loss of shareholder value," a loss that could reach "tens--possibly hundreds--of billions of dollars." Id. at 19, reprinted in 4 J.A. at 2760.

Indeed, the District Court itself appears to have conceded the existence of acute factual disagreements between Microsoft and plaintiffs. The court acknowledged that the parties were "sharply divided" and held "divergent opinions" on the likely results of its remedies decree. Final Judgment, at 62. The reason the court declined to conduct an evidentiary hearing was not because of the absence of disputed facts, but because it believed that those disputes could be resolved only through "actual experience," not further proceedings. Id. But a prediction about future events is not, as a prediction, any less a factual issue. Indeed, the Supreme Court has acknowledged that drafting an antitrust decree by necessity "involves predictions and assumptions concerning future economic and business events." *Ford Motor Co. v. United States, 405 U.S. 562, 578 (1972).* Trial courts are not excused from their obligation to resolve such matters through evidentiary hearings simply because they consider the bedrock procedures of our justice system to be "of little use." Final Judgment, at 62....

In sum, the District Court erred when it resolved the parties' remedies-phase factual disputes by consulting only the evidence introduced during trial and plaintiffs' remedies phase submissions, without considering the evidence Microsoft sought to introduce. We therefore vacate the District Court's final judgment, and remand with instructions to conduct a remedies-specific evidentiary hearing.

D. Failure to Provide an Adequate Explanation

We vacate the District Court's remedies decree for the additional reason that the court has failed to provide an adequate explanation for the relief it ordered. The Supreme Court has explained that a remedies decree in an antitrust case must seek to "unfetter a market from anticompetitive conduct," *Ford Motor Co., 405 U.S. at 577,* to "terminate the illegal monopoly, deny to the defendant the fruits of its statutory violation, and ensure that there remain no practices likely to result in monopolization in the future," *United States v. United Shoe Mach. Corp., 391 U.S. 244, 250 (1968);* see also *United States v. Grinnell Corp., 384 U.S. 563, 577 (1966).*

The District Court has not explained how its remedies decree would accomplish those objectives. Indeed, the court devoted a mere four paragraphs of its order to explaining its reasons for the remedy. They are: (1) Microsoft "does not yet concede that any of its business practices violated the Sherman Act"; (2) Microsoft "continues to do business as it has in the past"; (3) Microsoft "has proved untrustworthy in the past"; and (4) the Government, whose officials "are by reason of office obliged and expected to consider--and to act in--the public interest," won the case, "and for that reason alone have some entitlement to a remedy of their choice." Final Judgment, at 62-63. Nowhere did the District Court discuss the objectives the Supreme Court deems relevant.

E. Modification of Liability....

[We must also vacate the remedies decree because this] court has drastically altered the District Court's conclusions on liability. On remand, the District Court, after affording the parties a proper opportunity to be heard, can fashion an appropriate remedy for Microsoft's antitrust violations. In particular, the court should consider which of the decree's conduct restrictions remain viable in light of our modification of the original liability decision. While the task of drafting the remedies decree is for the District Court in the first instance, because of the unusually convoluted nature of the proceedings thus far, and a desire to advance the ultimate resolution of this important controversy, we offer some further guidance for the exercise of that discretion.

F. On Remand

As a general matter, a district court is afforded broad discretion to enter that relief it calculates will best remedy the conduct it has found to be unlawful.... And divestiture is a common form of relief in successful antitrust prosecutions: it is indeed "the most important of antitrust remedies." See, e.g., *United States v. E.I. du Pont de Nemours & Co., 366 U.S. 316, 331 (1961).*

On remand, the District Court must reconsider whether the use of the structural remedy of divestiture is appropriate with respect to Microsoft, which argues that it is a unitary company. By and large, cases upon which plaintiffs rely in arguing for the split of Microsoft have involved the dissolution of entities formed by mergers and acquisitions. On the contrary, the Supreme Court has clarified that divestiture "has traditionally been the remedy for Sherman Act violations whose heart is intercorporate combination and control," *du Pont, 366 U.S. at 329* (emphasis added), and that "complete divestiture is particularly appropriate where asset or stock acquisitions violate the antitrust laws," *Ford Motor Co., 405 U.S. at 573.*

One apparent reason why courts have not ordered the dissolution of unitary companies is logistical difficulty. As the court explained in *United States v. ALCOA, 91 F. Supp. 333, 416 (S.D.N.Y. 1950),* a "corporation, designed to operate effectively as a single entity, cannot readily be dismembered of parts of its various operations without a marked loss of efficiency." A corporation that has expanded by acquiring its competitors often has preexisting internal lines of division along which it may more easily be split than a corporation that has expanded from natural growth. Although time and corporate modifications and developments may eventually fade those lines, at least the identifiable entities preexisted to create a template for such division as the court might later decree. With reference to those corporations that are not acquired by merger and acquisition, Judge Wyzanski accurately opined in United Shoe:

> United conducts all machine manufacture] at one plant in Beverly, with one set of jigs and tools, one foundry, one laboratory for machinery problems, one managerial staff, and one labor force. It takes no Solomon to see that this organism cannot be cut into three equal and viable parts.

United States v. United Shoe Machine Co., 110 F. Supp. 295, 348 (D. Mass. 1953).

Depending upon the evidence, the District Court may find in a remedies proceeding that it would be no easier to split Microsoft in two than United Shoe in three. Microsoft's Offer of Proof in response to the court's denial of an evidentiary hearing included proffered testimony from its President and CEO Steve Ballmer that the company "is, and always has been, a unified company without free-standing business units. Microsoft is not the result of mergers or acquisitions." Microsoft further offered evidence that it is "not organized along product lines," but rather is housed in a single corporate headquarters and that it has

> only one sales and marketing organization which is responsible for selling all of the company's products, one basic research organization, one product support organization, one operations department, one information technology department, one facilities department, one purchasing department, one human resources department, one finance department, one legal department and one public relations department.

Defendant's Offer of Proof at 23-26, reprinted in 4 J.A. at 2764-67. If indeed Microsoft is a unitary company, division might very well require Microsoft to reproduce each of these departments in each new entity rather than simply allocate the differing departments among them.

In devising an appropriate remedy, the District Court also should consider whether plaintiffs have established a sufficient causal connection between Microsoft's anticompetitive conduct and its dominant position in the OS market. "Mere existence of an exclusionary act does not itself justify full feasible relief against the monopolist to create maximum competition." 3 AREEDA & HOVENKAMP, ANTITRUST LAW P 650a, at 67. Rather, structural relief, which is "designed to eliminate the monopoly altogether ... requires a clearer indication of a significant causal connection between the conduct and creation or maintenance of the market power." Id. P 653b, at 91-92 (emphasis added). Absent such causation, the antitrust defendant's unlawful behavior should be remedied by "an injunction against continuation of that conduct." Id. P 650a, at 67.

As noted above, see supra Section II.C, we have found a causal connection between Microsoft's exclusionary conduct and its continuing position in the operating systems market only through inference. See 3 AREEDA & HOVENKAMP, ANTITRUST LAW P 653(b), at 91-92 (suggesting that "more extensive equitable relief, particularly remedies such as divestiture designed to eliminate the monopoly altogether, ... require a clearer indication of significant causal connection between the conduct and creation or maintenance of the market power"). Indeed, the District Court expressly did not adopt the position that Microsoft would have lost its position in the OS market but for its anticompetitive behavior. Findings of Fact P 411 ("There is insufficient evidence to find that, absent Microsoft's actions, Navigator and Java already would have ignited genuine competition in the market for Intel-compatible PC operating systems."). If the court on remand is unconvinced of the causal connection between Microsoft's exclusionary conduct and the company's position in the OS market, it may well conclude that divestiture is not an appropriate remedy.

While we do not undertake to dictate to the District Court the precise form that relief should take on remand, we note again that it should be tailored to fit the wrong creating the occasion for the remedy....

VI. JUDICIAL MISCONDUCT

Canon 3A(6) of the Code of Conduct for United States Judges requires federal judges to "avoid public comment on the merits of [ ] pending or impending" cases. Canon 2 tells judges to "avoid impropriety and the appearance of impropriety in all activities," on the bench and off. Canon 3A(4) forbids judges to initiate or consider ex parte communications on the merits of pending or impending proceedings. Section 455(a) of the Judicial Code requires judges to recuse themselves when their "impartiality might reasonably be questioned." *28 U.S.C. § 455*(a).

All indications are that the District Judge violated each of these ethical precepts by talking about the case with reporters. The violations were deliberate, repeated, egregious, and flagrant. The only serious question is what consequences should follow. Microsoft urges us to disqualify the District Judge, vacate the judgment in its entirety and toss out the findings of fact, and remand for a new trial before a different District Judge. At the other extreme, plaintiffs ask us to do nothing. We agree with neither position. [The D.C. Circuit concluded that the district judge should be disqualified retroactively only with respect to the imposition of the remedy, and remanded the case for reassignment to a different trial judge.]

Notes and Questions

1. Both the government and Microsoft claimed victory after the D.C. Circuit rendered its decision. Which side was closer to correct? Is the D.C. Circuit's tying discussion consistent with your reading of Chapter 8, Section 2, of the Casebook? Could the D.C. Circuit have avoid fashioning a special rule of reason when the "tying product is platform software" by focusing its analysis on the special "one product" or "two products" issue, and if two products were found, retaining a *per se* analysis? Would there be any antitrust problem to selling two products together at a lower price than would be the case when each is purchased separately if the lower price were the result of efficiency gains from bundling the two together?

2. Compare the D.C. Circuit's rejection, as bordering "upon the frivolous," of Microsoft's claim that it has "an absolute and unfettered right to use its intellectual property as it wishes" with the Federal Circuit's *Xerox* opinion *infra*. The D.C. Circuit acknowledged that in technologically dynamic markets conduct remedies may be unavailing "because innovation to a large degree has already rendered the anticompetitive conduct obsolete (although by no means harmless)." What should be the standard for the awarding of structural relief in such a situation?

3. On June 8, 1998, the Federal Trade Commission filed an antitrust complaint against Intel Corporation. The FTC's press release summarized the agency's allegations as follows: "The FTC alleged that Intel illegally used its market power when it denied three of its customers

continuing access to technical information necessary to develop computer systems based on Intel processors, and took other steps to punish them for refusing to license key patents on Intel's terms."

One year later, the Commission and Intel entered into a settlement agreement. The FTC's staff's "Analysis of Proposed Consent Order to Aid Public Comment" describes the Commission's case and the terms of the consent order.

* * *

Analysis of Proposed
Consent Order to Aid Public Comment

The Federal Trade Commission has accepted for public comment an Agreement Containing Consent Order with Intel Corporation ("Intel") to resolve the matters charged in an administrative Complaint issued by the Commission on June 8, 1998. . . . The Agreement is for settlement purposes only and does not constitute an admission by Intel that the law has been violated as alleged in the Complaint or that the facts alleged in the Complaint, other than jurisdictional facts, are true.

I. The Complaint

The Complaint alleges that Intel has monopoly power in the worldwide market for general purpose microprocessors. According to the Complaint, Intel's market dominance is reflected in a market share approximating 80 percent of dollar sales, together with high entry barriers including large sunk costs of design and manufacture, substantial economies of scale, customers' investments in existing software, the need to attract support from software developers, and reputational barriers.

The Complaint alleges that Intel sought to maintain its dominance by, among other things, denying advance technical information and product samples of microprocessors to Intel customers ("original equipment manufacturers" or "OEMs") and threatening to withhold product from those OEMs as a means of coercing those customers into licensing their patented innovations to Intel.

A microprocessor is an integrated circuit that serves as the central processing unit (or CPU) of computer systems. Microprocessors are sometimes described as the "brains" of computers because they perform the major data processing functions essential to computer systems. Advance technical information about new microprocessor products is essential to Intel's OEM customers, who design, develop, manufacture, and sell computer system products such as servers, workstations, and desktop and mobile personal computers. Computer design and development require the effective integration of multiple complex microelectronics components (including microprocessors, memory components, core logic chips, graphics controllers, and various input and output devices) into a coherent system. To achieve such system integration, a computer OEM requires product specifications and other technical information about each component, such as the electrical, mechanical, and thermal characteristics of the microprocessor. OEMs also need advance product samples, errata, and related technical assistance in order to perform system testing and debugging, thereby assuring the high performance and reliability of new computer products.

Intel promotes and markets its microprocessors by providing customers with technical information about new Intel products in advance of their commercial release, subject to formal nondisclosure agreements. Such information sharing has substantial commercial benefits for Intel and its OEM customers. Customers benefit because the information enables them to develop and introduce new computer system products incorporating the latest microprocessors as early and efficiently as possible. Intel benefits because a larger group of OEMs can sell new computer systems incorporating Intel's newest microprocessors as soon as the new microprocessors are introduced to the market.

The Complaint charges that Intel suspended its traditional commercial relationships with three established customers -- Digital Equipment Corporation, Intergraph Corporation, and Compaq Computer Corporation -- by refusing to provide advance technical information about, and product samples of, Intel microprocessors. Intel did so, according to the Complaint, to force those customers to end disputes with Intel concerning the customers' asserted intellectual property rights and to grant Intel licenses to patented technology developed and owned by those customers. In at least one of the cases, the Complaint alleges that Intel also acted to create uncertainty in the marketplace about the customer's future source of supply of Intel microprocessors.

The computer industry is characterized by short, dynamic product cycles, which are generally measured in months. Time to market is crucial. Indeed, the denial of advance product information is virtually tantamount to a denial of actual parts, because an OEM customer lacking such information simply cannot design new computer systems on a competitive schedule with other OEMs. An OEM who suffers denial of such information over a period of months will lose much of the profits it might otherwise have earned even from a successful new computer model. Continued denial of advance technical information to an OEM by a dominant supplier can make a customer's very existence as an OEM untenable.

As a result of the commercial pressure exerted by Intel's conduct, Compaq and Digital quickly entered into cross-license arrangements with Intel. Intergraph was able to resist that pressure because it succeeded in obtaining a preliminary injunction from a federal district court requiring Intel to resume and continue supplying Intergraph with advance product information, part samples, and other technical support pending a judicial resolution on the merits of the claims in the lawsuit.

The alleged conduct tends to reinforce Intel's domination of the general purpose microprocessor market in at least three ways. First, the alleged conduct tends to give Intel preferential access to a wide range of technologies being developed by many other firms in the industry. To the extent that firms desiring to compete with Intel are unable to obtain comparable access to such a wide range of technology, they can be seriously disadvantaged, thus making it more difficult for them to challenge Intel's dominance. Second, because patent rights are an important means of promoting innovation, coercion that forces customers to license away rights to microprocessor-related technologies on unfavorable terms tends to diminish the customers' incentives to develop such technologies, and thus harms competition by reducing innovation. Finally, Intel's conduct tends to make it more difficult for an OEM to serve as a platform for microprocessors that compete with Intel's. Intel's actions ensure that Intel can act as a conduit for technology flows from one OEM to another. That is, an OEM that seeks to enforce its intellectual property rights against other Intel customers may face retaliation from Intel, as the Complaint alleges Compaq did when it sued Packard-Bell for patent infringement. The result is that OEMs find it more difficult to differentiate their computer systems from their competitors through patented technology. As a result, an OEM seeking to use non-Intel microprocessors is less able to offset the lack of an Intel microprocessor by the strength of its own reputation for offering superior technology in other areas. For all of these reasons, continuation of this pattern of conduct would likely have injured competition by entrenching Intel's dominant position.

The Complaint also alleges that Intel's exclusionary conduct was not reasonably necessary to serve any legitimate, procompetitive purpose.

Exclusionary conduct by a monopolist that is reasonably capable of significantly contributing to the maintenance of a firm's dominance through unjustified means has long been understood to give rise to serious competitive concerns. See, e.g., Lorain Journal Co. v. United States, 342 U.S. 143, 154 n.7 (1951); Eastman Kodak Co. v. Image Technical Services, 504 U.S. 451, 483 & n.32 (1992); Aspen Skiing Co. v. Aspen Highlands Skiing Co., 472 U.S. 585, 596 n.19 (1985); United States v. Grinnell Corp., 384 U.S. 563, 570-71 (1966); Barry Wright Corp. v. ITT Grinnell Corp., 724 F.2d 227, 230 (1st Cir. 1983) (Breyer, J.) (citing 3 P. Areeda & D. Turner, Antitrust Law, ¶ 626 at 83 (1978)).

Such conduct harms consumers, not only because competition brings lower prices, but also because competition is a powerful spur to the development of new, better, and more diverse products and processes. Unjustified conduct by a monopolist that removes the incentive to such competition by depriving innovators of their reward or otherwise tilting the playing field against new entrants or fringe competitors thus has a direct and substantial impact upon future consumers.

In the absence of a legitimate business justification that outweighs these concerns, such conduct constitutes a violation of Section 2 of the Sherman Act, 15 U.S.C. § 2, and therefore Section 5 of the Federal Trade Commission Act, 15 U.S.C. § 45. In issuing the Complaint, the Commission found reason to believe that such a violation had occurred.

II. Terms of the Proposed Consent Order

The Proposed Order would remedy all of the concerns embodied in the Complaint. The substantive prohibition, Section II.A., prohibits Intel from withholding or threatening to withhold certain advance technical information from a customer or taking other specified actions with respect to such information for reasons relating to an intellectual property dispute with that customer. It also prohibits Intel from refusing or threatening to refuse to sell microprocessors to a customer for reasons related to an intellectual property dispute with that customer. This provision is designed to prevent Intel from restricting access to microprocessor products, or advance technical information relating to such products, as leverage in an intellectual property dispute against a customer that is receiving advance technical information from Intel at the time the dispute arises. The Proposed Order does not impose any kind of broad "compulsory licensing" regime upon Intel. So long as it is otherwise lawful, Intel is free to decide in the first instance whether it chooses to provide or not provide information to customers, and whether to provide more information or earlier information to specific customers in furtherance of a joint venture or other legitimate activity. Moreover, the Order is limited to the types of information that Intel routinely gives to customers to enable them to use Intel microprocessors, not information that would be used to design or manufacture microprocessors in competition with Intel.

In short, Paragraph II.A. secures to Intel customers the right to seek full and fair value for their intellectual property, free from the risk of curtailment of needed advance technical information or product. With one exception, Intel will be required to continue providing information and product while the customer seeks any of a range of legal and equitable remedies available to it, such as damages (trebled or otherwise increased in appropriate cases), reasonable royalties, and attorneys fees and costs. These remedies will generally be sufficient to protect the customer in its exercise of its intellectual property rights. . . .

4. Intel appealed the grant of the preliminary injunction in favor of Intergraph Corporation (described in the FTC's statement supra), and in November 1999, the Court of Appeals for the Federal Circuit vacated the injunction. *Intergraph Corp. v. Intel Corp.*, 195 F.3d 1346 (Fed. Cir. 1999). The Federal Circuit concluded:

> Despite the district court's sensitive concern for Intergraph's well-being while it conducts its patent suit against Intel, there must be an adverse effect on competition in order to bring an antitrust remedy to bear. The remedy of compulsory disclosure of proprietary information and provision of pre-production chips and other commercial and intellectual property is a dramatic remedy for antitrust illegality, and requires violation of antitrust law or the likelihood that such violation would be established. In the proceedings whose

> record is before us, Intergraph has not shown a substantial likelihood of success in establishing that Intel violated the antitrust laws in its actions with respect to Intergraph. . . .

See In re Independent Services Organizations Antitrust Litigation v. Xerox Corp., 203 F.3d 1322 (Fed. Cir. 2000), infra.

Insert after *Kodak*, page 829:

IMAGE TECHNICAL SERVICES, INC. v. EASTMAN KODAK CO.
United States Court of Appeals, Ninth Circuit, 1997.
125 F.3d 1195.

Before: BEEZER and THOMPSON, Circuit Judges, and GILLMOR, District Judge.

BEEZER, J. Plaintiffs-Appellees Image Technical Services, and ten other independent service organizations ("ISOs") that service Kodak photocopiers and micrographic equipment sued the Eastman Kodak Co. ("Kodak") for violations of the Sherman Act. The ISOs alleged that Kodak used its monopoly in the market for Kodak photocopier and micrographic parts to create a second monopoly in the equipment service markets. A jury verdict awarded treble damages totaling $ 71.8 million. The district court denied Kodak's post trial motions and entered a ten year permanent injunction requiring Kodak to sell "all parts" to ISOs. . . .

This appeal raises questions relating to the application of antitrust principles upon a finding that a monopolist unilaterally refused to deal with competitors. We also address overlapping patent and copyright issues and their significance in the antitrust context. . . .

I

Kodak manufactures, sells and services high volume photocopiers and micrographic (or microfilm) equipment. Competition in these markets is strong. In the photocopier market Kodak's competitors include Xerox, IBM and Canon. Kodak's competitors in the micrographics market include Minolta, Bell & Howell and 3M. Despite comparable products in these markets, Kodak's equipment is distinctive. Although Kodak equipment may perform similar functions to that of its competitors, Kodak's parts are not interchangeable with parts used in other manufacturers' equipment.

Kodak sells and installs replacement parts for its equipment. Kodak competes with ISOs in these markets. Kodak has ready access to all parts necessary for repair services because it manufactures many of the parts used in its equipment and purchases the remaining necessary parts from independent original-equipment manufacturers. In the service market, Kodak repairs at least 80% of the machines it manufactures. ISOs began servicing Kodak equipment in the early 1980's, and have provided cheaper and better service at times, according to some customers. ISOs obtain parts for repair service from a variety of sources, including, at one time, Kodak.

As ISOs grew more competitive, Kodak began restricting access to its photocopier and micrographic parts. In 1985, Kodak stopped selling copier parts to ISOs, and in 1986, Kodak halted sales of micrographic parts to ISOs. Additionally, Kodak secured agreements from their contracted original-equipment manufacturers not to sell parts to ISOs. These parts restrictions limited the ISOs' ability to compete in the service market for Kodak machines. Competition in the service market requires that service providers have ready access to all parts.

Kodak offers annual or multi-year service contracts to its customers. Service providers generally contract with equipment owners through multi-year service contracts. ISOs claim that they were unable to provide similar contracts because they lack a reliable supply of parts. Some ISOs contend that the parts shortage forced them out of business. . . .

After remand [from the Supreme Court], the case proceeded to trial in the district court. Before closing arguments, the ISOs withdrew their § 1 tying and conspiracy claims. The remaining § 2 attempted monopolization and monopolization claims were submitted to the jury. A unanimous verdict awarded damages to the ISO's totaling $ 71.8 million after trebling. Ten ISOs were awarded damages covering lost service profits in the amount of $12,172,900 (before trebling) and six ISOs were awarded damages covering lost profits for used equipment sales totaling $ 11,775,400 (before trebling).

After accepting the verdict, the district court crafted a ten year injunction requiring Kodak to sell all parts to ISOs on "reasonable and nondiscriminatory terms and prices". . . .

II

Section 2 of the Sherman Act prohibits monopolies, attempts to form monopolies, as well as combinations and conspiracies to do so. The ISOs presented evidence in support of two § 2 theories: attempted monopolization and monopolization. They alleged, and the jury concluded, that Kodak used its monopoly over Kodak photocopier and micrographic parts to attempt to create and actually create a second monopoly over the service markets. . . .

Kodak primarily attacks the ISOs' monopoly claim because success would likely upset the "attempt" verdict as well. We now address Kodak's appeal against the background of the Supreme Court's opinion in Kodak and the extensive record developed at trial. . . .

[The Ninth Circuit concluded that Kodak had monopoly power in "all Kodak parts" markets for photcopiers and micrographics equipment.]

The second element of a § 2 monopoly claim, the "conduct" element, is the use of monopoly power "to foreclose competition, to gain a competitive advantage, or to destroy a competitor." Kodak, 504 U.S. at 482-83 (quoting United States v. Griffith, 334 U.S. 100 (1948)). The ISOs proceeded under a "monopoly leveraging" theory, alleging that Kodak used its monopoly over Kodak parts to gain or attempt to gain a monopoly over the service of Kodak equipment. The Supreme Court endorsed this theory in Kodak noting: "If Kodak adopted its parts and service policies as part of a scheme of willful acquisition or maintenance of monopoly power, it will have violated § 2." *Id.* (citations omitted). "Willful acquisition" or "maintenance of monopoly power" involves "exclusionary conduct," not power gained "from growth or development as a consequence of a superior product, business acumen, or historic accident." Grinnell, 384 U.S. at 570-71.

Kodak attacks the district court's monopoly conduct jury instructions as well as the ISOs' evidence establishing Kodak's exclusionary conduct. A challenge to a jury instruction on the grounds that it misstates the relevant elements is a question of law reviewed de novo. Caballero v. Concord, 956 F.2d 204, 206 (9th Cir. 1992). As noted, the jury's verdict will stand if supported by substantial evidence.

1. Kodak's chief complaint with the monopoly power jury instructions lies with Jury Instruction No. 29. That Instruction, entitled

"Monopolization - Monopoly Conduct," states in relevant part:

> [a] company with monopoly power in a relevant market has no general duty to cooperate with its business rivals and may refuse to deal with them or with their customers if valid business reasons exist for such refusal. It is unlawful, however, for a monopolist to engage in conduct, including refusals to deal, that unnecessarily excludes or handicaps competitors in order to maintain a monopoly.

Kodak argues that this instruction lacks objective standards and improperly includes within the prohibited activities a lawful monopolist's "aggressive" competition.

Specifically, Kodak challenges Instruction No. 29's "unnecessarily excludes or handicaps competitors" language. Kodak says that this language is based on a form of "monopoly leveraging" that we previously rejected in Alaska Airlines, Inc. v. United Airlines, Inc., 948 F.2d 536, 543 (9th Cir. 1991). In Alaska Airlines we did reject the Second Circuit's holding in Berkey Photo, Inc. v. Eastman Kodak Co., 603 F.2d 263 (2d Cir. 1979). Berkey Photo recognized liability under § 2 of the Sherman Act on a theory of monopoly leveraging involving a firm which used "its monopoly power in one market to gain a competitive advantage in another, albeit without an attempt to monopolize the second market." 603 F.2d at 275. In Alaska Airlines, we held that "monopoly leveraging" could not exist as a basis for § 2 liability in the absence of the defendant using its monopoly in one market to monopolize or attempt to monopolize the downstream market. 948 F.2d at 547. We characterized Berkey Photo's downstream monopoly requirement - "to gain a competitive advantage" - as too "loose." Alaska Airlines, 948 F.2d at 546.

Kodak accuses the district court of incorporating Berkey Photo's repudiated language into the court's instructions. We disagree. Instruction No. 29 required the jury to find that Kodak's monopoly conduct be undertaken "in order to maintain a monopoly" in the downstream market. Berkey Photo's watered-down standard does not go this far. Instruction No. 29 makes clear that the monopolies at issue are Kodak's alleged service monopolies and the Instruction required the jury to find that Kodak acted in furtherance of maintaining its service monopolies. Instruction No. 29's "unnecessarily excludes or handicaps competitors" language does not come from Berkey Photo, but from the jury instruction endorsed by the Supreme Court in Aspen

Skiing Co. v. Aspen Highlands Skiing Corp., 472 U.S. 585, 597, 611 (1985).

2. Kodak also objects to the attempted monopolization and monopolization jury instructions on the grounds that they fail to describe adequately the "essential facilities" doctrine, which Kodak contends is the controlling law in unilateral refusal to deal cases. Kodak asserts that this doctrine is the sole legal theory which could require Kodak to sell "all parts." Kodak argues that the essential facilities doctrine required the jury to find that Kodak's parts monopoly carries "the power to eliminate competition."

Kodak's challenge raises a novel issue: whether a monopolist is liable under § 2 of the Sherman Act for an anticompetitive refusal to deal only under an "essential facilities" theory, that is, only when the refusal involves something "essential" to the survival of competitors. As noted, Kodak would answer affirmatively; we reject this theory. Instead, relying on Kodak and Aspen Skiing, we endorse the ISOs' theory that § 2 of the Sherman Act prohibits a monopolist from refusing to deal in order to create or maintain a monopoly absent a legitimate business justification. We need not apply the essential facilities doctrine.

Section 2 of the Sherman Act prohibits a monopolist's unilateral action, like Kodak's refusal to deal, if that conduct harms the competitive process in the absence of a legitimate business justification. See Kodak, 504 U.S. at 483 n.32 (citing Aspen Skiing, 472 U.S. at 602). Unilateral refusals to deal often concern an "essential" facility. See Otter Tail Power Co. v. United States, 410 U.S. 366 (1973). In Alaska Airlines, we defined the essential facilities doctrine, generally, as: imposing "liability when one firm, which controls an essential facility, denies a second firm reasonable access to a product or service that the second firm must obtain to compete with the first." 948 F.2d 536, 542. A facility is "essential" if it is otherwise unavailable and cannot be "reasonably or practically duplicated." Anaheim v. Southern California Edison Co., 955 F.2d 1373, 1380 (9th Cir. 1992).

In Otter Trail Power Co. v. United States, the Supreme Court held that the defendant, Otter Trail Power, used its electrical utility equipment, an "essential facility," to gain monopoly power over all commercial electrical services. 410 U.S. at 377-79. Otter Trail Power generally sold both wholesale and retail electrical services. Later it refused to provide only wholesale electrical services to several municipalities which intended to supply retail electrical services to the ultimate customers. The Court held that Otter Trail

Power's refusal to supply "only wholesale" services eliminated competition in the downstream market for retail services as Otter Trail Power owned the only "facility" capable of supplying these services. The Court held that such "exclusionary" conduct violated § 2 of the Sherman Act. *Id.*

In Alaska Airlines, we interpreted Otter Trail as requiring plaintiffs proceeding under the "essential facilities" doctrine to establish that the controlled facility "carries with it the power to eliminate competition in the downstream market." 948 F.2d at 544; see, e.g., Twin Laboratories, Inv. v. Weider Health & Fitness, 900 F.2d 566, 569 (2d Cir. 1990) ("A successful 'essential facilities' plaintiff must prove that denial of access has caused it 'severe handicap' [in the market]."). Kodak faults the district court for failing to instruct the jury that to be liable under § 2, Kodak's exclusionary conduct must have "eliminated competition" in the downstream service market.

The Supreme Court has never explicitly held that a § 2 refusal to deal claim can only be established under the "essential facilities" rubric. In Kodak the Supreme Court never discussed the essential facilities doctrine; nor do any of the cases cited by the Court employ the essential facilities analysis. See 504 U.S. at 483 (citing Grinnell Corp., 384 U.S. at 570-71; United States v. Aluminum Co. of America, 148 F.2d 416, 432 (2d Cir. 1945), and Aspen Skiing, 472 U.S. at 600-605). Rather in discussing a firm's right to "refuse to deal with its competitors," the Supreme Court noted, citing Aspen Skiing, that this right "exists only if there are legitimate competitive reasons for the refusal." Kodak, 504 U.S. at 483 n.32. . . .

III

Our conclusion that the ISOs have shown that Kodak has both attained monopoly power and exercised exclusionary conduct does not end our inquiry. Kodak's conduct may not be actionable if supported by a legitimate business justification. When a legitimate business justification supports a monopolist's exclusionary conduct, that conduct does not violate § 2 of the Sherman Act. See Kodak, 504 U.S. at 483; Oahu Gas, 838 F.2d at 368. A plaintiff may rebut an asserted business justification by demonstrating either that the justification does not legitimately promote competition or that the justification is pretextual. See Kodak, 504 U.S. at 483-84 (citing Kodak, 903 F.2d at 618). Kodak asserts that the protection of its patented and copyrighted parts is a valid business justification for its anticompetitive conduct and argues that the district court's erroneous jury instructions made it impossible for the jury to properly consider this justification. Kodak attacks the district court's failure both to provide a "less restrictive alternatives" instruction, and to instruct as to Kodak's intellectual property rights. . . .

A. Least Restrictive Alternatives

Kodak argues that the district court erred by failing to instruct the jury that it was not to consider whether Kodak could have accomplished its business objectives through less restrictive alternatives. Kodak also questions the sufficiency of the ISOs' pretext evidence. The ISOs counter that Kodak waived its arguments regarding business justifications by failing to move for judgment as a matter of law. We disagree. To the extent that Kodak's arguments focus on the jury instructions and not the general sufficiency of the evidence, Rule 50(b) does not apply.

Kodak argues that monopolization, unlike tying, does not require consideration of whether the defendant could have achieved its aims through less restrictive alternatives. Kodak, however, cites no authority mandating an instruction requiring that the jury not consider "less restrictive alternatives." Kodak's argument rests on the combination of the district court's refusal to use Kodak's requested language and Kodak's disagreement with the "unnecessarily excludes or handicaps competitors" language of Jury Instruction Nos. 29 and 34. As a result of this combination, Kodak argues, the ISOs were able to argue a "necessity" standard and ask the jury to weight what Kodak did "against the alternatives."

As discussed above, the "unnecessarily excluded or handicaps" language was permissible under Aspen Skiing. Moreover, the district court's instruction here, Instruction No. 28, was very similar to both the language proposed by Kodak and the language endorsed by the Supreme Court in Aspen Skiing, 472 U.S. at 597. Jury Instruction No. 28 defines "exclusionary conduct" as impairing "the efforts of others to compete for customers in an unnecessarily restrictive way." The district court also instructed that: (1) Kodak could refuse to deal if valid business reasons existed and (2) the jury could not "second guess whether Kodak's business judgment was wise or correct in retrospect." Under these instructions the jury could not consider "less restrictive alternatives" without "second guessing" Kodak and thus violating the jury instructions. We presume that the jury followed the court's instructions. United States v. Alston, 974 F.2d 1206, 1210 (9th Cir. 1992).

Kodak next argues that the ISOs' primary arguments refuting Kodak's business justifications were "less restrictive alternative" arguments. Kodak focuses on the ISOs' attack on Kodak's quality control justification as one such "less restrictive alternative" argument. Kodak argues that because "the legitimacy of quality control is beyond reproach," the ISOs were forced to establish this justification, and others, were pretextual. The ISOs did establish pretext: they attacked Kodak's quality control justification on the grounds that it was pretextual, not because it was the least restrictive alternative. Counsel for the ISOs argued that Kodak's quality control justification was "a joke" because ISOs do not interfere with the quality of Kodak's service. We hold that the district court did not err in its instructions.

Kodak has waived its insufficiency of evidence claim on this issue by failing to move for judgment as a matter of law at trial. We review only for plain error. Cabrales, 864 F.2d at 1459. The ISOs' evidence suffices to support the jury's rejection of Kodak's business justifications, as the record reflects evidence of pretext. The ISOs presented evidence that: (1) Kodak adopted its parts policy only after an ISO won a contract with the State of California; (2) Kodak allowed its own customers to service their machines; (3) Kodak customers could distinguish breakdowns due to poor service from breakdowns due to parts; and (4) many customers preferred ISO service.

B. Intellectual Property Rights

Kodak also attacks the district court's business justifications instructions for their failure to properly detail Kodak's intellectual property rights. Kodak argues that the court failed to instruct the jury that Kodak's numerous patents and copyrights provide a legitimate business justification for Kodak's alleged exclusionary conduct. Kodak holds 220 valid United States patents covering 65 parts for its high volume photocopiers and micrographics equipment, and all Kodak diagnostic software and service software are copyrighted. The jury instructions do not afford Kodak any "rights" or "privileges" based on its patents and copyrights: all parts are treated the same. In Jury Instruction No. 37, the court told the jury:

> if you find that Kodak engaged in monopolization or attempted monopolization by misuse of its alleged parts monopoly . . . then the fact that some of the replacement parts are patented or copyrighted does not provide Kodak with a defense against any of those antitrust claims.

In Jury Instruction No. 28, the court stated, over Kodak's objection, that:

> such [exclusionary] conduct does not refer to ordinary means of competition, like offering better products or services, exercising superior skill or business judgment, utilizing more efficient technology, or exercising natural competitive advantages.

Kodak proposed to include "exercising lawful patents and copyrights" amongst the list of non-exclusionary conduct in Instruction No. 28, but the district court rejected that language.

Kodak's challenge raises unresolved questions concerning the relationship between federal antitrust, copyright and patent laws. In particular we must determine the significance of a monopolist's unilateral refusal to sell or license a patented or copyrighted product in the context of a § 2 monopolization claim based upon monopoly leveraging. This is a question of first impression.

1. We first identify the general principles of antitrust, copyright and patent law as we must ultimately harmonize these statutory schemes in responding to Kodak's challenge.

Antitrust law seeks to promote and protect a competitive marketplace for the benefit of the public. See Standard Oil Co. v. United States, 221 U.S. 1, 58 (1911); SCM Corp. v. Xerox Corp., 645 F.2d 1195, 1203 (2d Cir. 1981). The Sherman Act, the relevant antitrust law here, prohibits efforts both to restrain trade by combination or conspiracy and the acquisition or maintenance of a monopoly by exclusionary conduct.

Patent law seeks to protect inventions, while inducing their introduction into the market for public benefit. SCM Corp., 645 F.2d at 1203. Patent laws "reward the inventor with the power to exclude others from making, using or selling [a patented] invention throughout the United States." *Id.* Meanwhile, the public benefits both from the faster introduction of inventions, and the resulting increase in market competition. Legally, a patent amounts to a permissible monopoly over the protected work. See Zenith Radio Corp. v. Hazeltine Research, Inc., 395 U.S. 100, (1969). Patent laws "are in pari materia with the antitrust laws and modify them pro tanto (as far as the patent laws go)." Simpson v. Union Oil Co., 377 U.S. 13, 24 (1964).

Federal copyright law "secures a fair return for an author's creative labor" in the short run, while ultimately seeking "to stimulate artistic creativity for the general public good." Twentieth Century Music Corp. v. Aiken, 422 U.S. 151, 156 (1975) (internal quotations omitted). The Copyright Act grants to the copyright owner the exclusive right to distribute the protected work. 17 U.S.C. § 106. This right encompasses the right to "refrain from vending or licensing," as the owner may "content [itself] with simply exercising the right to exclude others from using [its] property." Data General, 36 F.3d at 1186 (quoting Fox Film Corp. v. Doyal, 286 U.S. 123, 127 (1932)); see Stewart v. Abend, 495 U.S. 207, 228-29 (1990)("nothing in the copyright statutes would prevent an author from hoarding all of his works during the term of the copyright.")

Clearly the antitrust, copyright and patent laws both overlap and, in certain situations, seem to conflict. This is not a new revelation. We have previously noted the "obvious tension" between the patent and antitrust laws: "one body of law creates and protects monopoly power while the other seeks to proscribe it." United States v. Westinghouse Electric Corp., 648 F.2d 642, 646 (9th Cir. 1981) (citations omitted). Similarly, tension exists between the antitrust and copyright laws. See Data General, 36 F.3d at 1187.

Two principles have emerged regarding the interplay between these laws: (1) neither patent nor copyright holders are immune from antitrust liability, and (2) patent and copyright holders may refuse to sell or license protected work. First, as to antitrust liability, case law supports the proposition that a holder of a patent or copyright violates the antitrust laws by "concerted and contractual behavior that threatens competition." *Id.* at 1185 n.63 (citation omitted). In Kodak, the Supreme Court noted:

> [we have] held many times that power gained through some natural advantage such as a patent, copyright, or business acumen can give rise to liability if "a seller exploits his dominant position in one market to expand his empire into the next."

504 U.S. at 480 n.29.

Case law also supports the right of a patent or copyright holder to refuse to sell or license protected work. See Westinghouse, 648 F.2d at 647. In United States v. Westinghouse Electric Corp., we held that "the right to license [a] patent, exclusively or otherwise, or to refuse to license at all, is the 'untrammeled right' of the patentee." *Id.*

2. Next we lay out the problem presented here. The Supreme Court touched on this question in Kodak, i.e., the effect to be given a monopolist's unilateral refusal to sell or license a patented or copyrighted product in the context of a § 2 monopoly leveraging claim. In footnote 29, previously discussed, the Supreme Court in Kodak refutes the argument that the possession by a manufacturer of "inherent power" in the market for its parts "should immunize [that manufacturer] from the antitrust laws in another market." 504 U.S. at 480 n.29. The Court stated that a monopolist who acquires a dominant position in one market through patents and copyrights may violate § 2 if the monopolist exploits that dominant position to enhance a monopoly in another market. Although footnote 29 appears in the Court's discussion of the § 1 tying claim, the § 2 discussion frequently refers back to the § 1 discussion, and the Court's statement that "exploiting [a] dominant position in one market to expand [the] empire into the next" is broad enough to cover monopoly leveraging under § 2. *Id.* By responding in this fashion, the Court in Kodak supposed that intellectual property rights do not confer an absolute immunity from antitrust claims.

The Kodak Court, however, did not specifically address the question of antitrust liability based upon a unilateral refusal to deal in a patented or copyrighted product. Kodak and its amicus correctly indicate that the right of exclusive dealing is reserved from antitrust liability. We find no reported case in which a court has imposed antitrust liability for a unilateral refusal to sell or license a patent or copyright. Courts do not generally view a monopolist's unilateral refusal to license a patent as "exclusionary conduct." See Data General, 36 F.3d at 1186 (citing Miller Insituform, Inc. v. Insituform of North America, 830 F.2d 606, 609 (6th Cir. 1987) ("A patent holder who lawfully acquires a patent cannot be held liable under Section 2 of the Sherman Act for maintaining the monopoly power he lawfully acquired by refusing to license the patent to others."); Westinghouse, 648 F.2d at 647 (finding no antitrust violation because "Westinghouse has done no more than to license some of its patents and refuse to license others"); SCM Corp., 645 F.2d at 1206 ("where a patent has been lawfully acquired, subsequent conduct permissible under the patent laws cannot trigger any liability under the antitrust laws.").

This basic right of exclusion does have limits. For example, a patent offers no protection if it was unlawfully acquired. Data General, 36 F.3d at 1186 (citing SCM Corp., 645 F.2d at 1208-09). Nor does the right of exclusion protect an attempt to extend a lawful monopoly beyond the grant of a patent. See Mercoid, 320 U.S. at 665. Section 2 of the Sherman Act condemns exclusionary conduct that extends natural monopolies into separate markets. Much depends, therefore, on the definition of the patent grant and the relevant market.

The relevant market for determining the patent or copyright grant is determined under patent or copyright law. See, e.g., *id.* at 666 (the patent's grant "is limited to the invention which it defines."). The relevant markets for antitrust purposes are determined by examining economic conditions. See Kodak, 504 U.S. at 462. . . .

Parts and service here have been proven separate markets in the antitrust context, but this does not resolve the question whether the service market falls "reasonably within the patent [or copyright] grant" for the purpose of determining the extent of the exclusive rights conveyed. Mallinckrodt, Inc. v. Medipart, Inc., 976 F.2d 700, 708-09 (Fed. Cir. 1992). These are separate questions, which may result in contrary answers. At the border of intellectual property monopolies and antitrust markets lies a field of dissonance yet to be harmonized by statute or the Supreme Court.

When an owner of intellectual property takes concerted action in violation of § 1, this dissonance does not threaten his core right of exclusion. See Brownell v. Ketcham Wire & Manufacturing Co., 211 F.2d 121, 129 (9th Cir. 1954) (listing acts giving rise to antitrust liability). Contrary to the ISOs' arguments, there is an important difference between § 1 tying and § 2 monopoly leveraging: the limiting principles of § 1 restrain those claims from making the impact on intellectual property rights threatened by § 2 monopoly leveraging claims. Where, as here, the claim involves a failure to act that is at the heart of the property right, liability depends largely on market definition and lacks the limiting principles of § 1. Under § 2, "behavior that might otherwise not be of concern to the antitrust laws - or that might even be viewed as procompetitive - can take on exclusionary connotations when practiced by a monopolist." Kodak, 504 U.S. at 488 (Scalia, J. dissenting) (citing 3 Areeda & Turner, Par. 813, at 300-302); see also Greyhound Computer v. International Business Machines, 559 F.2d 488, 498 (9th Cir. 1977) (otherwise lawful conduct may be exclusionary when practiced by a monopolist). Harmonizing antitrust monopoly theory with the monopolies granted by intellectual property law requires that some weight be given to the intellectual property rights of the monopolist.

The effect of claims based upon unilateral conduct on the value of intellectual property rights is a cause for serious concern. Unilateral conduct is the most common conduct in the economy. After Kodak, unilateral conduct by a manufacturer in its own aftermarkets may give rise to liability and, in one-brand markets, monopoly power created by patents and copyrights will frequently be found. Under current law the defense of monopolization claims will rest largely on the legitimacy of the asserted business justifications, as evidenced by the jury instructions approved in Aspen Skiing. . . .

3. We now resolve the question detailed above. Under the fact-based approaches of Aspen Skiing and Kodak, some measure must guarantee that the jury account for the procompetitive effects and statutory rights extended by the intellectual property laws. To assure such consideration, we adopt a modified version of the rebuttable presumption created by the First Circuit in Data General, and hold that "while exclusionary conduct can include a monopolist's unilateral refusal to license a [patent or] copyright," or to sell its patented or copyrighted work, a monopolist's "desire to exclude others from its [protected] work is a presumptively valid business justification for any immediate harm to consumers." Data General, 36 F.3d at 1187.

This presumption does not "rest on formalistic distinctions" which "are generally disfavored in antitrust laws;" rather it is based on "actual market realities." Kodak, 504 U.S. at 466-67. This presumption harmonizes the goals of the relevant statutes and takes into account the long term effects of regulation on these purposes. The presumption should act to focus the factfinder on the primary interest of both intellectual property and antitrust laws: public interest. Mercoid, 320 U.S. at 665 (citation omitted) ("It is the public interest which is dominant in the patent system."); Standard Oil, 221 U.S. at 58 (antitrust laws serve the public interest by encouraging effective competition).

Given this presumption, the district court's failure to give any weight to Kodak's intellectual property rights in the jury instructions constitutes an abuse of discretion. This error was, however, harmless. The ISOs maintain that Kodak argued protection of intellectual property as a business justification to the jury, which rejected this justification as pretextual. An error in instructing the jury in a civil case does not require reversal if it is more probable than not harmless. Jenkins v. Union Pacific R. Co., 22 F.3d 206, 210 (9th Cir. 1994). . . .

Phrased in these broad terms, Kodak's argument repeats the "free-riding" justification rejected, as a matter of law, by the Supreme Court. Kodak, 504 U.S. at 485. The Supreme Court held that preventing the ISOs from "exploiting the investment Kodak has made in product development, manufacturing and equipment sales" does not suffice as a business justification. *Id.* ("This understanding of free-riding has no support in our case law.").

Given the interplay of the antitrust and intellectual property laws discussed above, Kodak's contention that its refusal to sell its parts to ISOs was based on its reluctance to sell its patented or copyrighted parts was a presumptively legitimate business justification. See Data General, 36 F.3d at 1187. Kodak may assert that its desire to profit from its intellectual property rights justifies its conduct, and the jury should presume that this justification is legitimately procompetitive.

Nonetheless, this presumption is rebuttable. See *id.* at 1188. In Data General, the First Circuit reasoned that the plaintiff did not rebut the presumption by drawing an analogy to Aspen Skiing, where a monopolist made an important change in a its practices, which had both originated in a competitive market and persisted for several years. See Data General, 36 F.3d at 1188. Because competitive conditions had never prevailed in the service market, the First Circuit concluded that it would be inappropriate to infer "from [defendant's] change of heart that its former policies 'satisfy consumer demand in free competitive markets.'" *Id.* at 1188 (quoting Aspen Skiing, 472 U.S. at 603). As in Data General, we are not faced here with a simple comparison between the monopolist's market and the established competitive market found in Aspen Skiing.

The Data General court noted that the presumption of legitimacy can be rebutted by evidence that the monopolist acquired the protection of the intellectual property laws in an unlawful manner. See 36 F.3d at 1188 (citation omitted). The presumption may also be rebutted by evidence of pretext. Neither the aims of intellectual property law, nor the antitrust laws justify allowing a monopolist to rely upon a pretextual business justification to mask anticompetitive conduct. See Kodak, 504 U.S. at 484 (Because "Kodak's willingness to allow self-service casts doubt on its quality claim. . . . a reasonable trier of fact could conclude that [this justification] is pretextual.") (citation omitted).

Kodak defends its intellectual property rights "justification" against claims of pretext. Kodak argues that its subjective motivation is irrelevant. Kodak also contends, citing Olympia Equipment Leasing Co. v. Western Union Telegraph Co., 797 F.2d 370, 379 (7th Cir.), reh'g denied, (7th Cir. 1986), that a desire to best the competition does not prove pretext, nor does hostility to competitors. Kodak's argument and its accompanying authority stands for nothing more than the proposition that a desire to compete does not demonstrate pretext.

Evidence regarding the state of mind of Kodak employees may show pretext, when such evidence suggests that the proffered business justification played no part in the decision to act. Kodak's parts manager testified that patents "did not cross [his] mind" at the time Kodak began the parts policy. Further, no distinction was made by Kodak between "proprietary" parts covered by tooling or engineering clauses and patented or copyrighted products. In denying Kodak's motion for a new trial, the district court commented that Kodak was not actually motivated by protecting its intellectual property rights. Kodak argues that the district court should have allowed the jury to reach this conclusion.

Kodak photocopy and micrographics equipment requires thousands of parts, of which only 65 were patented. Unlike the other cases involving refusals to license patents, this case concerns a blanket refusal that included protected and unprotected products. Cf. Westinghouse, 648 F.2d at 647 (refusal to license patents); SCM Corp., 645 F.2d and 1197 (same); Miller Instituform, 830 F.2d at 607 (claim based on termination of license agreement). From this evidence, it is more probable than not that the jury would have found Kodak's presumptively valid business justification rebutted on the grounds of pretext.

Kodak argues that the existence of some patented and copyrighted products undermines ISOs "all parts" theory. To the contrary, as discussed above, the "all parts market reflect the "commercial realities" of the marketplace and the lack of identifiable separate markets for individual parts. The fact that Kodak did not differentiate between patented and nonpatented parts lends further support to the existence of these commercial realities. The jury accepted the "all parts" theory and found a scheme of monopolize the service market through Kodak's conduct. We hold that the district court's failure to instruct on Kodak's intellectual property rights was harmless. . . .[1]

IN RE INDEPENDENT SERVICE ORGANIZATIONS ANTITRUST LITIGATION v. XEROX CORP.
United States Court of Appeals, Federal Circuit, 2000.
203 F.3d 1322.

Before, MAYER, Chief Judge, and ARCHER and PLAGER, Circuit Judges.

MAYER, J. CSU, L.L.C. appeals the judgment of the United States District Court for the District of Kansas, dismissing on summary judgment CSU's claims that Xerox's refusal to sell patented parts and copyrighted manuals and to license copyrighted software violate the antitrust laws. . . . Because we agree with the district court that CSU has not raised a genuine issue as to any material fact and that Xerox is entitled to judgment as a matter of law, we affirm.

Background

Xerox manufactures, sells, and services high-volume copiers. Beginning in 1984, it established a policy of not selling parts unique to its series 10 copiers to independent service organizations ("ISOs"), including

---

[1] The Court then affirmed the findings below on all liability issues, revised and remanded specific damage awards, and affirmed various damage awards. The Court modified the injunction in various ways. District Judge Gillmore concurred in almost all of the majority's opinion, but she dissented with respect to two modifications of the injunction because "these modifications are unnecessary and significantly reduce the effectiveness of the injunctions."

CSU, unless they were also end-users of the copiers. In 1987, the policy was expanded to include all new products as well as existing series 9 copiers. Enforcement of this policy was tightened in 1989, and Xerox cut off CSU's direct purchase of restricted parts. Xerox also implemented an "on-site end-user verification" procedure to confirm that the parts ordered by certain ISOs or their customers were actually for their end-user use. Initially this procedure applied to only the six most successful ISOs, which included CSU.

To maintain its existing business of servicing Xerox equipment, CSU used parts cannibalized from used Xerox equipment, parts obtained from other ISOs, and parts purchased through a limited number of its customers. For approximately one year, CSU also obtained parts from Rank Xerox, a majority-owned European affiliate of Xerox, until Xerox forced Rank Xerox to stop selling parts to CSU and other ISOs. In 1994, Xerox settled an antitrust lawsuit with a class of ISOs by which it agreed to suspend its restrictive parts policy for six and one-half years and to license its diagnostic software for four and one-half years. CSU opted out of that settlement and filed this suit alleging that Xerox violated the Sherman Act by setting the prices on its patented parts much higher for ISOs than for end-users to force ISOs to raise their prices. This would eliminate ISOs in general and CSU in particular as competitors in the relevant service markets for high speed copiers and printers.

Xerox counterclaimed for patent and copyright infringement and contested CSU's antitrust claims as relying on injury solely caused by Xerox's lawful refusal to sell or license patented parts and copyrighted software. Xerox also claimed that CSU could not assert a patent or copyright misuse defense to Xerox's infringement counterclaims based on Xerox's refusal to deal.

The district court granted summary judgment to Xerox dismissing CSU's antitrust claims and holding that if a patent or copyright is lawfully acquired, the patent or copyright holder's unilateral refusal to sell or license its patented invention or copyrighted expression is not unlawful exclusionary conduct under the antitrust laws, even if the refusal to deal impacts competition in more than one market. The court also held, in both the patent and copyright contexts, that the right holder's intent in refusing to deal and any other alleged exclusionary acts committed by the right holder are irrelevant to antitrust law. This appeal followed.

Discussion

. . . As a general proposition, when reviewing a district court's judgment involving federal antitrust law, we are guided by the law of the regional circuit in which that district court sits, in this case the Tenth Circuit. We apply our own law, not regional circuit law, to resolve issues that clearly involve our exclusive jurisdiction. "Whether conduct in procuring or enforcing a patent is sufficient to strip a patentee of its immunity from the antitrust laws is to be decided as a question of Federal Circuit law." *Nobelpharma, 141 F.3d at 1068; see Midwest Indus., Inc. v. Karavan Trailers, Inc., 175 F.3d 1356, 1360 (Fed. Cir. 1999)* (en banc in relevant part) ("Pro-Mold and Nobelpharma make clear that our responsibility as the tribunal having sole appellate responsibility for the development of patent law requires that we do more than simply apply our law to questions of substantive patent law. In order to fulfill our obligation of promoting uniformity in the field of patent law, it is equally important to apply our construction of patent law to the questions whether and to what extent patent law preempts or conflicts with other causes of action."). The district court's grant of summary judgment as to CSU's antitrust claims arising from Xerox's refusal to sell its patented parts is therefore reviewed as a matter of Federal Circuit law, while consideration of the antitrust claim based on Xerox's refusal to sell or license its copyrighted manuals and software is under Tenth Circuit law.

A.

Intellectual property rights do not confer a privilege to violate the antitrust laws. See *Intergraph Corp. v. Intel Corp., 195 F.3d 1346, 1362 (Fed. Cir. 1999)*. "But it is also correct that the antitrust laws do not negate the patentee's right to exclude others from patent property." Id. "The commercial advantage gained by new technology and its statutory protection by patent do not convert the possessor thereof into a prohibited monopolist." *Abbott Lab. v. Brennan, 952 F.2d 1346, 1354 (Fed. Cir. 1991)*. "The patent right must be 'coupled with violations of § 2', and the elements of violation of 15 U.S.C. § 2 must be met." Id. "Determination of whether the patentee meets the Sherman Act elements of monopolization or attempt to monopolize is governed by the rules of application of the antitrust laws to market participants, with due consideration to the exclusivity that inheres in the patent grant." Id. at 1354-55.

A patent alone does not demonstrate market power. The United States

Department of Justice and Federal Trade Commission have issued guidance that, even where it exists, such "market power does not 'impose on the intellectual property owner an obligation to license the use of that property to others.'" *Intergraph, 195 F.3d at 1362* (citing United States Department of Justice and Federal Trade Comm'n Antitrust Guidelines for the Licensing of Intellectual Property 4 (1995)). There is "no reported case in which a court has imposed antitrust liability for a unilateral refusal to sell or license a patent . . . ." Id. The patentee's right to exclude is further supported by section 271(d) of the Patent Act which states, in pertinent part, that "no patent owner otherwise entitled to relief . . . shall be denied relief or deemed guilty of misuse or illegal extension of the patent right by reason of his having . . . (4) refused to license or use any rights to the patent . . ." 35 U.S.C. § 271(d) (1999).

The patentee's right to exclude, however, is not without limit. As we recently observed in Glass Equipment Development Inc. v. Besten, Inc., a patent owner who brings suit to enforce the statutory right to exclude others from making, using, or selling the claimed invention is exempt from the antitrust laws, even though such a suit may have an anticompetitive effect, unless the infringement defendant proves one of two conditions. First, he may prove that the asserted patent was obtained through knowing and willful fraud within the meaning of *Walker Process Equipment, Inc. v. Food Machinery & Chemical Corp., 382 U.S. 172, 177 (1965)*. See *Glass Equip. Dev., 174 F.3d at 1343*. Or he may demonstrate that the infringement suit was a mere sham to cover what is actually no more han an attempt to interfere directly with the business relationships of a competitor. See id. (citing *Eastern R.R. Presidents Conference v. Noerr Motor Freight, Inc., 365 U.S. 127, 144 (1961)*). Here, CSU makes no claim that Xerox obtained its patents through fraud in the Patent and Trademark Office; the Walker Process analysis is not implicated.

"Irrespective of the patent applicant's conduct before the [Patent and Trademark Office], an antitrust claim can also be based on [an] allegation that a suit is baseless; in order to prove that a suit was within Noerr's 'sham' exception to immunity, see *Noerr, 365 U.S.* at 144, an antitrust plaintiff must prove that the suit was both objectively baseless and subjectively motivated by a desire to impose collateral, anti-competitive injury rather than to obtain a justifiable legal remedy." *Nobelpharma, 141 F.3d at 1071*. "Accordingly, if a suit is not objectively baseless, an antitrust defendant's subjective motivation is immaterial." Id. at 1072. CSU has alleged that Xerox misused its patents but has not claimed that Xerox's patent infringement counterclaims were shams.

To support its argument that Xerox illegally sought to leverage its presumably legitimate dominance in the equipment and parts market into dominance in the service market, CSU relies on a footnote in *Eastman Kodak Co. v. Image Technical Services, Inc., 504 U.S. 451, 480 n.29 (1992)*, that "the Court has held many times that power gained through some natural and legal advantage such as a patent, . . . can give rise to liability if 'a seller exploits his dominant position in one market to expand his empire into the next.'" Notably, Kodak was a tying case when it came before the Supreme Court, and no patents had been asserted in defense of the antitrust claims against Kodak. Conversely, there are no claims in this case of illegally tying the sale of Xerox's patented parts to unpatented products. Therefore, the issue was not resolved by the Kodak language cited by CSU. Properly viewed within the framework of a tying case, the footnote can be interpreted as restating the undisputed premise that the patent holder cannot use his statutory right to refuse to sell patented parts to gain a monopoly in a market beyond the scope of the patent. . . .

The cited language from Kodak does nothing to limit the right of the patentee to refuse to sell or license in markets within the scope of the statutory patent grant. In fact, we have expressly held that, absent exceptional circumstances, a patent may confer the right to exclude competition altogether in more than one antitrust market. See *B. Braun Med., Inc. v. Abbott Lab., 124 F.3d 1419, 1427 n.4 (Fed. Cir. 1997)* (patentee had right to exclude competition in both the market for patented valves and the market for extension sets incorporating patented valves).

CSU further relies on the Ninth Circuit's holding on remand in Image Technical Services that "'while exclusionary conduct can include a monopolist's unilateral refusal to license a [patent] or to sell its patented . . . work, a monopolist's 'desire to exclude others from its [protected] work is a presumptively valid business justification for any immediate harm to consumers.'" 125 F.3d at 1218 (citing Data General Corp. v. Grumman Sys. Support Corp., 36 F.3d 1147, 1187 (1st Cir. 1994)). By that case, the Ninth Circuit adopted a rebuttable presumption that the exercise of the statutory right to exclude provides a valid business justification for consumer harm, but then excused as harmless the district court's error in failing to give any instruction on the effect of intellectual property rights on the application of the antitrust laws. It concluded that the jury must have rejected the presumptively valid business justification as pretextual. This logic requires an evaluation of the patentee's subjective motivation for refusing to sell or license its patented products for pretext. We decline to follow Image Technical Services.

We have held that "if a [patent infringement] suit is not objectively baseless, an antitrust defendant's subjective motivation is immaterial." *Nobelpharma, 141 F.3d at 1072.* We see no more reason to inquire into the subjective motivation of Xerox in refusing to sell or license its patented works than we found in evaluating the subjective motivation of a patentee in bringing suit to enforce that same right. In the absence of any indication of illegal tying, fraud in the Patent and Trademark Office, or sham litigation, the patent holder may enforce the statutory right to exclude others from making, using, or selling the claimed invention free from liability under the antitrust laws. We therefore will not inquire into his subjective motivation for exerting his statutory rights, even though his refusal to sell or license his patented invention may have an anticompetitive effect, so long as that anticompetitive effect is not illegally extended beyond the statutory patent grant. It is the infringement defendant and not the patentee that bears the burden to show that one of these exceptional situations exists and, in the absence of such proof, we will not inquire into the patentee's motivations for asserting his statutory right to exclude. Even in cases where the infringement defendant has met this burden, which CSU has not, he must then also prove the elements of the Sherman Act violation.

We answer the threshold question of whether Xerox's refusal to sell its patented parts exceeds the scope of the patent grant in the negative.[2] Therefore, our inquiry is at an end. Xerox was under no obligation to sell or license its patented parts and did not violate the antitrust laws by refusing to do so.

B.

The Copyright Act expressly grants a copyright owner the exclusive right to distribute the protected work by "transfer of ownership, or by rental, lease, or lending." 17 U.S.C. § 106(3) (1996). "The owner of the copyright, if

---

[2] Having concluded that Xerox's actions fell within the statutory patent grant, we need not separately consider CSU's allegations of patent misuse and they are rejected.

[it] pleases, may refrain from vending or licensing and content [itself] with simply exercising the right to exclude others from using [its] property." Data General, 36 F.3d at 1186.

The Supreme Court has made clear that the property right granted by copyright law cannot be used with impunity to extend power in the marketplace beyond what Congress intended. See *United States v. Loew's, Inc., 371 U.S. 38, 47-48, (1962)* (block booking of copyrighted motion pictures is illegal tying in violation of Sherman Act). The Court has not, however, directly addressed the antitrust implications of a unilateral refusal to sell or license copyrighted expression.

The Tenth Circuit has not addressed in any published opinion the extent to which the unilateral refusal to sell or license copyrighted expression can form the basis of a violation of the Sherman Act. We are therefore left to determine how that circuit would likely resolve the issue; the precedent of other circuits is instructive in that consideration. The Fourth Circuit has rejected a claim of illegal tying, supported only by evidence of a unilateral decision to license copyrighted diagnostic software to some but not to others. See *Service & Training, Inc. v. Data General Corp., 963 F.2d 680, 686, 23 (4th Cir. 1992)*. In reaching this conclusion, the court recognized the copyright owner's exclusive right to "sell, rent, lease, lend, or otherwise distribute copies of a copyrighted work," id. and concluded that "Section 1 of the Sherman Act does not entitle 'a purchaser . . . to buy a product that the seller does not wish to offer for sale.'" Id.

Perhaps the most extensive analysis of the effect of a unilateral refusal to license copyrighted expression was conducted by the First Circuit in *Data General Corp. v. Grumman Systems Support Corp.*, 36 F.3d 1147. There, the court noted that the limited copyright monopoly is based on Congress' empirical assumption that the right to "exclude others from using their works creates a system of incentives that promotes consumer welfare in the long term by encouraging investment in the creation of desirable artistic and functional works of expression. . . . We cannot require antitrust defendants to prove and reprove the merits of this legislative assumption in every case where a refusal to license a copyrighted work comes under attack." Id. at 1186-87. The court went on to establish as a legal standard that "while exclusionary conduct can include a monopolist's unilateral refusal to license a copyright, an author's desire to exclude others from use of its copyrighted work is a presumptively valid business justification for any immediate harm to consumers." See id. at

1187. The burden to overcome this presumption was firmly placed on the antitrust plaintiff. The court gave no weight to evidence showing knowledge that developing a proprietary position would help to maintain a monopoly in the service market in the face of contrary evidence of the defendant's desire to develop state-of-the-art diagnostic software to enhance its service and consumer benefit.

As discussed above, the Ninth Circuit adopted a modified version of this Data General standard. Both courts agreed that the presumption could be rebutted by evidence that "the monopolist acquired the protection of the intellectual property laws in an unlawful manner." *Image Technical Servs., 125 F.3d at 1219.* The Ninth Circuit, however, extended the possible means of rebutting the presumption to include evidence that the defense and exploitation of the copyright grant was merely a pretextual business justification to mask anticompetitive conduct. The hazards of this approach are evident in both the path taken and the outcome reached. The jury in that case was instructed to examine each proffered business justification for pretext, and no weight was given to the intellectual property rights in the instructions. This permitted the jury to second guess the subjective motivation of the copyright holder in asserting its statutory rights to exclude under the copyright laws without properly weighing the presumption of legitimacy in asserting its rights under the copyright laws. While concluding that the failure to weigh the intellectual property rights was an abuse of discretion, the Ninth Circuit nevertheless held the error harmless because it thought the jury must have rejected the presumptive validity of asserting the copyrights as pretextual. This is in reality a significant departure from the First Circuit's central premise that rebutting the presumption would be an uphill battle and would only be appropriate in those rare cases in which imposing antitrust liability is unlikely to frustrate the objectives of the Copyright Act. See *Data General, 36 F.3d at 1187 n.64.*

We believe the First Circuit's approach is more consistent with both the antitrust and the copyright laws and is the standard that would most likely be followed by the Tenth Circuit in considering the effect of Xerox's unilateral right to refuse to license or sell copyrighted manuals and diagnostic software on liability under the antitrust laws. We therefore reject CSU's invitation to examine Xerox's subjective motivation in asserting its right to exclude under the copyright laws for pretext, in the absence of any evidence that the copyrights were obtained by unlawful means or were used to gain monopoly power beyond the statutory copyright granted by Congress. In the absence of such definitive rebuttal evidence, Xerox's refusal to sell or license its copyrighted works was squarely within the rights granted by Congress to the copyright holder and did not constitute a violation of the antitrust laws.

Insert after Note 2, page 914:

On the subject of "flailing" firms, it is interesting to compare the results in the Boeing-McDonnell Douglas merger at the Federal Trade Commission in the United States, which in the final analysis raised no objections to the transaction, and the analysis of the European Commission's DGIV, which required the firms to promise to change certain business practices before the Commission was prepared to give a green light to the deal. See generally Official Journal of the European Community, L 336, 08/12/1997, page 16, for the report of the decision in Boeing-McDonnell Douglas.

Insert after *Hospital Corporation*, page 930:

Note on the *Staples* Case

In Federal Trade Commission v. Staples, Inc., 970 F. Supp. 1066 (D. D. C. 1997), Staples, the second largest office supply superstore in the United States with 550 retail stores, sought to acquire Office Depot, the largest office supply superstore chain, with over 500 outlets. The office superstore market was defined to include superstores selling "consumable" office products - *e.g.* paper, pens, file folders, computer discs and toner cartridges, but "consumable" did not include capital goods such as computers and office furniture. Defendants argued that the proper product market was all outlets selling office supply products, and in any such market, Staples and Office Depot accounted for only 5.5 percent of total North American sales. They also argued that the efficiencies of the transaction would lead to lower consumer prices and outweigh any possible anticompetitive effect. In that connection the parties emphasized a long record of office supply superstores cutting prices in order to increase market share, and claimed that track record showed that efficiencies would be passed along to consumers.

The proposed merger was the last of a series which had reduced the superstore category from 23 to 3. Office Max was third after Staples and Office Depot. Efforts by chains selling other products to expand into office supplies had not been successful.

The key question was whether office supply superstores constituted, as alleged by the government, an appropriate market or submarket, since functionally interchangeable products could be purchased at many outlets, including chains that did not emphasize office supplies but carried some items, and also at small stationery stores.

In seeking a preliminary injunction, the FTC had offered econometric evidence - more extensive than in previous cases - about prices in cities where a company owned the only superstore in town compared to cities where there were two or three competing superstores. In all cities reviewed, non-superstore outlets were present. The court summarized the Commission's approach as follows:

> First, the FTC presented evidence comparing Staples' prices in geographic markets where Staples is the only office superstore to markets where Staples competes with Office Depot or Office Max, or both. Based on the FTC's calculations, in markets where Staples faces no office superstore competition at all, something which was termed a one- firm market during the hearing, prices are 13 % higher than in three firm markets where it competes with both Office Depot and Office Max.
>
> * * *
>
> The evidence all suggests that office superstore prices are affected primarily by other office superstores and not by non-superstore competitors such as mass merchandisers like Wal-Mart, K-Mart or Target, wholesale clubs such as BJ's, Sam's and Price Costco, computer or electronic stores such as Computer City and Best Buy, independent retail office supply stores, mail-order firms like Quill and Viking, and contract stationers.

Staples' and Office Depot's internal documents confirmed the differences in price in one, two, and three superstore cities. In addition, upon request, District Judge Hogan visited and viewed many of the different types of retail formats and found that office superstores were very different in appearance, physical size, format, the number and variety of products offered, and the type of customers targeted and served than other sellers of office supplies.

Assuming an office supply superstore market, concentration statistics showed the merged company would have a dominant market share in 42 geographic markets across the country, with 100 percent in 15 metropolitan areas. In 27 other areas, post-merger market share would range from 45 percent to 94 percent. The average increase in HHI caused by the merger would be 2,715 points.

With respect to efficiency claims in defense of the merger, the court acknowledged that the government had changed its merger guidelines to allow the offer of an efficiency defense, but also noted that the Supreme Court, in *Procter & Gamble* (see Casebook, p. 986), concluded that "possible economies cannot be used as a defense to illegality in Section 7 merger cases." Despite the *Procter & Gamble* language, the district court assumed that efficiencies could be offered as a viable defense. Nevertheless, the court rejected the efficiency claims on grounds that those proffered were speculative and conjectural. The court noted the defendant claims of $5 billion dollar cost savings over 5 years, but observed that most of these alleged savings were undocumented, lacking backup sources and calculations. It further noted that the $5 billion figure exceeded by almost 500 percent the figures presented to the boards of directors of the companies when they were asked to approve the transaction, and were substantially greater than claims in the joint proxy statement/prospectus which was said to reflect the best currently available estimate of savings by management and was submitted to the Securities and Exchange Commission.

The court concluded that the Commission had shown a likelihood it would succeed after a full administrative trial and granted a preliminary injunction.

Note on AOL-Time Warner

America Online, the largest internet service provider ("ISP') in the United States with 25 million subscribers (about 50 percent of all subscribers) and 70 percent of total ISP revenues, sought to acquire Time Warner, a leading entertainment conglomerate with major holdings in magazines (Time, People, Sports Illustrated), copyrighted music (Warner Records), film and film libraries (Warner Brothers and New Line Cinema), and national network broadcasting (WB Network). Time Warner also was the second largest cable system in the United States with 12.6 million cable subscribers or approximately 20 percent of all U.S. cable television households. Time Warner was virtually the only cable provider in several major cities in the United States, including New York and Los Angeles. At the time the merger was announced in January 2000, it was valued at $183 billion, the largest merger in U.S. corporate history.

The merger raised significant competitive issues because the technology of internet connection was in the process of changing. Almost all residential users accessed the internet through a "narrowband" connection over standard telephone lines. "Broadband" internet access, offering faster service, a greater range of data, and more sophisticated programming through computers (including movies on demand and other entertainment), was expected to displace much of narrowband access in the several years after 2000. The vast majority of broadband access at the time of the merger was over cable, with upgraded telephone lines ("DSL") gaining ground but still a distant second. Long term, it is anticipated that wireless and satellite connections also would offer broadband services.

Time Warner was a majority owner of Roadrunner, the second largest provider of cable broadband ISP service in the United States, with about one million subscribers, while AOL with its enormous installed base in narrowband, and a small but developing base in broadband, was the most likely and most formidable future ISP presence in the broadband market. To the extent that AOL was in the broadband market, it provided access through DSL, but after the merger, would be expected to move aggressively into cable broadband connections.

The FTC approved the merger, but with extensive and somewhat unusual conditions. According to the "Analysis of Proposed Consent Order to Aid Public Comment," the Commission was concerned principally with two theories of possible anticompetitive effects: (1) the combination of Roadrunner with its cable broadband connections, and AOL with its DSL broadband connections, would have anticompetitive horizontal effects, particularly in areas of the country where Time Warner cable was dominant, and (2) the merger would decrease the incentives of AOL to promote and market access over DSL, the closest competitor to cable, particularly in Time Warner cable areas. With respect to both theories, the Commission was prepared to prove that wireless and satellite connections were not a sufficiently timely new entrant to curb AOL-Time Warner's post-merger market power.

A third theory related to interactive tv (ITV), an innovative technology at the time which combined television programming over computer connections with the ability of viewers to control the content of programs they see (*e.g.*, adding statistics or camera angles to sports events). Cable has distinct competitive advantages over DSL in providing ITV services, and AOL had recently launched AOL TV, a first generation ITV service. The concern was that after the merger, AOL-Time Warner would have incentives to discriminate against other ITV providers (*i.e.*, competitors of Time Warner content) from competing over cable with AOL's ITV service.

Under the terms of the antitrust consent order, which permitted the merger to be consummated, the combined companies were required to make cable broadband service available to an identified ISP (it turned out to be Earthlink) pursuant to terms and conditions evaluated and approved by the Commission. Within 90 days of making AOL broadband ISP service available over Time Warner cable to subscribers, Time Warner was required to enter into agreements to carry at least two additional non-affiliated broadband ISPs over its cable system on terms comparable to Earthlink. If Time Warner failed to enter into agreements within the time period, the Commission had the power to appoint a trustee with authority to enter into such agreements on Time Warner's behalf. Extensive ancillary provisions were designed to ensure that the contracts would not discriminate against competing ISPs and required that disputes be submitted to binding arbitration. In addition to the three ISPs that were required, the consent order permitted the combined company to decline to enter into agreements with other cable broadband ISPs because of technical limitations on the system or other good business considerations, but could not exclude or discriminate against other ISPs simply because adding competition over its cable systems would have an impact on the merged company's profits.

With respect to DSL, the order required AOL to market and promote DSL services in Time Warner cable areas at a comparable level and in the same manner as it promoted DSL services in non-Time Warner cable areas and not to discriminate in price between Time Warner and non-Time Warner cable areas.

Finally, as to ITV, the order prohibited Time Warner from interfering with an ISP competitor from making interactive features available when program content is delivered to viewers over Time Warner cable systems. Because the merger occurred in an exceptionally dynamic sector of the economy, the duration of the order was limited to five years from the time a final consent agreement was signed -- the shortest duration of an antitrust consent order in the history of the FTC.

At the time the proposed merger was under review, the press reported great concern on the part of competitors of Time Warner, particularly other movie and music companies, that their content delivered over AOL would not be treated on fair and equal terms with Time Warner material, and they sought anti-discrimination provisions. Given the size and market power of Time Warner at the content level and AOL at the ISP delivery level, such "vertical concerns" were understandable. Nevertheless, despite Time Warner's formidable market presence, it did not account in any segment of the entertainment industry (*i.e.*, movies, music, print) for more than about 20 percent of the market and faced powerful competitors (*e.g.*, Disney in movies, Bertelsmann in music) with products and artists that enjoyed strong consumer allegiance. Excluding such companies from the AOL system arguably would dissatisfy AOL users and therefore would not be likely to occur. In addition, the Commission apparently felt that content provisions precluding discrimination would not be necessary as long as competitors of Time Warner could reach viewers through Earthlink and the other ISPs on Time Warner cable as required by the consent order.

FEDERAL TRADE COMMISSION v. H. J. HEINZ CO.
United States Court of Appeals, District of Columbia Circuit, 2001.
246 F.3d 708.

Before: HENDERSON, RANDOLPH and GARLAND, Circuit Judges.

HENDERSON, Judge. On February 28, 2000 H.J. Heinz Company (Heinz) and Milnot Holding Corporation (Beech-Nut) entered into a merger agreement. The Federal Trade Commission (Commission or FTC) sought a preliminary injunction pursuant to section 13(b) of the Federal Trade Commission Act, to enjoin the consummation of the merger. The injunction was sought in aid of an FTC administrative proceeding which was subsequently instituted by complaint to challenge the merger as violative of, inter alia, section 7 of the Clayton Act. The district court denied the preliminary injunction and the FTC appealed to this court. For the reasons set forth below, we reverse the district court and remand for entry of a preliminary injunction against Heinz and Beech-Nut.

I. Background

Four million infants in the United States consume 80 million cases of jarred baby food annually, representing a domestic market of $865 million to $1 billion. The baby food market is dominated by three firms, Gerber Products

Company (Gerber), Heinz and Beech-Nut. Gerber, the industry leader, enjoys a 65 per cent market share while Heinz and Beech-Nut come in second and third, with a 17.4 per cent and a 15.4 per cent share respectively. The district court found that Gerber enjoys unparalleled brand recognition with a brand loyalty greater than any other product sold in the United States. Gerber's products are found in over 90 per cent of all American supermarkets.[1]

By contrast, Heinz is sold in approximately 40 per cent of all supermarkets. Its sales are nationwide but concentrated in northern New England, the Southeast and Deep South and the Midwest. Despite its second-place domestic market share, Heinz is the largest producer of baby food in the world with $1 billion in sales worldwide. Its domestic baby food products with annual net sales of $103 million are manufactured at its Pittsburgh, Pennsylvania plant, which was updated in 1991 at a cost of $120 million. The plant operates at 40 per cent of its production capacity and produces 12 million cases of baby food annually. Its baby food line includes about 130 SKUs (stock keeping units), that is, product varieties (e.g., strained carrots, apple sauce, etc.). Heinz lacks Gerber's brand recognition; it markets itself as a "value brand" with a shelf price several cents below Gerber's.

Beech-Nut has a market share (15.4%) comparable to that of Heinz (17.4%), with $138.7 million in annual sales of baby food, of which 72 per cent is jarred baby food. Its jarred baby food line consists of 128 SKUs. Beech-Nut manufactures all of its baby food in Canajoharie, New York at a manufacturing plant that was built in 1907 and began manufacturing baby food in 1931. Beech-Nut maintains price parity with Gerber, selling at about one penny less. It markets its product as a premium brand. Consumers generally view its product as comparable in quality to Gerber's. Beech-Nut is carried in approximately 45 per cent of all grocery stores. Although its sales are nationwide, they are concentrated in New York, New Jersey, California and

---

[1] Product volume in retail stores throughout the country is measured by the product's All Commodity Volume (ACV). Gerber's near 100 per cent ACV is impressive because virtually all supermarkets stock at most two brands of baby food. In at least one area of the country as many as 80 per cent of supermarket retailers stock only Gerber.

Florida.[2]

At the wholesale level Heinz and Beech-Nut both make lump-sum payments called "fixed trade spending" (also known as "slotting fees" or "pay-to-stay" arrangements) to grocery stores to obtain shelf placement. Gerber, with its strong name recognition and brand loyalty, does not make such pay-to-stay payments. The other type of wholesale trade spending is "variable trade spending," which typically consists of manufacturers' discounts and allowances to supermarkets to create retail price differentials that entice the consumer to purchase their product instead of a competitor's.

Under the terms of their merger agreement, Heinz would acquire 100 per cent of Beech-Nut's voting securities for $185 million....

II. Analysis

A. Standard of Review

We review a district court order denying preliminary injunctive relief for abuse of discretion, *National Wildlife Fed'n v. Burford, 835 F.2d 305, 319 (D.C. Cir. 1987),* and will set aside the court's factual findings only if they are "clearly erroneous."...

B. Section 7 of the Clayton Act

Section 7 of the Clayton Act prohibits acquisitions, including mergers, "where in any line of commerce or in any activity affecting commerce in any section of the country, the effect of such acquisition may be substantially to lessen competition, or to tend to create a monopoly." See *United States v. Philadelphia Nat'l Bank, 374 U.S. 321, 355 (1963)* ("The statutory test is whether the effect of the merger 'may be substantially to lessen competition' 'in any line of commerce in any section of the country.'"). The "Congress used

---

[2] Although Heinz and Beech-Nut introduced evidence showing that in areas that account for 80 of Beech-Nut sales, Heinz has a market share of about 2 and in areas that account for about 72 of Heinz sales, Beech-Nut's share is about 4, the FTC introduced evidence that Heinz and Beech-Nut are locked in an intense battle at the wholesale level to gain (and maintain) position as the second brand on retail shelves.

the words 'may be substantially to lessen competition' (emphasis supplied), to indicate that its concern was with probabilities, not certainties." *Brown Shoe Co. v. United States, 370 U.S. 294, 323 (1962)* (emphasis original); see S. Rep. No. 1775, at 6 (1950) ("The use of these words ["may be"] means that the bill, if enacted, would not apply to the mere possibility but only to the reasonable probability of the proscribed effect...."). "Merger enforcement, like other areas of antitrust, is directed at market power. It shares with the law of monopolization a degree of schizophrenia: an aversion to potent power that heightens risk of abuse; and tolerance of that degree of power required to attain economic benefits." Lawrence A. Sullivan & Warren S. Grimes, The Law of Antitrust § 9.1, at 511 (2000). The Congress has empowered the FTC, inter alia, to weed out those mergers whose effect "may be substantially to lessen competition" from those that enhance competition. See H.R. Rep. No. 1142, at 18-19 (1914). In section 13(b) of the FTCA, the Congress provided a mechanism whereby the FTC may seek preliminary injunctive relief preventing the merging parties from consummating the merger until the Commission has had an opportunity to investigate and, if necessary, adjudicate the matter.

C. Section 13(b) of the Federal Trade Commission Act

"Whenever the Commission has reason to believe that a corporation is violating, or is about to violate, Section 7 of the Clayton Act, the FTC may seek a preliminary injunction to prevent a merger pending the Commission's administrative adjudication of the merger's legality." *FTC v. Staples, Inc., 970 F. Supp. 1066, 1070 (D.D.C. 1997)....*

1. Likelihood of Success

To determine likelihood of success on the merits we measure the probability that, after an administrative hearing on the merits, the Commission will succeed in proving that the effect of the Heinz/Beech-Nut merger "may be substantially to lessen competition, or to tend to create a monopoly" in violation of section 7 of the Clayton Act. This court and others have suggested that the standard for likelihood of success on the merits is met if the FTC "has raised questions going to the merits so serious, substantial, difficult and doubtful as to make them fair ground for thorough investigation, study, deliberation and determination by the FTC in the first instance and ultimately by the Court of Appeals."... This specific standard was articulated by the court below, and it is a standard to which the appellees have not objected.

n6 In Beatrice Foods, two members of the court, writing separately from a denial of en banc review, included the quoted language from an unpublished judgment and memorandum issued earlier in the litigation.

In *United States v. Baker Hughes Inc., 908 F.2d 981, 982-83 (D.C. Cir. 1990),* we explained the analytical approach by which the government establishes a section 7 violation. First the government must show that the merger would produce "a firm controlling an undue percentage share of the relevant market, and [would] result[ ] in a significant increase in the concentration of firms in that market." *Philadelphia Nat'l Bank, 374 U.S. at 363.* Such a showing establishes a "presumption" that the merger will substantially lessen compctition. To rebut the presumption, the defendants must produce evidence that "shows that the market-share statistics [give] an inaccurate account of the [merger's] probable effects on competition" in the relevant market. *United States v. Citizens & S. Nat'l Bank, 422 U.S. 86, 120 (1975).*[3] "If the defendant successfully rebuts the presumption [of illegality], the burden of producing additional evidence of anticompetitive effect shifts to the government, and merges with the ultimate burden of persuasion, which remains with the government at all times." *Baker Hughes Inc., 908 F.2d at 983;* see also *Kaiser Aluminum & Chemical Corp. v. FTC, 652 F.2d 1324 at 1340 & n.12.* Although Baker Hughes was decided at the merits stage as opposed to the preliminary injunctive relief stage, we can nonetheless use its analytical approach in evaluating the Commission's showing of likelihood of success. Accordingly, we look at the FTC's prima facie case and the defendants' rebuttal evidence.

---

[3] To rebut the defendants may rely on "nonstatistical evidence which casts doubt on the persuasive quality of the statistics to predict future anticompetitive consequences" such as "ease of entry into the market, the trend of the market either toward or away from concentration, and the continuation of active price competition." *Kaiser Aluminum & Chem. Corp. v. FTC, 652 F.2d 1324, 1341 (7th Cir. 1981).* In addition, the defendants may demonstrate unique economic circumstances that undermine the predictive value of the government's statistics. See *United States v. General Dynamics Corp., 415 U.S. 486, 506-10 (1974)* (fundamental changes in structure of coal market made market concentration statistics inaccurate predictors of anticompetitive effect); see also *University Health, 938 F.2d at 1218.*

a. Prima Facie Case

Merger law "rests upon the theory that, where rivals are few, firms will be able to coordinate their behavior, either by overt collusion or implicit understanding, in order to restrict output and achieve profits above competitive levels." *FTC v. PPG Indus., 798 F.2d 1500, 1503 (D.C. Cir. 1986).* Increases in concentration above certain levels are thought to "raise[ ] a likelihood of 'interdependent anticompetitive conduct.' " *Id.* (quoting *General Dynamics, 415 U.S. at 497); see FTC v. Elders Grain, 868 F.2d 901, 905 (7th Cir. 1989).* Market concentration, or the lack thereof, is often measured by the Herfindahl-Hirschmann Index (HHI). See *Staples, 970 F. Supp. at 1081 n.12.*[4]

Sufficiently large HHI figures establish the FTC's prima facie case that a merger is anti-competitive. See *Baker Hughes, 908 F.2d at 982-83 & n.3; PPG, 798 F.2d at 1503.* The district court found that the pre-merger HHI "score for the baby food industry is 4775"—indicative of a highly concentrated industry.[5] The merger of Heinz and Beech-Nut will increase the HHI by 510 points. This creates, by a wide margin, a presumption that the merger will lessen competition in the domestic jarred baby food market. See Horizontal Merger Guidelines, supra, § 1.51 (stating that HHI increase of more than 100 points, where post-merger HHI exceeds 1800, is "presumed ... likely to create or enhance market power or facilitate its exercise"); see also *Baker Hughes,*

---

[4] The FTC and the Department of Justice, as well as most economists, consider the measure superior to such cruder measures as the four-or eight-firm concentration ratios which merely sum up the market shares of the largest four or eight firms." *PPG, 798 F.2d at 1503.* The Department of Justice and the FTC rely on the HHI in evaluating proposed horizontal mergers. See United States Dep't of Justice & Federal Trade Comm'n, Horizontal Merger Guidelines §§ 1.5, 1.51 (1992), as revised (1997).... Although the Merger Guidelines are not binding on the court, they provide "a useful illustration of the application of the HHI." *PPG*, 798 F.2d at 1503 n.4.

[5] To determine the HHI score the district court first had to define the relevant market. The court defined the product market as jarred baby food and the geographic market as the United States. *H.J. Heinz, 116 F. Supp. 2d at 195.* The parties do not challenge the court's definition.

908 F.2d at 982-83 & n.3; PPG, 798 F.2d at 1503.[6] Here, the FTC's market concentration statistics[7] are bolstered by the indisputable fact that the merger

---

[6] The FTC argues that this finding alone--that it is certain to establish a prima facie case--entitles it to preliminary injunctive relief under PPG. We disagree with the Commission's reading of PPG. In PPG, the Commission appealed the district court's denial of its request for a preliminary injunction to prevent PPG Industries, the world's largest producer of glass aircraft transparencies, from acquiring Swedlow, Inc., the world's largest manufacturer of acrylic aircraft transparencies. *798 F.2d at 1502.* After defining the relevant market and determining market share, the district court found that the merger would significantly increase the concentration in an already highly concentrated market. It also "found high market-entry barriers that would prolong high market concentration." Id. at 1503. On appeal, this court stated: "There is no doubt that the pre-and post-acquisition HHI's and market shares found in this case entitle the Commission to some preliminary relief." Id. This statement came, however, in the context of a case in which the appellants offered no rebuttal (other than the observation of rapid and continuing technological changes in the industry) to the presumption generated by the market concentration data on which the FTC based its prima facie showing. Id. at 1506. The court then noted the rule established in Weyerhaeuser that the FTC is entitled to a "presumption in favor of a preliminary injunction when [it] establishes a strong likelihood of success on the merits." Id. at 1507.

[7] The Supreme Court has cautioned that statistics reflecting market share and concentration, while of great significance, are not conclusive indicators of anticompetitive effects. See *General Dynamics, 415 U.S. at 498; Brown Shoe, 370 U.S. at 322 n.38* ("Statistics reflecting the shares of the market controlled by the industry leaders and the parties to the merger are, of course, the primary index of market power; but only a further examination of the particular market--its structure, history and probable future--can provide the appropriate setting for judging the probable anticompetitive effect of the merger."). In General Dynamics the Supreme Court held that the market share statistics the Commission used to seek divestiture of the merged firm were insufficient because, in failing to take into account the acquired firm's long-term contractual commitments (coal contracts), the statistics overestimated the acquired firm's ability to compete in the relevant market in the future. *General Dynamics, 415 U.S. at 500-504.*

will eliminate competition between the two merging parties at the wholesale level, where they are currently the only competitors for what the district court described as the "second position on the supermarket shelves." Heinz's own documents recognize the wholesale competition and anticipate that the merger will end it. Indeed, those documents disclose that Heinz considered three options to end the vigorous wholesale competition with Beech-Nut: two involved innovative measures while the third entailed the acquisition of Beech-Nut. Heinz chose the third, and least pro-competitive, of the options.

Finally, the anticompetitive effect of the merger is further enhanced by high barriers to market entry.[8] The district court found that there had been no significant entries in the baby food market in decades and that new entry was "difficult and improbable." This finding largely eliminates the possibility that the reduced competition caused by the merger will be ameliorated by new competition from outsiders and further strengthens the FTC's case. See *University Health, 938 F.2d at 1219 & n.26.*

---

[8] Barriers to entry are important in evaluating whether market concentration statistics accurately reflect the pre- and likely post-merger competitive picture. Cf. *Baker Hughes, 908 F.2d at 987.* If entry barriers are low, the threat of outside entry can significantly alter the anticompetitive effects of the merger by deterring the remaining entities from colluding or exercising market power. See *United States v. Falstaff Brewing Corp., 410 U.S. 526, 532-33 (1973); Baker Hughes, 908 F.2d at 987* ("In the absence of significant barriers, a company probably cannot maintain supracompetitive pricing for any length of time."); Horizontal Merger Guidelines, supra, § 3.0 ("A merger is not likely to create or enhance market power or to facilitate its exercise, if entry into the market is so easy that market participants, after the merger, either collectively or unilaterally could not profitably maintain a price increase above premerger levels."). Low barriers to entry enable a potential competitor to deter anticompetitive behavior by firms within the market simply by its ability to enter the market. *FTC v. Procter & Gamble Co., 386 U.S. 568, 581 (1967)* ("It is clear that the existence of Procter at the edge of the industry exerted considerable influence on the market."). Existing firms know that if they collude or exercise market power to charge supracompetitive prices, entry by firms currently not competing in the market becomes likely, thereby increasing the pressure on them to act competitively. See *Baker Hughes, 908 F.2d at 988; Byars v. Bluff City News Co., 609 F.2d 843, 851 n.19 (6th Cir. 1979).*

As far as we can determine, no court has ever approved a merger to duopoly under similar circumstances.

b. Rebuttal Arguments

In response to the FTC's prima facie showing, the appellees make three rebuttal arguments, which the district court accepted in reaching its conclusion that the merger was not likely to lessen competition substantially. For the reasons discussed below, these arguments fail and thus were not a proper basis for denying the FTC injunctive relief.

1. Extent of Pre-Merger Competition

The appellees first contend, and the district court agreed, that Heinz and Beech-Nut do not really compete against each other at the retail level. Consumers do not regard the products of the two companies as substitutes, the appellees claim, and generally only one of the two brands is available on any given store's shelves. Hence, they argue, there is little competitive loss from the merger.

This argument has a number of flaws which render clearly erroneous the court's finding that Heinz and Beech-Nut have not engaged in significant pre-merger competition. First, in accepting the appellees' argument that Heinz and Beech-Nut do not compete, the district court failed to address the record evidence that the two do in fact price against each other, and that, where both are present in the same areas,[9] they depress each other's prices as well as those of Gerber even though they are virtually never all found in the same store. This evidence undermines the district court's factual finding.

Second, the district court's finding is inconsistent with its conclusion that there is a single, national market for jarred baby food in the United States. The Supreme Court has explained that "the outer boundaries of a product market are determined by the reasonable interchangeability of use [by consumers] or the cross-elasticity of demand between the product itself and substitutes for it." *Brown Shoe, 370 U.S. at 325;* see also *United States v. E.I.*

---

[9] There are at least ten metropolitan areas in which Heinz and Beech-Nut both have more than a 10 per cent market share and their combined share exceeds 35 per cent. PX 781 at Ex. 1B.

du Pont de Nemours & Co., 351 U.S. 377, 395 (1956).[10] The definition of product market thus "focuses solely on demand substitution factors," i.e., that consumers regard the products as substitutes. Horizontal Merger Guidelines, supra, § 1.0; Sullivan & Grimes, supra, § 11.2b1, at 579. By defining the relevant product market generically as jarred baby food, the district court concluded that in areas where Heinz's and Beech-Nut's products are both sold, consumers will switch between them in response to a "small but significant and nontransitory increase in price (SSNIP)." Horizontal Merger Guidelines, supra, § 1.11. The district court never explained this inherent inconsistency in its logic nor could counsel for the appellees explain it at oral argument.

Third, and perhaps most important, the court's conclusion concerning pre-merger competition does not take into account the indisputable fact that the merger will eliminate competition at the wholesale level between the only two competitors for the "second shelf" position. Competition between Heinz and Beech-Nut to gain accounts at the wholesale level is fierce with each contest concluding in a winner-take-all result. The district court regarded this loss of competition as irrelevant because the FTC did not establish to its satisfaction that wholesale competition ultimately benefitted consumers through lower retail prices. The district court concluded that fixed trade spending did not affect consumer prices and that "the FTC's assertion that the proposed merger will affect variable trade spending levels and consumer prices is ... at best, inconclusive."[11] *H.J. Heinz, 116 F. Supp. 2d at 197.* Although the court noted the FTC's examples of consumer benefit through couponing initiatives, the court held that it was "impossible to conclude with any certainty that the consumer benefit from such couponing initiatives would be lost in the merger." *Id.*

---

10 Interchangeability of use and cross-elasticity of demand look to the availability of products that are similar in nature or use and the degree to which buyers are willing to substitute those similar products for one another. See *E.I. du Pont de Nemours, 351 U.S. at 393.*

11 Fixed trade spending consists of "slotting fees," "pay-to-stay" arrangements, new store allowances and other payments to retailers in exchange for shelf space and desired product display. Variable trade spending includes payments to retailers tied to sales volume and intended to insure a specific sales volume and lower shelf price.

In rejecting the FTC's argument regarding the loss of wholesale competition, the court committed two legal errors. First, as the appellees conceded at oral argument, no court has ever held that a reduction in competition for wholesale purchasers is not relevant unless the plaintiff can prove impact at the consumer level. Oral Arg. Tr. at 22, 28; see *Hospital Corp. of Am. v. FTC, 807 F.2d 1381, 1389 (7th Cir. 1986)* ("Section 7 does not require proof that a merger or other acquisition has caused higher prices in the affected market. All that is necessary is that the merger create an appreciable danger of [collusive practices] in the future. A predictive judgment, necessarily probabilistic and judgmental rather than demonstrable, is called for.") Second, it is, in any event, not the FTC's burden to prove such an impact with "certainty." To the contrary, the antitrust laws assume that a retailer faced with an increase in the cost of one of its inventory items "will try so far as competition allows to pass that cost on to its customers in the form of a higher price for its product." *In re Brand Name Prescription Drugs Antitrust Litig., 123 F.3d 599, 605 (7th Cir. 1997),* reh'g and suggestion for reh'g en banc denied (Oct. 8, 1997). Section 7 is, after all, concerned with probabilities, not certainties. *United States v. El Paso Natural Gas Co., 376 U.S. 651, 658 (1964); Brown Shoe, 370 U.S. at 323; Baker Hughes, 908 F.2d at 984).*[12]

---

[12] Although the merger's effects on the wholesale market for baby food are important to a determination of whether the merger is likely to reduce competition in the baby food market overall, we reject the FTC's argument here that the "wholesale competition" between Heinz and Beech-Nut is an entirely distinct "line of commerce" within the meaning of section 7 of the Clayton Act such that it must be analyzed independently from "retail competition." The Congress amended section 7 in 1950 "to make the measure of anticompetitive acquisitions the extent to which they lessened competition 'in any line of commerce,' rather than the extent to which they lessened competition 'between' the two companies." *Citizen Publishing Co. v. United States, 394 U.S. 131, 137 n.3, (1969).* Courts interpret "line of commerce" as synonymous with the relevant product market. See *General Dynamics, 415 U.S. at 510; Falstaff Brewing, 410 U.S. at 531-32.* The district court defined only one market--jarred baby food sold throughout the line of commerce in the United States. Thus, the proper "line of commerce" for analysis in this case is the overall market for jarred baby food, which includes both retail and wholesale levels. At this point in the proceedings, the wholesale market cannot be separated out for analysis without regard to the merger's effect on other levels of competition.

2. Post-Merger Efficiencies

The appellees' second attempt to rebut the FTC's prima facie showing is their contention that the anticompetitive effects of the merger will be offset by efficiencies resulting from the union of the two companies, efficiencies which they assert will be used to compete more effectively against Gerber. It is true that a merger's primary benefit to the economy is its potential to generate efficiencies. See generally 4A Phillip E. Areeda, Herbert Hovenkamp & John L. Solow, Antitrust Law P 970 at 22-25 (1998). As the Merger Guidelines now recognize, efficiencies "can enhance the merged firm's ability and incentive to compete, which may result in lower prices, improved quality, or new products." Horizontal Merger Guidelines, supra, § 4.

Although the Supreme Court has not sanctioned the use of the efficiencies defense in a section 7 case, see *Procter & Gamble Co., 386 U.S. at 580,*[13] the trend among lower courts is to recognize the defense. See, e.g., *FTC v. Tenet Health Care Corp., 186 F.3d 1045, 1054 (8th Cir. 1999),* reh'g and reh'g en banc denied (Oct. 6. 1999); *University Health, 938 F.2d at 1222; FTC v. Cardinal Health, Inc., 12 F. Supp. 2d 34, 61 (D.D.C. 1998); Staples, 970 F. Supp. at 1088-89;* see also ABA Antitrust Section, Mergers and Acquisitions: Understanding the Antitrust Issues 152 (2000) ("The majority of courts have considered efficiencies as a means to rebut the government's prima facie case that a merger will lead to restricted output or increased prices. These courts, however, generally have found inadequate proof of efficiencies to sustain a rebuttal of the government's case."). In 1997 the Department of

---

[13] In *Procter & Gamble Co., 386 U.S. at 580,* the Supreme Court stated that "possible economies cannot be used as a defense to illegality" in section 7 merger cases. The issue is, however, not a closed book. See *Staples, 970 F. Supp. at 1088* (collecting cases). Areeda and Turner explain that "in interpreting the Clorox language, moreover, observe that the court referred only to 'possible' economies and to economies that 'may' result from mergers that lessen competition. To reject an economies defense based on mere possibilities does not mean that one should reject such a defense based on more convincing proof." 4 Phillip Areeda & Donald Turner, Antitrust Law P 941b, at 154 (1980). They conclude that "the Court's brief and unelaborated language [in Clorox] cannot reasonably be taken as a definitive disposition of so important and complex an issue as the role of economies in analyzing legality of a merger." *Id.*

Justice and the FTC revised their Horizontal Merger Guidelines to recognize that "mergers have the potential to generate significant efficiencies by permitting a better utilization of existing assets, enabling the combined firm to achieve lower costs in producing a given quantity and quality than either firm could have achieved without the proposed transaction." Horizontal Merger Guidelines, supra, § 4.

Nevertheless, the high market concentration levels present in this case require, in rebuttal, proof of extraordinary efficiencies, which the appellees failed to supply. See *University Health, 938 F.2d at 1223* ("[A] defendant who seeks to overcome a presumption that a proposed acquisition would substantially lessen competition must demonstrate that the intended acquisition would result in significant economies and that these economies ultimately would benefit competition and, hence, consumers."); Horizontal Merger Guidelines, supra, § 4 (stating that "efficiencies almost never justify a merger to monopoly or near-monopoly"); 4A Areeda, et al., Antitrust Law P 971f, at 44 (requiring "extraordinary" efficiencies where the "HHI is well above 1800 and the HHI increase is well above 100"). Moreover, given the high concentration levels, the court must undertake a rigorous analysis of the kinds of efficiencies being urged by the parties in order to ensure that those "efficiencies" represent more than mere speculation and promises about post-merger behavior. The district court did not undertake that analysis here.

In support of its conclusion that post-merger efficiencies will outweigh the merger's anticompetitive effects, the district court found that the consolidation of baby food production in Heinz's under-utilized Pittsburgh plant "will achieve substantial cost savings in salaries and operating costs." The court also credited the appellees' promise of improved product quality as a result of recipe consolidation.[14] The only cost reduction the court quantified as a percentage of pre-merger costs, however, was the so-called "variable

---

[14] In addition, the district court described Heinz's distribution network as much more efficient than Beech-Nut's. It failed to find, however, a significant diseconomy of scale in distribution from which either Heinz or Beech-Nut suffers. 4A Areeda, et al., supra, P 975e1, at 73. In other words, although Beech-Nut has an inefficient distribution system, it can make that system more efficient without merger. Heinz's own efficient distribution network illustrates that a firm the size of Beech-Nut does not need to merge in order to attain an efficient distribution system.

conversion cost": the cost of processing the volume of baby food now processed by Beech-Nut. The court accepted the appellees' claim that this cost would be reduced by 43% if the Beech-Nut production were shifted to Heinz's plant, a reduction the appellees' expert characterized as "extraordinary."

The district court's analysis falls short of the findings necessary for a successful efficiencies defense in the circumstances of this case. We mention only three of the most important deficiencies here. First, "variable conversion cost" is only a percentage of the total variable manufacturing cost. A large percentage reduction in only a small portion of the company's overall variable manufacturing cost does not necessarily translate into a significant cost advantage to the merger. Thus, for cost reduction to be relevant, we must at least consider the percentage of Beech-Nut's total variable manufacturing cost that would be reduced as a consequence of the merger. At oral argument, the appellees' counsel agreed. This correction immediately cuts the asserted efficiency gain in half since, according to the appellees' evidence, using total variable manufacturing cost as the measure cuts the cost savings from 43% to 22.3%.

Second, the percentage reduction in Beech-Nut's cost is still not the relevant figure. After the merger, the two entities will be combined, and to determine whether the merged entity will be a significantly more efficient competitor, cost reductions must be measured across the new entity's combined production--not just across the pre-merger output of Beech-Nut. The district court, however, did not consider the cost reduction over the merged firm's combined output. At oral argument the appellees' counsel was unable to suggest a formula that could be used for determining that cost reduction.

Finally, and as the district court recognized, the asserted efficiencies must be "merger-specific" to be cognizable as a defense. That is, they must be efficiencies that cannot be achieved by either company alone because, if they can, the merger's asserted benefits can be achieved without the concomitant loss of a competitor. See generally 4A Areeda, et al., supra, P 973. Yet the district court never explained why Heinz could not achieve the kind of efficiencies urged without merger. As noted, the principal merger benefit asserted for Heinz is the acquisition of Beech-Nut's better recipes, which will allegedly make its product more attractive and permit expanded sales at prices lower than those charged by Beech-Nut, which produces at an inefficient plant. Yet, neither the district court nor the appellees addressed the question whether Heinz could obtain the benefit of better recipes by investing more money in product development and promotion--say, by an amount less than the amount Heinz would spend to acquire Beech-Nut. At oral argument, Heinz's counsel agreed that the taste of Heinz's products was not so bad that no amount of money could improve the brand's consumer appeal. That being the case, the question is how much Heinz would have to spend to make its product equivalent to the Beech-Nut product and hence whether Heinz could achieve the efficiencies of merger without eliminating Beech-Nut as a competitor. The district court, however, undertook no inquiry in this regard. In short, the district court failed to make the kind of factual determinations necessary to render the appellees' efficiency defense sufficiently concrete to offset the FTC's prima facie showing.

3. Innovation

The appellees claim next that the merger is required to enable Heinz to innovate, and thus to improve its competitive position against Gerber. Heinz and Beech-Nut asserted, and the district court found, that without the merger the two firms are unable to launch new products to compete with Gerber because they lack a sufficient shelf presence or ACV. This kind of defense is often a speculative proposition. See 4A Areeda, et al., supra, P 975g (noting "truly formidable" proof problems in determining innovation economies). In this case, given the old-economy nature of the industry as well as Heinz's position as the world's largest baby food manufacturer, it is a particularly difficult defense to prove. The court below accepted the appellees' argument principally on the basis of their expert's testimony that new product launches are cost-effective only when a firm's ACV is 70% or greater (Heinz's is presently 40%; Beech-Nut's is 45%). That testimony, in turn, was based on a graph that plotted revenue against ACV. According to the expert, the graph showed that only four out of 27 new products launched in 1995 had been successful--all for companies with an ACV of 70% or greater.

The chart, however, does not establish this proposition and the court's consequent finding that the merger is necessary for innovation is thus unsupported and clearly erroneous. All the chart plotted was revenue against ACV and hence all it showed was the unsurprising fact that the greater a company's ACV, the greater the revenue it received. Because the graph did not plot the profitability (or any measure of "cost-effectiveness"), there is no way to know whether the expert's claim--that a 70% ACV is required for a launch to be "successful" in an economic sense—is true.[15] Moreover, the number of data points on the chart were few; they were limited to launches in a single year; and they involved launches of all new grocery products rather than of baby food alone. Assessing such data's statistical significance in establishing the proposition at issue, i.e., the necessity of 70% ACV penetration, is thus highly speculative. The district court did not even address the question of the data's statistical significance and the appellees' counsel could offer no help at oral argument. ("I'm not aware of the statistical significance of the underlying study.").[16] In the absence of reliable and significant evidence that the merger will permit innovation that otherwise could not be accomplished, the district court had no basis to conclude that the FTC's showing was rebutted by an innovation defense.

Moreover, Heinz's insistence on a 70-plus ACV before it brings a new product to market may be largely to persuade the court to recognize promotional economies as a defense. Heinz argues that to profitably launch a new product, it must have nationwide market penetration to recoup the money spent on advertising and promotion. It wants to spread advertising costs out among as many product units as possible, thereby lowering the advertising cost per unit. It does not want to "waste" promotional expenditures in markets where its products are not on the shelf or where they are on only a few shelves.

---

[15] For example, a 5 cent piece of bubble gum introduced with a 90 ACV could appear as a failure on the graph because of low revenue but nonetheless be profitable. On the other hand, a high priced grocery product introduced with the same ACV could generate a lot of revenue (and thus appear as a "success" on the graph) yet be unprofitable.

[16] The graph evidence is also not useful unless we know the "sunk" costs in bringing the product to market and the manufacturer's fixed and variable costs in producing the product. Sunk costs are costs that have already been incurred such as research and development and promotional expenses, including brand name development. See Henry N. Butler, *Economic Analysis for Lawyers* 935 (1998). Fixed costs refer to those expenses that do not vary with output and will be incurred as long as the firm continues in business. Variable costs are those that change with the rate of output such as wages paid to workers and payments for raw materials. See id. at 920, 936; E. Thomas Sullivan & Jeffrey L. Harrison, *Understanding Antitrust and its Economic Implications* 19-21 (3d ed. 1998).

For example, in a metropolitan area in which Heinz has a 75 per cent ACV, every dollar spent on advertising is two or three times more "effective" than in a market in which it has only a 25 per cent ACV. As one authority notes, however, "the case for recognizing a defense based on promotional economies is relatively weak." 4A Areeda, et al., supra, ¶ 975f, at 77. The district court accepted Heinz's claim that it could not introduce new products without at least a 70 per cent ACV because it would be unable to adequately diffuse its advertising and promotional expenditures. But the court failed to determine whether substantial promotional scale economies exist now and, if they do, whether Heinz and Beech-Nut "for that reason operate at a substantial competitive disadvantage in the market or markets in which they sell" or whether there are effective alternatives to merger by which the disadvantage can be overcome. Id. at ¶ 975f2, at 78.

4. Structural Barriers to Collusion

In a footnote the district court dismissed the likelihood of collusion derived from the FTC's market concentration data. "Structural market barriers to collusion" in the retail market for jarred baby food, the court said, rebut the normal presumption that increases in concentration will increase the likelihood of tacit collusion. The court's sole citation, however, was to testimony by the appellees' expert, Jonathan B. Baker, a former Director of the Bureau of Economics at the FTC, who testified that in order to coordinate successfully, firms must solve "cartel problems" such as reaching a consensus on price and market share and deterring each other from deviating from that consensus by either lowering price or increasing production. He opined that after the merger the merged entity would want to expand its market share at Gerber's expense, thereby decreasing the likelihood of consensus on price and market share. In his report, Baker elaborated on his theory, explaining that the efficiencies created by the merger will give the merged firm the ability and incentive to take on Gerber in price and product improvements. He also predicted that policing and monitoring of any agreement would be more difficult than it is now, due in part to a time lag in the ability of one firm to detect price cuts by another. But the district court made no finding that any of these "cartel problems" are so much greater in the baby food industry than in other industries that they rebut the normal presumption. In fact, Baker's testimony about "time lag" is refuted by the record which reflects that supermarket prices are available from industry-wide scanner data within 4-8 weeks. See DX 617 at ¶ 86 (report of appellees' expert Jonathan Baker); see also Oral Arg. Tr. at 30 (statement by appellees' counsel that nothing in record reflects time lag is greater in baby food industry than in other industries). His testimony is further undermined by the record evidence of past price leadership in the baby food industry.[17]

The combination of a concentrated market and barriers to entry is a recipe for price coordination. See *University Health, 938 F.2d at 1218 n.24* ("Significant market concentration makes it 'easier for firms in the market to collude, expressly or tacitly, and thereby force price above or farther above the competitive level.'" (citation omitted)). "Where rivals are few, firms will be able to coordinate their behavior, either by overt collusion or implicit understanding, in order to restrict output and achieve profits above competitive levels." *PPG, 798 F.2d at 1503.* The creation of a durable duopoly affords both the opportunity and incentive for both firms to coordinate to increase prices. The district court recognized this when it questioned Baker on whether the merged entity will, up to a point, expand its market share but "then [with Gerber will] find a nice equilibrium and they'll all get along together." 9/8/2000 Tr. 1014. Tacit coordination

> is feared by antitrust policy even more than express collusion, for tacit coordination, even when observed, cannot easily be controlled directly by the antitrust laws. It is a central object of merger policy to obstruct the creation or reinforcement by merger of such oligopolistic market structures in which tacit coordination can occur.

4 Phillip E. Areeda, Herbert Hovenkamp & John L. Solow, Antitrust Law P 901b2, at 9 (rev. ed. 1998). Because the district court failed to specify any "structural market barriers to collusion" that are unique to the baby food industry, its conclusion that the ordinary presumption of collusion in a merger to duopoly was rebutted is clearly erroneous.

* * * * *

---

[17] In an oligopolistic market characterized by few producers, price leadership occurs when firms engage in interdependent pricing, setting their prices at a profit-maximizing, supracompetitive level by recognizing their shared economic interests with respect to price and output decisions. See *Brooke Group Ltd. v. Brown & Williamson Tobacco Corp., 509 U.S. 209, 227 (1993)....*

Although we recognize that, post-hearing, the FTC may accept the rebuttal arguments proffered by the appellees, including their efficiencies defense, and permit the merger to proceed, we conclude that the FTC succeeded in "raising questions going to the merits so serious, substantial, difficult and doubtful as to make them fair ground for thorough investigation, study, deliberation and determination by the FTC." *Warner Communications, 742 F.2d at 1162.* The FTC demonstrated that the merger to duopoly will increase the concentration in an already highly concentrated market; that entry barriers in the market make it unlikely that any anticompetitive effects will be avoided; that pre-merger competition is vigorous at the wholesale level nationwide and present at the retail level in some metropolitan areas; and that post-merger competition may be lessened substantially. These substantial questions have not been sufficiently answered by the appellees. As we said in Baker Hughes, "the more compelling the prima facie case, the more evidence the defendant must present to rebut it successfully." *908 F.2d at 991.* In concluding that the FTC failed to make the requisite showing, the district court erred in a number of respects. Regarding the contention of lack of pre-merger competition, it made a clearly erroneous factual finding and misunderstood the law with respect to the import of competition at the wholesale level. Regarding the proffered efficiencies defense, the court failed to make the kind of factual findings required to render that defense sufficiently concrete to rebut the government's prima facie showing. Finally, as to the contention that the merger is necessary for innovation, the court clearly erred in relying on evidence that does not support its conclusion. Because the district court incorrectly assessed the merits of the appellees' rebuttal arguments, it improperly discounted the FTC's showing of likelihood of success....

[In a concluding section, the Court of Appeals "weighed the equities." On the government's side, it cited legislative history and prior cases to the effect that denial of an injunction might prevent the government from ever undoing the anticompetitive effects of the merger. It assumed that the Beech-Nut manufacturing facility would be closed and its distribution channels closed. On the defendants' side, it recognized that the parties might abandon the proposed merger if they had to await full administrative litigation before the FTC and a possible appeal. The D.C. Circuit came down in favor of the government, noting that the alleged efficiencies would still be available after litigation.]

III. Conclusion

It is important to emphasize the posture of this case. We do not decide whether the FTC will ultimately prove its case or whether the defendants' claimed efficiencies will carry the day.[18] Our task is to review the district court's order to determine whether, under section 13(b), preliminary injunctive relief would be in the public interest. We have considered the FTC's likelihood of success on the merits. We have weighed the equities. We conclude that the FTC has raised serious and substantial questions. We also conclude that the public equities weigh in favor of preliminary injunctive relief and therefore that a preliminary injunction would be in the public interest. Accordingly, we reverse the district court's denial of preliminary injunctive relief and remand the case for entry of a preliminary injunction pursuant to section 13(b) of the Federal Trade Commission Act.[19]

---

18 "The most difficult mergers to assess may be those that combine both negative and positive effects: creating market power that increases the risk of oligopolistic pricing while at the same time creating efficiencies that reduce production or marketing costs." Sullivan & Grimes, supra, § 9.1, at 511.

19 Ed. The parties abandoned the merger shortly after the D.C. Circuit's decision was issued.

Delete Section 4 of the 1992 Horizontal Merger Guidelines, page 964 and insert the 1997 Revision:

Revision to the U.S. Department of Justice and FTC Joint Horizontal Merger Guidelines, 1997

Section 4. Efficiencies

Competition usually spurs firms to achieve efficiencies internally. Nevertheless, mergers have the potential to generate significant efficiencies by permitting a better utilization of existing assets, enabling the combined firm to achieve lower costs in producing a given quantity and quality than either firm could have achieved without the proposed transaction. Indeed, the primary benefit of mergers to the economy is their potential to generate such efficiencies.

Efficiencies generated through merger can enhance the merged firm's ability and incentive to compete, which may result in lower prices, improved quality, enhanced service, or new products. For example, merger-generated efficiencies may enhance competition by permitting two ineffective (e.g., high cost) competitors to become one effective (e.g., lower cost) competitor. In a coordinated interaction context (see Section 2.1), marginal cost reductions may make coordination less likely or effective by enhancing the incentive of a maverick to lower price or by creating a new maverick firm. In a unilateral effects context (see Section 2.2), marginal cost reductions may reduce the merged firm's incentive to elevate price. Efficiencies also may result in benefits in the form of new or improved products, and efficiencies may result in benefits even when price is not immediately and directly affected. Even when efficiencies generated through merger enhance a firm's ability to compete, however, a merger may have other effects that may lessen competition and ultimately may make the merger anticompetitive.

The Agency will consider only those efficiencies likely to be accomplished with the proposed merger and unlikely to be accomplished in the absence of either the proposed merger or another means having comparable anticompetitive effects. These are termed merger-specific efficiencies.[20] Only

---

[20] The Agency will not deem efficiencies to be merger-specific if they could be preserved by practical alternatives that mitigate competitive concerns, such

alternatives that are practical in the business situation faced by the merging firms will be considered in making this determination; the Agency will not insist upon a less restrictive alternative that is merely theoretical.

Efficiencies are difficult to verify and quantify, in part because much of the information relating to efficiencies is uniquely in the possession of the merging firms. Moreover, efficiencies projected reasonably and in good faith by the merging firms may not be realized. Therefore, the merging firms must substantiate efficiency claims so that the Agency can verify by reasonable means the likelihood and magnitude of each asserted efficiency, how and when each would be achieved (and any costs of doing so), how each would enhance the merged firm's ability and incentive to compete, and why each would be merger-specific. Efficiency claims will not be considered if they are vague or speculative or otherwise cannot be verified by reasonable means.

Cognizable efficiencies are merger-specific efficiencies that have been verified and do not arise from anticompetitive reductions in output or service. Cognizable efficiencies are assessed net of costs produced by the merger or incurred in achieving those efficiencies.

The Agency will not challenge a merger if cognizable efficiencies are of a character and magnitude such that the merger is not likely to be anticompetitive in any relevant market.[21] To make the requisite determination,

---

as divestiture or licensing. If a merger affects not whether but only when an efficiency would be achieved, only the timing advantage is a merger-specific efficiency.

[21] Section 7 of the Clayton Act prohibits mergers that may substantially lessen competition "in any line of commerce...in any section of the country." Accordingly, the Agency normally assesses competition in each relevant market affected by a merger independently and normally will challenge the merger if it is likely to be anticompetitive in any relevant market. In some cases, however, the Agency in its prosecutorial discretion will consider efficiencies not strictly in the relevant market, but so inextricably linked with it that a partial divestiture or other remedy could not feasibly eliminate the anticompetitive effect in the relevant market without sacrificing the efficiencies in the other market(s). Inextricably linked efficiencies rarely are a significant factor in the Agency's determination not to challenge a merger. They are most

the Agency considers whether cognizable efficiencies likely would be sufficient to reverse the merger's potential to harm consumers in the relevant market, e.g., by preventing price increases in that market. In conducting this analysis,[22] the Agency will not simply compare the magnitude of the cognizable efficiencies with the magnitude of the likely harm to competition absent the efficiencies. The greater the potential adverse competitive effect of a merger--as indicated by the increase in the HHI and post-merger HHI from Section 1, the analysis of potential adverse competitive effects from Section 2, and the timeliness, likelihood, and sufficiency of entry from Section 3--the greater must be cognizable efficiencies in order for the Agency to conclude that the merger will not have an anticompetitive effect in the relevant market. When the potential adverse competitive effect of a merger is likely to be particularly large, extraordinarily great cognizable efficiencies would be necessary to prevent the merger from being anticompetitive.

In the Agency's experience, efficiencies are most likely to make a difference in merger analysis when the likely adverse competitive effects, absent the efficiencies, are not great. Efficiencies almost never justify a merger to monopoly or near-monopoly.

The Agency has found that certain types of efficiencies are more likely to be cognizable and substantial than others. For example, efficiencies resulting from shifting production among facilities formerly owned separately, which enable the merging firms to reduce the marginal cost of production, are more likely to be susceptible to verification, merger-specific, and substantial, and are less likely to result from anticompetitive reductions in output. Other efficiencies, such as those relating to research and development, are potentially substantial but are generally less susceptible to verification and may be the

---

likely to make a difference when they are great and the likely anticompetitive effect in the relevant market(s) is small.

[22] The result of this analysis over the short term will determine the Agency's enforcement decision in most cases. The Agency also will consider the effects of cognizable efficiencies with no short-term, direct effect on prices in the relevant market. Delayed benefits from efficiencies (due to delay in the achievement of, or the realization of consumer benefits from the efficiencies) will be given less weight because they are less proximate and m ore difficult to predict.

result of anticompetitive output reductions. Yet others, such as those relating to procurement, management, or capital cost are less likely to be merger-specific or substantial, or may not be cognizable for other reasons.

Notes and Questions

1. The key to a successful efficiency defense appears to be proof that the claimed efficiency likely would be sufficient to reverse the mergers' potential to harm consumers in the relevant market. Mergers must be evaluated at the time they are consummated. How would the representatives of the merging companies produce evidence of this sort of procompetitive effect resulting from efficiencies? Would they have to rely on the structure of the market as an indication that any efficiency savings would be passed on to consumers, thereby countering the likely anticompetitive effect of the transaction?

2. Note that the efficiency defense is circumscribed in various ways. The efficiencies must be merger specific (i.e., they could not be achieved in some less anticompetitive way), substantial, verifiable, and will almost never justify mergers to monopoly or near monopoly. Should the opportunity to present an efficiency defense have been described in more generous terms?

3. In Philadelphia National Bank (Casebook, p. 875), the Supreme Court concluded that it was not permissible to justify anticompetitive effects in one market by pointing to redeeming virtues in a different market. Note 21 of the 1997 Guideline Revision recognizes that precedent, but goes on to say that the enforcement agencies, as a matter of prosecutorial discretion, will consider efficiencies in a different market if they are "inextricably linked." Can you imagines a set of facts that would satisfy the "inextricably linked" standard?

Insert after Note on Foreign Merger Regulation, page 1044:

On June 30, 1997, the Council of the European Union amended the Merger Regulation in several significant respects. See O.J. L 180, 9.07.1997, or <http://europa.eu.int/en/comm/dg04/lawmerg/en/131097.htm>. First, the Council lowered the thresholds used by the Merger Regulation to define which transactions have a "Community dimension," and are thus for the most part within the exclusive competence of the Commission, and which do not, and are thus the responsibility of the Member States. Four criteria now govern the

"Community dimension" determination: (1) the combined aggregate world-wide turnover of all the companies concerned must be more than ECU 2.5 billion (half the former requirement), (2) in each of at least three Member States, the combined aggregate turnover of all the companies concerned must be more than ECU 100 million (again, considerably lower than before), (3) in each of at least three Members States relied on for point 2, the aggregate turnover of each of at least two of the companies must be more than ECU 25 million, and (4) the aggregate Community-wide turnover of each of at least two of the companies concerned must be more than ECU 100 million. An exception to all of this applies if each of the companies involved achieves more than two-thirds of its aggregate Community-wide turnover within one and the same Member State. The overall effect of this change is to lower considerably the monetary thresholds that trigger Community competence and thus to bring many more transactions under the jurisdiction of the Commission.

A second change diminishes the importance of the difficult distinction between "cooperative" and "concentrative" joint ventures, because under the revised Merger Regulation all joint ventures are processed as mergers. The source of law that the Commission applies will continue to be Article 85(1) and (3) for cooperative ventures – those in which the participants continue to have an independent presence on the market – and the Merger Regulation for concentrative joint ventures. Nevertheless, this change will eliminate a great deal of confusion and forum shopping, and is certain to have been welcome in Europe.

Third, it is now perfectly clear that the Commission may attach conditions to a decision not to challenge a merger after only the first phase of proceedings. The Commission had been doing so, but the legal basis for its actions was not as clear as it might have been.

CHAPTER 10: SOME LIMITS ON THE REACH OF ANTITRUST—DIRECT REGULATION, FEDERALISM, AND COMITY

Section 3. "Comity" or Conflict with Foreign Sovereigns

Insert after *Hartford Fire,* page 1207:

The First Circuit issued an important decision finding that a criminal prosecution under Section 1 of the Sherman Act may be based wholly on extraterritorial conduct, as long as there were substantial and intended effects in the United States.

UNITED STATES v. NIPPON PAPER
United States Court of Appeals, First Circuit, 1997.
109 F.3d 1.

Before: SELYA, Circuit Judge, COFFIN, Senior Circuit Judge, and LYNCH, Circuit Judge.

SELYA, J. This case raises an important, hitherto unanswered question. In it, the United States attempts to convict a foreign corporation under the Sherman Act, a federal antitrust statute, alleging that price-fixing activities which took place entirely in Japan are prosecutable because they were intended to have, and did in fact have, substantial effects in this country. The district court, declaring that a criminal antitrust prosecution could not be based on wholly extraterritorial conduct, dismissed the indictment. See United States v. Nippon Paper Indus. Co., 944 F. Supp. 55 (D. Mass.1996). We reverse.

I. JUST THE FAX

Since the district court granted the defendant's motion to dismiss for failure to state a prosecutable offense, we draw our account of the pertinent events from the well-pleaded facts in the indictment itself. See United States v. National Dairy Prods. Corp., 372 U.S. 29, 33 n.2 (1963).

In 1995, a federal grand jury handed up an indictment naming as a defendant Nippon Paper Industries Co., Ltd. (NPI), a Japanese manufacturer of facsimile paper. The indictment alleges that in 1990 NPI and certain unnamed coconspirators held a number of meetings in Japan which culminated in an agreement to fix the price of thermal fax paper throughout North America. NPI and other manufacturers who were privy to the scheme purportedly accomplished their objective by selling the paper in Japan to unaffiliated trading houses on condition that the latter charge specified (inflated) prices for the paper when they resold it in North America. The trading houses then shipped and sold the paper to their subsidiaries in the United States who in turn sold it to American consumers at swollen prices. The indictment further relates that, in 1990 alone, NPI sold thermal fax paper worth approximately $6,100,000 for eventual import into the United States; and that in order to ensure the success of the venture, NPI monitored the paper trail and confirmed that the prices charged to end users were those that it had arranged. These activities, the indictment posits, had a substantial adverse effect on commerce in the United States and unreasonably restrained trade in violation of Section One of the Sherman Act, 15 U.S.C. § 1 (1994).

NPI moved to dismiss because, inter alia, if the conduct attributed to NPI occurred at all, it took place entirely in Japan, and, thus, the indictment failed to limn an offense under Section One of the Sherman Act. The government opposed this initiative on two grounds. First, it claimed that the law deserved a less grudging reading and that, properly read, Section One of the Sherman Act applied criminally to wholly foreign conduct as long as that conduct produced substantial and intended effects within the United States. Second, it claimed that the indictment, too, deserved a less grudging reading and that, properly read, the bill alleged a vertical conspiracy in restraint of trade that involved overt acts by certain coconspirators within the United States. Accepting a restrictive reading of both the statute and the indictment, the district court dismissed the case. See United States v. NPI, 944 F. Supp. at 64-66. This appeal followed.

II. ANALYSIS

We begin--and end--with the overriding legal question. Because this question is one of statutory construction, we review de novo the holding that Section One of the Sherman Act does not cover wholly extraterritorial conduct in the criminal context. See United States v. Gifford, 17 F.3d 462, 471-72 (1st Cir.1994).

Our analysis proceeds in moieties. We first present the historical context in which this important question arises. We move next to the specifics of the case.

A. An Historical Perspective.

Our law has long presumed that "legislation of Congress, unless a contrary intent appears, is meant to apply only within the territorial jurisdiction of the United States." EEOC v. Arabian American Oil Co., 499 U.S. 244 (1991) (citation omitted). In this context, the Supreme Court has charged inquiring courts with determining whether Congress has clearly expressed an affirmative desire to apply particular laws to conduct that occurs beyond the borders of the United States. See *id.*

The earliest Supreme Court case which undertook a comparable task in respect to Section One of the Sherman Act determined that the presumption against extraterritoriality had not been overcome. In American Banana Co. v. United Fruit Co., 213 U.S. 347 (1909), the Court considered the application of the Sherman Act in a civil action concerning conduct which occurred entirely in Central America and which had no discernible effect on imports to the United States. Starting with what Justice Holmes termed "the general and almost universal rule" holding "that the character of an act as lawful or unlawful must be determined wholly by the law of the country where the act is done," *id.* at 356, and the ancillary proposition that, in cases of doubt, a statute should be "confined in its operation and effect to the territorial limits over which the lawmaker has general and legitimate power," *id.* at 357, the Court held that the defendant's actions abroad were not proscribed by the Sherman Act.

Our jurisprudence is precedent-based, but it is not static. By 1945, a different court saw a very similar problem in a somewhat softer light. In United States v. Aluminum Co. of Am., 148 F.2d 416 (2d Cir.1945) (Alcoa), the Second Circuit, sitting as a court of last resort, see 15 U.S.C. § 29 (authorizing designation of a court of appeals as a court of last resort for certain antitrust cases), mulled a civil action brought under Section One against a Canadian corporation for acts committed entirely abroad which, the government averred, had produced substantial anticompetitive effects within the United States. The Alcoa court read American Banana narrowly; that case, Judge Learned Hand wrote, stood only for the principle that "[w]e should not impute to Congress an intent to punish all whom its courts can catch, for conduct which has no consequences within the United States." *Id.* at 443. But a sovereign ordinarily can impose liability for conduct outside its borders that produces consequences within them, and while considerations of comity argue against applying Section One to situations in which no effect within the United States has been shown--the American Banana scenario--the statute, properly interpreted, does proscribe extraterritorial acts which were "intended to affect imports [to the United States] and did affect them." *Id.* at 444. On the facts of Alcoa, therefore, the presumption against extraterritoriality had been overcome, and the Sherman Act had been violated. See *id.* at 444-45.

Any perceived tension between American Banana and Alcoa was eased by the Supreme Court's most recent exploration of the Sherman Act's extraterritorial reach. In Hartford Fire Ins. Co. v. California, 509 U.S. 764 (1993), the Justices endorsed Alcoa's core holding, permitting civil antitrust claims under Section One to go forward despite the fact that the actions which allegedly violated Section One occurred entirely on British soil. While noting American Banana's initial disagreement with this proposition, the Hartford Fire Court deemed it "well established by now that the Sherman Act applies to foreign conduct that was meant to produce and did in fact produce some substantial effect in the United States." *Id.* at 796. The conduct alleged, a London-based conspiracy to alter the American insurance market, met that benchmark. See *id.*

To sum up, the case law now conclusively establishes that civil antitrust actions predicated on wholly foreign conduct which has an intended and substantial effect in the United States come within Section One's jurisdictional reach. In arriving at this conclusion, we take no view of the government's asseveration that the Foreign Trade Antitrust Improvements Act of 1982 (FTAIA), 15 U.S.C. § 6a (1994), makes manifest Congress' intent to apply the Sherman Act extraterritorially. The FTAIA is inelegantly phrased and the court in Hartford Fire declined to place any weight on it. See Hartford Fire, 509 U.S. at 796 n. 23. We emulate this example and do not rest our ultimate conclusion about Section One's scope upon the FTAIA.

B. The Merits.

Were this a civil case, our journey would be complete. But here the United States essays a criminal prosecution for solely extraterritorial conduct rather than a civil action. This is largely uncharted terrain; we are aware of no authority directly on point, and the parties have cited none.

Be that as it may, one datum sticks out like a sore thumb: in both criminal and civil cases, the claim that Section One applies extraterritorially is based on the same language in the same section of the same statute: "Every contract, combination in the form of trust or otherwise, or conspiracy, in restraint of trade or commerce among the several States, or with foreign nations, is declared to be illegal." 15 U.S.C. § 1. Words may sometimes be chameleons, possessing different shades of meaning in different contexts, see, e.g., Hanover Ins. Co. v. United States, 880 F.2d 1503, 1504 (1st Cir.1989), cert. denied, 493 U.S. 1023 (1990), but common sense suggests that courts should interpret the same language in the same section of the same statute uniformly, regardless of whether the impetus for interpretation is criminal or civil.

Common sense is usually a good barometer of statutory meaning. Here, however, we need not rely on common sense alone; accepted canons of statutory construction point in the same direction. It is a fundamental interpretive principle that identical words or terms used in different parts of the same act are intended to have the same meaning. See Commissioner of Internal Revenue v. Lundy, 116 S.Ct. 647, 655 (1996); Gustafson v. Alloyd Co., 115 S.Ct. 1061, 1067 (1995). This principle--which the Court recently called "the basic canon of statutory construction," Estate of Cowart v. Nicklos Drilling Co., 505 U.S. 469, 479 (1992)--operates not only when particular phrases appear in different sections of the same act, but also when they appear in different paragraphs or sentences of a single section. See Russo v. Texaco, Inc., 808 F.2d 221, 227 (2d Cir.1986) ("It is a settled principle of statutory construction that [w]hen the same word or phrase is used in the same section of an act more than once, and the meaning is clear as used in one place, it will be construed to have the same meaning in the next place.") (citations and internal quotation marks omitted); United States v. Gertz, 249 F.2d 662, 665 (9th Cir.1957) (similar). It follows, therefore, that if the language upon which the indictment rests were the same as the language upon which civil liability rests but appeared in a different section of the Sherman Act, or in a different part of the same section, we would be under great pressure to follow the lead of the Hartford Fire Court and construe the two iterations of the language identically. Where, as here, the tie binds more tightly--that is, the text under consideration is not merely a duplicate appearing somewhere else in the statute, but is the original phrase in the original setting--the pressure escalates and the case for reading the language in a manner consonant with a prior Supreme Court interpretation is irresistible. See United States v. Thompson/Center Arms Co., 504 U.S. 505, 518 n. 10, (1992) (plurality op.) (flatly rejecting the idea, while construing language from a statute with both civil and criminal implications, that a court should "refrain in criminal cases from applying statutory language that would have been held to apply if challenged in civil litigation").

[The court here discussed the Supreme Court's opinion in Ratzlaf v. United States, 510 U.S. 135 (1994), and its own opinions in Strickland v. Commissioner, Me. Dep't of Human Servs., 48 F.3d 12, 21 (1st Cir.), cert. denied, 116 S.Ct. 145, (1995), and Strickland v. Commissioner, Me. Dep't of Human Servs., 96 F.3d 542, 547 (1st Cir.1996). All three supported the proposition that the same phrase, appearing in the same portion of the same statute, cannot bear divergent interpretations in different litigation contexts.]

The shared rationale of the Ratzlaf and Strickland cases reinforces the basic canon of construction and gives us confidence that we should follow the canon here. The words of Section One have not changed since the Hartford Fire Court found that they clearly evince Congress' intent to apply the Sherman Act extraterritorially in civil actions, and it would be disingenuous for us to pretend that the words had lost their clarity simply because this is a criminal proceeding. Thus, unless some special circumstance obtains in this case, there is no principled way in which we can uphold the order of dismissal.

NPI and its amicus, the Government of Japan, urge that special reasons exist for measuring Section One's reach differently in a criminal context. We have reviewed their exhortations and found them hollow. We discuss the five most promising theses below. The rest do not require comment.

1. Lack of Precedent. NPI and its amicus make much of the fact that this appears to be the first criminal case in which the United States endeavors to extend Section One to wholly foreign conduct. We are not impressed. There is a first time for everything, and the absence of earlier criminal actions is probably more a demonstration of the increasingly global nature of our economy than proof that Section One cannot cover wholly foreign conduct in the criminal milieu.

Moreover, this argument overstates the lack of precedent. There is, for example, solid authority for applying a state's criminal statute to conduct occurring entirely outside the state's borders. See Strassheim v. Daily, 221 U.S. 280 (1911) (Holmes, J.) ("Acts done outside a jurisdiction, but intended to produce and producing detrimental effects within it, justify a State in punishing the cause of the harm as if he had been present at the effect, if the State should succeed in getting him within its power."). It is not much of a stretch to apply this same principle internationally, especially in a shrinking world. See, e.g., Chua Han Mow v. United States, 730 F.2d 1308, 1311-12 (9th Cir.1984) (applying Strassheim principle to conduct in Malaysia involving drugs intended for distribution in the United States), cert. denied, 470 U.S. 1031 (1985); United States v. Hayes, 653 F.2d 8, 11 (1st Cir.1981) (similar); cf. John Donne, Devotions Upon Emergent Occasions, no. 17 (1624) (warning that "no man is an island, entire of itself; every man is a piece of the continent, a part of the main").

2. Difference in Strength of Presumption. The lower court and NPI both cite United States v. Bowman, 260 U.S. 94 (1922), for the proposition

that the presumption against extraterritoriality operates with greater force in the criminal arena than in civil litigation. This misreads the opinion. To be sure, the Bowman Court, dealing with a charged conspiracy to defraud, warned that if the criminal law "is to be extended to include those [crimes] committed outside of the strict territorial jurisdiction, it is natural for Congress to say so in the statute, and failure to do so will negative the purpose of Congress in this regard." *Id.* at 98. But this pronouncement merely restated the presumption against extraterritoriality previously established in civil cases like American Banana, 213 U.S. at 357. The Bowman Court nowhere suggested that a different, more resilient presumption arises in criminal cases.

Nor does United States v. United States Gypsum Co., 438 U.S. 422 (1978), offer aid and succor to NPI. Recognizing that "the behavior proscribed by the [Sherman] Act is often difficult to distinguish from the gray zone of socially acceptable and economically justifiable business conduct," *id.* at 440-41, the Gypsum Court held that criminal intent generally is required to convict under the Act. See *id.* at 443. Although this distinguishes some civil antitrust cases (in which intent need not be proven) from their criminal counterparts, the Gypsum Court made it plain that intent need not be shown to prosecute criminally "conduct regarded as per se illegal because of its unquestionably anticompetitive effects." *Id.* at 440. This means, of course, that defendants can be convicted of participation in price-fixing conspiracies without any demonstration of a specific criminal intent to violate the antitrust laws. See, e.g., United States v. Brown, 936 F.2d 1042, 1046 (9th Cir.1991); United States v. Society of Indep. Gas. Marketers, 624 F.2d 461, 465 (4th Cir.1980), cert. denied, 449 U.S. 1078 (1981); United States v. Gillen, 599 F.2d 541, 544-45 (3d Cir.), cert. denied, 444 U.S. 866 (1979). Because the instant case falls within that rubric, Gypsum does not help NPI.

We add that even if Gypsum had differentiated between civil and criminal price-fixing cases, NPI's reliance on it would still be problematic. Reduced to bare essence, Gypsum focuses on mens rea, noting that centuries of Anglo-American legal tradition instruct that criminal liability ordinarily should be premised on malevolent intent, see *id.* at 436-37, whereas civil liability, to which less stigma and milder consequences commonly attach, often requires a lesser showing of intent. There is simply no comparable tradition or rationale for drawing a criminal/civil distinction with regard to extraterritoriality, and neither NPI nor its amicus have alluded to any case which does so.

3. The Restatement. NPI and the district court, 944 F. Supp. at 65, both sing the praises of the Restatement (Third) of Foreign Relations Law (1987), claiming that it supports a distinction between civil and criminal cases on the issue of extraterritoriality. The passage to which they pin their hopes states:

> [I]n the case of regulatory statutes that may give rise to both civil and criminal liability, such as the United States antitrust and securities laws, the presence of substantial foreign elements will ordinarily weigh against application of criminal law. In such cases, legislative intent to subject conduct outside the state's territory to its criminal law should be found only on the basis of express statement or clear implication.

Id. at § 403 cmt. f. We believe that this statement merely reaffirms the classic presumption against extraterritoriality--no more, no less. After all, nothing in the text of the Restatement proper contradicts the government's interpretation of Section One. See, e.g., *id.* at § 402(1)(c) (explaining that, subject only to a general requirement of reasonableness, a state has jurisdiction to proscribe "conduct outside its territory that has or is intended to have substantial effect within its territory"); *id.* at § 415(2) ("Any agreement in restraint of United States trade that is made outside of the United States ... [is] subject to the jurisdiction to prescribe of the United States, if a principal purpose of the conduct or agreement is to interfere with the commerce of the United States, and the agreement or conduct has some effect on that commerce."). What is more, other comments indicate that a country's decision to prosecute wholly foreign conduct is discretionary. See, e.g., *id.* at § 403 rep. n. 8.

4. The Rule of Lenity. The next arrow which NPI yanks from its quiver is the rule of lenity. The rule itself is venerable; it provides that, in the course of interpreting statutes in criminal cases, a reviewing court should resolve ambiguities affecting a statute's scope in the defendant's favor. . . . But the rule of lenity is inapposite unless a statutory ambiguity looms, and a statute is not ambiguous for this purpose simply because some courts or commentators have questioned its proper interpretation. . . . Rather, "[t]he rule of lenity applies only if, after seizing everything from which aid can be derived, [a court] can make no more than a guess as to what Congress intended." Reno [v. Koray], 515 U.S. [50, ----], (citations, internal quotation marks, and certain brackets omitted); accord United States v. O'Neil, 11 F.3d 292, 301 n. 10 (1st Cir.1993) (describing the rule of lenity as "a background principle that properly comes into play when, at the end of a thorough inquiry,

the meaning of a criminal statute remains obscure"). Put bluntly, the rule of lenity cannot be used to create ambiguity when the meaning of a law, even if not readily apparent, is, upon inquiry, reasonably clear.

That ends the matter of lenity. In view of the fact that the Supreme Court deems it "well established" that Section One of the Sherman Act applies to wholly foreign conduct, Hartford Fire, 509 U.S. at 796, we effectively are foreclosed from trying to tease an ambiguity out of Section One relative to its extraterritorial application. Accordingly, the rule of lenity plays no part in the instant case.

5. Comity. International comity is a doctrine that counsels voluntary forbearance when a sovereign which has a legitimate claim to jurisdiction concludes that a second sovereign also has a legitimate claim to jurisdiction under principles of international law. See Harold G. Maier, Extraterritorial Jurisdiction at a Crossroads: An Intersection Between Public and Private International Law, 76 A.J. Int'l L. 280, 281 n. 1 (1982). Comity is more an aspiration than a fixed rule, more a matter of grace than a matter of obligation. In all events, its growth in the antitrust sphere has been stunted by Hartford Fire, in which the Court suggested that comity concerns would operate to defeat the exercise of jurisdiction only in those few cases in which the law of the foreign sovereign required a defendant to act in a manner incompatible with the Sherman Act or in which full compliance with both statutory schemes was impossible. See Hartford Fire, 509 U.S. at 798-99, 113 S.Ct. at 2910-11; see also Kenneth W. Dam, Extraterritoriality in an Age of Globalization: The Hartford Fire Case, 1993 Sup.Ct.Rev. 289, 306-07 (1993). Accordingly, the Hartford Fire Court gave short shrift to the defendants' entreaty that the conduct leading to antitrust liability was perfectly legal in the United Kingdom. See Hartford Fire, 509 U.S. at 798- 99.

In this case the defendant's comity-based argument is even more attenuated. The conduct with which NPI is charged is illegal under both Japanese and American laws, thereby alleviating any founded concern about NPI being whipsawed between separate sovereigns. And, moreover, to the extent that comity is informed by general principles of reasonableness, see Restatement (Third) of Foreign Relations Law § 403, the indictment lodged against NPI is well within the pale. In it, the government charges that the defendant orchestrated a conspiracy with the object of rigging prices in the United States. If the government can prove these charges, we see no tenable reason why principles of comity should shield NPI from prosecution. We live in an age of international commerce, where decisions reached in one corner of the world can reverberate around the globe in less time than it takes to tell the tale. Thus, a ruling in NPI's favor would create perverse incentives for those who would use nefarious means to influence markets in the United States, rewarding them for erecting as many territorial firewalls as possible between cause and effect.

We need go no further. Hartford Fire definitively establishes that Section One of the Sherman Act applies to wholly foreign conduct which has an intended and substantial effect in the United States. We are bound to accept that holding. Under settled principles of statutory construction, we also are bound to apply it by interpreting Section One the same way in a criminal case. The combined force of these commitments requires that we accept the government's cardinal argument, reverse the order of the district court, reinstate the indictment, and remand for further proceedings.

Reversed and remanded.

LYNCH, Circuit Judge (concurring).

The question presented in this case is whether Section One of the Sherman Act authorizes criminal prosecutions of defendants for their actions committed entirely outside the United States. Judicial precedents, culminating with the Supreme Court's decision in Hartford Fire Insurance Co. v. California, 509 U.S. 764 (1993), conclusively establish that Section One's jurisdictional reach extends, in civil actions, to foreign conduct that is meant to produce, and does in fact produce, substantial effects in the United States. The next question to be asked is whether there is any persuasive reason to believe that, with regard to wholly foreign conduct, Section One in the criminal context is not co-extensive with Section One in the civil context.

In answering this second question, courts must be careful to determine whether this construction of Section One's criminal reach conforms with principles of international law. "It has been a maxim of statutory construction since the decision in Murray v. The Charming Betsy, 2 Cranch 64, 118, 2 L.Ed. 208 (1804), that 'an act of congress ought never to be construed to violate the law of nations, if any other possible construction remains.'" Weinberger v. Rossi, 456 U.S. 25, 32 (1982). In the Alcoa case, Judge Learned Hand found this canon of construction relevant to determining the substantive reach of the Sherman Act, observing that "we are not to read general words [i.e., Section

One] ... without regard to the limitations customarily observed by nations upon the exercise of their powers." United States v. Aluminum Co. of Am., 148 F.2d 416, 443 (2d Cir.1945); see also Hartford Fire, 509 U.S. at 814-15 (Scalia, J., dissenting).

The task of construing Section One in this context is not the usual one of determining congressional intent by parsing the language or legislative history of the statute. The broad, general language of the federal antitrust laws and their unilluminating legislative history place a special interpretive responsibility upon the judiciary. The Supreme Court has called the Sherman Act a "charter of freedom" for the courts, with "a generality and adaptability comparable to that found ... in constitutional provisions." Appalachian Coals, Inc. v. United States, 288 U.S. 344, 359-60 (1933). As Professors Areeda and Turner have said, the federal courts have been invested "with a jurisdiction to create and develop an 'antitrust law' in the manner of the common law courts." I Areeda & Turner, Antitrust Law ¶ 106, at 15 (1978). The courts are aided in this task by canons of statutory construction, such as the presumption against violating international law, which serve as both guides and limits in the absence of more explicit indicia of congressional intent.

Here, we are asked to determine the substantive content of Section One's inexact jurisdictional provision, ""ommerce ... with foreign nations." 15 U.S.C. § 1. Because of the "compunctions against the creation of crimes by judges rather than by legislators," II Areeda & Hovenkamp, Antitrust Law ¶ 311b, at 33 (1995 rev. ed.), the constitution-like aspects of the antitrust laws must be handled particularly carefully in criminal prosecutions.

As the antitrust laws give the federal enforcement agencies a relatively blank check, the development of antitrust law has been largely shaped by the cases that the executive branch chooses--or does not choose--to bring. Accordingly it has been said that:

> novel interpretations or great departures have seldom, if ever, occurred in criminal cases, which prosecutors have usually reserved for defendants whose knowing behavior would be generally recognized as appropriate for criminal sanctions.

Id. at 34. This case does present a new interpretation. We are told this is the first instance in which the executive branch has chosen to interpret the criminal provisions of the Sherman Act as reaching conduct wholly committed outside of this country's borders.

Changing economic conditions, as well as different political agendas, mean that antitrust policies may change from administration to administration. The present administration has promulgated new Antitrust Enforcement Guidelines for International Operations which "focus primarily on situations in which the Sherman Act will grant jurisdiction and when the United States will exercise that jurisdiction" internationally. Brockbank, The 1995 International Antitrust Guidelines: The Reach of U.S. Antitrust Law Continues to Expand, 2 J. Int'l Legal Stud. 1, *22 (1996). The new Guidelines reflect a stronger enforcement stance than earlier versions of the Guidelines, and have been described as a "warning to foreign governments and enterprises that the [antitrust enforcement] Agencies intend to actively pursue restraints on trade occurring abroad that adversely affect American markets or damage American exporting opportunities." *Id.* at *21. The instant case is likely a result of this policy.

It is with this context in mind that we must determine if the exercise of jurisdiction occasioned by the decision of the executive branch of the United States is proper in this case. While courts, including this one, speak of determining congressional intent when interpreting statutes, the meaning of the antitrust laws has emerged through the relationship among all three branches of government. In this criminal case, it is our responsibility to ensure that the executive's interpretation of the Sherman Act does not conflict with other legal principles, including principles of international law.

That question requires examination beyond the language of Section One of the Sherman Act. It is, of course, generally true that, as a principle of statutory interpretation, the same language should be read the same way in all contexts to which the language applies. But this is not invariably true. New content is sometimes ascribed to statutory terms depending upon context. Cf. Robinson v. Shell Oil Co., 117 S.Ct. 843, 847 (1997) (depending on context, statutory term may have different meanings in different sections of single statute); 3 Sutherland, Statutory Construction § 60.04 (5th ed. 1995) (statutes with both remedial and penal provisions may be construed liberally in remedial context and strictly in penal context). As NPI and the Government of Japan point out, the Supreme Court has held that Section One of the Sherman Act, which defines both criminal and civil violations with one general phrase, "should be construed as including intent as an element" of a criminal violation. United States v. United States Gypsum Co., 438 U.S. 422, 443 (1978). Where

Congress intends that our laws conform with international law, and where international law suggests that criminal enforcement and civil enforcement be viewed differently, it is at least conceivable that different content could be ascribed to the same language depending on whether the context is civil or criminal. It is then worth asking about the effect of the international law which Congress presumably also meant to respect.

The content of international law is determined "by reference 'to the customs and usages of civilized nations, and, as evidence of these, to the works of jurists and commentators.'" Hilao v. Estate of Marcos, 103 F.3d 789, 794 (9th Cir.1996) (quoting The Paquete Habana, 175 U.S. 677, 700 (1900)); see also Kadic v. Karadzic, 70 F.3d 232 (2d Cir.1995). The Restatement (Third) of the Foreign Relations Law of the United States restates international law, as derived from customary international law and from international agreements to which the United States is a party, as it applies to the United States. [Judge Lynch then concluded that the Restatement served "as a useful guide to evaluating the international interests at stake."] . . . .

Restatement Section 402(1)(c) states that "Subject to § 403," a state has jurisdiction to prescribe law to "conduct outside its territory that has or is intended to have substantial effect within its territory." *Id.* § 402(1)(c). Section 403(1) states that, even when Section 402 has been satisfied, jurisdiction may not be exercised if it is "unreasonable." *Id.* § 403(1). Section 403(2) lists factors to be evaluated in determining if jurisdiction is reasonable:

> (a) the link of the activity to the territory of the regulating state, i.e., the extent to which the activity takes place within the territory, or has substantial, direct, and foreseeable effect upon or in the territory;
> (b) the connections, such as nationality, residence, or economic activity, between the regulating state and the person principally responsible for the activity to be regulated, or between that state and those whom the regulation is designed to protect;
> (c) the character of the activity to be regulated, the importance of regulation to the regulating state, the extent to which other states regulate such activities, and the degree to which the desirability of such regulation is generally accepted;
> (d) the existence of justified expectations that might be protected or hurt by the regulation;
> (e) the importance of the regulation to the international political, legal, or economic system;

(f) the extent to which the regulation is consistent with the traditions of the international system;
(g) the extent to which another state may have an interest in regulating the activity; and
(h) the likelihood of conflict with regulation by another state.

Id. § 403(2).

Comment f to Section 403 states that the principles of Sections 402 and 403 "apply to criminal as well as to civil regulation." *Id.* § 403 cmt. f. But, specifically naming the United States antitrust laws, the comment also says that for statutes that give rise to both types of liability, "the presence of substantial foreign elements will ordinarily weigh against application of criminal law." *Id.* The comment argues that legislative intent to apply these laws criminally should only be found on the basis of "express statement or clear implication." *Id.*

While the majority opinion accurately states that this comment is an expression of the clear statement rule, the comment also implies that there are special concerns associated with the imposition of criminal sanctions on foreign conduct. See also *id.* § 403 n. 8 ("In applying the principle of reasonableness, the exercise of criminal (as distinguished from civil) jurisdiction in relation to acts committed in another state may be perceived as particularly intrusive."). Indeed, most people recognize a distinction between civil and criminal liability; that the law of nations should do so as well is not surprising. And while Hartford Fire and earlier judicial decisions have found that the antitrust laws do apply, in the civil context, to foreign conduct, this antitrust common law is not the express statement of legislative intent that the Restatement suggests may be appropriate in the criminal context.

Also relevant to the present inquiry is section 415(2), which states that:

> Any agreement in restraint of United States trade that is made outside of the United States, and any conduct or agreement in restraint of such trade that is carried out predominantly outside of the United States, are subject to the jurisdiction to prescribe of the United States, if a principal purpose of the conduct or agreement is to interfere with the commerce of the United States and the agreement or conduct has some effect on that commerce.

Restatement § 415(2). Comment a to Section 415 states that the reasonableness principles articulated in Section 403 must still be satisfied. See id cmt. a.

Application of these principles to the indictment at issue here leads to the conclusion that the exercise of jurisdiction is reasonable in this case. Here, raising prices in the United States and Canada was not only a purpose of the alleged conspiracy, it was the purpose, thus satisfying Section 415's "principal purpose" requirement. Moreover, Section 415's requirement of "some effect" on United States markets is amply met here. The indictment alleges that NPI sold $ 6.1 million of fax paper into the United States during 1990, approximately the period covered by the charged conspiracy. In 1990, total sales of fax paper in North America were approximately $100 million. NPI's price increases thus affected a not insignificant share of the United States market.

These same factors weigh heavily in the Section 403 reasonableness analysis. Because only North American markets were targeted, the United States' interest in combatting this activity appears to be greater than the Japanese interest, which may only be the general interest of a state in having its industries comport with foreign legal norms. Japan has no interest in protecting Japanese consumers in this case as they were unaffected by the alleged conspiracy. The United States, in contrast, has a strong interest in protecting United States consumers, who were affected by the increase in prices. In this situation, it may be that only the United States has sufficient incentive to pursue the alleged wrongdoers, thereby providing the necessary deterrent to similar anticompetitive behavior. In another case, where the consumers of the situs nation were injured as well, that state's interest in regulating anticompetitive conduct might be stronger than it is here.

Other Section 403 factors also counsel in favor of the exercise of jurisdiction here. The effects on United States markets were foreseeable and direct. The Government of Japan acknowledges that antitrust regulation is part of the international legal system, and NPI does not really assert that it has justified expectations that were hurt by the regulation. The only factor counseling against finding that the United States' antitrust laws apply to this conduct is the fact that the situs of the conduct was Japan and that the principals were Japanese corporations. This consideration is inherent in the nature of jurisdiction based on effects of conduct, where the situs of the conduct is, by definition, always a foreign country. This alone does not tip the balance against jurisdiction.

For these reasons, I agree with the majority that the district court erred in dismissing the indictment.

DEN NORSKE STATS OLJESELSKAP AS v. HEEREMAC VOF
United States Court of Appeals, Fifth Circuit, 2001.
241 F.3d 420.

Before: JOLLY, HIGGINBOTHAM and EMILIO M. GARZA, Circuit Judges.

JOLLY, J. This appeal requires us to interpret the scope of the United States antitrust laws and their application to foreign conduct. The plaintiff is a Norwegian oil corporation that conducts business solely in the North Sea. It seeks redress under the United States antitrust laws against the defendants for an alleged anticompetitive conspiracy that supposedly inflated the plaintiff's operating costs in the North Sea. Supreme Court precedent makes clear as a general proposition that United States antitrust laws "do not regulate the competitive conditions of other nations' economies," *Matsushita Elec. Indus. Co. v. Zenith Radio Corp.*, 475 U.S. 574, 582, (1986). More specifically, today we are bound by the plain language of the Foreign Trade Antitrust Improvements Act (FTAIA). Thus, even though the plaintiff alleges that the antitrust conspiracy raised prices in the United States, it fails to assert jurisdiction under the antitrust laws because the plaintiff's injury did not arise from that domestic anticompetitive effect. Accordingly, we find that the district court properly dismissed the plaintiff's antitrust claims for lack of subject matter jurisdiction. It follows that we affirm the court's determination that the plaintiff lacked antitrust standing to bring these claims in United States federal court.

I

We begin with the basics. Sections 1 and 2 of the Sherman Act prohibit restraints of trade and monopolization. . . . The FTAIA, enacted by Congress in 1982 to clarify the application of United States antitrust laws to foreign conduct, limits the application of such laws when non-import foreign commerce is involved. The FTAIA states that the antitrust laws will not apply to non-import commerce with foreign nations unless the conduct at issue has a "direct, substantial, and reasonably foreseeable effect" on domestic commerce *and* "such effect gives rise to a claim under" the antitrust laws.

II

The plaintiff, Den Norske Stats Oljeselskap As ("Statoil"), is a Norwegian oil company that owns and operates oil and gas drilling platforms exclusively in the North Sea. The defendants are providers of heavy-lift barge services in the Gulf of Mexico, the North Sea, and the Far East. Only six or seven heavy-lift barges exist in the world. These immense vessels have cranes capable of hoisting and transporting offshore oil platforms and decks weighing in excess of 4,000 tons. During the 1993-1997 time frame, which is at issue in this suit, the three defendants controlled these barges. Between 1993 and 1997, Statoil purchased heavy lift barge services from the HeereMac and Saipem defendants in the North Sea.

Statoil alleges that the defendants conspired to fix bids and allocate customers, territories, and projects between 1993 and 1997. Under the alleged arrangement, the defendants agreed that HeereMac [a Dutch company] and McDermott [an American company] would have exclusive access to heavy-lift projects in the Gulf of Mexico, while Saipem [a British company] would receive a higher allocation of North Sea projects in exchange for staying out of the Gulf. The defendants also allegedly agreed to submit embellished bids on heavy-lift projects. As a result of this conspiracy, Statoil contends that it paid inflated prices for heavy-lift barge services in the North Sea. Statoil further argues that the conspiracy compelled it to charge higher prices for the crude oil it exported to the United States. Finally, Statoil asserts that purchasers of heavy-lift services in the Gulf of Mexico were forced to pay inflated prices for those services because of the conspiracy.

III

By way of background, it should be noted that in December 1997, the United States Department of Justice filed a criminal complaint against defendants HeereMac and Jan Meek, one of HeereMac's managing directors. The complaint alleged that the defendants conspired "to suppress and eliminate competition by rigging bids for the sale of heavy-lift derrick barge and related marine construction services in the United States and elsewhere." HeereMac and Meek submitted to United States jurisdiction and pled guilty to the charges. They agreed to pay fines of $49 million and $100,000, respectively.

Following the guilty pleas, numerous companies across the globe filed suit in United States federal court seeking redress for injuries stemming from defendants' conduct. The first of these suits was filed in the Southern District of Texas in June 1998 by Phillips Petroleum Company and three of its foreign-based subsidiaries.

On January 22, 1999, the court dismissed Phillips's claims for injuries sustained by its foreign subsidiaries relating to projects in foreign waters but allowed those claims asserting injury from projects in United States waters to proceed. While the court acknowledged the worldwide nature of the alleged conspiracy in its order, it nonetheless held that subject matter jurisdiction did not exist for those claims pled by foreign-based subsidiaries for injuries allegedly sustained on foreign platforms. Specifically, the court determined that those claims did not fall within the ambit of the United States antitrust laws because the claims did not arise from a direct and substantial effect on United States commerce.

Statoil filed this suit in the same court in December 1998. The court dismissed Statoil's complaint against the defendants on July 12, 1999. In its order, the court relied heavily upon its decision in the Phillips case and found no subject matter jurisdiction over the claims because "Statoil's damages arise from its projects in the Norwegian sector of the North Sea"; thus, the FTAIA's requirement that the effect on domestic commerce "gives rise" to the antitrust claim was not satisfied. *See* 15 U.S.C. § 6a(2). The court also held that the defendants' conspiracy "did not have a direct, substantial, and reasonably foreseeable anticompetitive effect on United States trade or commerce" under the FTAIA. *See* 15 U.S.C. § 6a(1). Finally, the court determined that "Statoil lacks standing to bring a claim under United States antitrust laws because its alleged injuries are not of the type that the antitrust statute was intended to redress." Statoil timely appealed the judgment.

IV

The issue presented to us is primarily one of statutory interpretation. Specifically, this appeal requires us to interpret the relevant provisions of the FTAIA to determine whether the defendants' conduct and Statoil's injury in the North Sea presents a justiciable claim in the federal courts of the United States.

It is not helpful that the federal courts have generally disagreed as to the extraterritorial reach of the antitrust laws and have employed assorted tests to determine the scope of the Sherman Act. The history of this body of case law is confusing and unsettled. However, as far as this appeal is concerned, our work is simplified by Congress' passage in 1982 of the FTAIA, which specifically exempts certain foreign conduct from the antitrust laws. This circuit has never interpreted the relevant portions of the FTAIA as they apply to global conspiracies and resulting foreign injury. Today, we take on this task, and make no claim that it is an easy one.

V

A

* * * [The court applied a *de novo* standard of review.] . . . We first outline Statoil's argument that United States antitrust jurisdiction encompasses the conduct and injury in its complaint.

B

Statoil argues that the FTAIA does not preclude the district court's jurisdiction over its antitrust claims. Specifically, Statoil argues that the FTAIA was enacted exclusively to ensure that the conduct providing the basis of the plaintiff's claim have the requisite domestic effects, and was not intended to preclude recovery to foreign plaintiffs based on the situs of the injury. Moreover, Statoil contends that Section 2 of the FTAIA was inserted only to ensure that the effect on United States commerce that provides jurisdiction is itself a violation of the antitrust laws; that is, the statute simply requires that there be some anticompetitive, *harmful* effect in this country--not just a positive or neutral domestic effect.

Addressing specifically the FTAIA's requirement that the domestic effect "gives rise" to its antitrust claim, Statoil primarily argues that, because the defendants operating in the Gulf of Mexico were able to maintain their monopolistic pricing only because of their overall market allocation scheme (which included agreements regarding operations in the North Sea), Statoil's injury in the North Sea was a "necessary prerequisite to" and was "the quid pro quo for" the injury suffered in the United States domestic market. Statoil alleges that the market for heavy-lift services in the world is a single, unified, global market; therefore, because the United States is a part of this worldwide market, the effect of the conspiracy, whether in the United States or in the

North Sea, "gives rise" to any claim that is based upon this conspiracy.

C

We must disagree with Statoil's arguments based on our reading of the antitrust statutes. Although we are controlled by the plain language of the statutes, we also find that the legislative history of the FTAIA and applicable case law supports our determination that the district court lacked jurisdiction over Statoil's claims. . . .

1

* * *

We begin by first noting that the Sherman Act itself applies only to conduct in "trade or commerce *with* foreign nations." 15 U.S.C. §§ 1,2 (emphasis added). The commerce that gives rise to the action here--the contracting for heavy lift barge services in the North Sea--was not United States commerce *with* foreign nations, but commerce *between* or *among* foreign nations--that is, between or among Statoil (a Norwegian corporation), Saipem (England), and HeereMac (The Netherlands). Therefore, we doubt that foreign commercial transactions between foreign entities in foreign waters is conduct cognizable by federal courts under the Sherman Act.[1]

As we have noted, the FTAIA states that the antitrust laws will not apply to non-import foreign conduct unless (1) such conduct has a direct, substantial, and reasonably foreseeable effect on United States domestic commerce, and (2) such effect gives rise to the antitrust claim.[2] The conduct

---

[1] This interpretation is further strengthened by the limits placed on Congressional power in the Constitution. Article I, § 8 of the Constitution gives Congress the authority only to regulate interstate commerce and "commerce *with* foreign nations" (emphasis added). Thus, even if Congress indeed intended to regulate purely foreign commerce in the Sherman Act, it was not empowered to do so under the Commerce Clause.

[2] The dissent, like Statoil, argues that Section 2 should be read to require only that the domestic effect give rise to *any* antitrust claim, not necessarily the plaintiff's claim. This interpretation contradicts the explicit intent of Congress to require that the effect must give rise to the particular injury claimed by the

of these defendants is foreign conduct that falls within the general parameters of the FTAIA and, thus, Statoil must show that the two specific requirements of the statute are met to establish subject matter jurisdiction over its claims.

We accept the contention that Statoil has sufficiently alleged that the defendants' conduct--that is, the agreement among heavy-lift service providers to divide territory, rig bids, and fix prices--had a direct, substantial, and reasonably foreseeable effect on the United States market. Statoil alleges that the conspiracy not only forced purchasers of heavy-lift services in the Gulf of Mexico to pay inflated prices, but also that the agreement compelled Americans to pay supra-competitive prices for oil [at least $165 million in U.S. commerce from 1993 to 1997]. These allegations are sufficient to satisfy the first requirement of the FTAIA.

However, Statoil fails to show that this effect on United States commerce in any way "gives rise" to its antitrust claim. Based on the language of Section 2 of the FTAIA, the effect on United States commerce--in this case, the higher prices paid by United States companies for heavy-lift services in the Gulf of Mexico--must give rise to the claim that Statoil asserts against the defendants. That is, Statoil's injury must stem from the effect of higher prices for heavy-lift services in the Gulf. We find no evidence that this requirement is met here. The higher prices American companies allegedly paid for services provided by the McDermott defendants in the Gulf of Mexico does not give rise to Statoil's claim that it paid inflated prices for HeereMac and Saipem's services in the North Sea. This is not to say that any antitrust injury suffered by customers or competitors of McDermott that arose from the anticompetitive

---

plaintiff in the suit . . . The dissent asserts that reading Section 2 as requiring that the domestic effect give rise to the plaintiff's claim renders the FTAIA's proviso redundant. Although giving the statute a clear understanding is difficult, we disagree with the dissent's reading. We read Section 1(B) to provide that the export commerce covered under the exception must be conducted by a person who is engaged in that export business in the United States. Section 2 provides that the defendant's antitrust effect on this export commerce described in Section 1(B) must give rise to the plaintiff's cause of action. The proviso, in turn, states that the recovery for injuries resulting from the conduct described in Section 1(B), which gives rise to the plaintiff's antitrust claim in Section 2, is limited to injuries occurring in the United States. Therefore, we fail to see the redundancy to which the dissent refers. . . .

effect in the Gulf of Mexico cannot be addressed. This means only that, while we recognize that there may be a connection and an interrelatedness between the high prices paid for services in the Gulf of Mexico and the high prices paid in the North Sea, the FTAIA requires more than a "close relationship" between the domestic injury and the plaintiff's claim; it demands that the domestic effect "gives rise" to the claim.

Statoil asks that we interpret the requirement of Section 2 that the domestic "*effect* " give rise to a claim under the antitrust laws as merely requiring that the defendants' domestic "*conduct* " (here, for example, agreements relating to the Gulf of Mexico) give rise to a claim. This interpretation is not true to the plain language of the FTAIA. Moreover, under such an expansive interpretation, any entities, anywhere, that were injured by any conduct that also had sufficient effect on United States commerce could flock to United States federal court for redress, even if those plaintiffs had no commercial relationship with any United States market and their injuries were unrelated to the injuries suffered in the United States. Such an expansive reading of the extraterritorial application of the antitrust laws was never intended nor contemplated by Congress . . . .

In sum, we find that the plain language of the FTAIA precludes subject matter jurisdiction over claims by foreign plaintiffs against defendants where the situs of the injury is overseas and that injury arises from effects in a non-domestic market. Although the plain language of the relevant statutes is clear and controlling, we nonetheless turn now to address briefly the legislative history of the FTAIA to illustrate how that history reinforces our interpretation of the extraterritorial reach of the antitrust laws.

2

[In this section of the opinion, the majority finds support for its conclusion that a foreign plaintiff injured in a foreign marketplace must show that a substantial domestic effect on United States commerce "gives rise" to its antitrust claim in the legislative history of the FTAIA.].

3

. . . To begin, we note that the only three federal courts that have addressed the narrow question before us interpreted Section 2 exactly as we have. *See Kruman v. Christie's Int'l PLC, et al.,* 129 F.Supp.2d 620

(S.D.N.Y.2001) (holding that the FTAIA permits jurisdiction "only where the conduct complained of had 'direct, substantial and reasonably foreseeable' effects in the United States and the effects giving rise to jurisdiction are the basis for the alleged injury."); *In re Microsoft Corp.*, 2001 U.S. Dist. LEXIS 305, at *37 (holding that, under the FTAIA, "foreign consumers who have not participated in any way in the U.S. market have no right to institute a Sherman Act claim."); *Sumitomo,* 117 F. Supp.2d 875, 876 (holding that "it is plain from the language of this act and bolstered by the legislative history that a private plaintiff cannot sue under the antitrust laws of the United States for injuries incurred as a result of international transactions that have an anticompetitive effect on a United States market if the domestic anticompetitive effect is not the same one that gives rise to the plaintiff's injury.").

We further note that we have found no case in which jurisdiction was found in a case like this--where a foreign plaintiff is injured in a foreign market with no injuries arising from the anticompetitive effect on a United States market. In those cases where the domestic effect on commerce did not give rise to the plaintiff's claim, courts have found subject matter jurisdiction lacking. *See, e.g., S. Megga Telecomm. Ltd. v. Lucent Technologies, Inc.*, 1997 WL 86413 (D.Del. Feb.14, 1997) (anticompetitive domestic effect of higher prices for United States consumers did not "give rise" to plaintiff's claim for lost sales to defendant); *The "In" Porters, S.A. v. Hanes Printables, Inc.,* 663 F.Supp. 494 (M.D.N.C.1987) (anticompetitive domestic effect (lost exports of United States exporters) did not "give rise" to plaintiff's claim for lost sales in France due to marketing sales agreement with defendant); *de Atucha v. Commodity Exch., Inc.*, 608 F.Supp. 510 (S.D.N.Y.1985) (conspiracy's effect on silver prices on United States exchange did not "give rise" to plaintiff's injury on London exchange).

On the other hand, in every case where jurisdiction has been found, the substantial effect on United States commerce has "give[n] rise" to the plaintiff's injury and claim under the antitrust laws. *See, e.g., Carpet Group Int'l v. Oriental Rug Importers Ass'n,* 227 F.3d 62 (3rd Cir.2000) (anticompetitive effect on domestic rug market "gives rise" to plaintiff's injury); *Caribbean,* 148 F.3d 1080 (monopolization of United States market for advertising in the Caribbean "gives rise" to plaintiff's claim of being blocked from that market); *Nippon Paper,* 109 F.3d 1 (collusion amongst fax paper producers resulted in higher prices for fax paper in the United States, which "gives rise" to the United States' claim); *Hartford Fire,* 509 U.S. 764

(conspiracy's effect on the United States insurance market "gives rise" to the plaintiffs' injury, the inability to obtain certain types of coverage in that market).

Finally, we note that none of the cases cited by Statoil in support of its interpretation of the FTAIA cast doubt upon our plain language interpretation of Section 2. Statoil cites *Pfizer v. India,* 434 U.S. 308 (1978), for the proposition that antitrust jurisdiction exists over foreign conduct like the commerce between Statoil and defendants in this case. *Pfizer,* however, was decided four years before enactment of the FTAIA, and the court's holding was limited to the question of whether a foreign government qualified as a "person" under the Sherman Act. *Id.* at 320. Statoil further maintains that *Caribbean Broadcasting,* 148 F.3d 1080, requires that jurisdiction be found over its claims. Initially, that case looks similar to today's case in that both the plaintiff and the defendant were foreign, and the defendant's international conspiracy had anticompetitive effects both inside and outside the United States. The critical difference, however, is that the effect on United States commerce in that case (that is, limiting to one radio station potential advertisers in the United States who wished to advertise in the Eastern Caribbean radio market) gave rise to the injury suffered by the plaintiff, a competing radio station-- that is, exclusion of the plaintiff from the market for United States advertising dollars. *Id.* at 1082, 1086. As previously explained, that is simply not true with Statoil's claims. Similarly, Statoil's reliance on *Nippon Paper,* 109 F.3d 1, is misplaced because the global conspiracy in that case had the domestic effect of raising fax paper prices in the United States, which gave rise to the government's claim under the antitrust laws. *Id.* at 2.

Simply put, Statoil has cited no case law to support an interpretation of Section 2 of the FTAIA different from the one we now adopt. This absence of such precedent, when considered with the plain language of the statute and evidence of congressional intent in enacting the FTAIA, reinforces our conclusion in this case.

VI

In sum, we find that the district court did not err when it dismissed Statoil's antitrust claims for lack of subject matter jurisdiction. Any reading of the FTAIA authorizing jurisdiction over Statoil's claims would open United States courts to global claims on a scale never intended by Congress. Without subject matter jurisdiction, United States federal courts are without power to entertain Statoil's claims. The judgment of the district court is therefore AFFIRMED.

HIGGINBOTHAM, dissenting. I agree that this is not an easy case, but I have no hesitation in concluding that the Foreign Trade and Antitrust Improvements Act does not here divest the federal courts of jurisdiction and that the plaintiff has standing. With deference to my colleagues, I am persuaded by the plain text of section 6a, as well as its statutory context, legislative history, and purpose.

The claim is that defendants allocated the market for hundreds of millions of dollars of commerce--an allocation that placed United States markets at the mercy of monopoly charges in an industry vital to national security. The charged conspiracy was no foreign cabal whose secondary effects only lapped at United States shores. The impact of the conspiracy was direct and substantial. Indeed, the participation of American business in the market allocation scheme was critical to its success. The plaintiff here is a foreign company, true enough, but it was injured by the same acts of defendants that injured American plaintiffs whose right to seek recovery of their losses the district court recognized in this litigation.

With the Foreign Trade and Antitrust Improvements Act, Congress set out to insulate United States business from its antitrust laws for certain business conducted outside the country. Its central purpose was to assist American business in competing abroad. This pass from antitrust restrictions did not extend to all conduct outside the United States. It stopped short of insulating conduct having direct and substantial effects upon American commerce and causing antitrust injury to that commerce sufficient to support a claim for treble damages.

I am not persuaded that when illegal conduct produces these domestic effects, that Congress intended to close the door to a foreign company injured by the same illegal conduct. That was not the law before this effort to assist American business abroad, and Congress did not intend to change it or do so unwittingly. I would reverse and remand for further proceedings.

I

A

Interpretation of a statute must begin with the text of the statute itself. [See Casebook, page 1196, note 6.] . . . Section 6a(1) requires an effect on (A) domestic or import commerce of the United States or (B) the export commerce of a person in the United States. Section 6a(2) requires that this effect "give[ ] rise to a claim under the provisions of sections 1 to 7 of this title, the Sherman Act, other than this section." The majority reads section 6a(2) to require that the effect "give[ ] rise to" *the plaintiff's* claim. It does not say that. It does say that the effect must "give[ ] rise to *a* claim." In other words, the effect on United States commerce must be sufficient to support a claim, an injury of some person in a way cognizable under the Sherman Act.

The literal text of the statute supports this conclusion. It reads, "gives rise to a claim." The word "a" has a simple and universally understood meaning. It is the indefinite article. There are many terms of art about which one can debate whether Congress uses the term as courts do, but this word is not one of them. If the drafters of the FTAIA had wished to say "the claim" instead of "a claim," they certainly would have.

The reference to "a" claim makes clear that the "effect" described by section 6a(1) must violate the Sherman Act--that is, harm competition. Section 6a(1) requires that the conspiracy have an effect on United States commerce; section 6a(2) requires that this effect either monopolize commerce or restrain trade in the United States, thereby giving rise to a Sherman Act claim. Section 6a(2) removes jurisdiction over conspiracies whose effects on United States commerce are beneficial or benign, even if they restrain competition in other parts of the world. That an injury that "gives rise to" an antitrust claim must be an injury caused by harm to competition is no light notion. It is a well established and fundamental tenet of antitrust law. Termed "antitrust injury," it is frequently encountered in enforcement action under the Clayton Act, by which Congress enlisted private enforcement in supplementation of governmental enforcement of the Sherman Act.

Thus, the literal text does not require that the effect on United States commerce give rise to the plaintiff's claim. At worst, the text is sufficiently ambiguous to allow for both the construction the majority offers and the construction I believe is correct. At the least, the majority cannot find support in a plain text argument.

Accepting that the text of the FTAIA compels neither the majority's reading or mine, we must enlist other aids in determining the meaning of the statute. In doing so, I conclude that the textual conclusion that "a" means "a" is supported by the statutory context of the FTAIA, which describes the function of the FTAIA and its animating purpose, and by the purposes of the antitrust laws in general; by the legislative history of the FTAIA; and by the sparse case law that interprets the FTAIA.

B

The FTAIA was enacted as Title IV of Public Law 97-290, entitled "Export Trading Company Act of 1982." Title I contains the congressional findings. Every single congressional finding relates to the importance of export business and the need to encourage export activity by American business. The statute then states: "It is the purpose of this Act to increase United States exports of products and services by encouraging more efficient provision of export trade services to United States producers and suppliers, in particular by ... modifying the application of the antitrust laws to certain export trade."[3] It could not be clearer that the FTAIA serves to exempt exporting from antitrust scrutiny, not to limit the liability of participants in transnational conspiracies that affect United States commerce.

The text of the FTAIA implements this purpose perfectly. The Sherman Act, prior to the enactment of the FTAIA, applied to conduct that affected domestic, import, and export commerce. Recall that section 6a(1) limiting the reach of the Sherman Act applies to conduct that affects (1) domestic commerce; (2) import commerce; or (3) export commerce, but only to the extent that American exporters are affected. One class of conduct is excluded: conduct that affects only foreign purchasers of American exports.

---

[3] FN10. § 102(b), 96 Stat. at 1234. The Third Circuit has recently cited this concluding language in that "Congress enacted the FTAIA for the purpose of facilitating the export of domestic goods by exempting export transactions that did not injure the United States economy from the Sherman Act and thereby relieving exporters from a competitive disadvantage in foreign trade." *Carpet Group Int'l v. Oriental Rug Importers Ass'n, Inc.*, 227 F.3d 62, 71 (3d Cir.2000).

This is the function of the FTAIA: to protect American exporters who monopolize or conspire to restrain export trade that does not harm United States commerce.

The purpose of the FTAIA offers no support for the majority's reading of the statute. It is undisputed that if proved, the conspiracy in this case would have direct, substantial, and reasonably foreseeable effects upon United States commerce. No American exporters are implicated by this suit. American exporting business can only be harmed by the alleged conspiracy in this case.

Indeed, interpreting the FTAIA as the majority wishes will impair the competitiveness of American exporters. Under the majority's view, an American cartel that fixes prices worldwide will be subject to Clayton Act suits by plaintiffs from around the world, but a foreign cartel that fixes prices worldwide will be subject to suit under the Clayton Act only from plaintiffs injured in American commerce. This interpretation of the FTAIA transforms a safe harbor for American exporters into a boon for foreign cartels that restrain commerce in the United States.

With respect to my colleagues, I fear that their reading of the FTAIA will hinder its purposes and reduce the effectiveness of the antitrust laws. Nothing in the text of the FTAIA, or the Export Trading Company Act of 1982 as a whole, or its legislative history, casts doubt on the importance of deterring restraints of trade that affect United States commerce. The Supreme Court has repeatedly recognized that the accent of the Sherman and the Clayton Acts is deterrence, requiring violators to pay full, treble damages, even if some plaintiffs gain a windfall or are foreigners. For example, in *Illinois Brick Co. v. Illinois,* [431 U.S. 720] the Supreme Court noted the importance of "vigorous private enforcement of the antitrust laws" and "deterring violators" and recognized that "from the deterrence standpoint, it is irrelevant to whom damages are paid, so long as some one redresses the violation." [*Id.* at 745-46.]

The Supreme Court in *Pfizer, Inc. v. Government of India* [434 U.S. 308] addressed a situation somewhat analogous to this case. The government of India sued several American pharmaceutical manufacturers under the Clayton Act for damages caused by a price-fixing conspiracy. Like Statoil, the government of India alleged a worldwide conspiracy that raised prices in the United States and abroad. Unlike in this case, in *Pfizer* the sales were made in the United States. In holding that foreign governments could recover under the

Clayton Act, Justice Stewart observed: "Treble-damage suits by foreigners who have been victimized by antitrust violations clearly may contribute to the protection of American consumers.... [A]n exclusion of all foreign plaintiffs would lessen the deterrent effect of treble damages." [*Id.* at 314-15.]

The logic underlying this conclusion is straightforward. Conspirators facing antitrust liability only to plaintiffs injured by their conspiracy's effects on the United States may not be deterred from restraining trade in the United States. A worldwide price-fixing scheme could sustain monopoly prices in the United States even in the face of such liability if it could cross-subsidize its American operations with profits from abroad. Unless persons injured by the conspiracy's effects on foreign commerce could also bring antitrust suits against the conspiracy, the conspiracy could remain profitable and undeterred.

It is no rejoinder that conspirators would simply choose to exclude the United States from any price-fixing conspiracy as long as American plaintiffs could sue. In at least some cases, including the United States in a price-fixing conspiracy is necessary to generate monopoly profits. Otherwise, arbitrage would rapidly equalize unequal prices around the globe as speculators resold goods purchased in the United States to buyers in high-price regions. Thus, a cartel may find it impossible to fix prices anywhere without a worldwide conspiracy. The Sherman Act can only deter these violations if it protects all parties injured by such a conspiracy. . . .

C

The legislative history also supports this reading of the statute and undermines the majority's interpretation of section 6a(2). . . . [Judge Higginbotham here argues that the Committee distinguishes between where the plaintiffs suffered economic injury and where, or whether, anticompetitive effects in the United States result from the conduct.]

D

I recognize that there is little precedent to guide our analysis of this question. Of the case law that does exist, there are no appellate court cases supporting the majority's holding. To the contrary, the majority must reconcile or distinguish the only other circuit court decisions interpreting the FTAIA, because all of them find jurisdiction present.

The majority opinion struggles, and I believe fails, to reconcile *Caribbean Broadcasting System, Ltd. v. Cable & Wireless PLC,* [148 F.3d 1080 (D.C.Cir.1998)], which involved a foreign plaintiff alleging monopolization in radio advertising in the Caribbean by a competing radio station. The defendant was also a foreign entity. Consistent with the reasoning of this dissent, the D.C. Circuit held that the FTAIA did not preclude jurisdiction, because the plaintiff showed that the foreign defendants' conduct had the effect of harming United States purchasers of advertising. It stated: "the alleged injury is to advertisers in the United States." Thus, based on the injury to advertisers in the United States, the court found jurisdiction over a suit by a radio broadcaster in the Caribbean. The D.C. Circuit did not require that the injury to American advertisers "give[ ] rise to" the plaintiff's cause of action; its determination that the injury gave rise to "a" claim was sufficient.

E

Finally, the majority's attempt to enlist the aid of the Commerce Clause and the canon of construction that creates a presumption against extraterritoriality is mistaken. . . . The majority is correct to note that the courts' historical willingness to apply the Sherman Act extraterritorially is not dispositive of this appeal, since the FTAIA, and not the courts' earlier interpretations of the Sherman Act, is controlling here. But precisely because the FTAIA applies here, the majority's reliance on the canon against extraterritorial application of statutes is misplaced. This canon operates when Congress has not clearly spoken on the issue of extraterritoriality. The FTAIA, however, explicitly addresses nothing other than extraterritoriality. We must be careful not to use such a canon when Congress is speaking directly to the relevant issue. Make no mistake: such canons reflect substantive presumptions about the content of laws. If courts apply substantive canons of construction against statutes that do speak to an issue, then it is the courts, not Congress, who are making the policy choices that form the content of legislation.

II

[In this section of the dissent, Judge Higginbotham explains that he would find that the plaintiff Statoil has standing.]

III

The antitrust laws have always given federal courts jurisdiction over conspiracies that adversely affect competition in the United States. The FTAIA limits that jurisdiction; but it does so by exempting American export conspiracies, not foreign conspiracies that injure American competition.

The majority opinion expresses concern that foreign litigants will flock to the United States for redress of their injuries in distant lands. The majority opinion, and the district court opinions it cites, seem to fear that the interpretation of the FTAIA that Statoil advocates makes the Sherman Act an antitrust regulation of foreign economies throughout the entire world, a paternalistic lawmaking enterprise that ignores the adequacy of foreign tribunals. But Congress has enacted no such thing. Congress enacted the FTAIA to serve the United States' narrow interest in vigorous domestic competition.

The text of the FTAIA may be inelegant, but it serves the selfish national interests of the United States: the FTAIA excludes from antitrust liability all conduct that has caused no antitrust injury to the United States economy; but it enlists all injured parties--foreign or domestic-- to assist the Department of Justice in deterring conduct that does harm the forces of competition in the United States. When a conspiracy causes a direct and substantial injury to competition in the United States, the Clayton Act recruits private parties to supplement the efforts of the Department of Justice in ending the conspiracy. The FTAIA ensures that parties injured by foreign aspects of the same conspiracy that harms American commerce are part of the phalanx of enforcers brought to bear by the Clayton Act. Thus, treble damages suits by parties who suffer antitrust injury from a conspiracy that has a direct and substantial harmful impact on United States commerce serve a single function: the protection of United States commerce. The FTAIA threatens no parade of horribles--it does nothing more than zealously protect competition in the United States while sparing from the docket of American courts suits involving conspiracies that affect only foreign economies.

In sum, I believe the FTAIA does not divest the federal courts of jurisdiction over suits by plaintiffs who suffer antitrust injuries from a conspiracy that also harms competition in United States commerce. Whether the harm felt in the United States is the source of the injury to the plaintiff is irrelevant; it is the effects on the United States that creates jurisdiction. Under the facts of this case, I would conclude that the district court had jurisdiction over the suit and that Statoil had standing to sue the defendants under the

Clayton Act. I respectfully dissent.

CARPET GROUP INTERNATIONAL
v.
ORIENTAL RUG IMPORTERS ASSOCIATION, INC.
United States Court of Appeals, Third Circuit, 2000.
227 F.3d 62.

Before: RENDELL and ROSENN, Circuit Judges, and O'NEILL, Senior District Court Judge.

ROSENN, J. This appeal arises out of an action under the Sherman Act alleging a conspiracy to restrain trade and monopolize the thriving United States market for oriental rugs. It requires us to determine, among other things, whether the Foreign Trade Antitrust Improvements Act ("FTAIA" or "the Act"), 15 U.S.C. § 6, divested the District Court of subject matter jurisdiction over this action. The plaintiffs are Carpet Group International ("CGI"), a Virginia corporation, and Emmert Elsea, a citizen of Virginia who is CGI's founder and sole shareholder. Elsea founded CGI with the objective of making imported oriental rugs available to retailers directly from manufacturers, bypassing importers at the wholesale level and thereby reducing rug prices to United States consumers. The defendants charged with antitrust violations are an association of importer/wholesalers of oriental rugs called the Oriental Rug Importers Association, Inc. ("ORIA"), several companies who are members of ORIA, and three individuals who are past or present officers and directors of ORIA.

In the District Court and on appeal, the defendants object to the Court's subject matter jurisdiction primarily on the ground that the plaintiffs' claims were barred by the FTAIA. They assert that the plaintiffs failed to establish jurisdiction under the Act because they have not proven that the defendants' actions did not involve or otherwise substantially affect United States commerce. The United States District Court for the District of New Jersey, acting on the report and recommendation of a Magistrate Judge, granted the motion of the defendants for dismissal of the action, and the plaintiffs timely appealed. We reverse.

I.

Firms involved in the oriental rug trade in the United States have traditionally utilized a narrow chain of distribution. In this carefully constricted chain, foreign rug manufacturers sell their goods to wholesalers in the United States, who import the rugs and then sell them to U.S. retailers. The retailers in turn resell the rugs to consumers. In the early 1990s, plaintiff Emmert Elsea conceived a plan by which retailers and consumers in this country could purchase oriental rugs more cheaply. He theorized that if U.S. retailers were to purchase rugs directly from foreign manufacturers, bypassing the wholesaler link in the chain of distribution, they could reduce the costs to themselves and, consequently, to consumers. Elsea founded CGI in order to facilitate his vision of a new chain of rug distribution.

In 1993 and 1994, CGI sponsored two trade shows in the United States at which foreign rug manufacturers were invited to display rugs and sell directly to American retailers. CGI expected to earn fees paid by the manufacturers for space at the trade show. In addition, Elsea, and later CGI, took U.S. retailers on buying trips to rug-producing countries in exchange for fees. On these trips, the plaintiffs arranged for the retailers to purchase rugs directly from foreign rug manufacturers. CGI's trade shows and buying trips were the mechanisms through which the plaintiffs attempted to effectuate their plan to assist American retailers in purchasing oriental rugs directly from the foreign manufacturer.

The plaintiffs claim that the defendants conspired to sabotage their efforts to facilitate direct sales between foreign manufacturers and United States retailers and, more specifically, conspired to wreck plaintiffs' trade shows. Plaintiffs' amended complaint alleges that the defendants used the following tactics:

> (a) threatening not to purchase rugs from any manufacturer who participated in the trade shows;
> (b) threatening not to purchase rugs from any manufacturer who sells rugs to any retailer on a buying trip;
> (c) threatening and retaliating, including expulsion from the association, against any ORIA member that participated in the plaintiffs' trade shows;
> (d) inducing the Carpet Export Promotion Council of India, the Export Promotion Board of Pakistan, and the Pakistan Carpet Manufacturers and Exporters Association not to subsidize the participation of manufacturers from those countries in the plaintiffs' trade shows;

(e) threatening not to sell rugs to retailers who participate in the buying trips sponsored by plaintiffs.

The defendants moved to dismiss the action for lack of subject matter jurisdiction. The defendants argued that the Foreign Trade Antitrust Improvements Act ("FTAIA"), 15 U.S.C. § 6a, deprived the District Court of subject matter jurisdiction under the antitrust laws by excluding the plaintiffs' claims from the coverage of those laws. . . . The District Court referred the motion to a Magistrate Judge. In accordance with circuit precedent, the plaintiffs introduced evidence to support their contention that the FTAIA did not apply to their claims and therefore did not deprive the District Court of jurisdiction.

A. The Jurisdictional Evidence.

The plaintiffs offered documentary evidence before the Magistrate Judge dealing with activity by ORIA and its members to convince foreign governments, foreign rug trade associations, and one domestic rug retailers' association not to provide financial assistance to the CGI trade shows. For example, ORIA wrote to the secretary of the Carpet Export Promotion Council of India ("CEPC") that in deciding whether or not to co-sponsor CGI's November 1993 Chicago trade show, the CEPC should consider that doing so would "possibly jeopardize a very friendly and prosperous relationship" between Indian rug manufacturers and American importers. In addition, defendant Hodges (the president of defendant Pande Cameron & Co. of New York, an importer/wholesaler) wrote to the chairman of the CEPC, expressing his opinion that the CGI 1993 show was "destined for failure," asking for the chairman's "comments and observations in lending CEPC support to this show," and requesting "the names of those exporters from India who plan on exhibiting." With respect to this last request, Hodges wrote: "These would be exporters, I can assure you we would avoid in any future business discussions." There is no evidence in this record that CEPC furnished Hodges with these names.

CGI planned another trade show in Washington, DC in August 1994. In March of that year, defendant Newman (the president of defendant Noonoo Rug Co.) wrote to the vice-chairman of the Export Promotion Bureau of Pakistan ("EPB") and the Pakistan Carpet Manufacturers and Exporters Association ("PCMEA") regarding this trade show, urging the PCMEA and the EPB "not to encourage nor support the 'renegade' activities and selfish motives of a few Pakistani trader/exporters and their American retail counterparts." Newman also noted that "[t]o do so would be to continue on the road leading to ill will and chaos." The PCMEA subsequently made efforts toward conciliation with ORIA. Its vice chairman wrote to ORIA informing it of PCMEA's decision not to officially participate in the Washington Fair being held in August that year, and of its request that the EPB not "give any facility to" the participants. He reiterated that "no manner of encouragement or patronage" would be provided by the Association to any firm desiring to participate in the fair. (JA.96).

On March 23, 1994, Hodges, acting in his capacity as ORIA president, wrote to the president of the Oriental Rug *Retailers* Association ("ORRA"), a United States trade association, regarding the August 1994 CGI trade show. He stated:

> Rumor has it that the ORRA has been approached by CGI to cosponsor this function. I think you are well aware of our sentiments regarding the purpose of this trade fair in undermining existing channels of distribution which have proven to be successful to all of us over the years. We would naturally hope that the ORRA would not entertain any thoughts whatsoever in being involved and therefore lending credence to [CGI].

Hodges further noted his belief that politicians directly involved with a child labor bill sponsored by Senator Harkin, a subject high on ORIA's lobbying agenda, would be invited to attend the CGI trade show. Hodges expressed fear that "all of our efforts in dealing with the Harkin Bill and responsibly trying to address child labor could be undone by any 'loose cannons' developing their own game plan." He concluded with the request that "through your leadership, ... the ORRA take a long and very close look at the negative ramifications in lending your name to this very damaging endeavor." Apparently after interim contact with ORRA, Hodges again wrote ORRA's president on March 28, 1995, expressing his sentiments "that Emmert Elsea's attitudes toward wholesalers [are] ... both incorrect and unhealthy," and of his concern with Elsea's approach toward eradicating child labor.

Significantly, the minutes of an April 1994 ORIA membership meeting show that "Dan and Gene," presumably a reference to Dan Hodges and Eugene Newman, had contacted the ORRA and obtained its promise not to endorse the August trade show as a group. The minutes also reflect that

"Gene" "urged the [ORIA] members who import from Pakistan, India and other countries to write the proper Export Promotion authorities in those countries and advise them not to participate in this show." The minutes of an August 1994 ORIA meeting reflect that this statement was amended to read "Gene Newman suggested that the individual members and not the organization" engage in this letter writing campaign.

In addition, the plaintiffs also offered one piece of documentary evidence intended to show that the defendants were boycotting domestic retailers and foreign manufacturers who supported the trade shows. These were handwritten notes dated May 25, 1994, taken by an unidentified rug retailer in Virginia, of a telephone conversation between the retailer and a representative of defendant Kelaty Rugs International. The notes describe the importer's representative as "irate," and record the retailers' fear that because of his cooperation with Elsea, "we will not be able to get rugs from anyone." Most significantly, the unidentified retailer stated "We are being dealt with from both ends. i.e., cannot get supplied in U.S.[,] also those who supply us from overseas will be boycotted by importers." The Magistrate Judge did not credit this evidence because it was unclear who wrote these notes. When the plaintiffs later objected to the Magistrate Judge's R & R before the District Court, they offered the declaration of someone named William Hirsch, in which Hirsch purported to authenticate these notes as his own. Although the defendants contend that this declaration was not submitted before the magistrate, plaintiffs claim it was submitted and the magistrate simply disregarded it.

Finally, CGI offered a declaration of Emmert Elsea dated July 17, 1997. Elsea made the following pertinent representations:

> 4. Joseph Zarnigin of Zarnigin Rugs, an ORIA member located in New York, informed me and Anne Williams that he would participate in the 1993 trade show except that doing so would jeopardize his membership in and benefits from ORIA.
> 5. DCC, Inc., an ORIA member located in New York, said he would purchase space in the 1993 trade show, but later refused to do so because ORIA strongly opposed the trade show.
> 6. Rug News[, a trade magazine intended for retail readership,] refused to accept advertising for the 1993 trade show.
> 7. Decorative Rug[, a similar magazine,] withdrew its acceptance of CGI's advertising on the grounds that it would

lose its ORIA customers if it allowed CGI to advertise. The publisher of Decorative Rug also stated that he was being pressured by ORIA to run unfavorable editorials concerning CGI.

8. Anadol Rugs, an ORIA member located in New York, executed a contract and paid a deposit for space in the 1994 trade show. The contract was not forged. Anadol cancelled [sic] its contract after its anticipated participation was revealed to ORIA, and, according to the president of Anadol, ORIA pressured it.

The Magistrate Judge recommended that the defendants' motion to dismiss for lack of subject matter jurisdiction be granted. He concluded that FTAIA governed the Court's subject matter jurisdiction and that the plaintiffs failed to establish jurisdiction under the Act because they failed to prove that the defendants' conduct had a direct and substantial effect on United States domestic commerce.

B. Additional Jurisdictional Evidence Offered To the District Court.

The plaintiffs subsequently filed objections to the Magistrate Judge's report and recommendation with the District Court. In so doing, both they and the defendants submitted additional evidence to that Court for its consideration. For example the plaintiffs offered additional evidence intended to show that ORIA and the individual rug importers had pressured independent trade publications to reject advertising for the trade show. They offered Elsea's contemporaneously written notes of a September 1993 telephone conversation with Ron O'Callaghan of Decorative Rugs magazine, an independent trade publication, in which he recorded that O'Callaghan "rejected his acceptance of" CGI's advertisements for the 1993 trade show. Elsea reported that O'Callaghan stated that if he printed the ads, ORIA and other importers would quit advertising, and that ORIA opposed the show and had pressured Decorative Rug magazine to run editorials against it. In response, the defendants offered a certification from O'Callaghan in which he denied that he made such statements, and specifically stated that none of the importers ever contacted him and threatened to quit advertising in his magazine if it accepted advertisements from Elsea for his Chicago trade show.

The plaintiffs also offered a letter from an advertising consultant reporting that when the consultant tried to place an advertisement in Rug News, another independent trade publication, she was told by Rug News official Les Stroh that the advertisement would not be accepted because the trade show would "damage the oriental rug importers." In response, the defendants offered excerpts from a deposition of Stroh, in which he testified that he never received any recommendation from ORIA not to accept ads from manufacturers. Stroh also denied ever having any conversations with anyone from ORIA pertaining to the acceptance or rejection of advertisements from manufacturers.

The plaintiffs also offered the minutes of a December 1993 ORIA executive board meeting, at which the board discussed CGI's November 1993 Chicago trade show. The minutes report a discussion concerning a memorandum that would be sent to all members about the operations of CGI, "which held a trade fair in Chicago last November where they had cut out the role of the importer in the chain of distribution." Lee Harounian, an ORIA board member, suggested that ORIA members "boycott" the manufacturers participating in the show. The executive board ultimately decided that this memorandum should not go to all members but to the board members only.

In addition, Elsea submitted a supplemental declaration in which he recounted that the owner of Istanbul Grand Bazaar ("IGB"), a company that both manufactures rugs in Turkey and imports them into the U.S. (and therefore is a member of ORIA), expressed interest in participating in CGI's 1994 trade show, but said he would not be the only ORIA member to do so. Elsea asserted that he informed IGB's owner that another Turkish importer/manufacturer and ORIA member, Anadol Rugs, also was participating. Subsequently, Elsea claimed, he received a fax from Anadol Rugs informing him that Anadol "had received a fax from ORIA concerning [its] participation in the trade fair." As a consequence, Anadol was "canceling" its participation in the trade fair. The fax, also offered as evidence, stated that Anadol "ha[s] no intentions whatsoever to attend this exhibit[ion]." The fax further admonished CGI to "please rectify this matter immediately, writing to [ORIA] that it was a mistake on your part." Neither Anadol nor IGB participated in the trade show.

The plaintiffs also offered evidence of ORIA's historical efforts to prevent foreign manufacturers from selling directly to U.S. retailers. In 1992, Pakistani rug manufacturers sold some rugs directly to Bloomingdale's department store, an American retailer. In September of that year, following this sale, then-ORIA president (and defendant) Isaac Etessami wrote to the Pakistani Minister of Commerce complaining of this practice, with emphasis on EPB's subsidization of Bloomingdales' promotion. The letter reminded the Pakistani minister of the "traditional, established and respected chain of distribution" in the United States, to wit, "MANUFACTURER/EXPORTER - IMPORTER/WHOLESALER - RETAILER - CONSUMER." The letter also admonished Pakistani exporters to concentrate their promotion sales efforts on American importers "and not attempt to involve themselves with retailers, who are the *importers*' customers." (Emphasis in original). The lengthy letter concluded with the exhortation: "Work with the American importer in promoting your rugs and not around him."

Finally, the plaintiffs offered a memorandum from the president of ORRA addressed to the ORRA board, written shortly after the president received the March 23, 1994 letter from then-ORIA president Hodges regarding potential ORRA sponsorship of CGI's 1994 trade fair. The memo read in part:

> Over the past year ORRA has made significant progress in mending fences with its sister organization ORIA.... Last year a letter went out under my signature that effectively distanced ORRA from [CGI].... The building process is slow. .... and it will come to a grinding halt, in my opinion, if we even entertain the notion of joining forces with [CGI].
>
> Both Dan Hodges and Gene Newman have gone on record requesting that ORRA continue to disassociate itself from Mr. Elsea's efforts.

In response, the defendants offered excerpts from the deposition of the ORRA president, in which she testified that nobody "at ORIA [told her] ... that moving away from an affiliation with another trade fair would improve relations."

C. Subsequent Proceedings.

[After a remand to the magistrate judge for consideration of the additional evidence and arguments, he again recommended dismissal; the district court adopted both reports and dismissed the complaint for lack of subject matter jurisdiction.]

II

Subject matter jurisdiction in this case rests, if at all, on 28 U.S.C. § 1337(a), which states that "[t]he District Courts shall have original jurisdiction of any civil action or proceeding arising under any Act of Congress regulating commerce or protecting trade and commerce against restraints and monopolies." On appeal to this Court, the primary question presented is whether the District Court possessed subject matter jurisdiction over the plaintiffs' antitrust claims in light of the FTAIA, which limits the applicability of the Sherman Act in certain circumstances. In addition to fervently disputing the plaintiffs' arguments, the defendants offer two additional arguments as alternative bases on which this Court might affirm the District Court's dismissal of this action. First, they argue even assuming the FTAIA does not apply, the plaintiffs have not established subject matter jurisdiction under the Sherman Act. Second, they argue that the plaintiffs do not have the "antitrust standing" needed to pursue their claims.

A

We first turn to the relevant provisions of the "inelegantly phrased" FTAIA. This statute, when parsed, states two requirements about when the Sherman Act, which falls within the jurisdictional ambit of 28 U.S.C. § 1337, applies. First, the initial sentence of Section 6a, along with its "import trade or commerce" parenthetical, provides that the antitrust law *shall* apply to conduct "involving" import trade or commerce with foreign nations (provided, of course, that jurisdiction is found to exist under the Sherman Act itself). 15 U.S.C. § 6a. Second, Section 6a(1)(A) states that the antitrust laws *shall not* apply to all other conduct involving trade or commerce with foreign nations unless such conduct has a direct, substantial, and reasonably foreseeable effect on (a) domestic trade or commerce, or (b) import trade or commerce with foreign nations. 15 U.S.C. § 6a(1)(A).

Here, the defendants attack subject matter jurisdiction "in fact," meaning they dispute the existence of certain jurisdictional facts alleged by the plaintiffs. When a defendant attacks subject matter jurisdiction "in fact," as opposed to an attack on the allegations on the face of the complaint, the Court is free to weigh the evidence and satisfy itself whether it has power to hear the case. . . .

In their complaint, the plaintiffs in this case allege a broad horizontal conspiracy among United States rug importer/wholesalers to restrain the domestic rug trade between foreign manufacturers and United States domestic retailers at plaintiffs' trade shows, and to restrain sales between foreign manufacturers and such retailers on buying trips abroad. They charge that the defendants' conduct restrained United States commerce, alleging threats not to purchase rugs from any manufacturer that participates in the plaintiffs' trade shows; threats not to purchase rugs from any manufacturer that sells rugs to any retailer on a buying trip; reducing or ceasing purchases of rugs from manufacturers that participate in plaintiffs' trade fairs or sell to retailers on buying trips; threats to retaliate, including expulsion from the association, against any ORIA member that participates in the plaintiffs' trade shows; and inducing the Carpet Export Promotion Council of India, the Export Promotion Board of Pakistan, and the Pakistan Carpet Manufacturers and Exporters Association not to subsidize the participation of manufacturers from those countries in the plaintiffs' trade shows.

Addressing the impact of the FTAIA to this case, the Magistrate Judge first determined that the plaintiffs were themselves not importers and, therefore, were not eligible for the "import trade" exception. The Magistrate Judge then addressed whether the evidence in the record supported a finding of subject matter jurisdiction under the statute.

The Magistrate Judge apparently found that the evidence plaintiffs introduced to back up their allegations was credible only with respect to the charge that they "attempt[ed] to induce or induc[ed] the Carpet Export Promotion Council of India, the Export Promotion Board of Pakistan, and the Pakistan Carpet Manufacturers and Exporters Association not to subsidize the participation of manufacturers from those countries in the plaintiffs' trade fairs." The Magistrate Judge held that this did not describe conduct having a "direct" and "substantial" effect on import trade or commerce. Accordingly, the Magistrate Judge and, subsequently, the District Court, held that this case fell under the FTAIA's exemption from the antitrust laws, and that subject matter jurisdiction was therefore lacking.

The District Court and Magistrate Judge both ignored significant additional evidence offered by the plaintiffs to back up their other allegations. . . . The District Court's opinion remanding the matter back to the Magistrate Judge . . . is troublesome [because the district court either did not realize that there was additional evidence or it did not consider that evidence]. . . . We believe that in the context of a challenge to subject matter jurisdiction which can be raised at any time during the course of the litigation, the District Court should have considered the additional evidence. . . . Yet without explanation, the District Court ignored the additional evidence and remanded the matter to the Magistrate Judge to consider only the additional arguments of the parties.

The Magistrate Judge held that this case did not fall into the FTAIA's parenthetical exclusion, i.e., did not "involve" import trade or commerce, because the plaintiffs in this case were not importers, but merely brokers. As plaintiffs observe, this is plainly an inaccurate reading of the FTAIA. It is an incorrect focus on the plaintiffs' function rather than *the defendants' conduct.* The FTAIA's exemption from the Sherman Act focuses on the latter's application to "*conduct* involving trade or commerce (other than import trade or import commerce) with foreign nations." 15 U.S.C. § 6a (emphasis added). The implication that the Sherman Act provisions "apply to import trade and import commerce is unmistakable." *Eskofot A/S v. E.I. DuPont De Nemours & Co.*, 872 F.Supp. 81, 85 (S.D.N.Y.1995). The proper inquiry was therefore whether the alleged *conduct by the defendants* "involved" import trade or commerce, not on whether the *plaintiff's* conduct, which is not being challenged as violative of the Sherman Act, "involved" import trade or commerce.

Congress enacted the FTAIA for the purpose of facilitating the export of domestic goods by exempting export transactions that did not injure the United States economy from the Sherman Act and thereby relieving exporters from a competitive disadvantage in foreign trade. . . . Thus, the Act's declaration of purpose states "[i]t is the purpose of this act to increase United States exports of products and services by," *inter alia,* "modifying the application of the antitrust laws to certain export trade." . . . The Act specifically excludes the importation of goods and domestic commerce from its antitrust exemption. "The Sherman Act does reach conduct outside our borders, but only when the conduct has an effect on American commerce." *Matsushita Elec. Indus. Co. v. Zenith Radio Corp.*, 475 U.S. 574, 582 n. 2 (1986).

> Since the FTAIA clearly states that the Sherman Act is not applicable to trade or commerce other than import trade or import commerce, the Sherman Act continues to apply to import trade and import commerce, thereby rendering the FTAIA's requirement of a direct, substantial, and reasonably foreseeable effect inapplicable to an action alleging an impact

on import trade and import commerce.

54 Am.Jur.2d § 18, at 77 (footnote omitted). Here, the plaintiffs' activities involved both buying trips abroad where manufacturers sold rugs to American retailers for importation into this country, and trade show sales in the United States where manufacturers sold rugs to American retailers. Therefore, the defendants intended their alleged conduct to subvert commercial activities that solely impacted domestic commerce. Plaintiffs charge that defendants engaged in a course of activity designed to ensure that only United States importers, and not United States retailers, could bring oriental rugs manufactured abroad into the stream of American commerce.

Even if this Court considered only the evidence presented before the Magistrate Judge, the latter erred in ruling that the defendants' conduct did not "involve import trade or commerce." The defendant association identifies itself as an organization of "rug importers"; the individual defendants are its officers and directors. Admittedly, the FTAIA differentiates between conduct that "involves" such commerce, and conduct that "directly, substantially, and foreseeably" affects such commerce. To give the latter provision meaning, the former must be given a relatively strict construction. The evidence before the Magistrate Judge dealt largely with efforts to prevent Indian and Pakistani export boards from giving financial assistance to CGI or to manufacturers who wanted to participate in CGI's trade shows. It also dealt with efforts to convince ORRA, the trade association of United States rug retailers, from sponsoring the shows. These are activities that arguably did not, standing alone, "involve" import trade or commerce, but that did relate directly to them.

Elsea's declaration, however, makes allegations that ORIA pressured Zarnigan Rugs, DCC, Inc., and Anadol Rugs, Inc., themselves ORIA members who were involved both in importing and foreign manufacturing, to refrain from participating in CGI's trade shows. This evidence was uncontested before the Magistrate Judge. These allegations directly involved both import and domestic commerce.

Significantly, *Mortensen* makes clear that because, in the Sherman Act context, jurisdictional facts are often closely intertwined with the merits of the claim, "it is incumbent upon the trial judge to demand less in the way of jurisdictional proof than would be appropriate at a trial stage." 549 F.2d at 892. Under this standard, the uncontested evidence in Elsea's declaration alone arguably should have been sufficient to remove the FTAIA as an obstacle to jurisdiction. Accordingly, the District Court committed clear error in ordering a dismissal of the action at this stage of the proceedings.

Furthermore, the foregoing conclusion finds even stronger support when one considers all of the evidence submitted before both the Magistrate Judge and the District Court, especially in light of *Mortensen*'s less stringent evidentiary standard. The plaintiffs have offered evidence that defendants took steps to: (1) prevent foreign manufacturers from selling to United States retailers, (2) prevent at least one American retailer from purchasing rugs directly from foreign manufacturers, (3) prevent foreign governments and trade associations from sponsoring trade fairs at which retailers could purchase directly from foreign manufacturers, and (4) prevent an American rug retailers' trade association from sponsoring the trade fairs.

Finally, the evidence offered by plaintiffs (including the evidence offered after the Magistrate Judge's initial report issued) reveals that the defendants' alleged conduct had its intended negative effect on CGI's trade shows and, consequently, had the effect of protecting the defendants' import and wholesale business. Accordingly, the evidence, taken as a whole, is sufficient to support the plaintiffs' allegations that the challenged conduct "involved" import trade or commerce. The crux of their case involves conduct in the United States, not conduct abroad. We hold that these activities are not the type of conduct Congress intended to remove from our antitrust jurisdiction when it enacted the FTAIA. The FTAIA therefore does did not divest the District Court of subject matter jurisdiction over the plaintiffs' claims.

B

The defendants next argue that even assuming the FTAIA does not divest the federal courts of subject matter jurisdiction over the plaintiffs' claims, the District Court nevertheless lacked jurisdiction under the Sherman Act itself. They contend that the plaintiffs have failed to demonstrate that the defendants' alleged conduct had a sufficient effect on United States interstate commerce. . . . . [Defendants argued that the plaintiffs had to demonstrate a "substantial" effect on U.S. domestic commerce to support the exercise of jurisdiction under the Sherman Act. The Department of Justice, as amicus curiae, said that all the plaintiffs needed to show was that the restraint either interfered with the sale of rugs in interstate commerce or had a "not insubstantial" effect on interstate commerce to invoke Sherman Act jurisdiction. Finally, the plaintiffs contended that their allegations of a horizontal group boycott are subject to a *per se* analysis, rather than analysis under the rule of reason, and furthermore, that effects on commerce should be presumed when a *per se* claim is presented, both for the merits inquiry and for subject matter jurisdiction.]

Traditionally, horizontal group boycotts are generally judged under a *per se* analysis. . . . The Supreme Court, however, has curtailed the application of the *per se* analysis in cases alleging concerted refusals to deal in recent years. Nevertheless, the plaintiffs' claims appear to fall within that class of cases that still enjoys *per se* analysis. They claim that the conspiring importer/wholesaler firms (themselves competitors, making this a horizontal boycott) engaged in a "naked" restraint by agreeing not to deal with manufacturers who sold to United States retailers directly, or with such retailers who purchased directly from manufacturers. . . . According to one commentator, a truncated antitrust analysis remains applicable to "concerted refusals that upon brief inspection are unlikely to have any purpose other than the reduction of market output and attendant price increases. In that case, condemnation is in order without any inquiry into [market] power." [Hovenkamp,]ANTITRUST LAW ¶ 2203a.

Similarly, this Court has stated,

> *per se* boycott cases usually contain three elements: "denial of something a competitor needs to compete effectively, defendants with a dominant position in the relevant market, and the absence of any plausible contention that the challenged behavior would 'enhance overall efficiency and make markets more competitive.' "

Rossi v. Standard Roofing, Inc., 156 F.3d 452, 463 (3d Cir.1998) . . . The defendants' conduct complained of fits this description. It can be characterized as having a "pernicious effect on competition" and lacks any redeeming virtue. . . .

Although "[t]he mere allegation of a concerted refusal to deal does not suffice because not all concerted refusals to deal are intentionally anticompetitive," *id.* at 463 (quoting *Northwest Wholesale Stationers*, 472 U.S. at 295, 298), it appears that the refusal to deal here at issue is predominantly anticompetitive. If the plaintiffs can prove at trial that the alleged conspiracy actually exists, the anticompetitive effect of such a conspiracy would be "immediately obvious." *FTC v. Indiana Federation of Dentists*, 476 U.S. 447,

458 (1986). There appears to be no reason for the defendants' action other than to protect the wholesaler/importer's role in the chain of distribution.

[The court here concludes that plaintiffs have alleged enough to invoke *per se* analysis.]

Moreover, the Supreme Court noted the broad reach of the Sherman Act and has made clear that a plaintiff's burden of establishing effects on commerce sufficient to confer jurisdiction under the Sherman Act is not great. The jurisdictional requirement of the Act "may be satisfied under either the 'in commerce' or the 'effect on commerce' theory." *McLain v. Real Estate Bd. of New Orleans*, 444 U .S. 232, 242 (1980). *McLain* controls when subject matter jurisdiction over domestic conduct is at issue. We reject the defendants' reliance on *Hartford Fire*, because it dealt exclusively with the extraterritorial applicability of the Sherman Act to wholly foreign conduct. The instant case deals primarily with conduct in the United States, namely concerted action by United States importer/wholesalers directly to affect the domestic retail oriental rug market. All the plaintiffs need demonstrate is "either that the defendants' activity is itself in interstate commerce or, if it is local in nature, that it has an effect on some other activity demonstrably in interstate commerce." *Id.*; *see also Mortensen*, 549 F.2d at 896.

No one claims that the conduct here at issue is "local in nature," and therefore no "effects" test even comes into play. Instead, we focus on whether the plaintiffs have proffered evidence that the defendants' anticompetitive activity is itself in interstate commerce. It is clear from the uncontradicted evidence presented that requisite nexus to interstate commerce exists here. ORIA is headquartered in New Jersey; several of the defendant wholesalers/importers are located in New York; the defendants wrote to the Rhode Island-based president of ORRA to dissuade that organization from co-sponsoring the trade shows; at least one retailer who was pressured not to associate with CGI is based in Virginia; Elsea and CGI are based in Virginia; and the trade shows took place in Chicago, Illinois and Washington, DC. In these circumstances, the plaintiffs therefore need not quantify the actual effect defendants' conduct had on interstate commerce to support federal jurisdiction.

. . .

Thus, because the plaintiffs have introduced evidence sufficient to show that the challenged conduct actually occurred in interstate commerce, we conclude that subject matter jurisdiction exists over plaintiffs' Sherman Act claims.

C

[In this section of the opinion, the court concludes that plaintiffs had adequately alleged antitrust standing. Their trade shows and buying trips could be "categorized as in competition with the rug importer/wholesalers. Elsea and CGI, by themselves, offered an alternative avenue of distribution to that offered by the wholesaler/importers. If the wholesaler/importers raised the prices at which they sold oriental rugs to domestic retailers, those retailers could go to CGI's trade shows and purchase rugs there directly from manufacturers. In other words, there is a cross-elasticity of demand between the plaintiffs' offering and the defendants' offering. The plaintiffs' trade shows offered retailers (and manufacturers) certain organizational efficiencies that previously could be provided only by distributing rugs through wholesaler/importers. They allowed the rugs to be brought across the ocean and made available to retailers. In so doing, the plaintiffs relieved retailers of the burdensome task of locating and contacting manufacturers abroad, dealing with a web of import and customs regulations, and surmounting potential cultural obstacles to doing business with Indian, Pakistani, Turkish, and possibly other foreign rug manufacturers." . . . "[T]he defendants' contention that they did not compete with Elsea and CGI is belied by their action to, at the very least, dissuade foreign and domestic entities from contributing financial support to the plaintiffs' trade shows. There is no logical explanation for the defendants' assiduous and persistent effort to preserve their role in the chain of distribution other than their belief that they were threatened by the plaintiffs' activities. Accordingly, we reject the defendants' argument and hold that the plaintiffs have antitrust standing."]

III

In summary, we conclude that the FTAIA is inapplicable and that the District Court erred in dismissing this case. Further, the plaintiffs have offered sufficient evidence to demonstrate that the activities of the wholesale importers were intended to and adversely did impact on domestic commerce by engaging in a course of anticompetitive conduct to ensure that only they, the importers, could bring oriental rugs manufactured abroad into the United States for distribution. We further hold that subject matter jurisdiction exists under the Sherman Act, and that the plaintiffs have antitrust standing. The order of dismissal of the District Court will be reversed and the case remanded to the District Court for further proceedings consistent with this opinion. Costs will be taxed against the appellee.

* * *

Insert after Note on Antitrust Cooperation Agreements, page 1211:

On April 17, 1997, the U.S. Department of Justice and the Federal Trade Commission announced the conclusion of the first International Antitrust Assistance Agreement made possible by the IAEAA. After publication in the Federal Register and a lengthy period of consideration, the agreement formally entered into force on April 27, 1999. The full text can be found at <http://www.usdoj.gov/atr/public/international/docs/usaus7.htm>.

Although the United States and the European Community have yet to conclude an agreement for direct enforcement cooperation under the auspices of the IAEAA, they have nonetheless managed to move forward under more conventional agreements. On June 4, 1998, representatives of the U.S. government and the European Community signed a new Agreement between the Government of the United States of America and the European Communities on the Application of Postive Comity Principles in the Enforcement of Their Competition Laws. The full text of the agreement can be found on the Department of Justice Antitrust Division's web page, at <http://www.usdoj.gov/atr/public/international/docs/1781.htm>. It commits both parties to greater use of the positive comity principle, under which one party may request another to take enforcement action against anticompetitive activities occurring within its territory in violation of its law, when those activities also have an effect on the other party.

CHAPTER 11: PRICE DISCRIMINATION AND THE ROBINSON-PATMAN ACT

Section 3. The Anticompetitive Effects of Price Discrimination

Insert after *Coastal Fuels*, page 1255:

IN THE MATTER OF MCCORMICK & CO. In 2000, the Federal Trade Commission added yet another twist to the interpretation of *Morton Salt*. McCormick was the world's largest manufacturer and distributor of spice products sold through supermarkets and other grocery outlets, and offered substantial discounts to some large supermarket chains but not to competing stores. Typically, McCormick's discounts were in the form of upfront cash payments that resembled the payments sometimes called slotting allowances in the supermarket industry. The payments commonly required that the customer allocate to McCormick a large portion, often as much as 90%, of the shelf space devoted to spice products.

The Commission's complaint alleged that each instance of discrimination involved a substantial price difference, over a substantial period of time, between competing purchasers in markets where profit margins were low and competition was keen - - circumstances that give rise to an inference of competitive harm within the meaning of *Morton Salt*. The Commission did not rest entirely on *Morton Salt*, however, but looked at a range of other factors to examine whether there was actual injury to competition. In its Analysis to Aid Public Comment, the Commission explained:

> While [the *Morton Salt*] inference may not be sufficient by itself in some circumstances to warrant bringing a case, in this instance, the inference is strengthened by McCormick's position as the largest supplier of spice and seasoning products in the United States and by the fact that McCormick typically demanded that customers allocate to McCormick the large majority of the space devoted to spice products. . . .

As alleged in the Complaint, disfavored purchasers consequently had few, if any, alternative sources from which to purchase comparable goods at prices and terms equivalent to those which McCormick provided to the favored purchasers.